# SOG: MISSIONS TO THE WELL

Dale Hanson

*SOG: Missions to the Well* by Dale Hanson

Copyright © 2025 Dale Hanson

All rights reserved. No part of this book may be used or reproduced by any means without the written permission of the publisher except in the case of brief quotations embodied in critical articles and reviews.

Although every precaution has been taken to verify the accuracy of the information contained herein, the author and publisher assume no responsibility for any errors or omissions. No liability is assumed for damages that may result from the use of information contained within.

Cover and interior design: Jacqueline Cook

ISBN: 979-8-9927534-0-0 (Hardcover)

ISBN: 979-8-9927534-1-7 (Paperback)

10 9 8 7 6 5 4 3 2 1

BISAC Subject Headings:

BIO008000 BIOGRAPHY & AUTOBIOGRAPHY / Military
BIO026000 BIOGRAPHY & AUTOBIOGRAPHY / Personal Memoirs
HIS027070 HISTORY / Wars & Conflicts / Vietnam War
HIS027180 HISTORY / Military / Special Forces

Published by Dale Hanson
P.O. Box 2870
Sitka, Alaska 99835

# Praise for
# *SOG: Missions to the Well*

"This book enables the reader to vicariously participate in several Top Secret, high-risk, deep-penetration missions of the legendary Military Assistance Command-Vietnam Studies and Observations Group (MACV-SOG), as experienced and witnessed by the author, himself a SOG reconnaissance team veteran. The book also delivers rare psychological insights of SOG personnel and of day-to-day life in SOG's Forward Operating Base 2 (FOB-2). A Must-Read!"

—**Ed Wolcoff**, Lieutenant Colonel (Ret), Former SOG Team Leader and Author of *Special Reconnaissance and Advanced Small Unit Patrolling: Tactics, Techniques and Procedures for Special Operations Forces.*

"A respected Special Forces combat veteran of the top-secret MACV-SOG, Dale Hanson draws upon his first-hand knowledge to write with an intensity only possible by a warrior who equally knows how to wield a pen. Well written and thoroughly engaging, it's an excellent read."

—**Maj. John Plaster**, Ret., Special Forces, SOG warrior and author

"After a SOGCast podcast interview with Dale Hanson about his incredible first SOG book, *Born Twice*, I told him that he had to write a second book as he had so many other SOG stories that deserved to be told by a brilliant and gifted writer. Being a man of his word, he said he would and the result is a powerful, well-written second SOG book which sheds more light on Dale's time running SOG missions with his beloved indigenous troops but also includes stories of great valor by fellow SOG recon men such as Edward Ziobron, a SOG recon man who's valor should have seen him awarded a Medal of

Honor. By SOG Mission of CCC. Thank you, Dale, write on sir."

—**John Stryker Meyer**, author of *Across the Fence: The Secret War in Vietnam*, *On The Ground* and *SOG Chronicles: Volume One*

"I have read many books written by my fellow SOG veterans, but Dale Hanson's style is unique, taking the reader into the reality of a SOG operator and the circumstances of SOG missions while not losing sight of the humanity of those involved. A SOG recon veteran, Dale has the experience and authority to give authenticity to his writing. *SOG: Missions to the Well*, is even more gripping and compelling than his previous book, *Born Twice*. Dale's newest effort has encapsulated our world of cross border missions and the teams that ran them and written them for readers to experience. Hard to put down, this book is full of irony, compassion, patriotism, dedication, dark humor and, of course, the warrior ethos. It reads like fiction but, as has been said, 'you can't make this stuff up!' Highly recommended."

—**John Padgett** MAJ (Ret), USSF Medical NCOIC Kontum 1970-71

"With his latest book, ex-SOG soldier Dale Hanson draws his reader deep into a fascinating landscape, because he understands that the world of special operations amounts to a modern-day samurai culture with its own bushido code. He describes the time when the rules of special warfare were being written in blood by super-secret units in which casualty rates consistently exceeded 100%. Go along on missions deep into enemy territory that brought moments of sublime natural beauty and sudden, wrenching bursts of almost incomprehensible violence and polished military skill. A world in which each Special Forces soldier understood that the mission was more important than the team, and the team was more important than him. Only someone who earned entrance to that secret and forbidden world can take you inside it to see the missions and meet the men who answered their country's call. As one who served and fought with Dale Hanson for years in SOG operations, I can tell you:

this is how it was, and this is why so many of these amazing Special Forces soldiers never got to tell their stories."

—**Michael Buckland**, Special Forces CCC RT Maine/Ford Drum Missions

"In his first book, *Born Twice*, Dale Hanson gave readers insight into the operations he ran into denied areas such as Laos. *SOG: Missions to the Well* is Hanson's second book on SOG Recon operations in Vietnam. In this new book, Hanson takes us inside the missions that other Recon Teams ran out of Command and Control Central. These intense missions are stories about the elation of success when a team made it out alive and the heart wrenching feeling of loss when they didn't. He writes about the hard reality of the combat the RTs faced on every mission and instills in the reader a feeling of what it's like when seconds count and help is an hour away.

— **Dennis J. Cummings**, author of *The Men Behind the Trident: SEAL Team One in Vietnam*

# CONTENTS

Chapter One: CCC Komtum ............................................................ 9

Chapter Two: RT Florida and Ben Het ........................................ 25

Chapter Three: Arizona Wire Tap ................................................ 52

Chapter Four: Florida POW Snatch ............................................. 89

Chapter Five: RT Maine: Hunter Killer ..................................... 119

Chapter Six: RT Hawaii Mission ................................................. 143

Chapter Seven: RT Florida and the Chinese Spy ..................... 171

Chapter Eight: Arizona in Juliet Nine ....................................... 194

Chapter Nine: Maine and an Hour of Hell .............................. 221

Chapter Ten: New York's Christmas Eve Mission .................... 240

Chapter Eleven: Cambodia and Ford Drum ............................ 258

Chapter Twelve: Delaware and a Downed Jet ......................... 287

Chapter Thirteen: Ziobron Leghorn Hatchet Force ............... 302

                RT Montana ............................................. 347

                RT Kentucky ............................................ 369

                RT Alabama ............................................. 399

Chapter Fourteen: Sebastian Deluca ......................................... 412

Chapter Fifteen: Saigon: The Continental Hotel .................... 422

Glossary ........................................................................................ 443

About the Author ....................................................................... 447

# CHAPTER ONE
## *CCC Kontum*

That morning—before the mission, before the choppers poked their way through the fog between us and Pleiku, before our team slogged our way to the air strip in our sterile uniforms and waited to be dropped far behind enemy lines—I stood before a mirror in the latrine with a camouflage stick in one hand and prepared to die. The electric charge of adrenaline I felt when we received this mission had not worn off; indeed, it resided in me as a tenant. This would be a hard one to survive.

We had taken a prisoner a few days before in the same area. We aimed for his thigh so he could not get away, but with him barely walking and blindfolded, and the enemy in full chase, we wondered if we would make it out at all. The Communists were aware of the closest LZ (we were in their own backyard) and it was a race for them to kill us during the chase or end it at the clearing. Casualties slowed us, and the North Vietnamese were right behind. They crashed through the brush shouting orders and sending rifle grenades in our direction. Covey arrived barely in time in his small airplane and directed gunships and fast movers, bringing death to the NVA. In the end, as the helicopters descended and we were boarding our captive, a bullet struck the prisoner in the center-left of his chest and killed him. His eyes rolled back to the whites, he slumped forward and rolled from the strut. Later, I was in the mess hall, still in my patchless, dirty uniform and I wondered if one of their own made careful aim and killed their comrade lest he be taken alive and talk.

We were going back to try again.

I started to smear on the camouflage. I had read of other men who faced certain or near-certain death and their demeanors. The New Testament tells of Christians sawed in half who did not deny their faith, of wicked kings whose knees "smote one against the other," and how Jesus in agony and about to die on the cross entrusted the care of his mother to a faithful disciple.

Secular history recounts a politician of a civil war in Europe on scarecrow-thin wobbly legs, vainly adjusting his checkered tie with shaking fingers. But his fingers could not recall how to make the knot. They fluttered about on the end of his palms like feathers of a wounded bird. Fingers, each with a separate mind, went their several directions in frenzied movement until his mind broke and his lips quivered and drool formed at the corners of his mouth, and they led him blubbering to the shooting stake.

And there was the missionary to South America with the long spear in his chest who said, "It is not foolishness to give up what you cannot keep to gain that which you cannot lose."

All of us in Special Ops faced death. Often. But we dealt with those demons. At night, alone in our beds, Death's boney hands spidered their fingers across our pillows and fastened tightly around our necks in nightmare. But we thrust them off, and when sunrise slid her red fingers through the slats, we harnessed ourselves and boarded those choppers. And no one ever mentioned the struggle in the night.

I began with the dark colored camouflage. We had captured a North Vietnamese sergeant on one of our missions. He took a round in the femur that broke the bone and sliced an artery. I talked with him in the dispensary in Kontum. "We see you," he said, "come from ground. Green hands and green faces. Think you be already dead. We no can kill. Afraid greatly."

I remembered his words. "If I die on this one, I will take a lot of them with me. They will think I came from the muck where roots and worms grow." At the mirror, I reversed the colors of the protocol. I made the recesses of my eyes and below my cheek bones very dark and highlighted my cheeks and forehead with light-green. With the lightest color of all, I placed short horizontal stripes. Teeth. Finished, I was a skull, a death's head in earth tones, rising from the ground.

"Choppers coming in," someone shouted at the door. I was ready.

\* \* \* \*

April 1969, Kontum, Vietnam. The airplane that brought us Green Berets that morning was sterile. It was a Hercules C-130 painted all black but with just a hint of dark green camouflage. No markings of nationality showed on the fuselage. Should this "Blackbird" be shot down, its connection to the United States was deniable. It flew classified operations: black ops missions to arcane places. En route to one of those missions, the day began by dropping off our handful of Special Forces commandos for a year tour of duty in SOG, "Studies and Observations Group," which, as a routine, was assigned some of the most hair-raising missions of any war.

The four-engine aircraft descended sharply. Dove almost. We came in from the east, out of the sun, dropping straight in for landing. Hot air over the darker rice paddies rose in invisible columns over the approach to the runway and bounced us like flak-tossed bombers of a previous war. A particularly violent jolt tossed us just before we crossed the Dak Bla River. Our rucksacks bounced on the deck between our legs. I looked across the aisle at the surprised looks of my mates. Had we had been hit? The pilot of our Blackbird had made no downwind or crosswind entry of a normal pattern lest he give the North Vietnamese gunners on the ridgeline hovering over their rockets time to shoot. There was testament to this. Among the vines and bushes that bordered the airfield, rumpled rusting wrecks of planes left over from the French experience yet lay where they fell. Those who tarried on the runway often remained forever. One tilted wing remained thrust skyward from a time-sunken fuselage, like an arm of a drowning person, clearly seen by anyone passing by on the road. Even the illiterate could read the message. The decal of the French Airforce yet remained on the tip of that wing—the tri-colors of France painted in concentric rings like a bullseye.

Kontum, a province as well as a town, hovered near the tri-border where Laos, Cambodia, and Vietnam touch. Hidden in those boundaries were half a dozen major communist sanctuaries. Infiltration routes coursed like veins through these highlands as platoons, companies, even regiments, trucked or walked along hidden paths. An additional army of conscripts pushed bicycles laden with massive bundles of supplies for the war in South Vietnam. Truck convoys brimmed with soldiers and munitions for the war in the south groaned under their loads as they labored in low gear over the hills and on roads freshly cut into the forest.

Mention Kontum to a local in Saigon or other place removed from battle? He would shudder, maybe flinch, the ashes falling from his cigarette. You would feel the tension within him. He would stop what he was doing (perhaps a chopstick of food paused mid-air before his open mouth) and would gaze into your face to imprint it in his memory. He would never see you again. His eyes would mist over, his body stiffen. "Oh, oh! *Beaucoup* VC there. Many, many *Cong San* around Kontum. You no go!"

The wheels of the Hercules lowered from the well with a rumble. Air hissed as the pilot lowered flaps. For a moment there was a sensation of floating, then a hard slam of contact with the pavement. Still taxiing on the main runway, the ramp lowered and bright sunlight flashed in. My eyes stung and watered in the glare. Nearing the terminal—a misnomer for it was a small, simple structure meant only to shelter from the monsoon rains—the loadmaster signaled that we would unload from the ramp and to please do so quickly.

# SOG: Missions to the Well

Two sergeants met us with a pair of three-quarter-ton trucks for the ride to Command and Control Central (CCC). We had never met them before but felt a kinship from the fellow Berets. Green Berets were a rare thing; there were more generals and admirals in the armed forces than Special Forces. We passed through the charm of the small city, the blend of French and Asian culture; trees planted for shade and beauty, villas, and cobbled streets. But at the edge of the town were a few empty houses, caved, leaning, some blackened by fire, others scarred by war. They bore broken, empty spaces where windows had been. French children had placed their soft fingers on the sills, stood on tip toes, and peered out as they heard the clopping of hoofs on the pavement. Once, a French boy watched an Asian boy his own age atop a large black water buffalo as the lad tapped the neck of the beast with a thin, limber stick to urge it along. The boy under the straw hat raised his head as he passed, proud of his responsibility for the beast, keenly aware of the small French boy at the window.

"Mama, I want to ride a buffalo and work in the paddies like that boy!"

Another time, the boy at the window at the edge of town heard the rumble and clank of tank treads, ran to the window and placed the fingers of both hands on the sill and peered out, awestruck with the massive power. The weight of the engines of war shook the road and shivered the house. A French soldier passing by on the monster waved at the boy. "Mama! Mama! Tanks! Soldiers!" he exclaimed, as trucks brimmed with helmet-clad soldiers drove by.

With the passing of the monsoons, columns went by more frequently, moving west to conflict beyond the highlands. The fighting grew nearer over the days. At night, artillery flashes outlined the nearby hills. And the boy's mother stood behind him at the window and wrung her hands and wished for France.

As we passed that way en route to our compound I noticed the house of the little French boy, whose small hands had curled over the sill as he watched the passing world on tiptoe. I saw windows empty of glass that stared outward like vacant, black eye sockets.

We crossed the Dak Bla, with its narrow, timbered bridge. Our slow-moving truck wheels thump-thumped over the wood planks with the sound of heart beats. On the other side of the river, the road took us to CCC but continued on all the way to Pleiku and forked to other destinations. It was two-lane road, narrow but wide enough for convoys to pass. Rice paddies and farmers' fields lay along its sides. Vietnamese girls wearing white áo dài rode by in the other direction in pedicabs. Young males with slicked down hair and sunglasses passed on small motorcycles, look-alikes of the latest movie stars. Tribesmen walked in file on the shoulder of the road, ever looking straight ahead. We had gone but a mile after the river to arrive. CCC could not be mistaken with its open minefields and fire, its sandbagged perimeter topped with concertina wire, and bunkers manned by guards in the shadowed recesses behind their machine guns. Our sergeants slowed before the gate, waved at the Chinese guards, and turned in. We had arrived.

They dropped us off at S-1, the personnel office, where we unloaded our gear to process in and receive our assignments. I recalled what we knew about C&C, and the awe we felt when in Nha Trang we saw that first Green Beret with the red SOG patch on his shirt pocket. He had blond hair and was thin in his rumpled fatigue uniform. His name was Kirshbaum. He walked past us and found an empty bunk at the far side of the billets. He was distant and hardened, quiet and removed. But here was someone alive. Soldiers actually lived who were in SOG—at least long enough to do business in headquarters before returning to Kontum. SOG was the most dangerous, most decorated, and most secret project of the war; so secret we would not be able to speak of what we had done for twenty years after the war. SOG, our most common acronym, would be the most decorated American unit in a hundred years, and our small Kontum company would be the most decorated company in American history. Coming into this we understood we would likely suffer one hundred percent casualties during our tour: all of us killed or wounded in the coming months. I looked at my brothers who I had trained with so long, and I imagined the vacuum each would make on my soul when it happened. I recalled the concern in the eyes of the little Asian man. "You no go."

I was one of the first to get an assignment. I told the captain that I wanted to be on a reconnaissance team. He paused over my paperwork and looked up at me. For a moment he reminded me of the words of that little Asian man with the misty eyes.

"I think they have an opening on one of the teams now," he said, but in his mind, he might have added, "With the casualties of those missions, they usually do," but the last he did not say aloud.

"Go over to Recon Company and see Sergeant Howard. He will set you up if they have an opening."

He walked me to the steps outside his door and pointed to a separate building across the parade field. "You can barely see the sign above the door from here. The first sergeant is Bob Howard. He is possibly the most decorated soldier in American history. They made him first sergeant to keep him out of the field so he doesn't get killed before he goes to Washington to receive the Medal of Honor. This is the third time he has been put in for it. Just thought you might want to know."

"Thank you, sir."

"Good luck."

I crossed the parade field and stood in front of the small building the captain indicated. A sign above the door simply said RECON COMPANY. The wood siding was sun-bleached the color of dry wasp nests or mummy wraps, but above the sign was a clear outline that had not faded in the sun. The shape was what a metal horseshoe might have made, had that symbol of good luck hung there for a time and had recently been taken down. My first consideration was it had been removed because luck had no bearing on the success of missions. As I paused there, an athletic man appeared at my side.

"What are you looking at?"

"Just wondering. I assume they did not take a good luck horseshoe off the wall. I took Bible Greek in college. That's the letter Omega."

As I said it, I remembered the various secret projects of the war and how many of them had Greek letters. I dimly recalled hearing about Project B-50. "Was there ever a Project Omega that operated out of here?"

Still looking at the unfaded place he simply said, "This building really needs painting!"

"Personnel said you were on the way. Come inside and we'll talk." Bob Howard was a powerful athletic man just under six feet with the slightest limp from a wound. A recent scar marked his right cheek and like Long John Silver in Treasure Island, it could be described as livid and white though not as long as one from a saber. He had the quality of speaking to those of us under the beret as equals. There was not a hint of arrogance in his voice. Heroism was the expected norm in Recon Company.

We went inside and he pointed to a chair. "My wife teaches Sunday School in our Baptist church in Alabama. She would be happy to know that one of us knows Bible Greek. I don't get home very often with my being overseas so much. Why did you leave college and come here? What do you want here?"

"Simply put, Sergeant Howard, I am very anti-Communism. I am convinced that it must be stopped before it enslaves the world. Unlike those hippies and the better-red-than-dead bunch that are protesting the war, I believe in it. As a Christian I am prepared to die if I have to."

Howard quietly listened to me, patiently waiting for me to finish. He was digesting my words.

"Also, I believe I am physically, emotionally and mentally prepared for this."

What I said apparently satisfied him and he proceeded to give me the overview of SOG operations and how the teams functioned.

"Each team has a leader called the One-Zero. He runs the team as he chooses. His leadership is based on experience, not rank. You may have a sergeant as the One-Zero and a lieutenant or captain under him as the One-One. Teams go by names of states in CCC and they seem to have an individual personality. I want to assign you to Recon Team Florida, but it is up to the One-Zero if he wants you on his team. Florida is one of my best teams and it is led by Master

Sergeant Norm Doney. He has had several tours in combat. But remember he has to approve you. Let's see if we can find him."

We stepped to the entry way of the office and looked across the parade field. "Oh, there he is now."

"Sergeant Doney," he said quietly and formally as he drew near us. "I think we have found the man you are looking for. This is Sergeant Hanson."

Doney firmly shook my hand, perhaps taking my measure as he did so, and looked directly into my eyes. He smiled a smile I would know as his "Doney smile;" one that I would know over the years as that of a leader, mentor, father figure, and as a friend. He was in his late thirties, just under six feet with dark hair and physically fit. He wore a black boonie hat with his pressed fatigue uniform complete with patches and rolled up sleeves.

"So, you're interested in recon, are you? Let's walk across the compound and find us a quiet place and we can talk about it."

Helicopters flew over low and drowned our words as we passed over the open compound with the American and Vietnamese flags. ARVN officers crisscrossed the square as we made our way to the perimeter. We stopped at the far side facing a small village in the distance. It was a Montagnard village, set into a canopy of trees bounded by shrubs leaving it barely visible. It consisted of three or four longhouses built on stilts. At night the villagers penned their livestock under the houses—cows, pigs, and fowl—and when the last child was counted, drew the log ladder into the building. Always someone watched in the night for the occasional tiger, and the not so occasional Viet Cong.

Doney pointed to a place for us to sit on the sandbags. I heard the grunt of a pig shoving its nose into the dirt for grubs and roots. The busy snorts originated in the bushes on the far side of our perimeter wire and I was glad the hog was not rooting in the mine field.

Doney saw me looking toward the village. "Most of the people are gone to forage or work in their fields. It is a very hard life for them. They are looked down on by the Vietnamese as being hill people and are not a part of their society, and the communists try to steal, tax them or conscript them. The North Vietnamese will come in and torture the head man; tie him to a stake and disembowel him as the village is made to watch. They will take a child and break all of his bones and say, 'We will be back tomorrow. We want this much rice and we want three of your men to join us as soldiers. If we do not get this we will take'—and here they will point at the most innocent and say, 'her.' That is their life. That is why their village is so close to us. Some of their young men work for us on our recon teams and in our hatchet force. They are some of the bravest, most loyal fighters I have ever known."

I looked at Doney as he said this. "That is why I am here, Sergeant Doney."

Doney reflected but a moment, smiled his Doney smile and said, "Well I can use you on Team Florida."

Doney glanced down at my pack. "I'll show you the Florida team house where the Americans stay and you can drop off your things. Then I will show you the layout of the camp."

For the next two hours we canvassed the base. He began on the recon side of the road.

"Each recon team has its own team room where the Americans live. Set it up as you like. You can get a carpenter in town to make you a dresser or trade with the Air Force for a thicker mattress. We do not have room inspections. Buy a small refrigerator or a fan or a tape deck and listen to music. Put a picture on the wall. Make a library. You need an oasis."

He pointed out the hooches where the Asian men stayed. "That one there is where our Florida people stay; that over there is the Montagnard mess hall. That big building is where communications, operations and the intelligence people work." We passed the motor pool, and the barracks of the Hatchet Force where the Montagnard fighters live. All the while as we walked Doney talked about RT Florida; his people, how he ran the team, his plans, and how he might differ from the other recon teams.

"I specialize in prisoner snatches. All teams try to get a prisoner when they can, but we train for it. When we are sent out for recon, we try to avoid contact and come back with the intelligence. But when we go out for a prisoner, we know we will have contact."

We crossed to the other half of the compound. "Those buildings on the right are the officers' quarters, that is the mess hall, that is the dispensary."

Doney thought he had showed me enough for one setting. "Let's go to supply and get you what you need at least for now. Tomorrow, we will get you squared away with supply and get your code name into the system. Sergeant Joe Morris is the other American on the team, and we will introduce you to the Indig. We have eight of them: four Chinese and four Vietnamese."

He glanced at his watch and we conducted ourselves to the mess hall for lunch. As we met them, Norm Doney introduced me to legends of Special Forces and in their absence, he told me of missions one could hardly believe possible were it not that to doers of them were among us.

Joe Morris was my height, slim, nearly skinny with red-brown hair and brown eyes—an all-American boy straight from a Norman Rockwell painting. A touch of nervousness was about him, hung like a thin shawl over his shoulders. "I don't know how we survive these missions," he said as he helped me carry my things from the supply building. "Every time we just barely make it back alive I tell myself, 'This is it. I am not doing this again.'"

He looked at the ground as we walked to our team house, lost in those words he said aloud to another person, words he thought he would never say. And he wondered if he should have said them at all.

"But you go, don't you."

He stopped and he looked at me. Sadly, and as if it were the first time he gave voice to his resolve to keep on, he softly said, "Yes, we keep on."

\* \* \* \*

I set up my web gear first of all. A pair of suspenders went over my shoulders and supported the heavy weight of ammunition we carried in our belts. I weighed mine: fifty-five pounds in all. Doney gave me the benefit of advice from years of combat. "You can't get enough in those pouches."

I used canteen covers with the linings removed to hold my ordnance. I put eight grenades in one canteen cover, which was the second container to the right as I throw with the right hand and did not want to change hands when seconds counted. Placing two twenty-round magazine clips flat in the bottom of the canteen covers held the rest high enough to be easily reached, and I could get eight magazines in a canteen cover. I placed the open ends of the magazines down, away from the rain, with the bullet tips pointing away from my body. I carried twenty-six in the field, six hundred rounds for my rifle. One held a canteen of water and the last one was for survival gear and a radio. Nothing was on the back of my belt. We never took our belts off in the field. Ever. A rope for a Swiss seat was coiled and snapped to the belt, ready to make a harness for those times when we needed to be hoisted out under a helicopter "on strings." A knife, smoke grenades, and field dressings for wounds were affixed to the shoulder harness. A compass was looped around my neck and clipped to my shirt. Food, extra ammunition and a Claymore mine occupied the recesses of my rucksack. My uniforms were sterile: no patches, tags of manufacture, or laundry marks.

The next dozen days were long and went at a fast pace, full of training which integrated me into the team. When I could get away to the range on my own, I worked on magazine drills, changing a magazine in my rifle for a new, full one. I placed two rounds in each of my magazines, fired the two rounds and when the bolt flew back, changed to the next magazine and fired it off. I shoot left-handed and although the weapon was designed for a right-handed person, the buttons worked better for me. Three seconds might be the goal for most, but after practicing my drill a thousand times or more I could do it in two seconds. My rifle never left my shoulder and my eyes never left the target as I changed magazines. I expected my hands to know what to do. I shot all of my life and was a good shot. The standard I placed on myself was that as I hurried through the drill, I still expected the rounds to be on target.

When the rest of the team ended the work day at the evening meal, Doney and I met alone for more training. He tutored and mentored me in the nuances of running a SOG team, and the lessons learned from a hundred battles. "After all, you said you wanted to lead a recon team."

I got to know my Asian fighters. Everything about them, their personalities and skills, how each functioned and contributed to the team, and I knew them as individuals. Nhok, my Chinese man with the grenade launcher, could shoot three rounds from his single-shot weapon and have all three in the air before the first one hit the ground-all on target. He was my scholar who rarely smiled. My intellectual.

Chin, my Chinese point man, always smiled when he talked with me. His was a smile at the very edge of laughter. The corners of his eyes crinkled, webs of a net full of joy. He carried an AK-47 rifle and wore a communist hat with the red star on the brim. Looking like the enemy he would encounter while on point bought him one second which also bought him life. It was he and Nhok who found the most auspicious way to write my name, Hanson, in Chinese. And how to write eternal life in Chinese characters so they could write the symbols in magic marker on my back so God could read it and take care of me in battle.

Noi was my handsome Vietnamese playboy; Hue, my interpreter who always looked like he just got out of bed; Ba, my tail gunner with his ready, open-mouth smile who invited me home to dinner to meet his family, and proudly showed me the underground bunker he dug in his house with the entrance hidden in a back room where his family practiced their dash for safety; Hiep, who should have been a tailor but worked for us to support his family; and the others with whom we each trusted with our lives.

We trained together until we functioned as one mind and did a few short "locals"—missions that were not over the fence in Laos or Cambodia. Doney had to remind me that fifty thousand Americans had been killed on locals, and not to forget that the tri-border area on this side of Indian country teemed with enemy too.

When each training day was over, I did not neglect my own personal workout. Much of it was makeshift as we had no gym. I used things on hand and supplemented with isometrics to keep what I had. I did dips and pullups at the high bar behind the club. Occasionally as I rested between sets, I walked over to the nearest bunker, coughed so the guard knew I was there and climbed up beside him. We talked in pidgin English. One evening I looked to the west beyond Kontum city and the highlands. It looked like the summer heat lightning I watched as a boy in Minnesota.

"Lightning?" I asked the tribesman at the window slat. He was puffing on a long-stem Montagnard pipe. He said something in the dark which I figured meant "What?" for it occurred to me he did not know the word lightning.

"What is that?"

"Aaah," he said in understanding, for I saw the red lighted bowl of his pipe move up and down. "That be Ben Het. Green Beret, same same you."

I recalled that Ben Het Special Forces camp was in that direction.

The flashing occurred again.

"That!" I said.

"Aaah," he said finally understanding to what I referred. "Aah, that be airplane. Bery, bery big airplane." He could not form the word "very."

I could see that he switched hands to hold his pipe and I made out his face from the glowing ember in the bowl. "VC come Ben Het. American call airplane. Boom, boom, *fini* VC."

His fingers rained down bombs in the shadows.

I heard shuffling outside the bunker. Boots climbed up the sandbags. Norm Doney entered the outpost. "So, you come here too, I see," he said to me.

Doney patted the Montagnard twice on his shoulder in greeting.

Faint light flashed over the hills toward Ben Het. "Reminds me of summer lightning," I said. "My friend here says those are bombs going off."

# SOG: Missions to the Well

Doney seemed to ponder the information. "It might just be harassment fire. But it might be something bigger. I shouldn't wonder if Team Florida might be involved in that over there."

The Montagnard drew a long puff on his pipe and I heard the crackle of the poor village tobacco and saw the increased glow. I noticed Doney's face in the dim red light. He was frozen in thought as he gazed steadily to the west, and I wondered if his words, "Florida might be involved in that over," were very prophetic.

Saturday, Doney and I made ladders. They were the first used in C&C and were always referred to as Doney ladders.

"We used them in Delta," he said, "and they worked fine. We could use them here," he said to justify our effort. With the challenging pace we had trained the last ten days, he gave the team the weekend off, but Norm and I built ladders. Our worksite was in a quiet, unused area behind the motor pool. Jan Novey, the old veteran of many battles, ran that area of the camp and got us what we needed. Jan was from Eastern Europe and fought the Nazis, then the Communists. He had been captured and tortured and finally made it to the United States and became a Green Beret and continued to fight Communism. His hands were deformed and nail-less from torture. Age and wounds slowed him down until he did what he could for the effort. Novey found what we needed. We laid out three long lengths of flexible wire cable, and cut lengths of hollow tubing for rungs, drilled and affixed them. When we had finished the first set, we could roll them up as a tube. One end could be snapped to the floor of the helicopter and unrolled into a ladder. A wounded soldier, too hurt to make it all the way up into the chopper, could snap in to whatever rung he was on. The Doney ladder could also be rolled up under him like a hammock from inside the chopper for the ride to base.

Monday morning the two of us demonstrated the ladder to Colonel Abt, the camp commander, and Bob Howard. We hung it from the water tower behind the motor pool and showed its uses, and how much easier it was to climb than a rope ladder. A full demonstration followed for the Americans and the chopper pilots.

*Dale Hanson*

The Doney ladders were added to the tools of C&C.

    I stepped back and studied our handiwork. Would I be a one of those wounded whose lacerated and crumpled body was too weak to climb one more rung; with my last failing bit of strength snapped in before passing out? It was with these thoughts I gazed on the faces of my brothers gathered under the water tower.

# CHAPTER TWO
## *RT Florida and Ben Het*

Staff Sergeant Kline's weary patrol made it to the far side of the clearing, where they were half hidden in the shrubs, and waited. Two Montagnard strikers next to Kline dropped to their knees and faced left and right, weapons at their shoulders. Rearward, the remainder of his people fanned in a half circle and faced their backtrail. For the first time in three days there was quiet behind them. The sergeant barely heard the low hum of the camp generator across the opening, but no sound from behind; no shuffling sounds of enemy passing through the thickness, no snapping twigs, no accidental muffled cough of an enemy tracker. The silence betrayed the weariness of the team. They heard their own soft panting breaths, the press of their knees in the dirt, the click of safety catches of the weapons. The tribesmen expected the bushes to part and North Vietnamese regulars to charge through.

Seven men made up the patrol: six Montagnard strikers and the American Green Beret. Relief from the pursuit was less than a hundred yards away. At the other side of the break in the trees lay

Ben Het Special Forces camp. The open space before the patrol was a cleared swath around the camp where the vegetation had been removed to create fields of fire to expose attackers. So close. But even here in sight of the fortification they were yet in danger. With the knuckle of one hand, Kline wiped a stream of sweat that stung his eyes. He felt the heaving of his chest as he caught his breath. It had been a near-run the last hour. His skin was clammy, slimy almost, from camouflage stick and sweat. A glance at the gate. They would have to navigate the mine field and concertina wire to the road and, fully exposed, make their way with pursuit close behind.

The sergeant's mouth was dry. He gathered as much moisture as he could, ran his tongue under his lips over his teeth so he could speak. "Let's do it," he said nearly to himself.

He keyed the handpiece of his radio. "Coming in," he said and was glad that in the dry desert that was his mouth he could even say words.

He began to replace the handpiece but remembered, "Bad guys right behind me. They are close."

"Roger. We will cover you."

They rushed from the tree line maneuvering to avoid the minefields, to the road and the gate. The last to leave the tree line walked backwards until they arrived at the gate. Only then did they lower their weapons.

"They are out there," he simply said to the first American he saw. "The place is thick with them. They were right behind us."

The captain met the team. "What do you have, sergeant?"

Kline glanced at his team. They stood erect, their clothing sweat-dark clinging to their bodies, and waited for instructions from their leader. A leader takes care of his people first. The captain noted the look. "Just the gist of it and you can take care of your people. We can get the rest when you are finished."

"Oh, they are out there for sure. There is movement everywhere. And there's more: We saw those tanks. They are the kind used in the World War and Korea. We got pictures. We heard them during the night."

# SOG: Missions to the Well

The captain nodded his head at the confirmation of what the other teams had reported. "We will get with you after you take care of your team." He turned to the Montagnard men. "Thank you," he said. "We will lay on a meal for you."

As they turned to go, Kline heard a few mortar rounds leave their tube and crash into the jungle in harassment fire.

Someone came from the commo shack. "Captain, I have friendly aircraft with unexpended ordnance. They will drop it into the ocean rather than land with it. Can we use it?"

"Kline, where did you say the bad guys were?"

He pointed. "Only a hundred meters in."

Night fell quickly. The bombers did not drop their ordnance into the ocean after all. Instead, they made a wide circle around the A camp and confirmed the coordinates of the target, making sure there were no friendlies in the area before the final run. In the mess hall there was only the sound of forks and spoons, then the loud, low jets passing with the sound of someone clearing his throat. As the patrol left the mess hall thinking of soft mattresses and sleep, the forest on the west side of the perimeter wire erupted in explosions. The men ran to the perimeter. Detonations began a hundred meters into the trees. Heavy bombs and napalm worked their way up the slope to the top of the ridgeline. Receding impact of bombs became muted by the leaves and distance. Napalm landing over the crest flashed white, but like summer lightning.

\* \* \* \* \*

The handful of Green Berets at Ben Het Special Forces Camp prepared for massive enemy attack. The signs were there. For days, patrols found evidence of heavy movement. Trails. Live sightings. The question on their minds was: Were those platoons and companies just passing through on both sides of the base as currents do passing a large rock in a stream or was Ben Het being surrounded? The Montagnard strikers were not privy to the maps and intelligence reports but knew all of this. Felt it. It was like Van der Post's, Story Like the Wind, when even nature was tense and expectant; animals and birds and later, villagers, fled before the unseen force. Tension was in the air. Strikers in camp studied the Americans with dark, unblinking, lingering eyes, and waited for information. Some brought their wives and children to the camp for refuge. This was information not to be ignored. The camp was not equipped for such a thing, but to send the families away invited desertion, as fathers would leave to care for their people.

The berets with their small teams had been slipping through the wire at night to assess the buildup. Scores of new trails marked movement from the sanctuaries in Laos and Cambodia. Countless platoons and companies flattened the grass and parted the vines. Prints of equipment-laden bicycles, trucks, and heavy-loaded vehicles full to the brim with crew-served weapons embossed their record into the soil. Tank tracks! Reconnaissance teams heard them. Heard them laboring in the night. One team even had a picture, but the higher-ups who did not live in the bullseye of Ben Het said, "No, you are hearing road building equipment. The pictures are unclear, sort of grainy. Could be anything. Besides, the People's Army of Vietnam has no tanks."

Then for several days it was pacific around the Special Forces camp. No sounds penetrated the perimeter to reveal PAVN lurking in the night. No black-clad infiltrators probed the perimeter to locate the camp's bunkers and machine gun positions. No enemy was seen on a patrol. It appeared the enemy had changed its mind and left the area. Or, rather, all was in place. Saigon said that the movement had bypassed them to other targets in the South.

Y Vahn, one of the strikers in the camp, whose life had been spent fighting the army of the north, and who had survived the battle of Dien Bien Phu, said, "No, no, sergeant. They be there." He waved his hand to show the whole horizon. "They just wait. Same same tiger, him wait for right time to strike. I feel him." Here he raised one hand like one feeling the air for its contents. "VC him crouch at water hole. Him very patient."

Pale, weary, saffron-yellow daylight pushed through the overcast and lay on the road. Far to the west, where it bent out of sight, a thin, tired layer of dust rose at the edge. Streams of villagers padded down the shoulder, leaving their villages and fields behind. They walked barefoot past the camp with their few possessions strapped on their backs. An old man with a wrinkled face, deeply furrowed like parched soil, leaned on his staff and lagged far behind. He waited for his woman to catch up. She took three or four steps, stopped and panted before looking up at her waiting husband then continued. She was like the woman in the gospels who was bowed together and could not stand upright. The grandfather, no, great-grandfather, had been plodding on ahead expecting her to be there behind him as she always had been before. But when he failed to hear the soft sounds of her shuffling feet he turned. She was at the edge of the road next to the shallow ditch. Her body swayed up and down with her effort to breathe. He must go on. It was the way of his people. But he could not leave her. Part of the time he watched her struggle to catch up, knowing in his soul that she would not be able to do so much longer and he wondered where it would be along this road that it would end, and would they have to leave her somewhere. But most of the time his eyes focused on the place where the road they had traveled disappeared in the distance, at that last corner they had taken together and his woman and companion of life could barely go on. Would the hated North Vietnamese or the cruel Viet Cong fill that space on the road they had just emptied?

Ahead of the old man, the distance between him and his people was becoming ever greater. Beside them was the ditch—a long open grave beside the road, always there, ready to receive them. The ancient father pondered for only a moment, for he was not a philosopher, but was there not such a ditch which followed all of us through the walk of life? Ahead of him, children carried younger siblings strapped across their chests. Sons and daughters of the old man and his wife walked; eyes fixed far down the road. They did not look back, could not, lest their hearts melt their resolve. They walked. Did not speak. Faces bland. No expression. Walked. None looked to the side. Fathers, grandfathers, with fixed eyes, focused on a faraway place—a place that might not exist at all.

## Dale Hanson

\* \* \* \* \*

Staff Sergeant Kline's dog was the first to sense they were under attack. Beau was a loose-boned mongrel bachelor rescued as a pup from the coils of a boa constrictor. It was Kline who saved him. He heard a snap of a bone and a croaking sound in the grass and saw the snake and the bulging eyes and floppy ears in the center of the encirclement. Kline grabbed the head of the constrictor and thrust the blade of his K bar knife through it, the blade crunching in the gravel on the other side. He unwrapped the small dog and blew breath into its nose. Death was close. The smell of snake remained on the pup. But life returned to the small body. The sergeant bent to give it one more breath of air and the little dog licked the Green Beret's nose.

He was Boa at first, named because of the boa constrictor, but when an old striker in the camp who had fought for the French watched the cocky walk of the animal, he told Kline, "He look like young boy, look, look for girl. He be Beau." And he was from then on. Beau became the camp mascot and was inseparable from Kline. Once, it was reported, Beau slipped out of the camp when Kline was doing reconnaissance near the border and joined him, slipping between the Montagnard strikers where they circled for the night. The sergeant was startled. He froze. Something weighed on his thigh. His first thought was a heavy head of a snake. Kline did not move. Then he heard a slight tapping on the ground next to him. Three taps. One. Two. Three. He was familiar with those taps. The tail of his dog made that sound when he curled next to him in the perimeter. He could count on Beau to be there when he spent the night in a bunker watching for North Vietnamese sappers trying to infiltrate the camp. The dog would search him out and tap his tail, three times. One, two, three. "Can I stay with you?" Kline would reach down and stroke the soft fur and, contented, his dog would lay the weight of his muzzle on his thigh. Beau had slipped through the wire, mines and trip flares and followed him into the field. Kline reached out his hand and stroked the slobbering muzzle on his leg.

# SOG: Missions to the Well

The day the siege began, Beau was trotting across the compound, his muscles loose under his skin. Mid step, he flinched sensing the North Vietnamese attack before the first explosion. It was that second just before a tornado hits in its fury, when air is sucked out to make room for storm. There was a slight break in Beau's stride. He relived that moment the constrictor threw its coils. Beau felt the change in air pressure of rockets descending on the camp. Then came the whoosh as heavy shells parted the air. Before the first round impacted on Ben Het and the long siege commenced, Beau dashed to the nearest cover and dove in. Soldiers crossing the compound were startled at Beau's out-of-character dash to safety. They had no time to ferret out the cause. The long battle at Ben Het began.

Rockets, artillery, and mortar rounds impacted throughout the base turning buildings into haystacks of wood splinters. A deuce-and-a-half truck was lifted into the air and fell crumpled on one side, the front wheels spinning in the air.

A Montagnard woman in a long black dress was carrying a load of firewood in her backpack when a string of explosions walked across the opening toward her. Like the dog, she sensed it all, felt the air suck out of the camp, perhaps even heard the projectile cut its way through the sky. She, with the stoic calm of her people, bent to her knees, her pack still on her back, and without spilling a stick of wood, stretched herself prone behind a low sandbag wall. An artillery round impacted it dead center. Sand and canvas flew from the place with hurricane force. It blasted the wall of a nearby building throwing a storage barrel next to it into the sky. The particles sandblasted the paint from the wall to bare wood leaving a still-painted silhouette where the barrel had been. The revetment where the mother lay, disappeared to the height of her knees. Debris rained down into her hair and greyed her pack. She caught her breath—for the concussion had knocked it from her—unfolded herself from where she lay, and with explosions still coming in, glanced for missing sticks of wood, and hurried on.

Enemy mortar-fire from the tree line joined the battle as many as ten North Vietnamese tanks rumbled toward the outer wire of the camp. Behind them, a full-regiment of screaming enemy regulars charged the base with their weapons. The treads of one tank caught in the barbed wire of the perimeter and wound itself into a ball where it helplessly lay, a ball of metal yarn with the cannon barrel thrust through like a knitting needle.

Special Forces men rushed toward the perimeter strapping on their web gear and gathered strikers to join the fight.

Green Berets shouted to their Montagnard strikers. "To the bunkers! Move! Move!"

One striker did not heed the orders. Near the center of the parade ground, he held his wounded arm at eye level with his good hand. In shock, with explosions falling around him, he stared at his massive wound without moving. A long white bone protruded through his flesh. His eyes were huge and fixed on his stick of bone. Blood poured into the ground. Fingers quivered.

Kline saw him.

He ran to him and turned his face away from his wound. "Hey, Go see *Bác Sĩ* now."

Kline took him by the shoulder and turned him toward the dispensary. "Doctor make number one. Go, go." And he shoved him in the direction.

The sergeant watched until he saw the soldier move.

The long siege had begun.

\* \* \* \* \*

We were leaving the mess hall, the place of eggs and bacon and hash browns and waffles with maple syrup, followed by the shallow dish of peach halves to end it all, when the staff sergeant from operations approached. Although we were among our own, he lowered his voice and said, "Mission for you, Norm. Briefing is at ten."

That was it. No Miss Moneypenny, or Doctor No, or Q or M. Just a simple statement. An hour on the clock. A place to go.

He waited for Doney to affirm that we got the message before he turned and walked away. I had that shot of adrenaline which all of us felt before our missions—not unlike the surge of excitement we felt at the door of the airplane as we jumped into the sky.

I glanced over at Joe Morris, then at Doney. It could be one of many targets but the most recent image in my mind was that of heat lightning in the west.

At ten we learned the target. C&C was not normally tasked with in-country targets in Vietnam, but rather Laos, Cambodia, and North Vietnam—significantly denied areas of enemy control. "Ben Het, as you know is under siege. PAVN has a tight cordon around them. There is constant incoming fire. They are reporting evidence of heavy tunneling under the perimeter leading into the facility. Saigon is concerned about those tanks being used by PAVN. Might we expect them to be used elsewhere? Is there movement and buildup for a nation-wide offensive?

"This is a mission the Mike Force is taking on as most of the fighting is in-country, but the higher-ups want more information than they can provide at this time.

"Your mission is to insert here," the captain tapped the map with his pointer, "west of Kontum and south of Ben Het. You will insert by Kingbee helicopter to an LZ you select. Your mission is to find and monitor infiltration routes, storage areas, truck parks, and evidence of tanks and long-distance weapons. Look for targets for our bombers.

"Questions? Good."

A staff sergeant with a limp gave the intelligence portion of the briefing. "Ben Het has been under assault by the crack 66th and 28th NVA regiments; formations of the ten-thousand-man First NVA Infantry Division which have been involved in several significant operations in the past. Until now it was believed they were in their sanctuary slightly north and west resting and refitting. The attack began using ten PT-76 tanks and 650 artillery rounds directed into the facility. It was followed by a full charge on the perimeter by elements of the full division. The camp is effectively surrounded by the enemy. There is ample evidence that the NVA is tunneling under the wire and outside fortifications in multiple locations around the camp." The briefer looked up from his notes. Finding no questions from us, he limped to his chair.

We received the logistics and communications portions of the briefing and the operations officer dismissed us with, "That is all. Good luck, gentlemen." The captain and first sergeant of Recon were there. Colonel Abt shook our hands and solemnly said, "God speed."

Florida was in the last stage of preparation gearing up for the show. For the remainder of that day and all of the next we coordinated with communications for call signs and frequencies, stocked up on provisions, and made final equipment checks. We had been well prepared for commitment before the alert. It was just a matter of fine-tuning it all. The last evening before we inserted, we three Americans walked to our familiar bunker behind the club. I heard the sucking crackle of the cheap tobacco in the Montagnard's pipe and I determined to buy him a supply from our small PX if they had any, perhaps Prince Albert in a can. We faced west. Somewhere on the other side of those blue-black hills, clearly outlined when bombs fell, lay our target. Tomorrow we would be there. The flashes would no longer remind me of summer heat lightning, or the old, silent, black and white movies, but would be in full color with the crescendo of war.

Morning found us at the metal helipad sitting on our packs. The deck was moist and slick from fog and the dew of the night. Ridgetops between us and Pleiku were erased in the overcast and we wondered how long it would be before the pilots could get through. But the H-34 Kingbees arrived with a flare. They did not wait for the fog to lift but threaded their way through a pass between the hills. In the distance they were without sound, a dot on the low horizon. The dot separated into three silhouettes. Far away the engines purred, but as they drew close, they rumbled. Over our eastern perimeter, just over the charcoal maker's hut, they swooped and dropped to a landing on the helipad. Before the rotor blades completed their last circuit, the pilots hopped from their choppers in scarves and sunglasses and I wondered if the lead pilot timed his leap so the last pass of the rotor blade lifted the scarf around his neck for his entrance. "We have arrived!"

The trio knew they were there to fly a mission, but our people had not told them what it was; no point in letting the enemy be aware by a slight slip of the tongue. Doney mollified the possibility of them thinking they were not trusted by telling them our mission was just laid on. One pilot was a double for the flamboyant leader, Nguyen Cao Ky, complete with thin mustache. Doney approached him with his map, placing his forefinger on a small white space in the mostly green paper.

The pilot shook his head and waved his hand back and forth. He spoke in good English. "Maybe you do not want to go in there. That LZ is too big. If it shows on the map, be sure Charlie is watching it. We know a place close by, been there before." He looked up at Doney. "Maybe here is better for you."

He and Doney hovered over the map, the American with his forefinger firmly fixed on the white place, the Vietnamese man sliding his own to alternate locations. In the end they agreed on a small opening in the trees. The pilot dipped his head in salute, turned to his people and raised one arm which said without words, "Mount up!"

We were barely aboard, Chin still on the strut hauling himself inside, when our fleet of three leaped into the air. Leaped! The craft leaned forward and sped toward the target. Although the Kingbee was large and heavy, capable of taking many hits, the power of the massive engines lent a feeling of being weightless as we raced to the west, banking left and right in turns around invisible pilons. We were airborne motorcycles, Harley Davidsons racing a winding course, swooping, diving, banking in tight turns. Having years behind the stick, our pilots were one with their machines. Their minds did not send the command to their fingers and on to the controls. Their minds were the will of the controls. They thought and the machine responded. What music coursed through their psyche? Ride of the Valkyries? A Vietnamese martial score?

Below us, all was thick and green. Steep highland ridges and dense valleys with fast-moving streams in them slid under us as we flew by. One could only guess how many soldiers peered through the breaks in the trees and sighted on us with their weapons. Waiting.

We grew near the pin hole in the green fabric of the central highlands that marked the place we would insert for our mission. The door gunner turned and shouted, but his words were snatched away by the wind. He pointed solemnly to a small opening in the green. His eyes narrowed. The levity of the morning was gone. I saw the white tops of his knuckles where his hands were frozen on the triggers. An enemy presence? A compromised LZ? Our destination? He nodded vigorously at me and gave me a thumbs up.

It was business. Straight and level, then coming in at speed. The door gunner crouched over his machine gun willing a target to appear.

Outside the door, only yards away, one of the other Kingbees dove by making a pass across the break in the forest to draw fire. Our turn next. Our Nguyen Cao Ky pilot banked hard and "S" turned, corkscrewing and sliding in, arriving with just a hint of pause. The moment the strut brushed the grass we leaped off and hustled to the thickness that lined the field. A pause only, and the chopper sped away, a dragonfly touching the surface of a pond.

We used the engine noise of the departing Kingbees to cover our rush to cover where we formed a tight circle and waited before dismissing the pilots who by now were in the next valley. Teams were often hit by a prepared ambush on an LZ. At times, as recon teams waited at an insert, they were alerted by the headlong rush of approaching enemy.

Ten minutes. No sign of enemy movement.

Doney caught Morris' eye and nodded toward the radio, "Dismiss the aircraft."

Morris removed the handpiece and in a whisper that was no more than air and could not be heard by the striker next to him, said, "Team okay. Good day."

We were on our own.

Doney clicked his tongue to Chin, our point man, and nodded

the direction he wanted him to go.

We were shadows sliding slowly in total silence. Our feet moved in braille. We felt the ground before we placed our feet, feeling to not make a sound, feeling with the care one would make to not place a foot on a sleeping viper. We looked for trails, especially leading to our small break in the trees, crossed a dry stream bed with its polished stones, and moved west. Part way up a slope we made a security stop. It was hot. The air was clammy. Around us the leaves were heavy and drooped. Birds were reluctant to fly and barely moved in the branches. We listened from our small perimeter. Quiet. I thought I could hear moisture evaporate into the air, but I wondered if I would ever hear movement in the soggy weeds. We listened. I heard Ba, close beside me, when he turned the top on his canteen.

Voices.

One moment there was no indication of another human. Then, voices. They were not crystal clear, for they were muted by the humidity. Dream-like voices hung above the ground like fog, weaving among the trees. Voices which were unafraid of detection. Voices with the tones of the Orient.

I glanced at Ba. He was looking in the direction of the speaking, his head craned forward, his mouth open. He slid his canteen into the cover leaving it unsnapped. At the front of the column Doney tapped his ear so Chin could see it and pointed to the side. His facial expression said, "Is it coming from there?"

Chin slowly nodded. The sign said, "Yes. And very close." The point man slowly slid his hand up for the rest of us to see and tapped the back of his head. "Enemy. Close by."

We waited, hovering over our weapons. I stared into the shrubs looking for anything to reveal the enemy. A shape. A movement. A color which did not fit. Twenty minutes or more, I neither saw nor heard a thing.

Doney signaled. We unfolded ourselves, moving like phantoms. Soundless. Coiled springs. We crept toward the source of the voices.

Nothing. Absolutely nothing. A yellow and black bird cocked its head and also listened.

Turtle-like, Chin slowly turned and looked back at the rest of us. His brows were raised in amazement. His features said, "I know they are out there, but where?"

We edged forward. Perhaps they had passed through. We looked for signs of PAVN but there were no clues they had ever been there. Doney gave a direction to the point man and we continued our reconnaissance.

Triple canopy forest lay its hand over us leaving us in constant twilight. In places, sunlight shone between its fingers and cast long shadows. "Just a few more hours of daylight at the most," I thought. Vegetation became dry and brittle as the day wore on. Notes of the birds carried a tone that said, "Come to the nest, darkness is on its way." At a listening stop we put water into the plastic bags with our prepared individual rations, let them soften, and ate. Ba gave me red pepper to add to mine. He rolled his eyes and waited to see if I could take its hotness. We composed a situation report for Covey in case we heard him in the area. It was written in code from a one-time pad and included the probable place we would remain overnight.

Faintly, perhaps in the next valley, we heard the hum of a small airplane. Morris crawled under his tarp with a penlight and the message and whispered our report with "team okay" at the end.

We were touch-close, tucked in a bamboo thicket we had chosen for our RON. I crawled forward and set up a Claymore mine. Doney did not like to use them in the RON for fear trackers could slip in, turn them toward the team, then rustle the bushes so we would unknowingly fire the mines on ourselves. I put a small piece of luminous tape on our side of the mine so we would know they remained facing the right direction. It was dusk, not yet dark. Ba faced our back trail with me next to him. Voices again! Ba flinched. I heard the brush of cloth when his body jerked in the dark. The voices were like those heard in a cheap hotel from the other side of a thin wall. Sentences came in fragments. It seemed only a thin line of bushes separated us from the speakers. The talking abruptly ceased. We waited to hear if it would begin again.

Ba slid over to me and whispered, "*Bac Viet*. North Vietnam.

They have accent. They no be VC."

"Certainly," I thought, "They aren't aware of us or they wouldn't speak so loudly. They might be holed up like we are, just on the other side of those bushes. Or," I reasoned, "they might be passing through on a trail." We leaned back against our packs.

It had been full dark for two hours. We were settled in—eight unmoving shapes, black shadows, a part of the vegetation. My last image before we could no longer see at all, was of Nhok leaned back against his rucksack with his grenade launcher across his legs, his hand around the comb of the stock. I memorized the shapes on my horizon against the slightly lighter skyline. I must have dozed. My eyes opened. I became fully awake. Someone was chopping wood. Minutes later, he was joined by other wood cutters. It came from below us in the valley. Loud talking filtered to us from the location; perhaps Asian loggers shouting to each other as they worked. The axe work continued for an hour. From the next ridge, not far from the wood cutters, I heard a low growl of a laboring truck engine.

Sometime after midnight I heard tapping sounds in the trees. They reminded me of the first rain showers on dry autumn leaves I heard outside my bedroom window when I was growing up. Not a mist or a cloudburst, but a modest rain that raises dust on a dry sidewalk and sends rivulets along an old, dry stream bed. The patter began farther up the ridgeline, worked its way down near us, edged along our RON, changed direction, and passed on. I thought it strange, listening to its passage, for it seemed to fall along a narrow path and proceed in a winding course, with no wind to steer it. I had a small piece of tarp and was about to cover my rifle to keep it dry when I realized no drops were falling on us.

"That isn't rain!" my brain shouted. "That's people moving out there. The sound is that of locusts which filled the skies in the old news reels about the dust bowl."

I felt Ba and Noi stir in their places on the other side of me. There was heavy movement in the bush—the trample of many people. Would the winding route of that passage of people turn on a signal and sweep through our RON?

I looked toward the shadowed area where I had placed my Claymore mine. I could not see the tape! I felt my heart stop. Had sappers slipped in and turned it around? But I remembered, its back was against a tree to protect us from the back-blast. From where I was, I could not see the tape. We waited.

The tapping of shoulders and trouser legs brushing against shrubs ceased. Quiet returned to the forest. Only the rustle of tree frogs and small night hunters disturbed the silence, leaving it for me to decipher them in the dark. At three in the morning the tapping resumed. It was close by. Perhaps fifty meters away. It began of a sudden, passed along our west side, and then faded away. We were fully alert for we could not discern if the marchers had stopped at our side or passed on into the night.

Morning came in lessening shades of grey and finally lay a veil of pale amber on everything. Norm Doney stared into the bushes. Catching my eye, he signaled me over and whispered, "They might be waiting for us out there. All that movement… I can't imagine they don't know we are here. I'm going to take Chin and find out. If we get in a fire fight you have the team. Joe has the radio and knows what to do. You decide if you should come and help or stay in place and wait for us to get back. If Chin and I are killed and you can't get our bodies, you know what to do. Take the team and make for the nearest LZ."

"Got it," I whispered back.

He signaled Florida to wait in place and took Chin to reconnoiter. They slipped out without sound, barely moving at all. I used all of my senses to follow their progress but the highlands had swallowed them.

Silence wrapped itself around us as we waited. My hands were clammy on my rifle. I used my ears most of all, straining for the sounds of struggle deep in the bushes. Once, I saw Nhok lean forward and slide his launcher from his knees, then relax again—something he thought he saw or heard. Even Hue, my hatless interpreter with his messed-up hair was intent. I saw a flick in the leaves. A single leaf brushed to the side, so slight a thing a breath may have done it.

## SOG: Missions to the Well

They arrived. It had been more than an hour. First, I saw Chin in his Chicom hat with the red star when he parted the vines and peered through at us. I was relieved to see his ubiquitous smile. Behind him, Doney slid through the bushes and joined us. Both of them had daubed their faces and hands with mud along the way. Their knees and elbows were dark with dirt.

Doney tapped his lips twice. We squeezed PIRs into our mouths. The only time we ever ate in our RON was when we were going to leave it. I retrieved my Claymore and we sterilized where we had spent the night. The enemy would not know that eight men had been there. A nod, and we rose to go. Chin looked back. No Billiken smile this time. He slowly parted the bush with his rifle barrel and Florida proceeded west.

Tension increased as we moved. We were sneaking, creeping up on an unseen enemy who was somewhere in front of us. We had slithered fifty meters or more when a troop of chattering monkeys swung noisily through the trees dropping seed pods and feces. We used their passage to speed our own movement for a few paces. I smelled something, a familiar smell I could not place. It hit me: It was the fragrance of the freshly mowed lawns I cut with a push mower as a boy. There was no time to ponder the anomaly. Having moved more quickly with the cover of the passing monkeys, we found ourselves at the lip of a fresh trail cut through the grass.

A hand signal—assault formation along the path. At the edge we dropped to our knees ready to fight. The One-Zero signaled Ba to cover one end of the path, and Chin and Noi to face the other direction. Abreast, we hovered in the last bit of cover. I heard the trail, actually heard it. Grass that was trampled flat in the night was in the process of standing upright. Soil that had been squashed by countless feet was swelling back to shape. Somewhere in the weeds along the path, water trickled to a new place. This was new, freshly made in the night, perhaps used only minutes before.

Doney signaled "take pictures." I slid out my camera and stepped on the trail. In places vegetation was worn away to mud and bore clear prints of boots: Bata boots, the footgear of the North

Vietnamese Army. I snapped pictures in both directions from where we stood. Norm glanced at his compass and noted the orientation for later entry in his log.

I was exposed on this trail. So recently had it been trod I fancied the smell of their perspiration. Soil that had been soggy before numerous footfalls squeezed it moved to its new stasis.

The tapping sound again! Heavy, hurried movement came from farther up the trail we were on. Noi spun around. He looked at Doney and me to be sure we also heard it. He placed his rifle to his shoulder and sighted at the place the path disappeared into brush. People were advancing toward us on this trail. Chin aimed his rifle toward the new threat. The footfalls of boots on the moist passage came from up the slope. They were closing fast. Doney looked up in that direction and jammed his notebook into his pocket. He looked over to me. "Go! Go! Now!"

With a single mind, we sprang from the trail, rushing for cover heedless we might be heard. We were moments, seconds from contact. In my dash from the track, I swept my foot across the dirt to erase footprints we may have left and saw a clear print of a Bata boot in the mud. It was a perfectly embossed empty boot print. A thin stream of water was trickling into the print and barely covered its bottom. The maker of that print had passed but minutes before. My camera was still out so I snapped a hurried picture as I dashed from the path. Just in time. A glance that was but a blur revealed the bushes being pushed aside as the first enemy entered the trail and came in my direction.

There was just enough time to lunge for cover, spin, and crouch in the bushes ready to shoot. Shrubs that were parted by my shoulders were still moving when the first enemy appeared. My knees made a snapping sound when they bent and I was surprised the lead soldier did not hear it. My concern we might have left our own footprints to be discovered on the path was moot, for the soldiers route-stepped at a quick march, never looking down. I heard their panting breaths in front of me. There were far too many of them to handle by choice, but any mistake would start the fight. They hustled by, mostly hidden except for snatches of blurred khaki cloth we saw through the breaks in the leaves. They continued on, one after another, not speaking or coughing. Rushing by. White rabbits of literature mumbling, "I'm late. I'm late. For a very important date."

The only date of urgency that might speed these platoons and companies so was the siege of Ben Het. No sergeants walked alongside to urge them on. There was the soft slapping of boots on the moist ground and swishing of fabric uniforms, then the silence the last soldier left behind. They were gone. They passed without rattling equipment or hint of a rear guard or stragglers in their wake.

We crouched without moving until we were sure they had passed. Doney made an entry in his notebook. He guessed the number of men who had gone by, the time, and direction of travel. He slid the notes into his shirt pocket and glanced back at the team. He signaled to use stealth and pointed the way for Chin. Until we were well clear of the path, we slipped away at a crouch, often walking backward, until we gained distance from the trail and could stand upright.

A hundred meters or more, with intervening shrubs and concealment, we made a security stop. We barely had time to sit and study the area in front of us before we heard hurried movement. Had our presence at the trail been undetected after all? Were they coming for us? They came from the ridgeline as before but with less tapping against the leaves, for all was worn away. Instead, we heard the rapid thudding of their boots in the wet soil, squishing where there was mud. They moved quickly—an urgent movement to a predetermined location. Then as before, they were gone.

We wormed our way west again looking for more intelligence on the enemy. To gather significant information, we needed to set up on a trail and see them with our eyes; count them, describe their weapons, how they moved, their alertness, and if we could, describe any patches worn on their uniforms. We would have to find a place where we could see all of that. So far, we had found several foot trails, a few high-speed trails, and it seemed they were making a road through the forest.

Engines. Trucks laboring up a grade, slogging with their loads.

Doney pored over his map. We would find a place and monitor the movement.

Another trail. This time it was hard-packed and high-speed. Footfalls and vehicles compressed the surface to clay. Along it, in the dirt of the shoulder, long, snake-like furrows were compressed into the soil. Bicycles. From the places it showed in the dirt, the tire marks cut deeply into the ground. Heavy-laden transportation bicycles. I guessed where they left the easy-going hard surface of the road and pushed their burden on the soft shoulder making room for large vehicles to pass. I would remember.

It was necessary to see the vehicles and troops and bicycles and describe them on paper. Perhaps a prisoner. . . .

Doney poured over his map, looking for a rise from which to monitor the trail and for a possible extraction point if we were in contact or had a prisoner.

Morris got a signal on his radio.

Florida moved deeper into the terrain, away from the road. From a security stop, Morris listened under his tarp.

"From Covey," Morris said as he emerged, "They have a team in trouble. Prairie Fire emergency. They want us to hole up."

We rose to find a defendable place removed from the labyrinth of trails.

A gunshot.

Hue had just taken a swallow and the canteen was yet at his lips. His eyes widened. The shot was close by, not the pop of an AK; more that of the SKS the trackers used. Hue slowly lowered his canteen. His bed head hair was straight up. Without turning his head, his eyes cast about left and right. His fingers inched over to his weapon and grasped it by the comb of the stock and only then lowered the canteen the rest of the way. Ba glanced at me and nodded the confirmation we all knew: We had trackers. They knew where we were.

Florida maneuvered along a shallow ridgeline and stopped. A gunshot. One round fired to alert enemy units in the area.

We changed direction and made our way to the east. Another

gunshot announced our move.

Fifty meters later we made a fishhook turn toward our backtrail. A rifle shot. Each discharge of the weapon directed enemy units in their pursuit.

Doney used every trick to confuse our pursuers and hide our passage, twisting our path, making false trails, once even following our own trail. Toward evening we fish-hooked, made our way up a gentle slope, and found a grove of thick trees with fields of fire below. We slid in and prepared to spend the night. We planned escape routes we would take if we had to evade in the dark. For the first time we heard no signal shots.

We remained touch-close in a blackness produced by the night and compounded by thick canopy. With the exception of the normal activity of a highland forest, it was quiet. Small creatures, both hunters and prey rustled in the leaves. Bamboo popped with the temperature. There was a flutter in the upper limbs of a tree that resembled wings of a bird caught in branches and I imagined a sparrow in the jaws of a lime-green mamba snake. Though in my mind I was compelled to analyze each sound I thought it a pacific enough night to expose trackers feeling for our passage.

Three times during the night we heard movement. It was farther away than before. Twice it was that hurried pace; troops heading for a destination where they were sorely needed, needed enough to march on new trails in near-total darkness. The third occasion involved cumbersome movement—twigs and breaking debris, loud brushing against branches at the side of the path. I imagined weary soldiers struggling and stumbling under heavy loads of weapons and ammunition. Although I could not see, I felt my head turn as my ears followed their movement as they passed.

Very early, long before the approach of dawn, when even night predators packed it in, a single gunshot broke the stillness. In a frenzy, frightened birds burst from a thicket. It came from below us, a little lower down the grade where we holed up. It was along our backtrail before that last fishhook we made before settling in. The tracker had found us.

I imagined a Montagnard tracker slowly straightening himself; painfully so, for he had been hours in a crouch, his hands and fingers touching the press of our marks in the forest floor, reading them in the black of this night. He was as a blind man reading the braille we had left behind, reading it as clearly as another man could in the day. Perhaps he would rise and sniff the air—for the incautious use of soap, or the anchovies in our rations, or that which only he would know. He would lower himself again, feel where our feet had bent the grass and where the edge of our boots had incised the soil; would sense the rise of the small hill which housed us and know its advantage; "They are there," he would conclude in absolute certainty.

Perhaps also, I wondered about the tracker. This was not even his war. He may have been taken by force from his longhouse, and an officer would say words, threats, which were clear to him, "Your skill for the safety of this village." And sadly, he followed the team. At a place he thought his task complete, he, with one deep breath, raised the rifle into the air and squeezed the trigger.

It was yet dark, but the enemy, in spite of that handicap, martialed its people into place. They tried to move with stealth and be on us before we were aware, but they stumbled, and broke dead branches as they moved without benefit of a trail. Enough shoulders swished against leaves to lend the sound of a whisper the length of the ridge. We listened to the movement. Tried to fix their location. If they were unsure where we were they might pass us by and we could evade from there.

Darkness surrendered slowly. Though we could not see the sky through the canopy, I hoped it would be clear with nothing to hinder help from the air—if it was available. The sounds of movement on the horizon ceased. I could no longer hear them. Perhaps, even now they were crawling toward us. I strained my ears to track them. Nearby, a bird rustled on the ground and with her feet, swept away dry leaves and grabbed a black bug. Another bird carried a worm to a nest. An insect made a sound as though its brittle shell were hollow. They masked the sounds for which I most listened, that of approaching enemy.

## SOG: Missions to the Well

Doney wrote a sitrep stating the events of the night as the rest of us squeezed rations into our mouths. All of our senses were alert; antennae ever searching. I heard a low hum in the next valley and hoped it was not truckloads of enemy. Morris slid under the tarp with Doney's report and whispered it to Covey. The answer was immediate. He slid from under the tarp.

"They want us to come out," he whispered.

Morris was holding the handset of the radio in one hand, his eyes on Doney as he said this. It was at that moment the North Vietnamese advanced toward us on line. All pretext of stealth was gone. It began with a single shot a hundred meters away. Another answered a distance from that. A third discharge came from our west. Shouts. Muffled orders. Trampling sounds to the north in the brush. Across a line to the north and to the west, the enemy shouted and tapped sticks together. Like hunters of old India, sitting astride bejeweled elephants driving the tiger to certain death, these sought to drive us to a place of ambush.

"Tell them they need to come right away. They are trying to push us into an ambush. Give them our coordinates. The enemy knows where we are."

Morris dove under the tarp and gave the information. I heard the muffled exchange with Covey from my place near the end of our line.

Norm signaled me over and showed me the map, ever mentoring me. "This is where we are. They are here," he said with his finger on the place, "and here. They are trying to drive us this way. They probably expect us to use that open area here to be extracted. They will be waiting. We'll find another." He waited to be sure I understood.

The enemy advance was closing on us quickly. I left one Claymore mine facing the place we spent the night with a primed ten-minute fuse in the well. With a glance back and a go-ahead nod from Doney, Chin led out, his face grim. We moved quickly to give us space. A hundred meters later, we made a radical change in direction. We slowed the pace, nearly a crawl, and evaded to the east. Stepping in the footprints of the one in front of us, as Ba erased the signs of our going.

The mine exploded to our rear and dozens of automatic weapons shot blindly into the bushes thinking they were under close attack. Shouting. A scream. Shouts of anger.

Doney looked at the map again and made an acute change in direction. He placed his hand on Chin's shoulder and pointed the way. His hand gesture was that of a meat cleaver parting the vines. He glanced back at Ba and signaled, "Hide our trail as we go."

I slid over to him. "I will be your eyes and cover you."

I saw the nervousness in Ba's face. A thin gold chain protruded from his lips and I knew he had his gold Buddha in his mouth. "Han Son, Han Son," he told me before, "If I die and VC kill me, if I have Buddha, him in mouth me, I go heaven same same you." He strapped his rifle to his back, bent to his knees and began to hide our passage. I had not time to tell him John 3:16.

We moved with stealth, changing directions prudently, with Ba hiding our tracks. At a place, the trees thinned and light poured through, leaving patches of pale yellow on the ground. I did not need the map to know this was the place printed in white depicting a large opening in the vegetation. The tapping of sticks behind us made a large arc and was clearly driving us to this area. We studied the area around the break in the trees. Among the varied and splattered colors of green that made up the bushes and tall grass, were areas of solid color—in shapes of men. They were grouped in clutches and formations along the edge. In places, men in ambush failed to be still. Their pith helmets moved under the sunlight, like mushroom swaying in a breeze.

We maneuvered away to the northeast. At a distance from the waiting enemy, we made a security stop. "Joe," he whispered, "Tell FOB to come now or it might be too late. Come with what we just made. Howard will know what I mean."

Morris answered back. "They got it. Another team is in trouble tying up assets but someone is on the way."

Enemy movement grew nearer. Underbrush cracked under their

advancing boots. Tall grass swayed. I did not think help would arrive in time.

I held up a Claymore and fuse.

Doney nodded. I put a ten-minute fuse into the well and Nhok rushed to the place the movement seemed most pressing and anchored it behind a tree facing the advance.

We maneuvered east at a rapid pace. I was crouched over Ba as he hid our trail, and I knew he could not keep up.

The Claymore exploded. There were loud shouts and what could only be cursing. They fired full-automatic in all directions. A few stray rounds slapped the leaves in the trees above us.

The communists crashed through the undergrowth nearly at a run. Without need of words, their headlong pursuit conveyed their rage, hatred, and hunger for revenge. They began to fire B-40 rockets toward us, some exploding in the trees sending shrapnel in an arc. I held up another Claymore with its 700 steel balls. I raised up a raised hand—five-minute fuse?

They were closing fast.

"Yes," he shouted back and I jammed it behind a tree facing the nearest advance. Nhok was firing round after round with his grenade launcher.

Fifty meters later we found a small opening in the trees, large enough for an extraction.

"Here!" Doney shouted.

I heard the rumble of helicopters.

"I hear you one-two-zero," Morris shouted into the handset.

The rumble grew louder.

"I will fire a pen flare to mark our location," he shouted into the handpiece so the pilot would know it was not small arms fire directed at him.

I shot the flare across the bow of the lead chopper. It was a Kingbee and I heard the unmistakable voice of the lead pilot in his blowing scarf and sunglasses.

Having fixed our exact location, the door gunner fired his machine gun around Florida trying to slow the advance.

A Kingbee skidded to a hover above us. The door gunner kicked out the Doney ladder, his hands never leaving his weapon. It unrolled; the last rungs swayed just above the ground.

Doney, Ba and I remained on the ground and shot into the bushes as the rest of the team climbed. Debris and dirt kicked up from the rotor blades matted in our hair and smarted our eyes. From the deck of the chopper, Nhok shot round after round into the swaying grass and bushes at the circling enemy.

Our legs were like rubber as we climbed those last rungs then lay on the deck of the craft panting for breath.

I remembered the ladder hanging over the side. I crawled to the edge and looked down. The door gunner was spraying the trees with the machine gun. Hot brass was falling on me and burning the back of my neck. As the Kingbee climbed to escape our peril, the ladder blew back in an arc. I wondered if the pilot would remember it twisting in the wind below us. I prayed it would clear the trees and not tangle and pull us down. To my horror, the bottom rungs slapped against the upper branches and thick limbs of the hardwood. Thick tree limbs thrust through the openings like claws seeking purchase. I thought with a sense of dread, "This is the end," but as the helicopter shuttered and paused, the rungs pulled free, the tree top sprang upright, and Florida, freed, flew east. I glanced at the door gunner. He had been holding his breath. His fingers were paused over his triggers as he forgot to shoot. Like mine, his eyes were frozen on the ladder rungs. The strong fingers of the forest lost their grip. He nodded at me and smiled.

I glanced over at Doney. He, like me, was watching his people, reading them. Morris sat with his back to the wall, his eyes closed; Nhok was without expression, always a scholar deep in thought. I noticed the pouches which held his M-79 rounds; he had only three left. Hue, our interpreter, the weak link in the chain, leaned back against the skin of the aircraft. His head nodded up and down; his hair was wild and straight. He was humming, looking around; nervously he tapped the deck with his foot.

Chin was looking at me with his full smile. He half-turned so I could see his back. He reached back and tapped it, then pointed at me. He tapped his back again. I knew what he meant. The words he and Nhok wrote on my back with felt pen, just high enough so God could see it: *"Han Son Cam Bow Ya Chin."* Hanson never die!

# CHAPTER THREE
## *Arizona Wire Tap*

There was a street that paralleled the Dak Bla River, set a row or two of houses in from its banks, that I considered to be main street. There was an aura about it I tended to describe even to those who knew it well. In the setting of the Orient, it had its comparison to the main streets of the small farm towns of the Midwest where I grew up. Not that they looked alike at all having no silos and feed stores, but both were simple, honest, statements of their communities.

To get there from our Special Forces camp, you drove through the "village" and past the open rice fields where one or two grey water buffalo paused behind an ancient plow and stared toward the road. You continued a mile to the shallow, wide Dak Bla with its sandy banks. Before sappers snuck in one night and blew the wood bridge, you crossed it hearing the tires thump over the timber planks like heartbeats or like the clop clop of hoofs when a farmer urged his cow across. The street was the first turn to the right and extended only a few blocks until the road bent left, leaving its charm behind.

We were on standdown after a mission, and we gave our

mercenaries, who we affectionately called our "little people," the day off. When I told them I was going to Kontum because I wanted to look in the shops and eat some good Asian food, that was it.

"Han Son, Han Son. We go with you. We take you number one. We show you best place."

Ba was my tail gunner when we were on mission. He was tall with high cheekbones and appeared to be North Vietnamese. His laugh was always soundless, his mouth wide open, and he tilted his head back in a gesture which suggested we might be pulling his leg. He was married with a small child, proud of his family. Ba brought me to his home to meet them. His wife cooked a Vietnamese meal of local fare—duck eggs, rice and herbs and shrimp taken from the ditch. That Ba would come with me to the heart of Kontum instead of going straight home spoke of his desire that I not go alone. Perhaps there was a danger of which I was unaware.

Two of my people were Chinese, Chin and Nhok. They insisted they also go. I always wondered if there were a Chinese section of the city as Saigon had Cholon. I wondered where they went on their off time.

That street had charm, Asian charm. But it was an allure that also bore the contribution of the French when they were there. Their mark left the street Eurasian. French landscaping and architecture blended with the breath of the Orient.

The street was cobblestone, sun-bleached and powdered with a brown-red dust, unlike the bloom of flowers. The bricks lent themselves to pedestrians and vehicles. Straining pedicab drivers peddled over the bumps with their boney legs, shells of men, gaunt and yellow with tuberculosis and the drugs of the Orient. They wheezed by and stopped out of breath and waited for a fare. It was late spring early summer and the flame trees that lined the road were in full red bloom. They were tall and arched over the street touching the flame trees on the other side. Nearly at the end, where the street turned, grew one coconut palm. Perhaps its first seeds came in on wind from the coast. The fronds spread from the common stock and in the center bore a clump of small, still-green coconuts.

At the very end of the lane where it bends between two buildings was a banyan tree. It brought Kipling and black panthers to my mind, and perhaps, in the old days, a place where a storyteller might sit and hold his listeners spellbound. He, as I imagined him, would get to an exciting place and pause—perhaps tap his long fingernails on the roots of this very tree, and wait until his listeners dropped a few coins into his hat to refresh his memory before he would go on.

The roots of a banyan tree are immense, the greater part above ground. They spread over the ground in every direction. The one at the end of the street in Kontum reminded me of an unwrapped mummy with its skin dried in numerous blue-grey folds, skin dry and shriveled over a bone frame and left to sag. The banyan roots seem to have no bark, just a skin, dried hard and powdered over with the dust of the street.

Tonal music played loudly inside the shops and the smells of ginger, cinnamon, and burning incense seeped from them to the sidewalk. "Come in, come in," the odors said. I bought a small jar of incense in one of the shops. Ba watched me unscrew the lid.

"Ba, it is to make your house smell good. You do not have to light it. Here, smell."

Ba inhaled a long whiff and rolled back his head in his wide soundless smile.

It was not expensive. It came from India and the container was of hand-carved lime-green soapstone. The carvings depicted several elephants around the whole. Each elephant held the leading one's tail with its trunk, until the very last one around the jar held the first elephant's tail. I was pleased with the sale. I bought it as much for the carving as the subtle fragrance.

We saw a restaurant near the end of the street. There was no sign, none was needed. The aroma of cooking food sent its finger through the open door and bade us inside. It was a busy place. Chattering locals filled the tables. Steam ghosted from the kitchen. I heard the sizzle from a large wok and the clatter of pots being washed at the back of the kitchen.

"How about here, Chin? Is this a good place to eat?"

"Yes. I eat here before. Very good place."

I turned to Nhok and Ba. "Okay, we eat here? You hungry?"

"Yes, hungry. We can get food inside and eat here," he said tapping a table outside on the cobblestones.

"You guys help me order food. You choose food for me . . . and I want to pay."

We went in.

Inside the glass case were large bowls of food. A pretty young girl in an *áo dài* waited for us to order. Behind her in a small open kitchen, a mama-san with her hair in a bun held a large ladle with both hands and stirred a huge kettle. On hearing our voices, she turned her body to better face us and continued to stir. Her face was stern, the young girl's mother?

Chin was talking. "Han Son this be number one for you. We get same same. This be called, *bun cha*. Lots of food. It be grilled pork, noodles, and herbs. You know lots of . . ." He looked over to Nhok for the English words.

"Cucumbers, water chestnuts, and green herbs," Nhok supplied.

I paid her and we sat outside.

For only a moment as we took our seats, I recalled it was just yesterday we were in the field behind enemy lines. The mission was to gather intelligence on the enemy. There were no targets to hit; gather information on the target area, learn what we want to know, then come back. And so, for four days we did so. We were not observed when we went in. We wandered nearly among them, spied out their trails and roads, monitored their activities, listened to their talk, and as far as I knew they never knew we were there. We made it to an LZ and made it back and not a shot was fired. Just four days of adrenaline. No tales to tell in the club. No close calls. No dogs on our trail. No signal shots. And when we made it back it would be an uneventful mission, what they called a dry hole. But it was a successful mission, no less so if we had to fight our way out.

"I think this is my favorite street in Kontum," I told them.

"Aah, Han Son," Chin said, "If you want to see beautiful street, you go city of Hue. It is very beautiful."

Nhok, who did not often speak, took over the conversation. "Oh, you go to city of Hue. It is very beautiful. The Perfume River is there and Minh Mang Street. The royal tombs and the Khai Dinh tomb are very large stone monuments. And the Imperial Citadel also. There are palaces. We have not seen it since the Tet Offensive but you never forget such beauty."

Ba listened as he fingered his Buddha necklace.

"Just remembered," I said. "We were talking about streets. There is a book I read about Vietnam when the French were here. He wrote one about Dien Bien Phu called *Hell in a Very Small Place*, but this one was called *Street Without Joy*. His name was Bernard Fall and he wrote as if the war was a long street and there was no joy on it."

Nhok was my Chinese scholar. He nodded his head as he absorbed each part of the imagery. "Nhok," I said, "I could see you writing books or poetry someday."

Our conversation veered to missions like our last one. We never talked about such things when we were away from the FOB. We were speaking quietly in the most general of terms with no one in earshot. "There is a place in the Christian Bible," I said, "where there were only 300 soldiers who had to fight an entire army of enemy who were called the Midianites. There were so many they were like locusts, *shau chau*, spread over the ground."

"Aah, *shau chau*, we know locusts. Go everywhere, eat everything," Nhok said.

"Yes, well, the leader of the good guys was a man named Gideon, and the people were nervous about fighting so many soldiers. In a dream God sent Gideon and a tiny recon team on a mission to sneak through the woods in the black of night to the enemy camp and listen. At the enemy lines they heard the enemy talk and learned the enemy army was terrified of Gideon's men. They would break and run at the first sign of battle." I waited to be sure they followed my words.

"With that information they went back and gathered their men. They made their way in the dark to the enemy's perimeter and when they got in place, Gideon gave the signal. They blew trumpets and made loud noise like a large army and shouted as in a charge and crashed through the brush toward the enemy. The enemy panicked and ran in the blackness and began to kill each other in the dark and Gideon won the battle. At the end they said, 'The battle is the Lord's.'"

Chin smiled. His eyes crinkled nearly shut. He looked at me and said, "Gideon must have been Chinese."

We were still sitting at the cobblestone walk, drinking tea. A small group of peasants gathered at the banyan tree and sat in a circle. Even to me, I could see their clothing was of the poorest. The cloth was thin, soil-brown, and threadbare. The dye had faded over days of labor and hot sun. There were four men and one woman. The woman and one of the men wore turbans on their heads; the others wore grass conical hats. All the men wore sunglasses. They were blind.

They sat on grass mats facing the street. She could see and slid musical instruments to the men: a drum, gongs of differing sizes, a wind instrument, bamboo castanets, and a two-string violin. They began to play and from their frail bodies came robust singing.

"Aah," Ba said, glad to be able to contribute to the conversation. "They be Xam singers," he said. "Vietnam have. They be bery poor people. Come to Kontum—sing, maybe make money to eat. I hear before when I was baby san." He nodded to an upturned conical hat propped to receive coins. "You like, put coin in. Bery bery poor people."

We listened for several minutes.

Nhok said, "They are very poor people. Sometimes when crops fail and the blind people starve, they go from village to village to sing for food. The music is simple country music, what Americans call, 'folk.' They are blind people. They sing simple songs about life, and hard work, and better times. Sometimes they laugh about hard times."

"What brings them to Kontum? All the villages here are Montagnard," I asked.

"Think maybe war do. Maybe so dangerous they must go away,

come here," Chin said.

We listened to several songs. Nhok explained the lyrics. "Farmer work hard, very hard, rain no come, no come, baby san crying, crying, only little rice, father work in field all day, empty, empty food bag, black birds come take, come take, all day chase birds from food, chase birds away."

I felt a sadness for the condition of the people, but in the back of my mind an unwanted cynicism crept in. I recalled our just-finished mission to gather intelligence, and the Bible story of Gideon, but it bothered me there were no nearby Vietnamese villages from which they may have come.

"Ba," I said, "Do me a favor, will you?"

I only had a limited amount of piasters left in my pocket and I pulled them out. There were certainly a thousand piasters left in the crumpled wad.

"Will you please put this in the Xam singer's bowl for me?"

Ba softly walked over to not disturb the performance and slipped it into the container. The nearest blind man in the thick sunglasses turned and seemed to watch the paper money fall.

I smiled to myself. "He can see," I thought.

"I need to get back to the FOB," I told my people. They were ready to leave also. Ba stretched, tilted back his head and smiled. "Hug your baby san for me, Ba."

"Thank you for your company," I said to the three of them.

The timing was perfect. As I stood to go, a jeep pulled up to the walk. It was Mike Wilson.

"I thought that was you," he said. "Hop in."

"Hey, thanks. Glad for the ride."

"What brought you here?"

"Just some time with my people. It's priceless. Only bought one thing: this little jar of room fragrance. I bought it because I liked the jar."

"You should put some in your socks."

"Wanna borrow it?"

Mike smiled.

"And you? What were you up to?"

He looked over to me as he shifted gears to enter the main road. He rolled back his head as he normally did when he spoke at length, but I sensed a new tension in his voice. "Getting ready to go on one, I think. Something is up, that's for sure. I was at the exchange and one of the guys from recon found me. 'Oh,' he says, 'I'm sure glad I found you. They want you back at the FOB.'

"I just looked at him. I could tell something was up because they were looking for me—something unusual was going on. As soon as we got outside, I waited for him to tell me more. I just stopped in my tracks. I wanted to know what was up, ya know, Dale. I looked around me so he got the point that no one was around to listen to us.

"I just waited. So, he said, 'Mike, I think Arizona is being committed for a mission. You guys are going in right away.'

"I was pretty worried for a minute. Like maybe one of the teams was in big trouble, maybe some of us were killed. Now, I know that a Bright Light team gets committed quick like that but we weren't on a Bright Light.

"The guy from FOB kind of looked up in the sky like he wondered if he should tell me more, but he finally said he thought they were taking a team out of the field and we were going to replace them immediately on the same LZ. They talked about doing a wiretap."

Mike went silent for half a mile and I waited for him to collect his thoughts.

He continued, "So I says to him to be sure. 'You mean, my team, Arizona?'"

"'Afraid so, Mike,' he says."

We were over the bridge now and crossing the fields. We were alone in the jeep and felt secure about talking about such things.

"We are going in heavy: four Americans and six Yards. That should tell you something."

I nodded to him. "Some teams want to go in heavy, like New York and California but so far, eight men is about max. Some of the more Sneaky Pete teams go in light so they don't get discovered. How did your people decide to go in heavy?"

"I think the team we're replacing is New York. They found big stuff. They found commo wire. That means battalions or regiments. Saigon wants to know what they are talking about. I don't have any information yet."

Mike pulled up at the Recon office and shut off the engine. We were not out of the jeep before two of his team members met us. Relief showed in their faces. Kyle Dean met Mike at the driver's side. "Oh, glad they found you. We have to hustle. We are going in." He glanced over at me and continued. "In two hours."

"Two hours." Mike Wilson simply repeated his words. He looked over at me, then back at his team mates. "Two hours," he said in disbelief.

Terry Minnihan, a big burly sergeant known as Twiggy whispered, "As close as I figure it, New York is coming out and we are going in on the same LZ. OP 35 out of Saigon just came in on a jet. A man in civilian clothes came in with a black suitcase handcuffed to his wrist and was met by Captain Mac. They went straight in to S-3. They just told Lt. Young, 'Have your One-One get the team ready to insert immediately and come with us.'"

"Doney was there and said he would get everything rolling," Kyle said, "And now you're here."

I took the jeep keys from Mike. "I'll do that. I can help you guys get ready, be your gopher; anything you need."

Far to the west, fifteen miles over the border of Vietnam into Laos, Recon Team New York was doing all it could to evade a pursuing enemy.

The eight-man team led by John St. Martin with Ed Wolcoff as the One-One had inserted into target Hotel Six the previous morning for an area recon. Soon after leaving the LZ and dismissing the air assets, the team sensed they were being tracked. It was subtle. There were no signal shots, barking dogs, or snapping branches, but the team was certain they were being shadowed. New York went into a defensive posture and set out Claymore mines as they waited for the situation to unfold. It was muggy and the air dampened the sounds of movement. A drop of sweat fell from St. Martin's forehead. New York froze in place. Ten minutes. The point man stiffened and craned his neck forward. An enemy unit parted the leaves and stealthily approached their position.

The point man tapped the One-Zero's thigh—an un-needed gesture. He saw the quiver of the branch also. "Shoot Claymore?" he whispered to St. Martin.

Several North Vietnamese appeared. Their eyes panned the area around them, then stopped, facing the waiting team.

"Yes," was the nod. Fourteen hundred steel balls shot through the foliage and into the oncoming force. The team immediately leaped to ascertain the damage and perhaps get a prisoner. But one Claymore had not been fired, and a new member of the team, a young Montagnard, turned to the point man and said, "This one too?"

"Yes," said the point man. The new soldier squeezed the trigger and sent another massive blast toward the enemy position. Unfortunately, the One-Zero was a foot directly behind the Claymore and the blast threw him in a full cartwheel into the air. He landed on his feet, stunned, but not otherwise wounded.

But the chance to capitalize on the exchange was over. Deeper into the brush loud movement came in their direction. "Break contact" was the unspoken order of the hour.

They moved west, evaded, and continued their mission toward a line of trees. As they approached, they noticed steps notched into the trunks of several of the tall trees. They were ladders for trail watchers to mount the tops and monitor the LZ on which they came. The tops were empty now; perhaps those very soldiers were cast down by the Claymores. The team continued until they found a small clearing. They maneuvered around it and found a road. It was oriented northwest to southeast in the direction of Cambodia. It was certainly a tributary if not the actual Ho Chi Minh Trail. New York sped across it and proceeded toward cover but discovered a wide trail that parallelled the road. A glance above the trail revealed a large coaxial cable strung along the trail. Such a cable was used to communicate between very large enemy units such as regiments and base areas. The trail would have been used to patrol and maintain the cable.

The Americans moved off the trail deeper to the north and communicated the information to the FOB. They found the area crisscrossed with trails and signs of heavy activity. Communication complete, St. Martin made several evasive maneuvers then finally found a suitable night defensive perimeter.

There was movement in the bush during the night but it passed by and they wondered if the Communists were able to pinpoint the position of the team for the night. There were faint sounds of truck engines in the direction of the road. Twice they heard chopping. Once they heard the shrieking of monkeys, but otherwise the night passed without event.

While still in the RON they received a message from SOG via the Leghorn relay site. "Find an LZ and remain in place. Prepare for exfil. New team will replace you at LZ. How copy?"

The One-Zero was puzzled and looked at the handset before he answered. "Roger, copy," he said.

There were signs of heavy enemy activity on the trails. They tried to bypass the line of trees and the trail watchers who were without doubt perched in their boughs. It was clear that FOB did not want further reconnaissance or enemy contact. New York moved with extreme caution in the direction of the field. With the area interlaced with trails it was difficult to maneuver without crossing one.

At a point they found themselves within eyeshot of a major one. Nine enemies walked down Laotian Route 96, a part of the Ho Chi Minh Trail. The front three were slightly ahead of the rest. The leader was reading a pamphlet. It seemed contact was inevitable. Wolcoff pulled the pin from a grenade and readied himself to throw. The team was tense, prepared to spring. St. Martin waited until they had to fire, but the lead group of three soldiers passed their position, the leader still engrossed in the pamphlet. The remaining six soldiers barely looked to the side as they passed patrolling their own backyard.

# SOG: Missions to the Well

The team waited, barely breathing, until it was certain the danger was gone. Wolcoff slipped the pin back into his grenade.

The eight men of the team found the field where they would be extracted. They set up security, made certain the enemy had not already secreted themselves somewhere to wait in ambush, and settled in to wait for Arizona.

CCC was a bustle of movement. At the other end of the compound, Kingbees descended on the pad. Arizona assembled in front of Recon, their weapons leaning across their open rucksacks. They stuffed rations into the spaces; Claymores, an extra canteen, and ammunition—much ammunition. Jim Young exited the S-3 with a black box under one arm and a folded map in his other hand. Someone had already gotten his weapon and pack.

"Radio?" he asked Twiggy.

"Got it, and extra batteries too."

The man in civilian clothes walked over to him. Young pointed to the civilian with his thumb. "Twiggy, this man is from OP 35 as you guessed. He is from General Electric. They've just invented a recording device just for us. It's a miniature tape recorder, what they call an eight-track recorder. It is top secret, as you saw on his brief case. We—that is you because you're my commo man on this team—are going to tap into the commo wire in the AO that PAVN is using to talk between their headquarters. It is voice activated and records when the device hears talking on the line then shuts itself off. This gentleman will show you how it works."

The two of them got on their knees over the recorder and the man in civies explained how to tap into the enemy wire and use the device. When he was finished, he stood and presented Twiggy with a manual.

"Questions?" he asked.

Twiggy shook his head. "Not much to it. Should be easy." Then he looked over at the readiness of the team with maximized weapons and ammunition. "At least my part of this is."

Colonel Abt was there. Captain Mac from S-3 stoically watched the preparation. Doney and most of us in recon hovered.

"Ready? Got everything? Remember, you are going in and St. Martin is coming out on the same LZ. They will brief you on how to find the cable and the enemy situation." Doney said.

Young stepped closer to his team and in a voice which could only be heard by his own people said, "Alright two lifts coming in. Twiggy with the radio, me, and the first three Yards in the column on the first lift. When we jump off, the last half of New York will get on that chopper. On the second Kingbee will be Sergeants Dean and Wilson with the rest of the Yards. They will jump off and the rest of New York will get on. Hopefully the NVA will think the recon team left on the LZ but not think we've replaced them."

He looked around at his people. "Everybody got everything? Okay, let's do it."

From the CCC helipad they rose and flew west to the Dak To launch site and the final preparations for the mission. They barely touched down before Covey reported all assets were in place. They proceeded to the target.

New York heard the low rumble of the helicopters in the distance.

"We hear you two six five degrees two miles. Popping smoke."

The Vietnamese pilot responded, "Roger. I see red."

"Confirmed red."

The first Kingbee sloped down to a soft landing on its wheels. Under the blast of blowing limbs and grass from the rotor blade, the first five men of Arizona hopped off and joined St. Martin and the lead half of his team. They ran, holding on their flop hats, and squinting their eyes against the debris.

"Not much time to talk," St. Martin said loudly to be heard over the engines. He placed his forefinger on a light-colored spot on the map. "We are here. This is where the road is. If it is not the Ho Chi Minh itself it is certainly a healthy branch of it. On the far side of it there is a maintenance trail, very well used. Above it is the coaxial cable. The place here is crisscrossed with trails. People everywhere. We had one firefight yesterday."

The first Kingbee had barely lifted off and the second was already descending on its heels. "They patrol that cable but I don't know how often they go by."

Young answered, his voice slightly rising with the increase of the second helicopter's noise. "Hopefully, they'll be aware you have been exfiltrated and not think you've been flipflopped. We are heavy in case we have to fight, but I hope we can move quietly like a small team."

The helicopter swooped in, this time hovering a foot or two above the grass. The back half of Arizona hopped off and the front half of New York with the One-Zero climbed on. The aircraft rose, banked to the east and climbed well above the hills.

Young pointed a direction to his point man. There was no reason to set up a listening post. It was imperative to distance themselves from the LZ.

They maneuvered a couple of hundred meters away from the field before they made their first security stop of any length. It was on a slight rise of ground that faced the LZ but did not leave them in silhouette, oval shaped with a long side facing their back trail. It was muggy. Sweat joined the camouflage grease on their faces and oozed down like crawling bugs. Insects stuck to the paste. Hair itched under their boonie hats. They resisted the urge to scratch through the cloth. They willed themselves to ignore their discomfort.

A buzz of insects dominated the air and shivered the leaves. Beyond their vision there was a steady shushing in the grass. They strained their eyes to see through the vegetation. Enemy patrols? Deer? A small troop of monkeys? An errant breeze?

The One-Zero nodded to the point man. They slowly rose. After the quiet of intent listening, the brush of their rucksacks sounded thunderous in their ears.

They picked their way through dry twigs and dirt clogs in the direction of the road and the cable. Just before the place indicated on the map where they might expect to find watchers in the line of trees, he halted his people in a security stop. Young and the point man bellycrawled forward until they found the place with steps cut into the bark. Their eyes scanned upward but found the limbs and platforms empty of men.

It was midafternoon before they found the road. They heard it before they saw it. Heavy-laden trucks passed with the groan of engines and the crunch of gravel under the tires. Minutes separated the vehicles, perhaps not to present a tempting target for a passing jet. They waited a short distance before the edge, listening for voices, nearby patrols, perhaps even a cough which might reveal a waiting ambush.

They needed to cross the road to find the cable along the maintenance trail on the other side. The most used protocol of crossing such a dangerous area was to line abreast along the axis and cross as a group, limiting the amount of time in a danger zone. The downside of that was leaving traces of passage along the full length of the crossing which a passing patrol could discover: scuff marks, even the unique boot prints of a SOG man. And furthermore, they could be counted.

Young had the team cross two or three at a time, with each group providing cover for the next. The down side was increased time exposed on the road, or worse, having the team split in two if a patrol proceeded down the road during the crossing. Nothing for it. The One-Zero, point man, and the radio man went first, followed by two more, then two, then Mike Wilson and the tail gunner. They covered all evidence of the crossing in the soil, on the road, and the ditch on the other side.

The point crossed the road to the maintenance trail on the far side. They watched for patrols on the path as well as the road.

In less than a minute they were across. A glance above revealed the cable: black, taut, and partly camouflaged. They maneuvered into the thicket, well into the woods to monitor the area. Michael Wilson and the two tail gunners slipped to the path to ensure there were no marks of the team's passage in the dirt.

They listened. Movement. Voices. The point man whispered to the leader, "*Beaucoup* VC. *Beaucoup, beaucoup*. Many, many."

There was a shuffle in the underbrush. Minutes later they heard the thumping of NVA Bata boots passing on the hard-packed trail. At a small break in the leaves, they saw the yellow-green cloth of a passing soldier on patrol.

They were too close to the trail. Young motioned the team deeper into the green.

Young told Twiggy, "We will set this up just like we would do a prisoner snatch. I will put you up there with the recorder and I will have Claymores directed to both sides of you. You will be close to monitor the recorder with one Yard. We will set up a defensive perimeter twenty meters behind. Got it? Ready?"

Twiggy held the device in his hands, his rifle slung across his back, and nodded. "We just have to find a place we can run my wire to the cable where it will not be seen. Maybe a tree alongside the wire."

They bellycrawled to the path. Wilson and two tribesmen took up security on one flank, Kyle Dean and two men on the other. They slid forward.

"There," Twiggy said, pointing to a slender tree next to the path. "I'll run it up the trunk and across into the wire."

"We have to work fast. I don't know how often they patrol. Very often if they think we came in on that LZ."

Flank security, and the center section arrived at the edge of the path at about the same time. But for a soft cough into an enemy patrolman's sleeve, they might have been caught at the edge of the path. The muffled cough was followed by the shuffle of a boot on hard-pack. Alerted, the recon team melted into the bushes and let them pass.

Twiggy quickly ran his wires up the tree and across to the coaxial and tapped in. He slipped down and set the device into the soil as instructed. He nodded its completion to the lieutenant. They slid back into the bushes a dozen meters. Twiggy turned on the machine. The spools of the recorder immediately began to turn. They did not have to wait long. The needle jumped. There were already voices coming across the device.

A dozen meters to either side, the flanks set up Claymore mines aimed down the path and road. It was unknown if the enemy was able to tell if their line had been tapped. At a silent signal the flanks slid back with the detonators of two Claymore mines.

Twiggy was glad to note that the turning of the spools could not be heard, nor the sound of the recording going off from the voice activation. He watched the needles as the tape responded. He and two Yards settled in close to the trail as the remainder of the team dropped back in a defensive perimeter, with two parts facing slightly to the flanks.

Arizona stayed in place the remainder of the day. Just out of sight, trucks passed by on the road at various intervals. One time they heard the steady crunch of gravel. There was no break in the sound. Twiggy peeked through a small opening in the vegetation. A long string of equipment-laden bicycles was being pushed along.

Toward dusk, with but an hour or two of daylight remaining in the day, the batteries gave out. Twiggy had to remember where he placed them in his clothing but found them. With great care he opened the case and slipped in a fresh pair. He glanced down. The first tape was nearly full. Communication among the enemy units was nearly continuous.

Young decided to pull deeper into the woods, away from the road for the night defensive perimeter. He was concerned about leaving the wires in the coaxial overnight. The unknowns were too great: whether the line was patrolled visually from the trail or if PAVN could become aware they were being tapped.

"Twiggy, let's take down the device tonight and set it up again in the morning."

The sergeant nodded. His features showed he had considered the same thing.

Arizona went a hundred yards deeper into the thickness and found a suitable place in a stand of fallen bamboo. They would hear the approach of trackers and there was an avenue through which they could evade.

Mike Wilson and two tail gunners slipped a half dozen meters down their back trail and set up a Claymore. Young glanced around. He was satisfied.

Twiggy examined the recorder. It was actually, for all of the top-secret nature of things, a rather simple thing. He even had a reverse tab. He held his breath and touched it for a micro-second. A tribesman was beside him. He tapped what he thought was "play," although there was no writing to show that was so. Voices. Clear voices. The volume was low but the words were clear.

The Montagnard's eyebrows raised in surprise. All of the little people in Arizona were Sadang, from the same tribe and village. All were well educated by missionaries and spoke several languages. "Aah, aah. *Bac Viet*." North Vietnam.

Twiggy slid over to the lieutenant. Without mentioning his transgression, he whispered, "We are halfway through our second set of batteries. They aren't holding up very well. I think we have only three sets."

Young nodded. He took the third set and held them under his armpit to keep them warm and ready to go in the morning.

It rained suddenly halfway through the night. It dropped its heavy contents for an hour. The mercenaries huddled under their thin tarps. The tarps were small sheets to not take up unnecessary space in their packs and the little people huddled with their feet drawn up, their knees at their chins. It passed as quickly as it came leaving only the drip, drip from the trees—the disconcerting tap which always sounded like movement in the bush. Rain was to be expected, if not overdue, for it was the monsoon season.

Morning, when it came, arrived sullenly and soggy. The vegetation smelled fecund, a womb of life.

Young tapped his mouth. "Eat" the gesture said. He did not like to eat when they were so close to the target, especially with the area so populated by troops, but the team was hungry. A distant drone of an engine came from over the hills and the team wondered if it was a new kind of vehicle in the enemy inventory, but it became recognizable as it neared: The familiar drone of an airplane. Young wondered if the enemy had the ability to locate radio transmissions so as Covey passed nearby, they gave the briefest of encrypted messages, "Team okay."

Twiggy was a big man: certainly 240 pounds, strong, powerful.

It took great care for him with his size to move with stealth through the bushes. But at mid-morning he was at his tree with his wires and box. The team, all around, was concerned with the dampening rain of the night that approaching enemies might not be heard on the bordering path or road. Only the stream of war-bound trucks revealed their approach with their engines groan and rattle of their frames in the occasional pothole.

Twiggy did not relish exposing himself for the setup. He saw the flanks had already laid out and camouflaged the Claymores and slid back from the trail with the detonators in their hands keeping watch. Twiggy grasped the end of the wire which tapped into the cable in one hand, glanced both ways down the trail, took a large breath, and sprang to the task. He saw a slight shake in his fingers but he willed them to the work. Completed, he plunged the ground stake into the dirt and slipped back into the thick vines. Looking one last time to be sure, he was certain nothing could be seen from the trail. He let out his breath.

Almost immediately, the needle bounced. It was not his own heartbeat being recorded, but voices activating the recorder, moving the needle, turning the tape; steady, continuous voices again. The team could only guess the source or purpose of the voices on the line; conversations between battalion commanders, secret orders, perhaps even the start of a sweep to find a SOG team. The flutter of the needle was insistent, frequent. The radio man was nervous; he fought the urge to look around him as it seemed he was centered inside the clockwork of the enemy. To move at the wrong time was to be discovered.

Arizona remained in place. Bugs which crawled on the backs of necks, paused, and bit remained un-slapped. Patrols marched or sauntered by depending on their purpose. Some passed noisily; others as silent and somber as those marching to an uncertain end, even their boots did not sound on the road. The recon men hidden along the path wondered when it would be that an alert private noticed an anomaly along the path and investigated to find an alert Sadang tribesman ready to fight; or a straggler chose that particular spot to "take care of business," or a passing company of men would halt for a meal.

Midafternoon. The sun had dried the road, and the feet of passing troops could be heard in the gravel to alert the men of their approach. Twiggy's second set of batteries had died. He slid the last set into the well. They were simple D batteries. With all of the technology of the top-secret device, it used everyday, store-bought D batteries.

"How are we doing?" the lieutenant asked when Twiggy slipped in the new batteries.

"Good," he whispered. "We are well into our last tape. After that we're done."

The lieutenant looked at the spinning spools of tape. Before his eyes he could see the speed becoming more and more slow, grindingly slow. The batteries were not holding a charge.

"Give me the old batteries. I'll have the little people keep them under their armpits to keep them warm. Maybe we can get some more life out of them."

The One-Zero looked at the device in disbelief and turned to go.

"While you're watching the dials, I'm keeping track of the traffic on the road. This is one busy place," he said, patting the notepad in his shirt pocket.

Radio traffic diminished the latter part of the day. It was sporadic, but seemed to occur in a frenzy of exchanges, then became quiet altogether. It was often followed by increased activity on the road. A cloud bank edged by overhead, bringing a dimness to the forest, but it did not rain, and the bank passed on.

Another look at the spools revealed a weary revolution. They inserted batteries that had been warmed under the armpits of the tribesmen. The slight new life in the batteries was scant help. But it seemed between breaks in the radio traffic, the device rested, and gained energy, however little, for the next recording.

Two hours later, light diminished a few shades. A light sprinkle fell but lasted only long enough to chill. About the time the haze passed overhead, the large sergeant signaled back; all the tapes are full.

It was a given, as the day began its surrender to dusk and night, they would not be exfiltrated until the morrow. The soldiers retrieved their recorder and Claymores, backed from the road, and made their way toward an RON. En route, they made a security stop where they ate and encrypted a message to transmit when the airplane passed over. The five letter code groups simply said, "Team okay. Mission accomplished. Need exfil in the morning."

"Roger, copy."

They found their way into a thicket with good concealment and defense and set up an early warning ambush. The earth was still moist from the brief shower of the day and they wondered if they would be able to hear the approach of trackers. So far, there had been no sign of dogs—a thing to be wondered about in an area so robust with enemy activity. There was a short-lived shower late in the night which left a gossip of drips to talk about it. A slim toenail of moon appeared which barely revealed the shape of the horizon, but it appeared only a short time before thin clouds covered it completely. They shivered for they were damp and clammy with sweat and night dew, and so passed the darkness.

Morning arrived grey and sullen. They squeezed indigenous rations into their mouths and waited. They possessed vital information on those spools which they could not jeopardize by exposing themselves or engaging the enemy. They would wait until the time came for them to be lifted out of the target.

Covey flew over. "Exfil confirmed. ETA 1000. Same LZ. How copy?"

Arizona wondered, "Same LZ? Doesn't that push our luck?" but Young whispered into the mic, "Copy."

The Kingbees arrived as stated; two of them, and without preamble. They simply arrived over the ridgeline, sloped to a low hover above the grass, and left with their charge. It was a speedy thing; in, out, and gone. Perhaps the enemy had been unaware they had ever been there and with the smooth departure did not know they had left.

They paused briefly at the launch site without getting off the

Kingbees and continued to the CCC compound outside of Kontum city. There had been no gunfights or need to evade trackers, yet they were tired; perhaps it was the very density of enemy in their constant proximity which wearied them. They looked forward to a shower, clean fatigues, and most of all the large steaks in the mess hall which awaited returning men.

The two Kingbees touched down, the weight of them pressing down the soft tires like a cushion.

Lieutenant Young leapt from the strut and turned to help his little people exit the door. When he next turned, Captain Mac from S-3 was standing in front of him. There was no "welcome home" look in his face—just a sentence: "Do you have the tapes?"

Young was startled for a moment at the abruptness. "Yes."

"Where?"

"In my rucksack."

The captain opened a black briefcase, the same one Young saw three days before.

"Put 'em in here."

Young did.

"What hand are you?"

"I'm right-handed."

"Give me your left hand."

Young did.

The captain took one step forward and snapped a handcuff on his left wrist and the other end to the handle of the briefcase.

"See that helicopter over there. You're getting on it. They will fly you to Pleiku and on to Saigon. You will be met at the airport. Understand?"

"Yes, sir."

"Go to it."

And that was it. Young walked to the waiting Huey in his dirty fatigues, web gear, rifle, grenades hanging from the harness, and a black briefcase cuffed to his left hand.

Pleiku was only two dozen miles by road from Kontum with an intervening line of tall highland hills between. Traffic passed during the day after the route had been cleared of road mines placed in the night by Viet Cong sappers. The Fourth Infantry Division stationed APC vehicles and tanks at intervals along the way. Some of the men from CCC grabbed a clean uniform, boots, and personal effects and raced to Pleiku for the hapless officer, hoping to get there before he left.

Two jeeps met the lieutenant when it touched down at the B team airfield at Pleiku. The men who greeted him were unsure what was going on—only to receive the soldier with the black satchel and have him ready for the next leg of his journey. They were cordial as he stepped off the helicopter but careful to not ask questions about his mission.

"I think Saigon would have liked to get you right to a plane from here, but they have to deflect one so we have a little time. Maybe we have time to get some of the grime off you and get you something to eat."

The thought made Young weary. His voice seemed sing-song to himself, wistful even, "That would be very nice," he said.

They arrived at the B team the same time as the jeep from CCC.

"Jim, we brought you a change of clothes and your personal things."

He cast a weary smile at them. A sigh. "And a toothbrush?"

"And a toothbrush."

"I am so grateful." He held up his arm, the one with the briefcase, "And there's this."

They let him shower. Twice. One shower was never enough to remove the grime, especially the greasy camouflage. It would be shower three or four that would discover the olive-drab grease inside the ear or behind it and the occasional mud or blood under the nails.

He felt clean. He was in his own fatigues, had his wallet and hygiene kit.

"We need to start back before they close the road. We'll take your rifle and web gear so you don't have to worry about it. They told us they have a late meal for you as the plane is still an hour out."

"Thank you," he said as he shook their hands.

# SOG: Missions to the Well

There was a delay getting the Blackbird to Pleiku B team for the transport to Saigon. The C-130 had been supplying an outpost tucked in a remote and contested area of Laos. The Green Berets there had been taking ground fire from a ridgeline and the Blackbird was forced to circle before descending for a crucial parachute drop. A slight wind across the perimeter eased its way toward the ridge and the source of the incoming mortar rounds; the drop needed to be low-level to prevent the chutes drifting across to the wrong side. It was mid-afternoon before the needed ammunition could be shoved out the tail gate and finally roll to a stop at the strip at Pleiku. It was late afternoon when they rumbled down the runway at Saigon.

At a remote, nearly out-of-sight area of Tan Son Nhut airport, a man in civilian clothes paced in front of his jeep, smoking impatiently. Finally, it seemed to him, he heard the hissing of the C-130 Blackbird as it taxied toward him stopping a dozen meters before the chain-link fence. He threw down his cigarette, squished it with his shoe, and waited with his hands clasped behind him.

"Lieutenant Young?" the man in civilian clothes demanded.

The civilian barely hid his anger at the lateness of the arrival.

Young did not miss the tone and impatience in the voice. "It would appear that I am the only one standing here with a briefcase handcuffed to his wrist. My name is Young."

The man stared for a moment at the soldier, uncertain how he should respond to the perceived incivility. "Chief SOG has been waiting patiently to interview you. I am to escort you to his location for your debriefing."

"You have a name?" Young asked.

True to a spy game, the civilian doubted that the officer had a need to know, but said, "Smith, Robert Smith."

Young thought to himself, "Yes, 'Bond, James Bond.'"

"Smith" looked disapprovingly at the officer's beret; SOG did not want the connection known between Special Forces and their Saigon offices, but he did not mention it. He would let the higher-ups do that one.

He had but a couple minutes to wait to be ushered in the large office. Chief SOG waited behind a very large mahogany desk. Various plaques were on the wall behind him. From a side office two Americans and two Vietnamese men entered the room, the latter seeming smarmy and insolent. None of the men congratulated him on Arizona's mission. They were down to business.

"Has this briefcase been out of your possession?"

"No sir."

An aid unhooked the briefcase from Young's wrist and opened the case. One of the Vietnamese men removed the tapes, his eyes lingering on them as a priceless and unique treasure. He nodded to Chief SOG.

"We will examine them and get back, Colonel Cavanaugh," said the other Vietnamese man.

They left the room and Chief SOG barely looked at the officer. "That's it then. We don't need you anymore."

Then, almost as an afterthought, what to do with the lieutenant standing before him, he said, "Just go to the safe house and wait there. One of these officers will get you a ride. That's all."

It was a half hour before the ride arrived from the safe house, the secret refuge where the Green Berets of Special Operations stayed when in Vietnam's capital city. As they waited, the officer reprimanded Young. He did not stand him at attention but his voice carried that tone "Lieutenant, we do not want to see those berets in Saigon. We do not want anyone to know there is a connection between Special Forces and this office. It would please us if we saw no Green Berets at all in this entire city. Understood?"

The driver was from House Ten, the secret hideaway in the city. His demeanor was a stark contrast to all that Young had encountered since he had left Hotel Six hours before. He was friendly and chatted. He was one of their own, a Special Forces man with several tours in the war, wounded, and filling out the remaining months of his tour.

As he drove, the bustle and flashing lights of Tu Do Street with its bars and whore houses, exhaust smoke from watered down gasoline and honking horns, and countless Vietnamese cowboys on their Honda motorcycles, morphed into wide, quiet streets where the wealthy French may have lived a pair of decades before. The street was called Nguyen Minh Chieu, and the address was Nha Muy. Every SOG man memorized the address to tell the cab driver: "Take me to Nha Muy, Nguyen Minh Chieu." On the reverse side of the house pass was the "walk on water card," which informed the reader that the bearer was on classified business and was not to be detained in any way. The reader was to expedite bringing him to the address on the reverse side. At times when exceeding curfew or being in a restricted area, angry military policemen were required to give the offender a ride to the safe house instead of a stockade.

They entered the high walled courtyard of the compound and parked. It was a secure place of refuge, but the security was discrete, nearly invisible, consistent with the confidential nature of it being a safe house. Inside they gave him a House Ten pass. As you entered, a tiny bar was to the right and a small dining area to the left. It was air conditioned; private bedrooms were on the second floor with thick Air Force mattresses on the beds.

SF men passing through and enjoying the hospitality of the house all knew its specialty: tender steak sandwiches. Young ordered one. He sat in a soft chair and visited with two soldiers passing through from CCN. Finding himself falling asleep, he excused himself, crawled between fresh smelling sheets, and was instantly asleep.

"They want you at Chief SOG's," said the voice through the fog of deep sleep where Young wandered in his dreams through a sparce Virginia forest playing cat and mouse with a wary deer. "You have an hour. We can do a small breakfast for you. It isn't much, but it will put something on your bones."

He showered and ate. House Ten had a jeep and they dropped him off at the entrance of OP-35. Young slipped his beret into his side pocket before he went inside.

It did not take them long to get to business. The Vietnamese man was first to speak. He wore black slacks and a white dress shirt. He had a slight lisp and, Young thought afterward, hissed rather like a snake. "*Trung Úy* Young (Lieutenant Young), this be number ten. No have, nothing. This be all white. Just noise. Nothing here. Empty.

No have."

"What!" It was an exclamation, not a question.

Young could say nothing. He knew the tapes were full. They were recording, he saw it. The needles jumped. It activated by voice and stopped when the voices did. But he could say nothing.

Chief SOG's aid held up his hand in a "stop" gesture.

"Your mission was for nothing. The Vietnamese got nothing from your tapes. You must have done it wrong."

There was a pause in the conversation where they perhaps expected Young to offer an excuse or apology. It did not come.

Cavanaugh's voice ended the meeting. "That's it then. You are excused from here. Make it back to base as best you can."

Young turned and saluted the Colonel, pivoted, and left the room.

The SOG man was disgusted. Angry. He knew those tapes were full. Headquarters did not even provide a way back to camp. At the door of the building, he carefully donned his beret; flash squared just over his left eye and pressed it down over his right temple. He hailed a taxi and gave the driver the address, "*Toi di Nha Muy, Nguyen Minh Chieu.*" All the way back to the safe house, the image of the lisping Vietnamese man played over and over in his mind—a hissing deadly viper.

The manager of House Ten was adept and linked him up with a special ops plane heading for Kontum. With a final steak sandwich and a prayer for his safety, he was off. There was gall in his heart; headquarters treated him as if everything was his fault, that the mission was an utter failure. As the airplane taxied to his location, he heard the familiar hissing of the hydraulics and he could not erase the image of the accusing, lisping voice.

At Kontum his people greeted him. In his absence, Kyle Dean and Michael Wilson cared for the team. They were rested, refreshed, and in readiness for whatever lay ahead. He gave his people the day off. Twiggy went to a hatchet force as he felt his skills were more suited there. Young checked with S-2 to see if there was added debriefing to be done. His only uncertainty was how much to confide in his other Americans that their effort was considered a failure by the higher ups, that getting nothing of value on those tapes was the fault of the team. In the end, he did not tell them.

He should have known, should have guessed anyway. He had been back at FOB Kontum only two days when, as he walked across the compound, he caught the briefest look of a man in civilian clothes entering S-3 carrying a black briefcase.

"That could be anything," he warned himself, but his experience in Saigon had not left him without suspicion. So, when one of the guys from S-3 found him in the Huckleberry Inn with Wilson and Dean, he was not caught entirely off guard. He was summoned for a warning order. "You have a mission."

It was the same civilian standing next to Captain MacClanahan that gave Arizona the recorder a week before. Young was certain he had another in the container at his feet.

MacClanahan was direct but anticipated the misgivings his officer would have. "Lieutenant Young, Saigon wants you to go back in there and try again. This comes from higher up, not from me. They want you to go in on the same LZ, go to the same place, and do it again."

Young did not realize his mouth was open. "The same LZ New York came out of, that we went in on, and the very same one we used to come out. Saigon wants us to go in and use that same place a fourth time. Do they want us killed?"

"Lieutenant, Saigon must have their reasons. We just follow orders. You can refuse."

"And go to the very same place to tap in?"

"They have their reasons."

"When?"

"Day after tomorrow." Young could tell his superior did not like it either.

There was a silence which the captain understood to mean that he was not refusing to go.

"Briefing 0800 tomorrow morning, brief back 1400 tomorrow afternoon. Insert by Kingbee next morning."

"Yes sir."

"All right. This gentleman wants to go over the device with you again.

Seeing it was his show, he stooped and pulled the eight-track from the case. "Okay, I am going to show you again," he said, as one who would instruct a person who just could not get it. "This is how you set it up. I can show you the dials later. It is important you put the ground in the dirt. It's a simple ground. You could even use a bayonet for an antenna. Just shove it into the ground and hook the wire to the hilt and use that. But the ground must be moist. SOG recommends that you urinate on it."

The lieutenant stared at the technician in unbelief. "Here I am on the Ho Chi Minh Trail trying to set this thing up before anyone walks by, trying to work fast, my fingers are shaking, and you want me to unbutton my fly, stand on the side of the road and urinate on this? I just want to get this straight. Is that what you want us to do?"

He swallowed. "It was just a suggestion, Lieutenant."

Jim Young assembled his people. "We are going back into H-9, same LZ, same spot on the trail to do the same thing. The mission comes from higher up. I have briefing and brief back tomorrow so that will tie me up some. I want you two to go to the range in the morning. You know what to do. In the afternoon we will prep our gear. Next day we go in. Kyle, I want you to lay on a vehicle for tomorrow."

The Kingbees arrived early and the pilots checked with intelligence about the area and the location to insert Arizona. A brief shower breezed by, a rumor of coming monsoon rain. Twenty minutes before insertion, Covey eyed the landing zone from an oblique angle at a distance but saw no activity. He had assets stationed over the next line of hills, far enough away to not tip off the Communists. The One-Zero had grave misgivings about coming back this way and was concerned they would to be hit during the landing. Along with the machine gunner of the helicopter, his own people's weapons bristled from the door in anticipation.

Nothing occurred. The field was strangely still. Not a bird. Even the debris tossed by the rotor blades seemed heavy and sullen as they descended. Young almost thought, "This is deathly quiet." The two H-34s spiraled neatly to a dive ending just above the grass, and Arizona hopped from the struts and dashed to the closest cover. By the time the engine noise faded, they were in a circle several dozen meters into the vines and shrubs, weapons thrust out like a wary porcupine.

The thick forest was without sound or movement. The absence of bird or animal often suggested the presence of people. Only flying insects, and few of them, were present, their shapes revealed against the grey sky. The men rose and maneuvered away from the field.

As before, they moved west to the place where steps had been carved into the trunks of trees so trail watchers could climb and monitor teams such as Arizona. Young and the point man bellycrawled to the place and studied the treetops. They were empty of men. The team leader thought of something, "Had they been recently used?" He crawled forward until he was under one of the tall platforms. He slid a finger along one of the carved steps. His finger drew wet mud from the grooves. They had recent use. Perhaps the watcher had learned what he wanted to know, climbed down and was reporting even as he looked.

But there was ample sign of enemy around them. Two of the Montagnards had far better hearing than the rest. One at the rear of the column clicked his tongue. Wilson looked at him. He placed a forefinger into the air, tapped his ear, and with his thumb and fingers formed a mouth that opened and closed in speaking. "I hear talking," the gesture said.

They crossed the several trails as before. They had recent use. Twice they froze in place as they heard enemy units pass by. PAVN still was present.

More talking. This time they all heard it. The point man looked back and whispered, "*Beaucoup* VC."

They were careful to not go directly to the road but frequently changed directions. By afternoon they knew they were approaching it. A heavy truck groaned by. They heard a tailgate slam when it bumped over a pothole. They set up security to ensure the slam was indeed from a pothole and not from letting off troops to sweep in their direction.

At the edge of the road, they set up security and monitored it for activity. Saigon insisted they use the same position as before. Was someone waiting on the other side?

A half hour.

He had the last two sections of the team cover left and right as the first rushed across the trail. They penetrated ten meters into the thickness and Young brought the second section over. Then the third. It had rained that morning and the edge of the road had lost its hardness and their passage could be seen in the soft ground. He got the attention of the last section to cross, pointed to the ground and made a wiping motion with his hand: "Clean it of tracks."

They nodded and rushed across, the tail gunner glancing down to be sure the earth was sterile.

A safe distance from the road and the path, they formed a perimeter. Before they set up the Claymores and recorder, he went forward to be sure they were at the correct place. He recognized the area but wanted to be sure.

He saw where the soil had been pressed where they crawled to the coaxial the last time they were there. He bellycrawled to the site. He recognized the tree. It had the mark where Twiggy affixed and camouflaged the wire. He looked up.

The wire was gone!

Young looked around. Could he be mistaken as to the location? No. He was positive.

He made his way back to his people. "Mike, crawl over to that place where you set up your Claymore last time. Are you positive we are at the same place?"

It was not five minutes and he was back. "It is. I even found the place where I put my elbows."

Young felt cold air crawl up the back of his neck. He could nearly hear alarm sirens sounding in the trees. He had only to replace the vague intuition he felt with plain words, sentences and paragraphs to articulate the thoughts.

"Kyle, you go over to where you were. Tell me if it is the same exact place."

He came back minutes later with a very small wrapper in his fingers. "Positive," he said. "I had a piece of gum when we were here before, and I pushed the wrapper deep into the dirt with my finger. I dug it out. Here it is."

The leader took a long, deep breath, and said, "Gentlemen, we need to get away from this place. Now."

They moved with absolute stealth. Although the soil was moist with the beginning of the monsoons, they made certain where to place their feet. They moved at the pace of the tail gunner, only as quickly as he could perfectly hide their passage. Mike Wilson and one other of his Sadang Yards covered the rear, watching for trackers as the tail gunner was bent to the task. They changed direction often, for a time moving obliquely to the road.

The three Special Forces men briefly gathered at a security stop, the first halt since the road. Their heads were close together so they could whisper. "Here's the deal. They know that we are here. They knew that we were coming. There is a mole in SOG HQ that told them we would be here and that we were recording their communication. The coaxial wire is gone.

"I think our people in Saigon got a lot of information on those tapes we made, but one of the Asians told Chief SOG there was nothing on them, maybe erased them. Whoever the mole is told Charlie we were coming. They insisted on what LZ we came in on and that we go to the same exact place to record. The only thing that saved us so far, I think, is that they didn't expect us so soon.

"Perhaps we can salvage this mission. We need to evade anyone who comes for us first of all. Maybe we can do a trail watch and monitor the traffic, maybe get a prisoner if the situation presents itself. That's about it. Questions?"

At first there were none, but then Wilson reminded the other Americans of something he was noticing. He pointed up at the rolling, boiling clouds above. "We are losing our weather fast. We could get in trouble."

The others looked up as well. The day became darker even as they spoke.

"Let's get a little more distance from the road and find a good RON. We will make one more security stop to eat and contact the radio relay site, if possible, then go to a night perimeter."

They made the briefest of transmissions with the relay: "Team okay. Wire gone. Weather deteriorating."

They found an adequate location to spend the night on the military crest of the nearby hill that was distanced from the trail. Truck traffic on the road could barely be heard with the distance and vegetation. They had cover and concealment under a stand of bamboo and settled in. Three of the team, Mike Wilson, the tail gunner and Mui with his M-79 watched the rear. Three Claymores were laid out in the most likely avenues of approach. Jim Young placed the point man where the team would leave the circle and escape and evade if needed. They leaned back against the trees on their rucksacks and waited.

They heard the rain come before they felt it: hard, heavy, unrelenting rain. It came through the trees, pelting the leaves sounding like a thousand sheets of paper shredding and tearing. The wind with it did not blow it, it pushed, shoving its solid grey shoulders through the branches. Everything was grey, water-grey. Then it fell on the team. It reminded one of being in a shower with the water coming on full blast. The team was instantly drenched, soaked and incapable of becoming more wet.

It did not abate.

The horizon was gone. Kyle Dean could not see Michael Wilson fifteen feet away. The interpreter's voice could not be heard by the One-Zero. The monsoon hit. The rain would continue until it decided to quit, until it had used up all of the water in Southeast Asia. Recon teams in the past had endured ten days at a time in which they could not move, could not dry themselves, only to be rescued during a break in the weather with trench foot and other serious medical problems.

## SOG: Missions to the Well

They leaned back, some with small squares of tarp, some with only the umbrella of the tree branches to hinder the downpour, to wait, confident only in that the enemy was also under the deluge.

It rained all night. It did not stop or diminish. In the morning the Americans crawled over to their people and signed them to take something to eat, then returned to their place. It rained all day, all afternoon. It continued through the next night.

When morning arrived, there was no difference from the night other than everything was just a slightly lighter dark. To look toward the next soldier was to view him through a fish tank removed of any fish.

It rained all day without letting up.

Most of the men sheltered their weapons under their tarps. They endured the pounding water; their skin hurt like a burn. It was sensitive to touch, a Chinese water torture of nature. A few of the little people felt the pain of the incessant drops and curled up fetal style under their squares of tarp.

It rained all night. Their ears hurt with sound of the deluge. Their shoulders were raw and felt like the skin had worn off.

It rained the next morning. The sky brightened slightly and tried to deceive the soldiers that there was a sun above the monsoon. Then, late morning it stopped. It shut off. A giant spicket had been turned. Their vision was returning as the saturated air lost its volume. A tribesman in the center of the column could actually see the tail gunner at the end of the column. He was still there. He had not left.

Daylight arrived with the sound of dripping in the trees, and the moving flood on the ground that flowed like a stream to lower ground. It seemed daylight had arrived and was pushing her shoulders through the curtain of water to greet the day.

A glance at the ground. Two or three inches flooded the ground, unable to seep into an already saturated soil. The runoff swirled, looking for a place to go.

Wilson at the rear with the tail gunner remarked, "At least our tracks are gone."

It would be hours before they could walk on the ground. It was relatively certain the enemy had not snuck up on them the last two and a half days. It would be safe to stand, to stretch, and to see to the status of their weapons. Jim Young stood and could barely unbend his legs. His people also stood. They were rusty hinges barely able to unfold. In time they could move. They tested their gear. A rifle cartridge can expand slightly in the cold and not eject in a firefight. They replaced the bullet in the chamber with one they had kept warm in their pocket. The M-79 man broke the action of his weapon and slid the round back and forth to ensure it would not jam. "Eat," Jim signed.

They remained in place all afternoon. It was pointless to move. The world around them was dripping and soggy. A few birds flitted in the trees, their eyes peering at the ground, looking for drowned things or for burrowed things that had been forced to the surface by the water and lay exposed. A few animals began to move about. Some, when they passed in front of the circle of men, seemed self-conscious when the shuffle of their feet disturbed the water and presented new sound. The paws of larger creatures pressed the ground like sponges, squeezing out water into a sink.

The sky seemed to clear but the clouds that moved seemed to pass over with a purpose and the soldiers wondered if it did so to make room for the next torrent of rain. Unless something intervened, Arizona would try for an exfil.

They ate. Mike Wilson shared his indigenous rations with his Yards. He put water inside the pouch—there was plenty of water—and let the rice and anchovies with hot pepper and green peas soften. He looked at the water near his feet. He was becoming an expert, he thought, of gauging monsoon water. The level above the ground was diminishing. At first, he watched twigs float on the surface like tiny toy boats and slide toward lower ground. Just at the range of his vision he saw a small creature, perhaps a mouse, struggle not to drown, but it found shallower water where its feet could touch, and so hurried away in its grey matted hair.

He had squeezed the first bite into his mouth when the trees crashed to the front. Loud continuous crashing. Trees broke. Limbs snapped. Water splashed as if platoons of men charged through the brush heedless of discovery. The sound was as if tanks crashed toward them, but without engine noise or clanking treads.

The team was instantly alert, taking whatever cover they could find—behind a tree, a fallen chunk of bamboo, and for those who had nothing else, they lay on their bellies in the water behind their rucksacks. Every weapon was trained toward the charging adversary.

Kyle Dean exclaimed to the striker beside him, "Elephants, it has to be elephants."

It did sound like elephants charging, breaking all before them, but then crashing in the trees joined the charge on the ground. The attack of the unseen adversary grew close. The team prepared to shoot.

"Huuh, huuh, huuh," sounded from the source of the crashing.

The Montagnard next to the Dean exclaimed in discovery, "That not be elephant. That be ape-man. Them be ape."

But there were no apes in Southeast Asia. Special Forces teams in the past encountered what stateside were called sasquatch, abominable snowmen, or yeti. The charge arrived at the edge of visibility. They had but a glimpse: tall, black, hairy, ape-like creatures perhaps six feet tall. The creatures grabbed chest high shrubs and shook them, turned and went away, the splashing of their feet fading as they left.

The men looked side to side at each other and nervously smiled.

The sky was blue. It did not bear the ominous grey that covered it between the attacks of rain. Water no longer ebbed but disappeared completely. Birds of prey circled above, twisting, dipping, diving. The sound of an airplane passed among the birds. Covey.

Arizona marked their position using a "shiny"—a mirror of all things, that which required sun. Covey gave them an azimuth toward a small opening which seemed workable and arranged for a pickup.

Most of the day was spent maneuvering toward the place. Their feet made new sounds which they could not avoid. It was not a matter of not stepping on dry twigs. Each step was a squish in the sponge of earth. They passed two trails, unmarked by passage in its mud. They heard no sounds indicating an enemy presence. By mid-afternoon they found the break in the forest. It was small, but adequate for a Kingbee to lower itself; small enough for the team to monitor for ambush.

The two Kingbees descended and lifted with the team. "You be just in time," said the door gunner. "You look, look there."

A glance to the southeast. The sky was dark grey, heavy with monsoon rain. The sky carried a week of moisture in its grasp, struggled in the direction the team had just been, and the sluggish movement of the cloudbank showed it could not hold on much longer.

They leaned back against the shell of the helicopter in their soaked clothing. Thoughts went through Young's mind. He thought of the debriefing he would have to give: civilians with black briefcases, eight-track wire taps, Ho Chi Minh Trail, Saigon OP 35, spies, enemy mole in our own HQ. Oh, and the apes."

The choppers sloped down to the strip outside CCC. More than the dry clothes and the steak, he thought of the debriefing to come and what he might say.

"I better not mention the apes."

# CHAPTER FOUR
## *Florida POW Snatch*

I heard the press of his boots in the dirt off to the side as I hung with both hands on the pull-up bar that was behind the club. It was dark, but not fully so; just enough starlight to produce faint shadow and outline the sandbag revetment and perimeter against the dim sky. The source of that foot step stopped in the shadow a couple dozen meters from me. I noted the place, then glanced in the other direction toward the bunker. I had a moment of alarm when I saw a red dot similar to those in single-point rifle scopes, but it moved in an arc and ended at the mouth of the nearly invisible Montagnard sentry. It glowed as he puffed his cigarette and I knew he was awake. Sappers had probably not passed by him leaving one of their own in the shadows to run a knife between my ribs as I exercised under the horizontal bar.

    I worked out in privacy at the end of the day but always felt vulnerable in this secluded area. It was the only high bar in the FOB and was located in a removed unlighted part of the camp. I carried nunchaku in the small of my back, behind my belt and felt confident

I could handle any attack except a projectile.

I glanced again at the place where the boots scuffled and wondered if he shuffled to let me know he was there. I was on my third and last set of pull-ups, three sets of thirty-five. The other portions of my workout were finished for the night. I pushed to see how many reps I could get from this last one. Thirty-six . . . thirty-seven . . . thirty-eight. I struggled on this one, my chin frozen just under the bar. I glanced again into the shadows and dropped to the ground.

I faced the shade and waited.

"Hey, Dale, it's me, Joe," he said. "I didn't want to interrupt you."

Joe Morris was my roommate and, along with MSG Norm Doney, we were the Americans of Recon Team Florida. "Norm wants me to remind you that you're scheduled to leave for One-Zero School tomorrow. We'll be giving you a ride to Kontum Airport in the morning."

Someone opened the back door of the club and framed Joe in the square of light. With his red hair flopped over his forehead and slim carriage, he was the picture of the all-American boy, freckles and all. The reason Norman Rockwell used the skinny black-haired boy with his hair parted in the middle and slicked down with hair oil as the model for his paintings was that Joe was not around then, perhaps not as yet born. Joe was nervous before all of our missions, as were we all, but he went out on them time after dangerous time. I hoped he knew how much he contributed to the war to end Communism in this part of the world.

"Joe, let me show you something. Come with me." As we walked, I remembered an open mortar pit that could not be seen in the darkness. "Watch for the pit. Remember, one of the guys keeps his python in it."

We walked a few dozen steps to the perimeter where the sentry from security company kept watch under the corrugated tin roof. A strong odor of Vietnamese cigarette smoke replaced the fresh night air. I coughed to let him know we were coming up and he shuffled inside to let us know he was awake.

"A quiet night? You must have *fini* all VC." Even in the faint starlight I saw the shine of his gold tooth and knew that he was smiling.

"Joe, look toward the west, past Kontum and those foothills." The sky was just a fainter shade of darkness. "What do you see?"

He was unsure what I pointed out.

"Look carefully."

I waited as he studied the greyness. Certainly, he thought he was missing something.

"What do you see?

I sensed that he turned toward me. "I don't see anything."

"Exactly," I said, "There is nothing there beyond the range of hills." To our right were the lights of Kontum city and beyond that, northwest of the city, one of the bases sent up a flare, but to the west in the direction of Ben Het, the sky was axle grease dark. "You see the 'nothing' in that direction—you did that Joe."

There was silence as he wondered what I meant.

"You and I and Doney and Team Florida did that on our last mission. I often came here during my workouts to catch my breath and talk with my Montagnard friend here and we watched that horizon."

I wondered how to best explain it to my fellow team member. "When I was a boy, I used to pedal my bike to one of our lakes in northern Minnesota and sit by the shore as it got dark, I would listen to the loons and just look across the lake. It would still be hot from the day and the water was flat calm. I would sit on the shore or in one of the boats moored nearby and think about French Voyagers in their huge canoes and about fishing for walleye or camping in canvas wall tents with a campfire and just daydream. Across the bay, just over the hills flashing lights often appeared like distant thunderstorms and I thought I would be really in for it if I didn't get home on my bike before the rain hit. Only there was no thunder. The distant flashing left the hills in outline. Sometimes one flash covered the whole sky on the other side of the horizon. Sometimes it would glow in several places. At times the whole sky beyond the Black Bay hills would flame up beginning on one side and ending in the other. One after another it flashed like a war going on with tanks and cannons. But there was no sound of thunder with the flashing to go with the battle that I imagined 'over there.' There was no sound and my dad told me when I asked him about it, 'That is heat lightning.'"

I glanced around me for danger as was my habit but sensed only the tribesman near us who listened to our conversation. "Joe, every night that I would do my pull-ups here at the bar, I would climb up to this bunker and shoot the breeze with the men on guard duty and we would look over to the west. On the other side of those hills is Ben Het. They had been under siege for weeks. The sky over those ridges flashed every time I came here. Hundreds of flashes, no, there were thousands of them, as the Communists sieged the camp, the base returned fire, and the B-52s did their best as they dropped their bombs. Ben Het was far enough away that we could not hear anything and it was just like heat lightning that I remembered. Once when the generator was out and our camp was dead quiet, I heard the faintest of rumbling from the ferocious fighting on the other side of those ridges.

"See how quiet it all is? There are no flashes from incoming rockets or bombs." I looked over to where I thought Joe stood next to the opening of the revetment. "You had something to do with this quiet, Joe. You and me and Team Florida. We were there among the enemy and found the artillery that killed our people and made those flashes. I would stand here before that mission with my Montagnard friend and watch, all the while knowing what was happening. One time I heard him sadly say, 'I have people there.'"

I waited for him to speak. When he did, he was speaking as much to himself as to me. "That was a close one. We almost didn't make it back," he said. "They have all been close."

"Joe, Doney told me they diverted a hundred B-52s to drop their bombs on what we found. It broke the back of the siege. What was left of the enemy regiments limped back into their sanctuaries in Cambodia to heal. That evening after we took care of our little people and were debriefed, Doney said he was going to sit on the wall for a while. I should have gone with him. I think he went to this very place where we are tonight and watched the result of those thousands of bombs—how the strike destroyed the enemy's ability to make war. I wonder if he, like me, marveled at the peaceful sky after the Arc Light. And no one knows the roll we played in all of that. Except us, Joe.

"The other night I came here during my workout and looked to the west. Just about where Ben Het is located, I saw stars in the sky.

"Anyway, Norm told me that was the very day that the siege on Ben Het ended. The enemy artillery and heavy mortars and gathered troops were destroyed. The wounded enemy regiments slithered off into their sanctuaries across the border. And, Joe, the quiet we see over those hills tonight was in a large part because of what you did."

Doney checked out the recon jeep and the three of us drove to the airfield located on the far side of Kontum. From there I would be transported by a classified airplane to the top-secret school in Long Thanh for the three-week One-Zero school. We passed through my favorite section of Kontum: its cobblestone street with red-flowered trees on both sides whose long arms reached across the avenue and like lovers, their fingers of branches on one side of the street held fast to those on the other side. Sandalwood incense and the spicy odors of the cooking of the Orient wafted through the air. Shops enjoyed a vibrant trade and I enjoyed the loud chatter of vendors and shoppers and music played on transistor radios. A few peasants in white shirts sat at slim-legged tables on the sidewalk and rolled noodles around chopsticks as they ate Chinese soup.

Our timing was perfect as we arrived at the strip because we saw the plane on the horizon, a small dot making a straight approach. I retrieved my duffle from the back of the jeep and we walked to the tarmac as it touched down on the strip. It was a C-130 Hercules, painted all black with no national marking or numbers of identification. The Blackbird was clandestine and deniable. Its crew were all senior officers and NCOs. Its four engines never shut down as it pulled off the active runway and headed to a siding. Doney nudged me forward.

"They will not want to stay here long and draw fire."

Doney looked at me in his paternal way. "I will see you in three weeks. You will do fine there and you may have a One-Zero slot waiting for you when you return."

"Be careful while I am gone," I told him as he shook my hand. I thought a single tear sparkled from one corner of his eye. "But that could not have been," I thought.

Joe stepped forward and shook my hand. "And you be careful too, Joe."

The huge ominous looking airplane rumbled down the strip toward us, growling and hissing as it came. It slowed as it made its turn and a crewman threw open the starboard door and waved to me. It had not fully stopped but the signal was, "Hurry and board." I ran across, threw my bag inside, and climbed in. I scanned around me. Although the Blackbird was a huge four-engine craft with jet assist and a ten-person crew, I was the only passenger. I had barely sat down in one of the canvas seats before we were airborne and climbing over Kontum and the enemy rockets set in hollowed bamboo tubes ready to discharge at the airfield should we have remained too long. Below us, shrinking quickly, was the district city with its red-tiled roofs, and the Dak Bla River which as I looked, shrunk from being a winding blue ribbon into a thin string.

"Yours is almost the last stop of our day," the crew chief said as he handed me a coffee. "After that we go to our nest for the night . . . unless we get called for something." I knew we could not talk about our specific missions, but we were aware of what the other did. During the flight to Long Thanh my mind wandered to an imaginary flight path they might have taken before they picked me up. Perhaps they dropped ordnance to an A team under fire, resupplied a CIA team in a remote valley in Laos, or parachuted a team into Cambodia. It made my flight to One-Zero School pass quickly, those straying thoughts and my concern for leaving Doney and Joe Morris to do a mission without me. I hoped they would not be committed before I returned.

## SOG: Missions to the Well

It was four in the morning. The sky was black over the FOB and still. The flutter of a moth trapped against his window woke Doney just before the soft knock on his door. "Sorry to wake you so early, Sergeant Doney, but they want you at the TOC. You have a mission."

"Now?"

"I am afraid so. It came from Saigon."

"You don't mean the Bright Light people? You mean RT Florida."

"That's what they said." The sergeant delivering the message looked to the side and lowered his voice. "I think they want you in today. Briefing is at six."

"I will alert my team." Doney dressed and stepped out of his hooch. His boots crunched the gravel as he walked. All was dark over the camp, but a few miles down the road toward Pleiku, the 4th Infantry Division experienced a probing of their perimeter. Doney stopped and looked toward the base. The crisp air carried the crackle of small arms fire and the rapid hooting sounds of descending parachute flares. A few lines of tracer fire marked the place.

On his walk to the TOC there was little sign of life, and he considered that the very quietness lent a form of security, for the slightest sound of enemy intrusion would be detected by the guards. A sentry shuffled in his enclosure giving life to his shadow.

A bat hunted under the street light at the gate. Across the street a generator turned on and hummed at the mess hall. Doney entered one of the barracks which was divided off into a half dozen team rooms. He paused at Team Florida's door, softly knocked twice and went in.

The room was dark and he left the hall door open to see inside. Joe Morris was asleep on the far side of the room, his head buried in a pillow. Doney cleared his throat so he would not startle the sleeping man. "Joe. Joe."

There was no sound.

"Joe," he said slightly louder. "Joe."

There was rustling in the bed. "Hunhh! What?"

"Joe, it's me, Doney."

"What?" said the startled voice.

"It's me. Its Doney. I'm afraid we have a mission."

There was a small lamp on the table. "Watch your eyes. I'm going to turn on the light."

Joe squinted. "It's night. It's dark. A mission?"

"Something has come up and they want us right away. I have a briefing at six. I want you to get the team together and get them ready. I will know more later. Are you awake now?"

Joe stared into the shadows across the room and pulled himself from slumber. "I'm awake." He swung his legs from the bed.

It was seven when Doney left the Operations Center accompanied by a Vietnamese lieutenant in a red beret. He straightened himself at the door where Morris waited. Doney motioned him away from the entrance. "Sergeant Morris, let's talk over there."

They stopped in an open area near a Conex container a couple dozen meters from the front gate. Doney waited as a Montagnard man wearing a loin cloth wearily passed with his family. They walked on the shoulder of the road in single file with nearly empty packs. They were silent and faced ahead and one could wonder if joy ever came to their fires. A pedicab passed by in the other direction filled to capacity with white-shirted women in conical hats. One of the women was old with black teeth and sunken eyes. The others were young and chattered brightly together. Joe waited for Doney to speak. Something was up. Although they were standing at a solitary place, the team sergeant did not talk until the area was clear of people.

"Sergeant Morris, we sometimes get missions we do not expect or fully know the reason for them. We have to adapt and carry them out. We've been given such a mission and our task is to fulfill it. I wish we had Sergeant Hanson with us for this one. We have trained for this as a team. Now we have to piece this together with what they're giving us."

He turned to Joe Morris. "Saigon wants a prisoner from a certain area and they want him now. In the strategic scheme of things SOG needs information that only a person from that area can tell them, and that means a prisoner. We are the recon team that specializes in and practices prisoner snatches. We have our immediate-action drills and our protocol. But Sergeant Hanson just got on the plane for One-Zero School and that leaves us short. But SOG HQ has assigned us help for this mission.

"To fill out our numbers they have attached a Vietnamese lieutenant, a Vietnamese sergeant and two *Chieu Hoi* privates who know the area. At least the Vietnamese are LLDB, their Special Forces."

Joe stared with his mouth open.

"Two *Chieu Hoi* coming with us! You mean two ex-NVA soldiers who changed sides and are working for us now. How do we know they won't change sides again?"

"We don't, Sergeant Morris. I suppose Saigon thinks we need special help for this one. On this mission they might be the best assets of all. Who knows the enemy better than they and who, more than they, do not want to be caught by them."

Joe looked at the ground, unconvinced. His face was moon-white against his brown eyes. "Some of our teams have been wiped out by them too."

"Yes, that is too true. You and I will have to be vigilant on this. You have the radio and I like you close to me. But this time, I want you near the rear next to Ba and Nhok so you can keep an eye on things toward the front. It'll just be you and me as the only Americans on this. Understand?"

Joe nodded.

"I will have Chin at point followed by me and the Vietnamese lieutenant, then Hue, our interpreter. In the middle I want Noi with the *Chieu Hoi* and the LLDB sergeant. I want them between the *Chieu Hoi* so they can't signal each other. You will be right behind the *Chieu Hoi*.

"I want everyone together at ten hundred at the training room and I will give the order of march and go over the immediate action drills and how we on Team Florida set up for a prisoner snatch. We will go to the range this afternoon to practice it all. Tomorrow, we go in. I will do a visual reconnaissance at noon today. Got it?

"Sergeant Morris, I want you to get our people ready and I will get Lieutenant Vinh to prepare his people and give him the schedule."

Joe's mouth was dry, too dry to answer.

"See what you need from supply also."

Team Florida waited at the Dak To launch site for word to go in. Nothing living moved in the area, not even a bird. It was early in the day. Full heat had not arrived to bake the asphalt of the strip and create heat waves to drift ghost-like from the danger in Laos. Troops sat on their packs and leaned against the side of the mortuary building and did not talk. Ba, the tail gunner, a devout Buddhist, played with his Buddha on the chain which hung from his neck. Should he die "out there" he hoped his people could bring his battered body home to his wife and she would find the gold Buddha firmly clinched between his teeth. Chin, the point man of the team, reclined at the other end of the line wearing his Chicom hat complete with Communist red star, and an AK-47 across his lap. These items were his "edge," buying him that crucial second when he met the enemy on his turf.

Joe Morris held his breath. He had never had an easy mission. "Across the fence" was a thing to be survived "by the skin of one's teeth," as Job in the Old Testament said. He scanned the people around him. Each was lost in his own particular world into which he escaped before a mission. Would the urgency of this mission, the order to "Go now," be amended or canceled at the last minute? What intelligence did Saigon have that they did not share with team Florida that warranted infiltration by a SOG team into this particular forbidden area of Laos at this specific time? What was it that intelligence needed so badly? Would Covey find the area compromised, their wings Swiss-cheesed with 12.7 bullets and troops of the special North Vietnamese regiment especially trained the eliminate SOG people be waiting when they landed?

It rained lightly and briefly during the night. The morning sun glistened on the trees and meadow grass as Covey made a pass over the area of operations. Perhaps the wetness of the night would reflect on a windshield, a helmet, a wet rain-slick or even a line of gun barrels. Betrayal of this mission lay as heavy on Covey's mind as it did on the other Americans.

Joe peeked over at the *Chieu Hoi* next to him. He was young, certainly not twenty. His face was without wrinkles or facial hair and his eyes were bright and open wide and pinballed about as a small boy's do when entering the gates of a carnival for the first time. "He cannot know the utter danger of this mission," Joe thought.

Ba noticed the American studying the young man. He dropped his rucksack and shuffled over. "Him very young man. Him too young to die in field."

Joe studied the man's face again and visualized him at a school function and wondered how he could walk the distance from North Vietnam, through Laos or Cambodia under exploding bombs and battles en route and seem unmarked by hardship.

Ba spoke softly with the young soldier, out of the hearing to the second *Chieu Hoi*. The young man was open and forthright, even naïve with his answers.

Ba turned to Joe and said, "Soldier, him name be Lam. Him say he never do fight before. *Cong Sahn* take him, draft him, and him see American on first mission and *Chieu Hoi*. Him never have battle before. This is first time him. Him not baby san but him young same same."

Joe watched as Lam turned and faced ahead. He stroked the stock of his rifle and waited for the event to begin.

Noi, the handsome Vietnamese member of Florida was on the other side of Lam next to the second *Chieu Hoi*. That ex-NVA was much older, nearly Doney's age. The boney fingers of his hands were wrapped around his rifle like a python. The team would not know but the grip was to mask a nervous tremor he felt going on this mission to an area from which he had recently escaped. His cheekbones were large and prominent and his face tapered to a narrow chin, drawing his skin tight with long wrinkles along both sides of his mouth. His eyes were nearly slits in the folds of skin, the whites of which were jaundice yellow. Around the corners of his eyes webs of wrinkles extended downward and joined those around his mouth. His teeth were stained yellow from extended time in the elements. From his cheekbones down, the older man's skin was deeply browned by the sun, but above, about where a PAVN pith helmet would shade, his skin was pale and moist like cheese. Unlike his fellow *Chieu Hoi*, he knew fully well what lay in store.

Miles to the north and west, Cobra gunships and a pair of fast movers signaled their arrival on standby. Covey radioed the launch site. "Ready to go. Load up."

Joe lay back against his rucksack along with the team. He counted the people for the hundredth time. "Eleven. Eleven of us. Enough of us to make a good prisoner snatch as we always practiced. Lieutenant Vinh was a familiar figure in camp. Slim, 'strack,' with tailor-tight trousers. He was professional, spoke good English and was friendly with Americans. I know Sergeant Tran also. But I have never before seen these *Chieu Hoi*."

Doney and the lieutenant were in the control tower listening for traffic and the all-clear to infiltrate into forbidden territory. Below them on the ground, the rest of the recon men sat in a row under the shade of the building in the line of march. Sergeant Morris studied his people. Each person was a chapter of a psychology book manifesting how men faced fear and danger by their posture, faces, and gestures. In particular he studied the men who had fought for the enemy short months ago and tried to read them. Could he read their secret thoughts and intentions through their posture and mannerisms? They were fit and professional in appearance, faced ahead, never interfacing with the rest of the team. Did they have a mission Team Florida knew nothing about? Did they pull into themselves as he himself did when facing a dangerous mission? Or were they not bothered at all, and were stoic with hearts and nerves of cold stone?

Giving up looking for clues, he determined the only safeguard to the unknown was to be vigilant and professional. Joe leaned back and recalled, "Just yesterday morning Doney woke me for this one and we are here already." Friday passed at bullet speed. Morning was taken up with supply and mission prep. At eleven RT Florida sat before a chalkboard as Doney gave the line of march, immediate action drills and described how they set up for a prisoner snatch with the assault element, the two flanks for early warning and security, and the command element with the radio. About noon they ate, then spent the afternoon at the range practicing immediate action drills and setting up the snatch with the new members of the team. All of that squeezed into one day.

That night Joe Morris slept fitfully with dreams of enemy who would not die but kept coming and coming, laughing and taunting, calling him by name, "Joe. Joe. Here Joe," and he carried a wounded prisoner on his back and his feet were stuck in the ground and he could not move. Then Doney rapped his knuckles on the door and though it was morning and closer to the danger of the field, he was glad to be awake and distanced from the dreams. They ate, boarded the choppers and now waited under shade of one of the three buildings of the launch site, a mortuary of all places.

A screen door slammed at the control tower as Doney and Vinh exited and walked briskly to the waiting team. "Let's go Florida. Mount up!"

The choppers hissed and rumbled to life. Covey landed on the strip and taxied to the group of men.

The men grunted as they rolled to the side with their heavy packs and pushed off the ground with their arms and staggered to their feet. Doney pointed to the second helicopter in the line. "Joe that is your ride," and he watched as the American and the tail element boarded with the two *Chieu Hoi* and the LLDB sergeant. He studied their faces. The Vietnamese sergeant seemed satisfied with the two men who switched sides. Doney boarded last and waved the readiness of the team to lift off.

The RPM increased and blew the steel plates of the helipad clean of sand. Each helicopter shuddered like a retriever about to be released from its leash. They lifted and leaned forward as they climbed and proceeded west. Doney looked over the shoulder of the door gunner as they gained altitude and saw the medic in the chase chopper which flew to their side lean toward him and wave. The hand said, "If you need help, I will be there." Doney raised one hand to say "thank you."

A half hour into the flight to the target in Laos, the older *Chieu Hoi* crawled on his belly to the opening next to the crew chief and his mounted machine gun and peered down at the passing terrain. He saw the contour of the ground and winding streams and fragments of roads which poked through the forest and read them as a map, a familiar one. He sensed nearness to familiar ground and what he now suspected was their goal. He uttered a loud sigh, closed his eyes and leaned back. His hands trembled as he gripped his weapon. Doney saw it and took note.

A "Charlie Model" made a pass over the LZ to draw fire and was followed by the first Huey carrying Recon Team Florida thirty seconds behind. Those who sprang from the struts of the first lift and ran to cover scarcely cleared the small opening in the trees before the second lift descended to a hover and discharged the remainder of the team. Using the noise of the engines to mask sounds of their movement, Doney's people moved briskly from the landing site and circled into a small perimeter.

The day was windless. Insects buzzed and brushed the leaves with their dry paper wings. A few birds hopped place to place on the ground and scratched the humus with their thin feet. A large bird fluttered above the team and settled on a limb and cocked its head as it studied the men below. But the team filtered out those natural sounds and listened instead for those of human origin. The men of Florida all faced outward intently searching with their eyes. Doney was convinced the LZ was clear of ambush but knew also that the SOG hunters often waited for the teams to commit themselves away from where they came in and dismiss the assets before they sprang in attack.

Doney nodded to Morris. It meant, "Radio Covey and dismiss the assets."

The target was on a certain kilometer of the Ho Chi Minh

# SOG: Missions to the Well

Trail—the thoroughfare, the blood flow of the war in the south which carried the battalions of fighters and truckloads of the material of war. They had selected an insertion point far enough away from the main road that it would not telegraph their intentions. But that sensible choice lengthened the time to arrive at the target without being discovered along the way. Although Saigon wanted a prisoner ASAP, Doney knew from his experience success meant getting to the target without being detected and such a thing could not be hurried.

Doney softly clicked his tongue. Chin slowly turned his head and received the direction he was to go. He soundlessly rose and the team proceeded, never breaking a twig, their eyes stripping the vegetation around them for sign of enemy.

Chin stopped often. He never moved until every leaf and blade of grass yielded its secrets. As Doney had instructed, "We have a long way to go to get to the Ho Chi Minh Trail, but we will never arrive unless we avoid the enemy." Nothing escaped the eyes of the Chinese point man. Every sound was evaluated. No odor was dismissed. From time-to-time Chin statued himself when what was before them was uncertain until the anomaly was resolved. The men who followed behind him often lowered themselves to a squat, weapons pointed toward the uncertainty and froze until some subtle movement ahead had passed. Once, a deer passed a dozen yards ahead, bent to a morsel of grass then passed on without alarm.

Doney was pleased with his people for they moved as a practiced unit with stealth and vigilance. Joe Morris wondered if he himself was giving too much attention to the ex-NVA. It seemed to him the old *Chieu Hoi* was the most vigilant of all, peering deeply into the undergrowth as if he expected to meet someone. "But then, "he reasoned, "Who more than he would know how well the place was patrolled so close to the main trail, the lifeline of the Communist effort to win the war."

Midafternoon, they stopped in a security circle and ate, squeezing rations from their prepared bags. Their surroundings were death-quiet with no sign of PAVN. Timid animals which would be alarmed by movement of trackers and scurry ahead in the bushes did not occur. The One-Zero wondered if it was too quiet, but then they still had a distance to go before they neared the road where patrols would be more concentrated. He prepared a situation report for Morris to encode and give to Covey when he passed; an hour or two before they found a place to RON. When he finished the message, he gave it to Noi to give to Morris. He would not have both Americans close together on this mission. One burst of rifle fire could take the two of them out and leave the rest to the mercy of PAVN.

An engine hummed as Covey passed over the next ridge. Doney signaled a security stop. On his belly and with a poncho draped over him to mute any sound, Joe used a faint light and breathed out the message from a one-time-pad, giving the location of the anticipated RON and intelligence of the day. Florida never transmitted or ate from where they would hole up.

The night passed without indications of movement around the RON. Only the occasional chirp of a tree frog and a flutter of wings disturbed the night.

Morning was mostly clear and the sky was saffron-yellow with a few thin streaks of blood-brown cloud, the colors of Buddhism. They were still a distance from the main road where they expected a heavy concentration of patrols and security for the trail. It was imperative, however, that they close the distance to the road. Doney wanted to change direction more often to confuse the enemy as to their target, but they ever drifted toward the Trail and their goal could not be hidden from an alert enemy.

By midafternoon they encountered significant movement. Chin and Doney tried to decipher if the passage of forces was routine or if the patrols were looking for Florida. Doney did not dismiss the possibility of a mole like the one in Project Gamma. Deeper into the day they watched patrols and larger units pass on some of the paths and wide trails. Those soldiers were fully uniformed and carried their arms ready at the port. The uniforms matched the color of the foliage but their faces were easy to observe from where Florida hid, nearly white and spectral under their pith helmets. They moved with purpose, never speaking, with expressionless faces as if their souls had been sucked from them. These were professional soldiers of the army of North Vietnam.

Doney selected an RON site from the map and they fish-hooked, changing direction, and arrived at a small knoll in a bamboo thicket. There was cover to hide the team yet allow them to observe the approaches. Curled dry bamboo leaves littered the slope. In the darkness, the most skillful tracker would have difficulty approaching the wary team silently. They were in their small touch-close circle at twilight when even the creatures of the bamboo forest settled in for the night. A few birds wrapped their wings over a nest of young, as nearby, other fowl perched on limbs and chirped among themselves, avian philosophers pondering where the light went at night. At a place among the high branches, a songbird uttered a single peep, the final good night at the knoll. Ba and Noi scoured the backtrail for any hint of followers, their backs rigid in tension. Only when the light dimmed and vision was replaced by hearing to alert of danger did their bodies relax and fold to the contour of tree trunks. Doney took mental stock of the day. Trails were more abundant and traveled, patrols more frequent, and he knew they were approaching the Ho Chi Minh. Tomorrow they would expect passing enemy units and more trails, some of which they might not see until they were at their threshold.

Morning arrived with the sound of thrashing in the bushes. The were startled to alertness. Had a force approached in the night and prepared its assault? Doney held his carbine in one hand and with the other, eased open the canteen cover which held his grenades. He showed no alarm, only readiness to meet the challenge. Seconds later, Chin smiled and made a sign: A mongoose and snake were in mortal combat. There was a hiss, what seemed to be a growl, thrashing and finally, silence.

They ate in place as Doney prepared a sitrep for Covey when he flew in the area. Ambush was always a possibility when a team left the RON in the morning. PAVN might have pinpointed the team when they settled in for the night, then stealthily brought in units to surround and ambush them when they left the RON. Doney sent Chin and Nhok ahead on their bellies to probe ahead before the team as a whole rose and proceeded toward the target. Doney looked back and gave a signal to his people: one hand, palm down in a washing motion which meant, "sterilize the site." He did not want the enemy to see where they had been and count their numbers.

Throughout the day they encountered trails which paralleled the main road and a half dozen times froze in place as patrols passed. Some were fully uniformed North Vietnamese regulars with their ranks supplemented by others in black pajamas. There was often a shout in the distance and one-time sounds which seemed to emanate from a loud speaker. At a security stop, when they listened and squeezed a meal and all was quiet, they heard truck engines hundreds of meters in to the west.

"Tomorrow, we will be on the trail," Doney mouthed to Joe on the other end of the line.

They found a place to RON with good cover and concealment. There was less dry debris to warn of approach in the night. Everyone sensed the nearness of the main highway and knew contact was imminent. Lam looked toward every sound and wondered at its source. The older *Chieu Hoi* was an old hand at war. His feet were drawn up near his buttocks where he sat with his weapon lain across his lap and his thoughts were curled up in the blankets of his mind. Morris positioned himself slightly inside the circle where he could monitor the new members of the team. Doney lay out two avenues of escape from the RON should they be probed and have to escape and evade. Florida waited for morning.

It sounded like rain; tiny rain drops faintly tapping dry leaves. It reminded Doney of a soft summer shower in the Midwest when it is carried by a breeze and drops its shimmering moisture, then moves on. They were small waves of tapping, then silence, followed by a drip or two which lagged behind the rest. Several times during the night they heard it, the tapping sound which began on one side of the team and moved along a flank before it disappeared in the distance. Although the night was not fully overcast and Morris could not clearly see the faces of his team mates, he knew all of them were alert and though they could not see in the dark, their eyes followed the tapping nonetheless, their heads turning as they followed the sounds around them. There was no rain.

Morris did not think it was possible for him to doze even for a minute, for his neurons shot back and forth inside their channels like terrified trapped mice frantically seeking an opening, but at a time well before morning someone was standing directly above him. He did not hear the shuffle of movement that brought the person to drift like a phantom, but he was there. This was not a dream. Enough light filtered in to recognize the figure. It was the older *Chieu Hoi*. The man stood alert, facing the tapping sounds around him.

Joe's mouth was open in a gasp. How did he get past the others and arrive to hover over him? Did he come to silently kill this red-headed American then slip into the bamboo forest and join his comrades? Morris inched his finger into the trigger guard of his rifle and prepared to ward off an attack. He wondered if Doney at the other end of the perimeter were alive at this moment.

The old *Chieu Hoi*'s knees cracked as he bent toward him and said in a hoarse whisper, "*Beaucoup* VC. *Beaucoup* VC." The older man wore no hat and Joe felt those jaundiced eyes looking down on him. The tone of his voice was of controlled anxiety and of one giving information. "Sergeant," he whispered in measured English, "VC everywhere. Many. Many VC."

The old soldier's head panned about and Morris was convinced now if he never was the tapping sounds were passing patrols moving through the underbrush. Unsure what to do, he reached out in the darkness and gently patted the man's forearm, "I know." The *Chieu Hoi* raised himself and slowly turned to go but stopped. He bent close to Joe and whispered, "My name is Bao."

He shuffled his way back to his place in the circle and faced the renewed tapping in the bamboo, his finger on the trigger guard. Joe watched in the faint light as the man's head panned and followed the passage of troops. He thought of the tone of sadness in the whisper of the older man. "My name is Bao." Was the man thinking, "No one knows or cares that I am here. My name is Bao."

With the greyness of the morning and better visibility. Doney gave the team a "wait and be very still" sign as he sent Chin and Nhok to recon around the RON. It was an hour before they returned and gave the location of lingering patrols. He signaled for them to squeeze out something to eat and prepared a sitrep for Joe. He and the lieutenant conferred with Chin regarding the enemy presence as He passed the message to Joe. If Covey arrived the message said, "Will arrive target and attempt snatch. Assets available?"

They slipped from the night hideaway on a side Chin deemed to be free of enemy and contoured the side of a gently sloping ridge which led in the direction of the Ho Chi Minh Trail. Twice the point man froze and held his clinched fist behind him so Doney could see. He signaled with his palm down in a pressing-down motion and the team lowered themselves to a squat. He placed his free hand to the back of his head, "Enemy." He looked back at Doney for instructions. Chin dropped his pack and crawled to the suspect area. Ten minutes later he returned and reported to Doney and the lieutenant, "*Bac Viet* be there. It be listening post."

Twice they changed direction and twice waited as patrols passed on established trails. Florida maneuvered away and came to a narrow path and stopped. It faced the direction they wanted to travel. "This be animal trail. No people do. Maybe deer have. Florida can use no problem," Chin whispered. Doney considered for only a moment; recon teams never used enemy trails but this was unlikely to be ambushed by PAVN and they needed to get to the target. He nodded his approval and Chin led the way. They moved at a faster pace and the way was nearly soundless with only an occasional brush of leaves against a shoulder.

Truck engines moaned under their heavy loads passing west to east, and no more than a couple hundred meters away. Chin looked back and smiled. They were there. They were at the Ho Chi Minh Trail. They halted in a thicket a hundred meters from the shoulder and set up a security stop. As the team waited for them, Chin, the lieutenant and Doney scouted to the road to make a final inspection.

In a thicket a dozen meters from the road, next to a shallow ditch which lined the road the three took up post and waited. This portion of the way was hard packed and did not reveal clues of what had passed on the way to the war in the south. The soles of countless Bata boots and many hundreds of convoys wore it smooth and did not tell its secrets. Vehicles could meet and pass here, but with difficulty. The surface before them was straight for fifty meters but had a bend at either end where the road and that which was on it disappeared from view. If they ambushed at this location, they would not know what lay around the corner; passing patrols, convoys or even a bunker that was often spaced along the way.

The road was empty of traffic at the time and he said to the two men with him, "I would like to know what is around those corners, if there are any bunkers." He checked his watch. "It is early enough in the day, that if we got a prisoner now, we have time to get him to an LZ before dark."

The lieutenant seemed lost in his thoughts as he stared at the bend and imagined the dangers beyond it. Without looking up he said, "If we catch one now, we have time. I think if we take time and look around corners, we do not have time today." After a moment he added, "If VC have bunkers, they talk and make noise, but we have heard nothing. I do not think there are bunkers around the corner."

They watched for traffic the next hour. It was slight with no large units or convoys passing. They passed knowing they were in their own sanctuary and were lax with security. "Let's do it," Doney said.

They joined the rest of the team a hundred meters off the trail. "This is it. Joe, you will be right here by yourself with the radio. You are our lifeline. When things happen, we will all rally here. Watch for us so we don't go by you."

Hue translated for the Asians on the team., "It will be like we practiced in Kontum."

Doney pointed at the Vietnamese sergeant. "You and two of my men will be at the bend of the road on the right. If you can do it without being seen, you will alert us when VC are coming. When we get in contact you must hold off all enemy until we have prisoner secured and are off the road. Understand? That is most important.

You must hold off enemy."

Hue translated it and the three men affirmed they understood.

"At the other bend is Lam and two more of my people. You have same mission."

Hue translated and they said that they understood.

Doney pointed at Bao, the lieutenant, and Chin. "You will be with me at the ambush. I have two Claymore mines to take out everyone in the column except the one I want as a prisoner. When I blow the Claymores, all VC will fall down except the one that I want in the middle. Do not shoot him." He paused to be sure they were clear in what would happen. "If there is no column, I will just shoot the NVA in the leg or shoulder and we will run out and secure him. Chin and Bao will be security when I do it. This is not new. It is just as we trained it. Understand?" They nodded when Hue finished translating.

"And Joe, you had a response that the air assets were not committed elsewhere, so we are good there."

"Yes, Covey is up."

Midday, they were wormed into the thicket beside the road, invisible to those who were on it. Their view was clear the full length of the gravel highway all the way to the bends on either side, and with the stillness of the day, engines of oncoming vehicles or the tread of boots in the gravel would alert them of approach. Doney never used Claymore mines in the RON because the stealthy enemy could sneak in and turn them around to face the team, but he had two of them for the ambush. They were placed to take out two swaths of an enemy column leaving a gap in the center between the coverage of the two blasts. He would wait until his target was in that void before he pressed the detonators. Perhaps his prisoner would be dazed by the blast and easy to manage and shooting him in the leg with his silenced Hi Standard .22 pistol would not be necessary and the prisoner could walk.

Doney was placing the last bit of vegetation in place to complete the hide and decide how he would lunge from it without entangling in vines when the first element came down the road. A twinge of nervousness coursed through them because they had finished just in time. Had the enemy troops arrived minutes earlier Florida might have been found still secreting themselves. The column was large, far too large to engage, and the only fear left was that of being discovered. As simple a thing as one soldier stepping to the bushes to relieve himself could unmask them. The enemy formation was at least a company and they moved by their platoons with sergeants walking at the flanks. In addition to the munitions they carried, the sounds of men on the march: the swish of fabric, thumping of half empty canteens, clacking metal clasps and wood rifle stocks, and occasional cough were also carried along.

They passed and were nearly at the next bend where three of his people were poised as security. An airplane passed over. Perhaps it was Covey, and Doney watched as the column split in two halves and dashed into the bushes at the sides of the road. They remained in the shrubbery until the spotter plane was gone and a soldier in a pith helmet walked to the center of the way, removed his helmet to better hear the receding engine, then shouted a command. From the two sides of the road the troops reformed and at another command continued on.

"Close," Doney thought. "They might have just as well dashed into the cover where we were hiding."

Twice more in the hour, units passed. They were trucks in a long column and too many for their attention. Doney glanced at Bao. His head was down and his eyes closed, and Doney recalled the adage that people sense your presence if you look at them or make eye contact. He glanced at the man's hands where he held his rifle. They were steady and did not shake.

Nothing moved for the next twenty minutes. Doney was getting a cramp. He tried to reposition himself. A cramp would not do if he were to shoot and spring to the road and wrestle a prisoner. Chin saw it and grinned. "Papa san." He teased. "Old man."

Gravel crunched.

The four of them looked to the right. One single uniformed soldier boldly walked down the center of the road. He was stocky.

His chest was out as he carried his rifle slung over one shoulder.

"Perfect," Doney thought. "Had he carried his rifle in his hand, I would shoot him in that shoulder to keep him away from his weapon. As it is I need to shoot him in the leg and run out and grab him. He is by himself. Maybe we can grab him and be off the road with no noise before anyone knows we were here." He trusted Chin to be aware of the *Chieu Hoi*, and Doney slowly slid the silenced pistol through the opening he had prepared in the bush.

Pffft! The small bullet went true, striking the man in his thigh just as he was putting his weight on the leg. With a grunt of pain, he crumpled to the ground. The NVA tried to stand but the shock in his wounded thigh would not support him. Doney charged from the bushes and was on him in seconds. But the soldier immediately recovered from the pain, turned and faced the American. The stocky man was agile and powerful, a much larger man than most Asians. He twisted from Doney's grip and swung at him with his fists. Desperation and rage marked the enemy's face. For one moment he was free of Doney's grasp and he tried to swing his rifle from his shoulder.

Three loud shots from behind Doney ended all chance of taking this man prisoner silently—and they were distinctive M-16 rounds at that. One of the rounds struck the Asian's ammo pouch with a loud "whack!" The second hit him in the pectoral muscle and the third hit the man square in the chest. Doney flipped him over and placed flex cuffs on his wrists before the man could resist. Pain, anger, and fierce hatred for the American showed in the wounded man's eyes. "We need to get him off the road and into the bushes before VC comes," Doney said in a loud voice.

Shouts from the bend. From around the corner, heavy automatic fire erupted. It was the distinctive popping sound of numerous AK rifles and an RPD machine gun, followed by B-40 rocket fire. The three men left to secure the flank and hold off enemy attack to the center folded without a shot. They ran headlong down the center of the road toward Doney and the prisoner.

"VC! VC! Many VC come road."

They shouted, "Maybe hundred VC come!" Their eyes were wide and terror marked their faces. When they reached the ambush site they did not stop in their running, but fled through it without pause and charged into the brush and disappeared leaving Doney on his knees caring for the prisoner.

Bao and the lieutenant were returning fire as Norm Doney finished placing a compress on the chest wound lest he die before they get to an LZ and looked up. The road was filled with charging shooting soldiers. Bullets whizzed past kicking up dirt on the road and shredding the leaves around them. "Chin, turn the Claymores toward them. Now!"

Some of the front ranks of the charging force stopped to shoot, as others ran around them using the ditches to continue their charge at the team. Two or three soldiers in khaki and pith helmets knelt to the side where the backlash would not hurt their comrades and fired B-40 rockets at the four men on the ambush site.

A rocket exploded next to Doney sending shrapnel over his body. A large fragment struck him at the orb of his right eye and face. He heard the slap of the impact as the force spun his head to the side. His nose ran. Blood and clear liquid streamed down his cheek. For a brief millisecond, he ran the back of his hand over the place: blood and clear fluid. "I lost an eye!"

"Chin," he yelled again, "Turn the Claymores down road toward VC!"

Doney glanced at the two other men of his attack element. Both the lieutenant and Bao were shooting down the road.

Chin shouted from the road, "All *fini* sergeant."

"Come back. Shoot Claymore at VC.

Doney hoisted the prisoner over his shoulder. "Let's go!"

He staggered with the weight and stumbled into the bushes just as the Claymores went off. But moments later another B-40 exploded and he heard a muted cry. He glanced back. Chin had a massive wound on his forehead at the hair line which may have pierced his skull. One arm hung limp but he held his rifle with the other and moved zombie-like off the road, walking backward and shooting with his AK held under his armpit.

"Bao," he shouted to the *Chieu Hoi* who was fully engaged shooting at the oncoming force, "Help Chin. Come follow me."

The ambush team melted into the thick undergrowth and made for Joe and the radio. Doney's vision blurred and he did not know if it was from weariness or losing sight, but he sighted on the next bamboo tree and said to himself, "I will make it that far," and when he arrived at the place, he chose the next landmark and continued on.

Bao came from his shell of silence. He knew in his heart which side he was on. Blood poured down Chin's face and into his eyes. "*Dung lai! Dung lai!*" he shouted to those ahead of him. Doney looked back. Bao took Chin's cravat and mopped the blood from his eyes and tied it around his forehead and the wound. He looked at Doney and said, "Okay now."

The shooting at the road diminished and brush cracked from milling troops at the thicket. Shouts of orders filtered from the road as they organized the care of their casualties and for pursuit.

Doney staggered with the weight on his shoulder but strode as fast as he could. His vision blurred with the effort and he gasped for air. Exhausted, he dropped to his knees and set the prisoner down on the ground just as the four men of the snatch element joined Joe Morris and the radio. Doney leaned back and gasped for air. "Joe, come with me with your camera. A dozen meters away they arrived at the wounded soldier. Take a picture of him." The soldier had a sucking chest wound and was looking about with wide searching eyes. Drainpipe sounds came from his open mouth. "We will get a bandage on that and get him to an LZ."

Doney looked at the small group around him. "It appears we have a split team, but we have to get out with the prisoner. Sergeant Morris, get on the radio and get with Covey. We have casualties and a prisoner and need an immediate exfil."

The answer was immediate. Covey was in the area and had an LZ picked out. It was close by and assets were on the way. With the wounded NVA hoisted over his shoulder, they moved briskly in the direction. Chin continued to bleed through the cravat on his forehead. It streamed down his face and into his mouth. He blew the blood that streamed into his mouth and slung his rifle over his shoulder so he could use his bandana to mop the flowing blood and clear his eyes. Chin insisted he stay on point and lead as he always had. No wound could alter his resolve, not even a wound which exposed his brain.

Bao was nearly touch-close as he followed the wounded Chinese point man. His rifle ensured the area ahead was free of enemy, and without a spoken word, assumed the care of the wounded man. Doney was close behind, at times correcting the direction to their exfiltration site. As the thickness of the undergrowth and bamboo thinned, Doney stopped and faced Joe. "Tell Covey we are at the LZ but have a split team so they don't fire them up."

At the edge of the clearing Doney reached into his side pocket and pulled out a panel. "Use this to signal Covey. So far Charlie hasn't found us and might not know where we are. I don't want to use a pen flare and tell them."

Engines sounded at the horizon. Doney dropped to his knees and let down the prisoner. The man's eyes fluttered and he struggled to breathe as blood entered his lungs. He looked up at his captor."

"Soon, you have *bác sĩ*," he assured him.

The Communists had clearly arrived. Florida knew they would be pursued. By now they must know that they had one of theirs as a prisoner. PAVN would martial everything to destroy them at the LZ. They could only hope for help to quickly arrive and join the battle. Small arms fire came from a broad swath at the opening in the bamboo for they were unsure of the exact location of the team. It gained in intensity as more platoons joined the first to arrive. Muffled shouting filtered through the bamboo on one flank, cracking bullets puncturing the leaves, and assaulting men crashing through the brush announced full scale attack.

Covey radioed, "We picked up part of your team at another LZ. The third part will join you shortly. We see panel."

"Roger then, we have heavy small arms fire and pressure from two-seven-five degrees. See panel?"

"Copy. I will give marking rounds for assets."

"Roger. Other element of split team has just joined us. You are free to engage."

"Copy. Pop smoke."

"Smoke out."

"I see red."

"Good copy."

"Assets inbound. Heads down."

There was a roar of engines as an F-4 Phantom flew directly overhead. It flew low just above the bamboo and had the adversary on the ground been aware of its gunrun they might have engaged it with their rifles. But it was gone before they could raise their weapons leaving a swath of death behind it from its 20 mm cannons and payload of bombs. Some enemy soldiers died in the act of raising their weapons to their shoulders. The dense forest erupted in white explosions and flames. Black smoke rose between breaks in the trees. Screams of agony and angry shouting filled the path of the first Skyhawk.

The second made its pass just behind the first with heavy bombs, napalm, and more cannon fire. The run was danger-close as Doney had directed, and bits of tree limbs, clods of earth, and chunks of objects wrapped in cloth fell as rain on the LZ.

The F-4s made the run twice more before the Cobra gunships relieved them with their miniguns and other ordnance. Huey helicopters followed the last gunship and began a descent to exfiltrate RT Florida. Doney ran over to Joe, the first time they had been talk-close on the mission.

"Joe, you and the ones who got split from us and joined us here go on this first lift. The rest of us will go out with me on the next one."

Joe wiped some fallen debris from his eyes and hair, nodded and started to go. "Hey," he said in a voice of sudden realization. "I lost my hat back there."

Doney stopped and smiled. He put a hand on Joe's shoulder and calmly looked him in his eyes and said, "Well, Joe, do you want to go back and get it?"

The second helicopter arrived only seconds after the first and lowered to the ground as Cobra gunships kept the tree line free of enemies. The One-Zero motioned Bao and the lieutenant to board first. Doney lowered the bleeding prisoner from his shoulder to the deck and struggled inside as the others slid the prisoner in away from the open door. Doney's eyes filled with fluid and he mopped his eyes with his cravat just as the chopper lifted. But Chin was not yet inside. He had one usable arm and grabbed the strut. They lifted into the air with him hanging with one hand. With one arm he did a pull-up far enough to throw one leg over the strut and straddle it.

They were a hundred feet in the air when a Charlie gunship radioed the situation. "You have a man hanging outside on a strut." The first consideration was that a courageous enemy had attempted to crawl aboard to take down the craft. Doney looked around him. Chin was missing. Doney was horrified. With his fluid-covered eyes he thought he himself was the last to board.

"Grab my feet," he shouted to the closest person as he scrambled to the opening on his belly, reached over the edge and pulled the wounded man inside.

They flew directly to Kontum with the prisoner, landing in the CCC compound. Half the compound hugged the exhausted team and shouted their greetings. Medics came with two vans for the wounded. First sergeant Robert Howard brought his ubiquitous tub of soft drinks and beer submerged in ice water. It was here that the team first felt the exhaustion that had been masked inside by adrenaline. They were hugged and congratulated.

Chin did not want to be carried to the aid truck but walk instead. He would walk all the way to the dispensary to be attended to. He took a few steps in that direction. Dizziness made everything swirl around. He felt weak. His legs became rubber and began to fold under his weight. A medic who walked beside him, read the signs and grabbed his shoulder. Someone cradled him and folded him into the stretcher which had been carried beside him, ready for just this moment.

Doney daubed the blood and fluid from below his eye as he spoke. "Prisoner is wounded, sucking chest wound. I hope he makes it."

They slid him off the deck of the chopper, an easy thing, as the surface was slick with blood. Though the prisoner was large, Bob Howard carried him in his arms like a child taking him to the nearest medic's van. The man's eyes were covered with a bandana for security, and though the man could not see, Howard felt the fear and flutter of his heart and the shaking of his whole body. Howard sensed also the soldier gave up being in charge of his own destiny and succumbed to that of his captors.

That afternoon the medics gave Doney the good news. The eye was not harmed; it was not fluid of the eyeball leaking away. The repair of the damage would have to be done elsewhere. "You have a duct that is severed. Those are tears."

Shortly after, just before Doney and the lieutenant were about to be debriefed, Howard stopped him in the hall. "Bad news, Norm. It was that sucking chest wound. After all that you guys did, he died."

# CHAPTER FIVE
## *RT Maine Hunter Killer*

It was a phenomenon. Most soldiers liked the popular music that came out in those years of our war. A crazy thing. The song writers and musicians did not like us, despised us, mocked us, and the lyrics could have been the propaganda of the other side, yet we played their music in the club. What would have been reprehensible when spoken, was accepted and admired when sung. Like other servicemen throughout the war zone, we listened to the songs, sang the lyrics, tapped the beat on the stocks of our rifles, and played them on our reel-to-reel tape decks, sometimes with the volume sounding outside our hooches.

Some of us were passing by RT Maine's team room and heard one of those songs outside. A knot of Montagnards had also been walking by and stopped as the first beats of Creedence Clearwater Revival sifted through the window screens. One of the Yards smiled at his fellow Bahnar tribesmen from the same village. I saw his open mouth. As a child his upper teeth had been filed to the gums as was the custom of his people, but with the prosperity of working for

Special Forces, that gap had been replaced with one white tooth which spanned the gap of the four missing teeth. His companion smiled in return. Gong music flowed in their blood. The beat brought them to their longhouse deep in the hardwood forest, where varied sizes of bronze gongs played in unison, the trong drums joined in turn, then the gord zither and a bamboo xylophone, and finally the melody played on a sao flute. One of the Bahnar bent forward and shrugged his shoulders to the rhythm. They laughed and shuffled away.

Maine's hooch was the first team room in the building. Screen windows lined across the front. A fan softly blew through the room and passed through the screen with the music. The space inside was filled with boxes: ammunition, C-rations, indigenous rations, grenades, thin tarps, all that was needed for a mission in the field. Sherman Miller was hunched over, loading magazines, preparing his gear. His head bobbed to the music. Without realizing, with each beat, he slid one bullet into a magazine he held in the other hand. At a point in the song, he stopped altogether and listened to the lyrics.

*I see the bad moon a-risin'*
*I see trouble on the way*
*I see earthquakes and lightnin'*
*I see bad times today*

*Don't go around tonight*
*Well it's bound to take your life*
*There's a bad moon on the rise.*

Miller slipped in a few more rounds as John Fogerty came to the last verse.

*Hope you got your things together*
*Hope you are quite prepared to die*
*Looks like we're in for nasty weather*
*One eye is taken for an eye*

*Don't go around tonight*
*Well it's bound to take your life*

# SOG: Missions to the Well

*There's a bad moon on the rise.*

"Well, that's cheerful," I said as we entered the hooch.

Miller rarely talked. He said, "Huh."

"Huh," could mean "Talk louder, I can't hear you," or "You can say that again," or "I don't get it." But that was his conversation of the day, and he went back to loading magazines. He was the demolition-engineer of the team; he could build anything or blow it up. Abstract concepts had no place in foundational things such as fuses and det-cord and timed-pencils. Things did not disturb him. He was solid and unshakable in combat. In the corner, next to a pair of metal ammo cans was his P.O.W. stove with a cube of C-4 explosive, just enough to cook a meal and a packet of indigenous rations. He liked fish and squid best. Our conversation ended, he turned from where he squatted loading magazines and busied himself cooking a snack.

Baker, the team leader, was inspecting the Yards' work in another hooch. Everything else that needed doing for the mission had been done.

Mike Buckland finished the last touches to his web gear. He draped it over the back of a chair, stood and stretched.

"About finished?" I asked.

"Just."

"Tomorrow?"

"Yes. Weather is good. Clear and hot like today."

Dennis Bingham glanced around the room and its pre-mission clutter. He preferred a more Spartan place. "Want to go for a walk. There is air conditioning at the club. I can buy you a Coke."

"I could use a break. I think I'm finished here. Just the last-minute things to do as a team."

The club was in two halves. The larger half was screened in and faced the perimeter. A stage took up one corner where floor shows and special services were held. Connected by a single door, was the other section, The Huckleberry Inn. It was dimly lit with a full-sized bar at the far end and a dozen round tables and chairs. It was at those tables many of the recon people hashed over events across the fence and scrawled notes of lessons learned and strategies on napkins and let out the tensions of their ordeals. To the side of the bar was a tiny post office where everyone could pick up mail. It was usually manned by someone who was recovering from wounds and not quite ready to return to the field.

I ordered seven soft drinks, naming them off to the person running the club that day. The cooler where they kept the drinks was only a point or two above freezing. A vapor cloud escaped it when he opened the door.

"This will give you guys a brain freeze, guaranteed," he said.

I gave him the required seventy cents, cradled five cans under one arm and carried the other two in my free hand. The day was steamy. I set the cans down and watched the sides perspire. Drops of moisture slid down like tears and puddled on the table. Cans, when we opened them, did so with a hiss that sounded like sprung trip flares. I felt the spray against my face, moist and cool. Around the table were some of the guys with whom I arrived in April. It seemed distant history now; driving past the wrecked French fighter airplanes along the road; the first look at the busy main street of Kontum, the smell of saffron and ginger, the Asian music that reached out from open shop doors, and our truck tires as they thumped across the planks of the Dak Bla bridge.

Most of us had already had serious experience fighting the enemy. Compared to any other unit in Vietnam we would be considered seasoned. Still, there was much to be learned, many things to be experienced on the forge of war before we considered ourselves fully tempered. Any SOG man was aware of the unfathomable danger one faced being out there thinking he knew it all.

We were discussing that over our soft drinks.

"I remember Doney teaching me the rules the old timers figured out which must never be broken. 'Do so at the peril of your life.' When he thought I had learned all the tricks of our trade, both from him and the other old timers, he gave me that Doney grin. 'But you can break any rule as long as you know you are breaking it and have a compelling reason to do so. It is when you do not know you are breaking the rule at all that will get you killed.'"

Mike Wilson tilted back his chair. He threw back his head and lowered his eyes turtle-like as his manner was, and drawled, "It is like we have to know how to never make a mistake in the woods, to know it so well, that you do not have to think when the pressure is on. You just do the smart thing."

"Like a reflex," one of us added.

Randy Rhea was quietly listening. Seven of our bunch had been roommates for nearly a year before we came to CCC. He was wholesome and very smart. With his gentle smile and slight nod, he added his amen to our conversation.

Ferry Cross the Mersey was playing over the speakers in the background.

"My kind of music," I said.

Dennis slowly nodded with his cherubic smile. He was the only one of us who had not been over the fence on a SOG mission. Over the half hour we talked, he listened, taking it all in, writing it on the invisible notebook of his brain, next to the encyclopedic recall of the hundreds of books he had read. His cheeks were rosy and smooth, he never needed to shave. Dennis hung on our words. His feet shuffled under the table. We knew him well: All his life he wanted to be a Green Beret and to be in mortal combat. Of those of us who trained together and arrived at the same time, he was the only one yet to feel that electrical charge of adrenaline course through his body on one of those deadly missions.

"I think I will be going out on Uemura's team in a few days," he said, "I can't wait until my foot leaves that helicopter skid and touches the enemy's backyard." I watched Dennis' face and knew that precise moment was being lived on the screen of his mind.

"And I want that first firefight. I want the bullets to go both ways—green tracers and red. I want that CIB," he added, pointing to the cloth badges on our shirts.

"Be careful, Den, they have bulldogs in the enemy's backyard," one of the guys said.

Mike Buckland added, "There is something about that first step off the Huey. Are you going to step off onto a golf course or on a mine or on a snake?"

Another one of the guys, it might have been John Plaster or Ralph Rodd; "I hear they are stretching wires across some of the LZs like spider webs. You can't see them from the air. They tie empty C-ration cans to the trees. At each end of the string, they slide grenades with the pins removed into those C-ration cans. Dozens of them. When the chopper drops down to let the team off, they settle into the strings and a dozen grenades slam the team."

"I guess that way they don't have to have a bunch of watchers at every LZ," I said.

Mike looked over at him. "Gee, thanks. I'm going in tomorrow."

"We never know what we will find," I said. "I think I mentioned it to some of you before, but we were settling into an opening filled with elephant grass about ten feet tall. Just as we were about to land, I saw a cobra snake looking well above the tops. Its hood was fully flared and it turned its head like a periscope."

Randy cringed. "Those cobras with the hood spread always remind me of Pharoah in Egypt and that hat with the hood that spread over his shoulders. I wonder if they did that on purpose so people would fear Pharoah."

"A cobra has to have two thirds of its body on the ground to lift the rest of itself up, so that snake had to be twenty-some feet long," I continued. "We were descending on it. The front of the struts nearly touched it. For sure, the pilots must have seen it in their windshields. Can you imagine what it must be like to have a huge snake in your windshield? It was white, must have been old, against the glass with the black dots like eyes on the hood. Imagine what it must have been like if it struck at the pilots and they heard the thump on the plexiglass inches from their faces. We touched down and ran for the trees in the direction I last saw the serpent. But it was gone. I dreamed about it when we got back. You never know what's on an LZ."

Maine departed the next morning. We watched them. Perhaps

we saved the event in our minds. We might not see them again this side of eternity. It was the custom among us to see our brothers off. We patted the shoulders of the tribesmen. Called them by name if we could; Andre, Kiet, Nhut, Suih-Kim, and the rest. We smiled, looked directly into their eyes and wished them well. We said our parting words. Placing the palms of my hands together as they did, I told them I would pray for them. We watched as the choppers rose from the dark dust cloud that lifted under the rotors, like a modern-day phoenix, and climb, skirting Kontum city on their westward journey.

Alone, I walked to the far side of the camp to a vantage point and watched as the fleet grew smaller and finally disappeared.

Maine left the Dak To launch site fairly early that morning. The day was clear. Baker picked out a landing zone the day before. He appraised it obliquely from the side—an opening about fifty meters across. Usually, an opening of that size made it probable there were watchers, ready to ambush or announce the arrival of a team. But Baker and Sneaky Pete Air Force, the small group of Birddog pilots who flew for SOG in Kontum, circled the area at a discrete distance and found no indication of enemy.

"Okay, that one then," Baker said.

"Our mission," Baker told his team, "Is to find a battalion base camp ... here," he said placing his finger on the map. "Saigon thinks it may be abandoned, and PAVN may have gone on to another location. They want to know for sure. No point bombing a base that is no longer there, I guess."

He looked around at the other Americans. There were no questions.

"That's it then. Just the eight of us. The LZ looks like a grassy field. No sign of enemy so far."

The Hueys made a straight-in approach to a gliding hover into the field. Buckland spotted the grass waving below, like the pictures of Kansas wheat fields he remembered from school. The grass bent and swayed from the push of the rotor blades and he readied himself for a short hop into the knee-high grass and the sprint to the trees.

He saw the skids slap the top of the blades of grass and bent his knees for the jump. He would be the third out: Kiet the point man and former NVA, then Baker, then himself. To his side he saw his point man leap from the skid—and disappear. Completely. Then Baker followed, Buckland had a faint image of the One-Zero's head above the grass.

Mike jumped. This was no golf course. It was a field of very tall elephant grass with chest-deep water. To the side he saw the point man gasp and sputter. He had gone fully under. Murkey water filled Kiet's lungs. In a moment of terror, the little Montagnard choked and struggled to stand, heaving for breath. The depth was to his neck. The Americans cast about to locate their people. Only the nearest tribesmen could be seen in the thick vegetation. Water was to the necks and chins of his people. It would be left for Miller to find those at the rear of the column.

They sputtered and loudly coughed. They splashed and thrashed about. Only the wash of the helicopters and the engine noise hid their struggle. Americans buoyed up their little people, keeping them above water.

Baker hissed above the splashing water, "Everyone got their weapons?"

All were accounted for. The mercenaries gained control of themselves. They held their weapons above their heads. Around them was a wall of grass. The direction to go?

Baker glanced up at the sun and from it pointed the direction to the point man. With the noise of the departing choppers, they started off, feeling the bottom before placing their feet, trying to move without sound.

Ten minutes to reach firm ground. Having heard the engines, would enemies have guessed what was occurring, rushed to the edge, and waited to pick them off? Waited as they crawled out with muck pouring from them, unable to move speedily against the weight of the water and drag of the thick grass. They waded in and dragged themselves to the closest cover. Grey and dripping with muck, they hovered as a pack and listened for enemy.

## SOG: Missions to the Well

Ten minutes. Baker signaled to tend to their gear. They held their weapons, stock-up, and watched brown water pour from the barrels. Half at a time, they secured their gear as the rest watched the tree line.

Ready, and a nod from Baker, Buckland radioed the "Team okay, good day" message and the assets were dismissed. Maine rose from their small circle and crept forward on their mission, Kiet, the former NVA soldier on the point, Baker and Buckland close behind.

They proceeded north in the direction of one of the tributaries of the Communist lifeline to the war in the south and the targeted base area. They were soggy and chaffed in their wet fatigues at the start. Were they not looking for enemy as they moved, each might have noticed faint steam on the soldier in front of him as stagnant pond residue evaporated from his clothing, the drying uniforms taking on lighter and lighter shades of green. Maine proceeded with stealth. The Ho Chi Minh Trail and all its resources and ability to martial forces at them, was especially fraught with danger.

The terrain was steep, hilly and mountainous, more jungle than forest. Rains occurred the week before and the ground had not again become brittle and noisy on which to walk. They moved with stealth. That which allowed them to move quietly, allowed also the enemy to maneuver around them soundlessly.

Baker led his people toward the objective: the NVA battalion base camp. He would have changed direction more often to confuse the enemy as to their objective, but the terrain itself channeled them. Even then, they zig zagged when they could to throw off the enemy. They made security stops, listening for any sign of trackers, their eyes scouring the foliage ahead.

Sometime after midday, the lead man pointed out a slim green highly venomous snake on a tree limb. It lay body length along the limb nearly invisible. The limb extended neck height across their way. It was a tri-pacer, one of the three-step snakes whose bite could kill before the anti-venom kit could be taken from a wrapper. He gently lifted the limb with his rifle barrel and looked back at Baker to be sure he saw it. Kiet gently lifted the limb and passed under it to the other side. Baker followed suit, then Buckland until all of Maine passed under. Any tracker team who followed the SOG people and was not alert would lose one point man as they did so. To a slim snake.

The quiet was uncanny. They were deep into enemy territory. It was that moment of utter stillness just before a tornado fills its chest with air, looks across the prairie, then lets it out in furry knocking down barns and silos. But no enemy. So far. Perhaps all was being positioned. The eerie silence made them all the more cautious. Maine moved toward their objective, their heads casting about. Waiting.

But nothing occurred. No signal shots to inform the team "We see you." No movement in the brush. No birds rocketed from the trees alarmed by approaching soldiers.

It was late afternoon before they found it. Having emerged from a steep valley the lay of the land flattened as they moved north. They had not patrolled far from the lowland when the point man abruptly stopped. He froze.

Baker moved up to him.

The point man nodded not taking his eyes from the point of concern. "There," he whispered.

Baker did not see it at first, but then the vegetation was too perfect, set in rows in places. Bunkers.

It was at least a battalion-size base camp: the objective SOG headquarters deemed so important they risked sending one of their teams to learn the simple answer to "Was it occupied, being used today?"

Had it not been for a narrow cross trail before which they stopped and studied the foliage beyond it, they would not have seen through the camouflage., They were on it before the shapes of structures revealed themselves. They backed into a thicket and surveilled. Utter stillness. No sign of ambush. No soldier coughed in the distance; the sound covered with a sleeve. No safety slid off the weapon of a nervous soldier. No faint squelch of a radio.

Still the team waited. A not-swatted mosquito drank from one bare neck. Ten minutes. Nothing.

## SOG: Missions to the Well

Baker looked at his point man. He had been NVA, served in their army. What did he think? Deserted?

Kiet caught his eye. Slowly he raised his eyebrow. "Strange," the eyes said, "But I think maybe VC *fini*, gone."

They crossed the trail.

There were numerous log structures. Each of them was two-thirds buried into the earth. Grass and shrubs grew on the tops and along the sides for camouflage except for the ports from which they could fight. The buildings were in good repair and had been recently used. There were many of them built in long rows rather than in a circle or square. Except for the command bunker, each could accommodate twenty soldiers.

Inside were tables and benches. Along the outer walls were the places the fighters slept: thick pads of dry grass were arranged on the floors for beds. The grass was not moldy and grey, but dry, haymow fresh.

The structures were the same: in good repair, freshly emptied of men, but ready for their return. Otherwise, the bunkers were sterile, everything of personal or military value was taken. There was nothing of intelligence value in them.

Baker and his men looked for commo wire or other signs the battalion could communicate with other units. There were none. They looked for signs to indicate the direction the enemy might have gone but found none.

Buckland marveled. They had gone only about fifteen hundred meters, barely over a mile from their LZ before they arrived at the target. Had the place been occupied, the force here might have heard the team's insert and struggle in the murky water and ended it at that water's edge. As near as he could calculate it, they were only a klick from the Ho Chi Minh Trail, a half a mile.

But the absence of enemy ended then. Signal shots. They came from the direction of the main trail. Maine would now be the hunted. First there was a solo signal shot, then it was answered by others, left and right along the trail.

The men of RT Maine listened. Kiet faced the direction of

the road. His body was rigid, straight, and alert. His body was an antenna.

More signal shots from the area of the trail, North Vietnam's super highway. The shots were barely muted by the vegetation. The enemy was close.

Baker gathered his team and prepared to evade but listened a moment for the enemy's locations and intentions.

From places along the trail, they heard the moan of large truck engines, followed by the dropping of tailgates. The enemy response was fast. There were at least three places where truckloads of soldiers stopped. It took no effort to imagine a hundred men in khaki lining the ditch waiting for the command to move out.

Maine looked to their leader for instructions. They glanced up in the direction of the trucks. The enemy's command to advance must have been given. Already, they heard bamboo clackers as the enemy advanced in line. Kiet looked at Baker, a look that said, "These are not regular soldiers, these are the counter-recon teams who are trained to kill SOG people."

The One-Zero pointed the direction to go to his point man and glanced about to ensure his people were all prepared to follow. He double clicked his tongue for the signal, and the team began their evasive maneuvering.

The hunter-killer team seemed to be aware of the location of the team and maneuvered with deliberation in their direction. Perhaps the bunker complex had been monitored as the team approached. Perhaps even the very infiltration into the elephant grass had been observed. The enemy response was immediate and deliberate. Maine had not been ambushed—yet.

The hunter-killer team did not rush. They did not exercise significant noise discipline either. Indeed, Maine heard the tapping of bamboo sticks from time to time, non-elite units might do so to keep their own forces on-line or to drive a prey to a certain place, but it dwelled in the minds of the recon team: the enemy wanted the team to know they were there. Most apparent of all, Maine knew they were being driven. Slowly. Inexorably.

## SOG: Missions to the Well

Baker used every strategy he knew to evade his pursuers. They changed direction, sometimes radically. They fish-hooked. They even switched back on their own direction risking encountering a wing of those who pursued them on line.

Twice they left powdered CS gas on their back trail for the tracker dogs to sniff up their noses and ruin them for a time.

It was late in the day. The information Saigon wanted had been learned. Since then, the team's movement had been hide-and-seek. Avoid and evade until they could be extracted from the target area. The enemy had made no effort to close with them. It was clear they had something in mind.

A glance at the sky and time of day. There would be no exfiltration today unless it were a Prairie Fire emergency. The team found a place which was suitable and likely for the group to wait for morning. They ate and prepared a situation report in case Covey flew over.

Within the hour they heard the low hum of the Covey airplane just over the hill. It flew parallel to the Ho Chi Minh Trail. Lurking enemy might conclude they flew over to monitor activity on the trail and were not checking the welfare of a secret SOG team hidden in the bushes.

"Team okay. Have trackers. Significant enemy unit," Buckland transmitted.

With less than an hour of workable light with which to maneuver, Baker led his people out of the fake RON. They fish-hooked directly toward the enemy and the Ho Chi Minh Trail, the least likely location for the team to spend the night. As was the custom of SOG units, they circled touch-close. Baker gave his people a rally point in the event they were hit and separated in the night. At the side of the circle facing their backtrail, he placed a Montagnard with canister round in his M-79. He gave the point man the most likely avenue to leave the RON if they had to evade in the dark.

Maine settled in for the night. They were ear shot from the Communist main road into the war. Perhaps, even as the Kontum men waited for the day with eyes closed only for minutes at a time, even then, enemy platoons and companies were assembling to find and destroy them on that very road.

Maine did not sleep in the normal sense of the word. It was the rest in which the soldier closes his eyes for a time, but his senses do not turn off, rather become more acute. With diminished sight in the darkness, acute hearing takes over. The soldier lays back, perhaps with his head and back propped against a tree and does not move until morning. He hears his own breath, the rustle of cloth, the slightest breeze that bends the grass. He will open his eyes and without moving his head glance across the shades of black and grey, note "all is well," and shut them again.

From time to time during the night they heard the groaning of heavy trucks as they crawled along the road. There were other faint sounds below them on that thoroughfare only five hundred meters away, perhaps routine on the trail; the slamming of a heavy truck door, a shout between two sentinels on duty, a cry in the night—someone having a bad dream. Otherwise, the recon team wore the blanket of tension and the thickness of jungle. The utter silence, apart from the road sounds, whispered to the team "danger is about." Normal night creatures remained in their burrows, nests and thick boughs. Nothing scratched the earth for grubs and larvae or slithered through the grass for prey. The muffled sound of a night owl's powdered wings was absent this night. The tiny circle of men did not miss those clues.

Baker tapped his people awake. The gesture was not needed. With the perceived movement during the night, he wanted to leave the RON and evade as early as possible. He tapped his lips twice in the signal to eat and composed a sitrep for Buckland to transmit should Covey fly over. They would not wait for his arrival, however.

The team began to maneuver away from the RON and the trail with its trucks of men. "Perhaps," he thought, "I can catch the enemy sleeping and be gone before they know it. I need to still discover if I can where that battalion went."

They had not gone a half hour before they heard enemy movement. "That commander had not been asleep and caught off guard," Baker thought, "He will be a difficult one to deal with."

They heard the clacking of bamboo sticks together, and the soft passing of troops through the brush. They were not coming rapidly, just following, pushing slightly.

Then they heard movement from both flanks. They were being pushed in a "Y" formation by at least three platoons with another in reserve behind the other three.

Baker shifted his movement in a new direction. The enemy did the same. They were followed by a very skilled and disciplined pursuer. It took great training to move units of men in line through dense jungle.

Baker changed direction again. Baker conferred with Kiet, his point man. "Yes, *Trung Sĩ* Baker. That be *Bak Viet* number one fighter. Him very good."

Covey flew in the area. They heard the engine. The covey rider was Howard "Karate" Davis, who went through 11-F school with Buckland. Part of his training related to counter-recon teams.

At a nod Buckland gave the message.

"Team okay. Movement in our direction. Highly skilled adversary, perhaps counter-recon force."

All maneuvering failed to shake the enemy. It was as if they read Baker's mind. Perhaps scouts, as silent as phantoms, hovered like vapors about the team and transmitted their every movement.

Clearly the counter recon team had them surrounded on three sides. The deepest part of the "Y" steered the team and made no attempt to close with them. The two flanks prevented Maine from veering too radically to the sides unless they broke directly through one of the flanks. They were being pushed in a specific direction.

Twice when they laced their backtrail with CS powder, they heard the yelping of the hounds. Even the dogs were trained. They did not bay or bark as they followed the team.

To fishhook was out of the question. To do so was to place the team deep into the "Y" and effectively surround themselves.

At a break they poured over the map. It seemed plain on the map: In one direction was a rocky cliff face, fully exposed to the enemy. The other was a large valley, slash-burned and exposed. In either place Maine could be annihilated by the NVA.

Throughout the day the team attempted to shake their followers. The options were few and clear.

They were in their fake RON when Karate Davis flew over the area. Buckland gave him the sitrep. "Tracked and surrounded by highly skilled counter-recon force. Need certain exfil tomorrow."

They were touch-close, each memorizing their dim grey surroundings, preparing perhaps for death if that phantom chose that night to slip in and take them. Miller slid next to the tail gunner for added security to the rear. Buckland and Baker were next to each other in the thicket. A thought occurred to Mike and he slipped over to the One-Zero.

"You know, Dave, I don't think they will hit us in the RON tonight."

There was a moment of quiet as Dave Baker waited for the rest of it.

"They have been pushing us to a place where they can get us all. They might lose some of us in the dark if they hit us here and we scatter. They could have surrounded us today somewhere in the bush and still some of us might get away. I think they want all of us with no escape. They have been shoving us along like sheep. I think they will hit us tomorrow when they get us to that slash-burn or the cliffs."

Baker, with the last shades of day remaining, slowly nodded. "Maybe. Maybe. It is the only thing. We will have Covey plan for exfil."

Faintly in the distance, farther away than the night before, they heard traffic on the road. Some heavy-laden trucks groaned through with their heavy loads. But some trucks appeared to stop. Two or three minutes they stopped then continued on and they heard the changing of gears from low to high. It took little for the two Americans to imagine platoons of soldiers leaping from the vehicles and shunting in the direction of RT Maine.

To Buckland he said, "Let Miller know what we have said. Have him and his tail gunner go a space on the back trail and lay out plenty of CS powder."

They passed the night without incident, without movement around them. The enemy commander left them alone perhaps to sleep, confident the day would be his. Maine was not, however, fooled by the truce. The calm was but Rudyard Kipling's "Kaa"—the huge python as it circled Mowgli with its coils and softly hummed, "Sleep. Go to sleep, go to sleep."

At very first light Maine was ready. Baker prepared a coded sitrep for Covey when he passed over the area. They were confident Karate would arrive early for their last transmission stated they expected imminent attack. They were correct. The SCU had but the first bites of food when they heard the hum of the airplane in the distance.

Mike Buckland got into a prone position and breathed the message. "Team okay but will need extraction today or will be overrun. Will wait response. How copy?"

In a half hour they had the answer. Covey had to decode the sitrep, transmit it, and wait. FOB was quick with the answer. "Assets prepared. Exfil 1300 to 1400 hours at your suggested LZ."

Team Maine knew they would be pushed, however slightly, to a determined place of ambush where the enemy expected it would all be over for the special ops team. Maine decided the only option was to initiate the fight themselves in a location they determined; to decimate as many of the North Vietnamese as possible, then to hold out until the assets arrived with their arsenal and scoop them up by helicopter. The choice of where to attack the unsuspecting enemy was imperative to gain great advantage as they were outnumbered twenty to one. The logical option was the field, the large slash-burn, at a place before it became a killing field. The enemy commander would assume his adversary was in the open without cover. The Green Berets must surrender or be destroyed.

The team moved out of the RON later than the day before and allowed the enemy commander to press them as before. Closer to mid-day Baker altered their direction and increased the pace of movement to give them time to find the best position for a frontal attack and to arrive well before the hunter-killer team.

Near the edge they found a better than nothing site: a slightly lower area of ground set in knee-high grass for cover, and a line of chest-high bushes for concealment. From there, at a signal, the fight would begin with first fire from the recon team. The Yards and Americans slid to their stomachs behind the line of shrubs, their weapons trained on the back trail and waited for the signal to shoot.

It was not long before they heard the enemy approach. Twigs snapped, grass brushed loudly against khaki pant legs. Someone coughed, another talked loudly. Sounds of the two wings of the "Y" revealed platoons to either side of the leading force. The team did not look up above the grass. The enemy was far too close. Had they dared a glance above the tall reeds they could have read the features on the faces of the soldiers. They remained crouched, ready to pounce.

At a place or two it was possible for the Americans to peer through the waist-high bushes. The adversary was a fully equipped force, moving with weapons at the ready, relaxed but alert. Their uniforms were complete and in good order. The soldiers were well-groomed and healthy, a well-trained enemy.

The force was larger than a company; perhaps it was the battalion for which they had been looking. One of them, a slightly older officer, shouted to several others around the perimeter and pointed directly at the team hidden behind the bushes. A shot of adrenaline exploded in the Americans. But the commander did not raise his weapon or show alarm. He was inviting his subordinates to lunch, and the place he chose was the very line of shrubs behind which Maine hid. The enemy force stopped directly in front of Maine with the wings of the "Y" wrapped around their sides.

Nine officers sauntered to the other side of the bushes and sat only fifteen feet from the secreted team. Maine had a furtive glimpse through the twigs and leaves to see the nine. In addition to the overall commander, they appeared to be the commanders of the various elements of the force. Chinese officers were among them.

## SOG: Missions to the Well

They sat in a small circle and broke out their field rations and began to eat. They conversed loudly in Chinese and Vietnamese. Buckland and Baker lay directly opposite the officers. Andre, the team interpreter, who was fluent in several languages, lay on one side of Buckland and listened carefully to the conversation. Kiet, the ex-NVA and indigenous team leader, lay on the other side of Baker and waited for the fight. He imagined the horrors which awaited him if he were captured. Some of the officers were only five feet away from the SOG men on the other side of the bushes. The Montagnards feared even their breathing could give them away.

It was up to Baker to initiate the attack. Perhaps he hoped to hear helicopters arriving from the other end of the valley before he gave the command. But the stalemate continued for forty minutes. The enemy talked, ate, laughed, all the while remaining ignorant of death a dozen feet away.

One voice on the other side of the shrubs seemed to command. It was more husky than the rest, mature, confident. His sentences were wrapped with the authority of experience. He was prophetic in his words—the day would unfold as he decided. The Americans could imagine him raising one forefinger into the air as he spoke those words, and those around him uttered soft agreement as he said them. His controlled enthusiasm filtered through the thin branches to the recon team on the other side. They would snuff out that voice first of all.

At the end, it was not a decision Baker made, nor the purr of distant rotor wings, nor a cough behind the bushes which began it all. One of Montagnards could no longer handle the tension. Knowing his M-79 was of limited effect at the close range, he drew his .45 pistol and pulled back the slide on an already cocked weapon. The sound was unmistakable.

The nine officers on the other side of the bushes froze instantly. But only for a second. Without a command they sprang to their weapons. The sound of a sliding bolt could not be mistaken. It could only be hostile on the other side of the bushes. If there was a cry of shock and alarm it was lost in the explosion of movement a dozen feet from the team. Food was backhanded away in the mad scramble for their weapons and a wild attempt to stand.

They never made it to their feet. The SOG people were prepared to take out that command element. Baker clicked his tongue to shoot, an unnecessary thing. Buckland had already selected the commander and sent several rounds into his stomach and chest. The bullets dragged the cloth of his shirt into the holes with them and threw him back with the impact. The fingers of his hand were wrapped around the grip of his pistol, half still in the holster. Before the commander had fully fallen, Buckland went to the next officer, and the next, and the next. In three seconds, Recon Team Maine destroyed all nine officers.

Maine turned their firepower on the enemy around them. With deliberation and controlled bursts, they began to eliminate the groups of soldiers, who remained in shock twenty yards away. Most of them did not have time to stand before SOG firepower threw them down. Their commanders lay in a heap in front of three Americans and five Montagnards. Dozens of the hunter-killer team were slammed to the ground by the team's well aimed bullets. Sui-Kim sent round after round from his M-79 to explode among them. There was contorted movement in the grass and moaning among the enemy to bring further chaos into their ranks.

The senses, not needed at the time to survive, will sometimes indel their own perceptions of an event into memory, to be ever buried or recalled at another time. They would recall the air on that abandoned field was saturated with the smell of cordite, the gun powder of explosions and thousands of rounds; the smell of salt, iodine and metal from the great amounts of blood which sprayed from wounds or seeped into the grass, spreading like crawling fingers. The smell of adrenaline and fear hovered over prone bodies like escaping spirits revealing the very last thoughts when they fell. And there was the odor of feces; some had been shot in the stomach. Mixed in the roar of gunfire and explosions were cries and shouts of fear. There was the blur of tossed soldiers; images of the senses "present and accounted for" to be called forth unbidden long after the mission on a quiet evening when the soldier lays on his back in the darkness and relives it all.

It was perhaps a half minute in which soldier after soldier fell before sergeants took control. They shouted loud commands above the explosions. An aged sergeant screamed orders as he pointed in the direction of the team. Soon return fire was directed in the direction of the Kontum men. It came from both flanks of the "Y." But Maine was in a slight depression and the bullets of one leg of the "Y" hissed over their heads and hit their comrades on the opposite side of the "Y." They were shooting each other.

Buckland got on the team radio. A glance around him showed chaos among the enemy force, a situation which they could not hope to continue. Already, the sergeants among them were gaining control and organizing a response.

Covey responded immediately to Buckland's call. He shouted to Baker and gave him the thumbs up sign: help was nearby.

"Covey, Covey, this is Thunderbolt. We are in a very heavy firefight. Trying to break contact. About to be overrun."

"Roger Thunderbolt. Extraction units are close to pick you up. How can we direct our help. Mark position."

RT Maine threw out green smoke. Not the most visible in the jungle but the first one grabbed from the harness.

Covey immediately answered, "I see green smoke. I say again green."

Mike Buckland shouted to Baker. He gave the thumbs up and pointed down the slash-burn. "They are coming in to get us now. How do you want to work the assets?"

"Tell them to work the tree line to our smoke. I'll get us moving down the valley for pickup."

Baker shouted to Miller and his people at the other end of the tiny line of people. "Up! Move out."

The eight men rose as one and rushed down the slash-burn, Miller and the two Yards at the rear firing steadily into the North Vietnamese.

A pair of SPAD fighter planes passed low overhead and dove at the enemy in the tree line spraying them with all of their ordnance. The location of the enemy erupted in explosions and heavy machine gun fire. Return fire became sporadic and desultory.

"Thunderbolt. Be advised. Slicks coming in for pick up. Valley sides are steep and the Hueys want to pull you out on strings. How copy?'

Before answering he shouted the question to Baker as the team ran down the valley. He stopped his people. "Hey, everyone got extraction rigs on?" he shouted and patted his own to be sure they understood.

"Good to go," he shouted to Buckland.

They were still getting sporadic fire from the trees. The pair of A1 fighters sent bombs and 20 mm cannon fire on them. Cobra gunships were on their heels sending in their rockets and machine gun fire, smothering the enemy. Certainly, a hundred enemy died in the runs.

Information came from the slick helicopters. "Two lifts out on strings. We will do four on each."

Baker pointed to Sherman Miller. "You and the three little people on your end will go on the first lift. Go!"

The timing was perfect: the choppers sloped to a hover as they tossed the ends of four ropes. Miller and Baker helped the Yards make the loops in the swaying life lines and ensured they were all snapped in. Baker stepped back and gave the "okay, snapped in" signal. Buckland radioed, "First lift snapped in, ready to go," and before the words were fully spoken the Huey lifted off. It rose swiftly, banked away from the enemy position, and climbed aloft.

Like timed trapeze artists, the second helicopter slipped into the field at the heels of another brace of war planes and two Cobra gunships. Its rotors flattened the grass as four more ropes unfolded themselves from O rings anchored in the chopper's floor and bounced on the ground. The two Americans ran to the lines, tied loops for the little people, and snapped Andre and Kiet into them. They, last of all, snapped themselves in.

Buckland confirmed into the handset, "Hooked and ready," and immediately they were whisked into the air.

Mere seconds after their feet left the ground, Baker and Buckland glanced down. The wind shrieked past their ears at eighty miles an hour as they climbed away from the battlefield. The SPADS made another pass far below them, tiny toy airplanes against the dark green of the forest. They seemed to be playthings down there, needing just a little boy to guide them with his fingers on their backs and make airplane sounds. But then they saw the results: white and orange flashes, grey smoke that rose in columns, and secondary explosions. It was over. A ridge closed its curtain over the stage they had left.

A new fear always attended coming out on strings following the immense feeling of rescue from near-certain death. Snatched from jaws is not an imperfect analogy. It is replaced by the realization that one is suspended a mile in the air by one thin rope. One does not dare to kick one's legs; you realize there is nothing there. If it is possible you cling to a soldier hanging on the next string. At least if your rope fails—cut part way by a bullet or frayed on the edge of the helicopter door—there is a chance one of the two will hold.

Maine, like other recon teams that have gone back to base this way, will freeze at the altitude, be pelted and stung by rain at eighty knots, spun in the air until dizzy and sick, and on arrival at Dak To launch site, discover their legs are asleep and they cannot stand because the harness had stopped the flow of blood. They will be hugged by the Bright Light team and helped from the ropes. Ice cold soft drinks will be thrust into the hands of the little people. They'll be told how glad those at the launch site are to see them and that they made it back, until at the end they are helped to waiting helicopters for the last leg to Kontum, this time riding inside.

Kontum was the place of collapse and refitting. The Americans looked after their people first of all: showers, hot food, taking care of gear after a mission, and a bed and soft pillow. For the Americans it was all of those things and more. There was always the debriefing with the intelligence people. Maine had much to report. They were certain they encountered a hunter-killer team, and that the rumored Chinese were indeed in the fight.

On their way to the S-2, Andre the team interpreter, who spoke English, Vietnamese, French, and three Montagnard dialects, stopped the Americans.

"Sergeant Baker, Sergeant Buckland, think something important. Remember enemy talk, talk on other side of bushes? This is what them say."

He waited to see if they had time to listen before their meeting.

"Those nine men were all commanders. Three of them were Chinese. The number one leader was Chinese man. They talk like they were there to hunt for SOG teams. He was," here he paused to remember the right word, "specialist—man who is trained to do that. He was very confident. He told the other officers that they would capture at least one American as POW by dark."

The two American stopped and listened in the middle of the parade field.

"The Chinese man said he had set a trap to catch our team and that we were falling for it. He said they would be promoted in the People's Liberation Army when this was over."

Andre looked at the Americans. "Very interesting, huh?"

Maine's Americans made their way to the debriefing thinking to themselves, "Chinese. hunter-killer teams. What we suspected about a special regiment are true."

# CHAPTER SIX
## RT Hawaii Mission

I woke to the crump of the landing gear being lowered for arrival at Kontum and my return to CCC. That sound, I realized, was the same a mortar round makes when it leaves the tube in a thicket. I was fully awake. How could I have fallen asleep after what I had seen? I was sitting in a canvas folding seat of a black ops airplane of Air America, the largest airline in the world. It was, to be sure, a legitimate airline of "tickets please," checked baggage, and scheduled flights, but all of that was just a facade—a very massive cover for its real purpose: the clandestine operations of the CIA and special ops.

The captain who flew this Curtiss C-46 might have been the inspiration for the comic strip Terry and the Pirates who fought evil, cruel tyrants across China and that part of the world. He did not tell me all as I sat up front with him, but he said he flew with Chennault's Flying Tigers against the Japanese in the last big war, and he supported Chiang Kai-Shek and the Kuomintang against the Communists of Mao. I was confident the Terry who held the yoke of this airplane had not ended his war against the Fu Manchus of the world. He was long in the tooth but his hand was still steady on the controls and his resolve was constant. I knew the dark side of Air America supported forces which opposed the Communists in South East Asia, CIA and Special Forces outposts and covert missions. But any confirmation that he was involved was spoken with the twinkle in his eye and a wry smile.

The co-pilot of this flight was younger than the captain and could also have been the inspiration for his counterpart in the series. In the comic strip his real name was Charles C. Charles but went by Hotshot Charlie. He had taken the wire from his pilot's hat and let it sag, limp and tired looking. The dye of his weathered coat had worn in places to the original leather. Where the sun had bleached it on the back and shoulders, the garment was pale. On one shoulder the original deep brown which had been untouched by the sun was yet visible; an ancient patch had been there and removed. Its shape remained like a memory that had seen it all and refused to go away. For these two men there were no surprises left in life. I was honored to be invited to visit with them on the flight deck.

There was no other crew, no sidekick to render adulation or esoteric information the others would not know. Nor was there a long-limbed monkey to scamper across the instrument panel until it was needed to complete the disguise of one of them at the mouth of the narrow alleyway of a marketplace—a monkey in a red Turkish hat that sat on the shoulder of an organ grinder.

Nor was there an arch-fiend and nemesis known as The Dragon Lady hidden among the baggage. It was just the three of us SOG people coming from One-Zero School at Long Than after three weeks of intensive training followed by a mission for the Australians.

That mission was only two days distant in my mind and memorable. As point man, I spent a great deal of time moving on my belly avoiding countless booby traps as I made my way into enemy outposts and perimeters, crawling so carefully I found a waiting enemy sentry by smelling his breath. Once, as I crawled toward an enemy perimeter, I found myself strike-close to a deadly viper. It was asleep. In my stealth it lay undisturbed. Unaware of my presence, its hood was not raised as it lay in the sun. Its color matched the rock and it further camouflaged itself by stretching itself along a crack in the rock, blending into its contours. I never took my gaze from its veiled-over eyes as I maneuvered away without waking it.

Our flight took us over an outpost hidden in the jungle. As far as I know no map reflected its existence. The pilot made a maneuver called a pilon, a very steeply banked turn in a circle which seemed anchored from an invisible column in the air. The co-pilot removed his cap so it would not be caught in the wind and lowered an arcane bundle from a long rope to a waiting man in camouflage.

I had been napping when they let the wheels down for landing and I recall the last image in my dream. It was a long patch of white that weaved in and out like seaweed in the brush of current. It was sinister: a long, white, livid scar. And I recalled the captain calling me over to the flight deck. "Hey Sarge, look at this," he said pointing through the window, "What do you think that is?" We were over the South China Sea and it was shallow there. You could see the sand showing through the shallows close to the shore.

"I'll give you a hint," he said. "That strip of white is two miles wide and six miles long and sonar tells me it is a thousand meters thick."

I stared at the site and all I could think was a sandbar until he said the word thick.

"Give up?"

I looked over to his grinning face.

"Those are sea snakes. It is a mating frenzy. Who knows where they all come from."

I thought of that deadly, writhing mass and shuddered. I recalled the shock of coming upon that cobra on the rock, and now the gathered lethality of that weaving horde of snakes.

The image of the pilots working undercover in a Mideastern marketplace must have impressed my mind because in my cat nap I remembered an event when I was a young boy in northern Minnesota. It was summer. Hot. I recalled a man with a beard of stubble on the sidewalk turning the crank of a street organ. Out of it came music one hears at a carnival. He was missing an arm and the sleeve was pinned to his shoulder. From the sides of his black eyepatch a thick white scar showed. A small "Veteran" sign at the base of the stand had been written in Crayola. He had a monkey that sat on his shoulder and was tethered with a thin chain. He sold popcorn and small bags of peanuts. The monkey's eyes were dark against its white face and watched me as I passed by. When it appeared that people would go by him by without buying anything, the disabled man would quietly say, "The monkey eats peanuts."

We flew straight in at Kontum, no downwind or cross-wind leg to alert the enemy in the hills to prepare their rockets. "We will get you as close to the gate as we can before you jump off. We won't be pausing to collect a few rounds." He pointed to the low line of hills just outside the city. "Know what we call that over there? Rocket Ridge."

We taxied to the front of the terminal as the old captain went back and tossed open the door to let me out. "God bless you son. Stay safe."

I still had my pack on my back and was making it for the team room when Norm Doney met me. He was mopping his cheek under his right eye with a rag and blinked. He saw the wonder in my face and answered my unasked question.

"It's nothing. Got shrapnel just under the eye and it cut a tear duct, so I am always crying. They say they can fix that in-country."

He saw that I was still perplexed. "Oh, you didn't know. Florida had a mission just after you left. I got this from a B-40 rocket. Chin was wounded too, once in the shoulder and a good one on his forehead. He's back from the hospital now."

"Changes," he said. "Here, I'll walk you to the team room."

I waited for Doney to tell me about his mission. He did not. Instead, he brought me up to speed of the needs of the day.

"Sergeant Howard left to receive the Medal of Honor and they have appointed me to be the new first sergeant of recon company. You are going to be the One-Zero of Florida until Sergeant Worthley comes back to take his team. We might slide you to another team then.

"He hasn't told me officially yet, but Sergeant Morris wants to go to the commo section. He has not had an easy mission yet. I can read it in his eyes.

"Chin and Nhok are finished with recon. They are the last of the Chinese. There was a time we had companies of them. Our two might be the last of them left alive to fight. It was overdue for them to retire from war."

Doney daubed the tears which ran down his cheek.

"You have a skinny team now. Joe will be gone too. You might want to recruit or use a straphanger if you get called for a mission. Ken Worthley will be back in a month. I will be here to help you. I heard you did well in One-Zero School. Visit me in my office and I can fill you in on anything you need."

I saw Chin and Nhok near the front gate.

"Han Son, Han Son," Chin shouted when he saw me. Chin had his wide, ubiquitous smile and hugged me. Nhok smiled and took my hand.

"Chin, I heard that you were wounded very bad. I am surprised you are back so soon."

"Yes, *Bác Sĩ* fix me. I wounded here," and he lifted his short hair so I could see the raised whitish scar at the hairline. "Doctor, him put scar there so nobody see. Very bad wound. Doney say him see my brain."

Nhok, who normally never spoke, said, "Hanson, Chin him lie. Doctor him look and he no find brain."

I laughed. "Where are you going now?"

"We go to village and eat. Han Son you come with us. Good food."

The village was just outside our gate, hugging our mine-filled perimeter with its bunkers, and machine guns. Although CCC might receive an occasional rocket, and they in turn suffer the impact of a near miss, they felt secure next to us and remained like a young monkey clinging to the chest of its mother with its arms wrapped around her neck for its safety and nourishment. Calling it a village was a bit of a misnomer. On either side of the street, closest to the main road, were the shanty bars and buildings where the women worked and slept. The next tier of buildings housed a tailor shop, a place to buy cheap books and music tapes which were printed in Korea, and one or two places to buy food. At the edge of the road were the bars with comfortable chairs and couches and young women of negotiable affection. The newest music from the States drew in customers just as the swaying flute charms the cobra from the basket. To many soldiers, it was a place to relax away from the base. Helen's was a well-known establishment. Although no one ever saw her with a cigarette, Helen had a heavy, husky voice of a woman who may have smoked heavily for decades. Her English was pedestrian and perfect as she called out to passing GIs.

Suzie's was her competition on that side of the road. At Suzie's, they would place a drop of perfume on the side of the beer can so men would think of women as they drank. No GI ever met anyone named Suzie.

On our walk through the village, we passed The Green Door. It was the first bar on the right side of the road and competed for business with the other side of the road. The door was open as we walked past, but even open, I saw the door was painted army green on both sides. Through the open door I saw the bar on the far end of the room and paintings on the wall and bamboo curtains muting the outside sunlight. Music played from the stereo and wafted to us on the road. I stopped as I heard the song. It was a song of a dozen years before and the style was unlike any music heard on AFVN radio. Although I did not drink or frequent bars, I smiled. The song was its namesake sung by Jim Lowe. I was perhaps in third grade when I heard it.

"Just a minute, Chin. I want to listen to this. I haven't heard this since I was a boy."

*Midnight, one more night without sleepin'*
*Watchin' till the mornin' comes creepin'*
*Green door, what's that secret you're keepin?*

# SOG: Missions to the Well

*There's an old piano*
*And they play it hot behind the green door*
*Don't know what they're doin'*
*Wish they'd let me in*
*So I could find out what's behind the green door*

I looked over at my Chinese warriors. I knew that they would not understand my surprise at the song. I wondered if they would be interested in knowing about speakeasy places.

"Just a minute more. I want to hear the rest."

*Knocked once, tried to tell them I'd been there*
*Door slammed, hospitality's thin there*
*Wonder just what's goin' on in there*

*Saw an eyeball peepin'*
*Through a smoky cloud behind the green door*
*When I said, 'Joe sent me'*
*Someone laughed out loud behind the green door*
*All I want to do is join the happy crowd behind the green door*

I know that I was smiling. "I'll tell you guys about it later," I said.

It was just a place to eat. Nothing was fancy; no chandeliers, refined tables or chairs, and no menus. The tables were of wood made in the carpenter shop in town, plain and unadorned. A few locals ate at tables along the wall. By their dress, I guessed some of the girls eating were from Helen's or Suzie's or The Green Door. A few prints and one painting hung on the walls. Nearest the kitchen hung a frameless print. Its pages were yellowed and curled up by the haze of kitchen grease. There was one I recognized from a studio in Kontum. It portrayed a Vietnamese girl in a white dress. Her head was bowed and she held a set of dog tags in her hand. Its chain spilled from her fingers as the life of someone she loved had. A tear rolled down her cheek. The artist captured light and shadow and the tear seemed separate from the paper, a real thing.

"Nhok. Tell me about the painting."

"Han Son, her husband be soldier. Him die. She own this place. This be good place. Safe place to eat."

"Good. I will have the same thing you get. You can order for me? I want to pay for us all."

A Vietnamese cook worked in the small kitchen, barely visible in the steam. His face was down to his work and I heard the sizzle of vegetables in the wok. In minutes we had large bowls steaming before us. Various green and red plants, shrimp, and red meat were tangled in long lengths of noodles. Centered in the bowl was a large, boiled egg. Chopsticks and a large spoon leaned in the bowl slanting toward our waiting fingers.

"Sergeant Doney told me that you will not be going to the field anymore."

"Yes," Chin replied to my statement. "We *fini* now. Doney get us jobs in supply shop. We lucky to live this long. Many, many Chinese man die in this war."

He rolled up a wad of noodles on his chopsticks and ate. "How many times do Chin and Nhok almost die? Many, many. Green Beret is most dangerous in Vietnam, in all Asia. If we still fight, we die for sure."

I ate a spoonful of goose egg and noodle.

Nhok, who I usually pictured in a classroom giving a lecture to scholars said, "I was in the next helicopter when they take Chin out of jungle. It lifted from ground before Chin get all way in. I watch him hang from strut with one hand. Chin do pull-up with one hand so he could get his leg over top. Then Doney see him and pull him in." Nhok cast his eyes downward and tapped the table with the fingers of one hand and could not go on.

"I am very glad you will be safe in the supply room. I will not be as safe in the field without you, but I am glad you are safe."

We ate for a few minutes without talking. There was a small dish of something fried dark-brown, nearly black and crispy. A shallow dish of their pungent soy sauce was next to it.

"What is this," I asked.

Chin looked up at me and smiled with a string of noodles hanging from his mouth. "Han Son, no ask, just eat."

They watched me as I dipped it in the sauce and brought it to my mouth, watched until the chopstick was clear of my mouth and empty of food. They watched without moving. Nhok held a spoon half way to his mouth, suspended in the air until my morsel was gone. Chin stopped chewing until he was sure that I had swallowed it all. I nearly expected him to say "Open" to be sure I ate it.

"Well, what did I eat?"

The two men looked at each other and smiled.

"Sometimes, better you not ask," Nhok said.

"I just thought of something," I said, "Who will write Han Son Kam Bow Ya Chin on my shirt when I go in the field now?"

It was just the lightness Nhok needed to take him from the memory of seeing Chin dangling by one hand a thousand feet in the air. He laughed. "You just come supply before mission and we do every time."

I was in the Florida team room working over my web gear, cleaning my rifle, and getting everything combat ready. What did I eat that so amused Chin and Nhok that they would not tell me? I found mud and dry weeds stuck in the openings of my ammo pouches from my mission at Long Than. Our policy on Florida was to never take our web gear off in the field. We left the back bare so we could lay back with it in place. On the mission for the Australians, I spent significant time on my belly crawling toward enemy sites. Having my grenades and magazines in front made it difficult to crawl low to the ground and I wondered how those who fought there arranged their gear.

I was sitting on my bunk pulling debris from the pouches when Joe came in. "Hey man, I'm glad you are back," he said.

We talked about One-Zero School and our mission finding the headquarters for the Viet Cong.

Joe was distracted. I could see it. He often looked away, peering into the void of the bare, shadowed corner of the room. He did not add to our conversation. Sentences hung in the air like little ghosts waiting for an answer. I held my web belt in my lap and waited for him to talk.

"I'm quitting recon," he simply said. It was as if he had finalized his decision at that moment, although he had been quitting for several days.

"My nerves are shot. I have not had a mission where we did not barely make it back. All of us get killed or wounded during our tour. I haven't been on a dry hole mission yet." He looked down at his hands in his lap. "Look at my hands. They shake. My stomach churns when I think of going out there."

I set my work down on the bunk beside me.

"I think we all feel that way. You are not alone. I am glad you are going to take a break. You have done more than enough, Joe."

He looked at me with his dark-brown eyes and pale face. "I have to go tell Doney. I'm not looking forward to that."

"Joe, I think he knows you're coming," I said.

Some of us were talking in the Florida team room. I was still overhauling my field gear after One-Zero School. I hung my web belt over a chair back with the straps facing out as I worked. We were catching up on the events of the last three weeks while I had been away. We covered the various missions our people had been on and our casualties. We recapped the details of the missions, the after-action reports, and lessons learned. While our missions were top-secret from the rest of the world, knowing those details was crucial to our own survival. In recon, it was expected that we would know and discuss the details of previous missions. Great courage and resourcefulness marked recon's exploits; all done in secrecy known only to other SOG people like us.

"One might just as well take the danger and challenges of James Bond, Colonel North, or Matt Helm, take out the beautiful women, then change the casbah or rocket site hidden on a deserted tropical island, replace all that with jungle, leeches and snakes and you have us. Oh! And we do not have the soundtrack in the background to urge us on." Such was the sentiment I was conveying to the others.

"Did James Bond ever have leeches or prickly heat?"

My friends smiled.

Dennis expanded my thoughts. "I wonder if he ever sweated," he said.

"Yes, and did he ever wear camouflage stick on his face for ten days and sweat through it until it was a paste and his face was a red rash when he got cleaned up."

"Yes, and a beautiful woman in a towel would see him as he removes the sticky goop from his face and say in a dreamy voice, 'James!'"

"Or 'Dennis!'" Mike added, teasing him.

I sat on my bunk. We had only two chairs in the Florida hooch and the bunks to sit on. Mike Buckland leaned back in a folding chair with its back propped against the wall. His fingers were interlaced around a can of Coke. He leaned forward and handed one to me. Out of habit, I ran my thumb in circles around the top to clear it of any traces of feces from the rats living in the big warehouses. It opened with a loud pfssst. Condensed water rolled down the can and the back of my hand.

Dennis had tea. He, Mike, and I had been roommates for the year of training at Bragg. His face was cherubic, what I imagined angels possessed. It was what the artists of old portrayed in their paintings: a pair of them suspended in the air above the Lord, each with a trumpet in his hands. If one were to look closely, one of cherubs would look just like Dennis Bingham. His hair was fair and the skin of his face was moon-pale with cheeks the color of pink flowers. We teased him all that year when he had been our roommate in training group. "You never have to shave. Not fair." Dennis was utterly wholesome. He never uttered a curse, never complained.

It did no good to quote from literature as a proof-text for anything. It seemed that Dennis had read them all and remembered the content. "I read a book a day," he once said. He was not trying to impress us but rather stating a fact. I often quoted Scripture as my primary authority. Dennis said, "I read that too, cover to cover."

A boom of an artillery round sounded. Our conversation stopped mid-sentence. We all looked skyward toward the ceiling and waited. We heard the crack of the sound barrier as it passed overhead. It was not incoming. The speaker continued, "Where was I?"

"Snakes," I said, "We were talking about snakes."

Each of us conjured up an image of snakes and suppressed a shudder.

Dennis remembered carrying a stout stick as a boy on the farm flailing the grass side to side as he walked in the fields just to be sure.

"I wonder if it comes from Lucifer in the Garden of Eden that sends the shock of electricity down our backs. God, after the temptation of Eve, said, 'On thy belly shalt thou crawl and dust shalt thou eat all the days of thy life.' They have no legs and we can see them move, sometimes in a straight line without pushing off the curves of its body."

I took a large swallow from the can. "I remember when I was little on the farm reaching under the house for my toy tractor and having a garden snake explode into action and shoot out of there. I think it was sunning itself on the metal frame when I reached for the tractor. I remember the shock to my system to this day. I was little, only a few years old, but I remember after that, I always probed the area with a stick before I reached for my tractor."

Michael Buckland, having spent all of his life in Alaska had no snake experience but Dennis nodded his head and smiled. He seemed to be recalling another of his own encounters with a cottonmouth in the swimming hole.

"Before I forget, flying here from One-Zero School we passed a gigantic mass of sea snakes. I didn't know that many snakes existed in the world. The Air America pilot said they were in a mating frenzy. They were the most poisonous snakes in the world."

Dennis smiled. "There are sixty species of sea snakes," he said. "They are from the cobra family. They fall into two main groups, true sea snakes and sea kraits. They are highly venomous."

I sat upright on the edge of my bunk. Mike tipped his chair back on its two legs and listened. "The true sea snakes are related to Australian cobras. The ones around here are related to Asian Cobras. They are way more venomous than the land cobras."

Mike leaned forward. "Dennis, how do you know this stuff?"

"I just remember things."

Dennis smiled at our amazement. His cheeks became crimson.

"Oh, I'll tell you something else about sea snakes," he said. "They need to drink water like everything else. They swim in an ocean of water. But they really can't drink salt water. They must have fresh water. Some actually crawl to land at night to drink. But mostly they go to the surface of the sea to drink because fresh water is lighter than salt water and there is a layer of fresh water at the top. Also, they will go to the top and drink when it rains."

"You amaze me, Dennis."

He shrugged his shoulders. "I guess I just don't forget things. The one thing I really had to work on since I was young was that I wanted to be a Green Beret. I studied. I exercised. I ran several times a day to get in shape. This is what I always wanted to be."

He looked down at his hands as if a script were there. "I always wanted to go on one dangerous important mission before I died."

He looked up from his hands. A glow had come over Dennis' face. He smiled. "I am going—finally—on my first mission. I'm strap-hanging with Team Hawaii. Glenn Uemura is taking the team. It is his first mission as the One-Zero. Sergeant Delima will go on the mission just to observe and be there for Glenn. I will take the radio."

He smiled broadly. "I need to get over there."

He walked to the door with his cup of tea. His eyes were bright with excitement and his mouth was parted in a full smile. Dennis was about to do what he had prepared for since he was a small boy. My joy for him was tempered. I recalled in the Bible how the martyr Stephen was said to glow just as he was about to die.

"Oh, Dennis, what is your target?"

He paused with his hand on the door frame and looked both ways down the hall. "Juliet Nine," he whispered.

Mike and I looked at each other. Juliet Nine was a target of dread. It swarmed with enemy. Recon teams were decimated there. Many SOG men were consumed in its bowels. Juliet Nine was a place to die.

Joe Morris left Doney's office. At the outer door of the building, he paused and stared ahead. Before him was the courtyard between the buildings with the painted flag pole near the center. The flags hung limp in the still air. In the distance, helicopters, in the work of war, passed by with a soft rumble as Vietnamese and American soldiers crisscrossed on their way to the various buildings. A couple of maids chatted as they walked by. But none of this was noticed as Joe stood in the entrance. His emotions churned inside. He felt guilt that he might be deserting the guys in recon. But most of all, he felt relief, immense relief.

He had dreaded telling Doney what he had decided and had not looked forward to that time. "Being in recon is voluntary, after all," Joe reminded himself. He finally ginned up his courage, took a long breath, tapped on the door and went in.

Doney smiled at him and waited. It was as if Doney knew why he was there.

Morris was disgusted with himself, for he began his first sentence with a stutter. When he got it all out, he said, "I need to get out of recon, at least for a while. I am going to get killed if I don't get out. They have a place for me in the commo shack."

Joe should have known. Doney was sympathetic and understanding. He dabbed the wound under his eye with his handkerchief as he talked. Doney did not hug him, but his eyes did. He felt like he was Joey—a boy, not Joe Morris the sergeant, and Doney was a father who cared deeply for him.

"You have done more than your share. You have been brave and calm in the field. You deserve a rest."

And that was that. He was out of recon. There would be a safer billet in the com shack. He might just make it home in one piece.

And then Glenn Uemura met him halfway across the field.

"Joe, I've been looking for you. I'm going on a mission. It's my first time as the One-Zero of RT Hawaii. Bill Delima will go as the One-One just to be there to observe and help. This will be his last mission before he goes stateside. I asked Dennis Bingham to strap-hang and take the radio. We have a good team."

Joe waited for his friend. They had been together through jump school and training group and went through commo school together. Glenn paused a moment and studied his friend before he went on.

## SOG: Missions to the Well

"Joe, I want you to come with me on this one. I really want you to come."

He was not thirty steps from the recon office and telling Doney that he was through going into "Indian Country." Joe Morris would have been surprised at himself. There was not a moment of hesitation when he answered Glenn Uemura.

"Yes, I will go with you. Of course."

Relief showed on Uemura's face.

"I'll get my gear from the team room."

Uemura smiled and turned to join his team.

Morris looked down at his hands. They were stone calm. No surge of electricity shot through him. A friend needed help on a mission. That is all there was to it. Commo would have to wait for Joe Morris.

It rained during the night. Not a downpour, but enough to weigh the clouds into a soggy blanket over the target. Team Hawaii—four Americans and six Cambodians—waited under the dripping eaves of the radio shack of the Dak To launch site. If it continued to drizzle and remain overcast, they knew the choppers and support craft would not be able to needle through the fabric of low clouds. Covey reported intermittent showers. They would give it a few hours, then decide.

By midday a faint glow showed through the overcast. But the conditions needed to improve before they could insert and have time left to maneuver before darkness. They continued to wait. Some of the tribesmen slept. Others stared into that space a Cambodian goes to wait. Two hours later the fog thinned over the launch site and a degree of brightness appeared over Eastern Laos.

Delima and Uemura left the control tower and joined the team. "Almost good to go," Uemura told them. "It is clearing over the target. Assets are on the way, about half an hour. It should be good when we get there."

Joe Morris stood and stretched. He felt calm and steady. He stood next to Dong, the Cambodian point man. He was taller than most Cambodians and he stood out. Joe wondered if he was perhaps the son of a French GCMA, a Special Forces soldier and a village woman. Some of those special troops spent an entire tour in one remote village, adopting their ways, training the men, even taking a wife.

Dennis stood briefly but remained near his radio. Joe glanced at him. He looked soft and not in shape, but he knew that could not be the case. Joe could not fathom the enthusiasm Dennis had to go on this mission. Maybe after this one that would change; when you think your heart will burst in fear and you can hear it beat in your ears like a drum, or worse, you get hit by something in a firefight and discover it was something that flew out of the soldier next to you when he got hit. "Oh, well, first mission," he thought.

Morris studied the guileless face and thought, "Dennis Bingham will never look weathered and old."

It was after three o'clock and the layer of mist parted over Juliet Nine. The choppers began their startup. "Packs on, let's go," Glenn shouted.

Forty-five minutes later the team dropped between the trees to the selected landing zone. A Charlie model gunship made a low pass in front of the Hueys to draw fire but received none. The lead chopper was one minute behind it and dove with Uemura and half the team, followed seconds later by the second lift. Juliet Nine was a place where choppers were blown out of the sky just as they flared to land. The door gunner was tense, frozen over his machine gun expecting incoming fire which could cut his craft in two. But no ambush was sprung. The small field was deceptively pacific and empty of men. The helicopters climbed and broke east. Door gunners who were tense and frozen by adrenaline thawed and breathed again.

Uemura's people ran from the danger of the LZ to the closest cover and sunk from view. In the past, many teams never got past this initial landing. But it was also not unlike PAVN to wait until air support had left the area before they struck in fury. Hawaii waited and watched with the thought, "I know they are out there somewhere, just waiting for us. Where are you? Where are you hiding?" They used all of their senses to locate secreted enemy. Nothing. No sound of movement. Not a twitch of a twig or color that did not belong.

Delima's eyes scoured the bushes. He knew the reputation of this target. Juliet Nine was known as being saturated with them. He saw no sign. "Except," the seasoned One-Zero thought, "Except, there's no sign of any life at all. Not the twitch of a bird or bug. It's as if nature itself senses danger."

Delima glanced ahead where Uemura waited at the other end of the tight circle of men. Delima would not interfere. He was just there to observe and be there. It was Glenn Uemura's team now. Delima did not even take a rifle; only a .45 pistol.

Glenn Uemura clicked his tongue at his point man. He slowly faced him and signaled, "I see no VC." Glenn turned to Dennis and signed, "Radio Covey, 'Team okay, good day' and release the assets."

The team moved out. It was late in the day. They would not get far before they would have to find a place to hole-up, but it was necessary to distance themselves from where they inserted. Surely, in this densely packed staging area, PAVN would have heard the helicopters.

Knowing the reputation of Juliet Nine, they moved with maximum stealth, stopping often to assess their surroundings. There was no sign of enemy. The point man's eyes were fixed to the front, almost willing the leaves to part and reveal a shirt sleeve or rifle stock. At a place, Delima stood straight and looked upward into the sky. "Where are they? I know they are around us somewhere." The silence was that of a tornado one minute before it sends its fury. "I know they are out there. Where are they?"

Uemura led his people, avoiding danger areas, stopping, listening, trying to guess the intentions of the elite regiment that staged here. His little people were well-trained and alert. They too knew the enemy had to be nearby. Uemura looked for clues in the deportment of his strikers who were raised in the jungle. They did not wonder "if" but "where." Each of them moved with a finger in the trigger guard and a thumb on the safety.

Bingham mirrored the movements of the Cambodians as he navigated the dense vegetation. He was calm and alert. Each step was that of a panther approaching prey, ready to strike. The camouflage on his face barely hid his excitement.

Both Uemura and Delima were aware of the hour and limited time to maneuver. Perhaps they had two hours. The One-Zero made a security stop and motioned for Hawaii to eat, half of them at a time. He prepared a sitrep for Dennis to relay when they heard Covey. Still no sign of enemy. The overcast and rain caused the late insertion into the target giving them little time to distance themselves from the LZ and find an ideal place to RON. He would pick a place in the next hour.

No desired place revealed itself to hole-up the night, but they found a huge fallen tree with dense thicket to hide and give them some cover. With waning light, it would have to do. They set out Claymores and memorized the shapes of their surroundings and settled in. The SOG men were amazed they found no trace of enemy in the densely populated sanctuary. Except for a singular flutter of a warbler bird on a limb as it crawled into its nest for the night, all was absolutely quiet. Uemura entered the events of the day into his notebook. In the stillness he could hear the pencil lead scraping across the paper, like foraging sparrows scratching in the leaves. He looked to the soldier near him to see if he could hear it. He plotted his location. They were only a little more than half a klick from the LZ they came in on—about seven hundred meters.

They were curled up, wrapped in darkness and protected slightly by the fallen log. They were perplexed they had not been attacked already in this notorious place that ate SOG teams. Perhaps even now their forces were wrapping around RT Hawaii like a python, preparing to squeeze and take them in the morning. Was it possible that the enemy regiments were not aware of them being there?

Some of them lightly slept, listening, even as they dozed, for movement in the grass.

Eleven o'clock it happened. They heard the whooshing sound of a descending artillery round followed by the crash and explosion. Debris and shrapnel shredded the branches and leaves of a nearby tree. It was big stuff, much larger than a mortar or small rocket.

## SOG: Missions to the Well

It was followed by another explosion, then another, and another, and another. From absolute quiet, the North Vietnamese announced their presence: a series of rounds in a straight line along one side.

They had no cover or hole to dive into—only the fallen log or their rucksacks to give them any protection. The series of explosions ended to the west, but a moment later a second line of explosions began on the other side of the team. One explosion flashed next to them and Joe Morris saw in the blink of light Chu's hand raised into the air next to him. The courageous Cambodian arced his hand toward Morris, found his hand in the darkness and raised it high into the air with his own. Morris did not know the significance of the gesture. He wondered if the tribesman was lifting his hand in prayer, bringing Joe into the presence of God. Chu kept their hands raised throughout the shelling. "Whoosh . . . BOOM. Whoosh . . . BOOM." The rounds bracketed them on both sides. They were heavy artillery rounds. Clearly the enemy somewhere in the darkness knew where they were.

That was it. The team had been bracketed. Hawaii waited for a signal from Uemura to escape the center in the darkness before the enemy sent in the coup de grace. But they did not send more artillery rounds down the middle of the brackets and the SOG men remained huddled close to the earth. Nothing followed the dozen rounds. No charging enemy crashed through the brush in the darkness to wipe them out. The racing hearts of the team slowed, but they no longer slept. At a minimum PAVN would arrive in the morning to check the results of the barrage. Uemura decided that when they arrived, Hawaii would not be there.

Uemura had them awake and ready to go as soon as they could safely maneuver, when gray replaced the darkness. Morris looked around him. Thick branches had been torn from the trees and scattered around the team. One standing tree had been splintered lengthwise. The color of the heartwood was wound-red. Leaves of plants and shrubs were shredded on both sides of the team. Strikers found debris on the rims of their flop hats. It smelled like new mown lawns back in the "world." But the odor of cordite explosives floated in the air with it to remind them of the cause of it all. Uemura made a sitrep relating the events of the evening and intentions of the day. They squeezed in a few mouthfuls of indigenous rations and left the RON, alert for the possibility the enemy may have surrounded the fallen tree.

Dong, the point man moved bent over, mantis-like. He made no sound, disturbed no bush, missed nothing in his search. Glenn Uemura followed him nearly touch-close, both of them trying to pass through the cloth of ambush the enemy may have woven during the night.

Dong froze. Two NVA soldiers appeared fifteen feet away. They were the point of an enemy patrol coming down a high-speed trail. Because of the thick vegetation the point man had not seen the trail until they were nearly on it. Soundlessly the two soldiers walked down the path with their rifles on their shoulders. Any movement would betray the team. They could only freeze and hope the soldiers would pass by.

"Don't look in their eyes," Dong thought. For a moment it seemed the soldiers might go by, oblivious of the presence of the team. "Don't look into their eyes. They are so close. How can they not see us?"

One of the two soldiers flinched mid-stride. Out of the corner of his eye he noticed the point man breath-close to him. He affected to be unaware of the SOG men and faced straight ahead, willing himself to not look toward the team. He made a half step of decision and clamped his mouth closed. The muscles of his cheek bulged. He ripped his rifle from his shoulder and spun toward the team. The One-Zero and the point man were ready and shot, killing him and the soldier one step behind him. Immediately shouts and sporadic fire commenced from up the trail. Heavy AK-47 fire sprayed the bushes around the fallen men, for they did not know the location of their attackers. Uemura pointed a direction and Dong rushed that way to distance themselves from the trail. Hawaii moved nearly at a run to separate themselves from the patrol.

Shouting and rifle fire grew from all quadrants. A loud howl and angry shouts indicated the North Vietnamese discovered the two bodies and tracks of the team. They gave rapid chase. Muffled shouts of orders penetrated the thickness. The Communists used high-speed trails, and forces rushed along them to overtake Hawaii. They gathered in the north and west and began an organized pursuit.

Uemura had the point man change course often and they moved nearly at a run, from the signal shots and breaking branches. Twenty minutes later it seemed they had succeeded. Joe noticed Dennis gasping for breath with the exertion of the escape and the heavy radio. They halted to renew their energy and assess the enemy activity.

"We are compromised for sure. They were not pleased when they came across their dead comrades. We can try to get out of here or we can continue the mission," Uemura thought. Joe and Dennis edged to him whisper-close. Although it was entirely up to him, he asked, "What would you gentlemen want to do?" He looked at Dennis. "What do you think, Dennis, extract or continue the mission?"

Dennis panted but felt excitement more than the peril. He simply replied with the mantra of Special Forces: Break contact and continue mission. "I want to continue the mission."

Uemura thought only a moment. "We will continue if it is at all possible."

Hawaii rose to its feet. They maneuvered toward a ridgeline in the east but signal shots sounded close in that direction. They altered their course and heavy movement came from the new direction. Signal shots! Answering shots came from other quadrants. Heavy movement crashed through the forest in several places. The only avenue left open was toward the LZ from which they came.

"This mission has changed to fighting for our lives," he said to himself as he scanned the trees. He gave the point man a heading of travel, to the place they came in yesterday afternoon.

Ten minutes later Hawaii changed direction again. They moved quickly, pushing through the brush. "Put distance between us and Charlie," the leader thought. They panted with the exertion. Uemura looked at his people. If they were hit now, they could not hold a rifle steady. Uemura halted the column. They would catch their breath and assess movement around them. As their breathing became under control, Dong, faced the team in alarm. They all heard it: many men just out of their sight thrashed their way through the brush toward the team. The recon team squatted lower in the weeds and faced the direction of the pointing finger. They leveled their weapons. A heavy patrol veered and passed through the foliage parallel to them. By the sound of thrashing through thigh-high bushes it seemed they would pass by. They prepared to fight. They were close. Some of the Cambodians dared not slide the safeties on their weapons lest the enemy hear the click. They followed the progress of the patrol through the brush by the sounds of them pushing through bushes and swishing ferns on their trouser legs. They listened, awaiting the signal. The sounds diminished. The patrol went by and disappeared.

Sergeant Uemura gave it ten minutes and signaled to move. This time stealth was more important than speed.

More signal shots. They came from several quarters.

The team was being driven. Alarm sounded in Dennis' mind. Though it was his first mission it was clear to him that the team was being pushed to a purpose. He recalled after one of the intelligence classes at Fort Bragg, Dale Hanson, Mike Buckland and he were talking about Sun Tzu's book The Art of War and specifically where he wrote: "Never completely surround enemy for they will fight in desperation. Always give them an outlet of escape, for them to flee . . . but of course have an ambush there." These distant thoughts whispered in his mind as the recon team sped toward the LZ.

They were pushed, driven, maneuvered. They were the tiger. PAVN was the force riding the elephants, beating the drums, pushing Hawaii to the waiting big-bore rifle.

Dennis was exhausted with the pace as they pushed through the thick brush and he struggled under the weight of the radio. His feet were cement blocks. Chu saw it and tugged his sleeve.

"Dennis, see if you can get Covey on the radio," Glenn Uemura called.

Dennis was hurrying with the rest of the team, speaking as he walked. He was out of breath. He willed himself to speak clearly into the set. There was no point in the whisper as the enemy was aware of their location.

"Nothing," he answered, "No contact at all."

Uemura thought, "We can either make it to the LZ or we will have to wait at the first defensive location we find, ambush, and fight until help comes."

Twenty minutes later Dong stopped and held up his hand behind him. Light shone brighter as the canopy thinned and trees gave way to shrubs and thickets before becoming open field. It was either a place of rescue or certain death.

Uemura: "Dennis, get Covey on the radio."

Minutes later he answered, "No contact. Nothing."

"Keep trying. Don't quit. Keep on until you get them."

The team set up at the edge of the opening, just inside far enough to be hidden yet see the field. "Anything yet?"

"Nothing."

"Keep trying."

The team squatted in a defensive circle. They panted. Their rifles bobbed up and down with their breaths. Sweat rolled down their faces and into their eyes. Their hair crawled with rivulets of sweat and as it coursed downward it felt like crawling bugs.

"Still nothing," Dennis said.

Glenn digested the information. Without radio, no help would be on the way. "Put out Claymores. Get behind something and be ready to fight," he told his people.

"Keep on the radio," he told Dennis.

The SOG men prepared their defense and waited. It had been an hour since they arrived at the edge of the LZ.

"Got them!" Dennis said with excitement in his voice.

"Tell Covey our situation: that we are hard pressed and about to go into contact."

Dennis bent back into the radio and gave the message.

Uemura heard the static in the radio as he keyed. Dennis slowly looked up; the handpiece held in the air like something he did not recognize.

"What?" Uemura asked.

"They can't come. The assets are already on another Prairie Fire. They said to go high and dry. They will get to us when they can."

Delima crawled over to the One-Zero to listen. "Well, we can't go high and dry. We are here and can't move," Glenn said. "We will just have to wait in place."

He took a long breath. "Put out all of the Claymores. Prepare to fight here."

They waited in place for the next four hours. It seemed the enemy decided to go home. All was silent around them. There were no signal shots, no shouts, no sound of soldiers barging through the wait-a-minute vines, snapping twigs and brushing leaves as they came. It was quiet, deadly quiet. A bird with red wings stopped at a low limb and looked down on the Cambodians, tilting its head side to side, then flew away. Nothing else.

The radio came to life. Dennis had the volume low and put the handpiece to his ear. "They're coming for us. They want us close to the edge of the field. Covey wants smoke."

An airplane engine hummed in the distance. Covey was in the area. The sound of the airplane grew closer. "Choppers and assets are on the way, nearly on scene. Throw smoke. Choppers will be coming in."

"Smoke out."

"I see red."

"Affirm, red."

The rumble of helicopters came from the east.

"Get your first lift onto the field."

Heads down against flying debris and brown grass, Dong and the first half of the team ran to the field just as the first helicopter swooped down.

It had been the moment for which the North Vietnamese waited. Incoming AK rounds poured in from all directions. Rifle grenades exploded in the trees and on the field. A line of green tracers cut through the running men. Bullets struck Dong and he went down.

The lead helicopter stopped its descent and climbed away from the explosions.

"Get on the radio and tell them we are under fire," Joe screamed. Dennis was already talking to Covey, his body half-bent over the handpiece to shut out the loud explosions which muted his words. Recon Team Hawaii was returning fire in every direction. Rifle grenades exploded in the trees. Lines of green tracers arced over the heads of the team.

Joe and Chu were next to Dennis as he shouted their situation in the handpiece. An explosion went off in the tree next to them. Dennis groaned and fell to the ground, his hand tight around the handpiece. His body shook. In seconds he lay unmoving on his back, his blue eyes open, facing the sky.

Uemura rushed to his side. Numerous wounds covered his body. A large piece of shrapnel was lodged in his neck. Glenn pulled it out and spoke into the unseeing eyes. "We will get you out. You will be okay, Dennis. Hang in there."

But he was gone. His eyes glazed over. In seconds his ruddy face paled.

Joe put his hand to his friend's lifeless head. Dennis' hat fell away half-filled with the results of another massive wound.

Uemura ran to the edge of the field. He looked back. "Joe, get the radio from him."

Morris bent over his teammate. With both hands raised into the air, he thought, "What to do?" He pulled the handpiece from fingers that refused even in death to relinquish their duty.

"I'm sorry, Den," he tearfully said, as he rolled the body over without ceremony. He slid the straps over one shoulder and felt the warmth of his body. It took both hands to wrestle the second strap. He braced his feet and pulled it with a groan. The pack came free and Joe landed on his back. He stood to a half-crouch and strapped it on himself

Glenn ran stooped over to where the point man lay. Machine gun bullets pierced both lungs. Glenn rolled him to his back and watched as he struggled to breathe. With effort, he sucked air that had to pass through the blood which was filling his lungs. The eyes which had never shown fear in countless battles relinquished it all to panic. He reached for Glenn's hand and held it tightly. He convulsed in his last gasps and died.

The recon team returned fire with all they had but the line of assault hard pressed them. They were about to be overwhelmed.

"Fire your Claymore," he shouted to a Cambodian near him.

"Joe, bring me the radio," Uemura screamed."

He scrambled to him with the handpiece extended. "I have bad guys nearly on top of me. I need support right in front twenty-five meters," he shouted into the set.

"That's way too close," Covey answered back, "That is more than danger close."

"We are going to be dead anyway. Put it on me. It's on me!"

"Give me another smoke for the Cobras and fast movers."

He fumbled for a smoke grenade and found none. He only had pen flares.

"Shooting a pen flare," he said.

"Roger copy. Heads down!"

"Heads down," he shouted above the explosions. "Fire all Claymores."

Covey worked the Cobras and fast-movers around the perimeter trying to smother the incoming fire. It would diminish in one side and erupt on the other as fire from above suppressed the first.

Another SOG man went down. A Cambodian. He lay in a heap where he left cover and entered the grass, a dozen meters from the Huey. They were close with gaining manpower. Hawaii was engaging with all of their weapons: with rifles and M-79s, and by throwing grenades. They would be overrun if nothing intervened.

"Give me the radio," Glenn shouted. He sensed incoming was being suppressed and the choppers could make a pass.

A sudden roar of helicopter blades masked out all other sound as the first craft returned and swooped in. Delima ran out with a few Cambodians with the intention of helping them get in and limit the time on the ground. But as he turned at the door to help the first one in, the door gunner grabbed his harness and pulled him aboard, followed by three who scrambled inside. Before he could turn and jump off, the pilot thrust the controls and they leaped into the air.

Incoming erupted from another quadrant of the LZ and fast movers swept in with their ordnance. Shrapnel and pieces of trees whizzed over their heads and the tracers of incoming bullets ceased.

"Second lift coming in. Get ready. Get on the field," someone shouted over the radio.

Uemura grabbed Dennis' limp body by the harness and tried to drag him. The body was limp and far too heavy. He could not budge it. It seemed Dennis' body contoured to every dip in the ground and anchored there. Joe grabbed the other strap and pulled. Even then, they barely moved him through the grass. They pulled and gasped for air and pulled again.

Next to them, a wounded Cambodian shouldered his rifle and grabbed Dong's harness with both hands and dragged him, tugging and walking backwards. He pulled yard by yard, falling and grunting as he dragged.

The helicopter hovered next to them. The door gunner poured rounds into the tree line. The Americans drug Dong's body the last yards. Blood was on the grass and he slid easily. They hoisted him to the metal deck. They turned and grabbed Dennis but the two of them could not lift him all the way in. Wounded Chu jumped out and lifted Dennis' legs with his uninjured arm. They struggled with the weight and limpness. The door gunner saw that the effort was keeping them under enemy fire. He released the handles of the machine gun and grabbed Dennis' web harness and pulled and the four of them heaved him inside. The pilot immediately lifted off and flew east over the LZ to avoid incoming fire which renewed in that quadrant.

Sergeant First Class Delima sat with his back to the skin of the aircraft. His arms were over his knees and his head was bowed and rested on his hands. This was his last mission. In all of his time in country he had never had an American killed, until now.

Glenn Uemura was emotionally crushed at losing Dennis. It was his first mission as a One-Zero. Under his leadership, the very first mission, he lost someone. It was of no comfort that he could not have done anything differently and changed it. But seated there with his hand clasped on Dennis' foot, he resolved, "I will never lead a team again. I will go on missions with others, but I will not lead. Never again."

They were at altitude flying over the side of the field. Joe was near the door. Below him the fast movers were working their ordnance. White flashes of a napalm run shone on the tree line followed by huge billows of smoke. He saw five-hundred-pound bombs fall in the trees where Hawaii had been only minutes before. The limbs of the canopy swayed in the impact, and he saw waves of energy flow outward in concentric circles. For a moment Joe wondered, "Can a person see energy, actually see energy?" But the thought did not remain in his mind. He was alive. Once again, he had cheated death. He was alive.

# CHAPTER SEVEN
*RT Florida and the Chinese Spy*

The Communists were on us the moment our feet touched the soil of our target in remote Cambodia. It is likely they had been expecting our arrival: a panther waiting on its haunches at a water hole, just another khaki-colored log at the edge, but ready to spring. Trail watchers, hearing our helicopters that morning might have said, "Oh there they are. We didn't expect them in this rain, but they arrived as our agents said they would."

An event of war and espionage which occurred weeks before and far away from our landing zone had its ripple effect on us seven commandos in Cambodia. That genesis occurred when a Communist mole, a double agent was "eliminated with extreme prejudice." The man's name was Thai Khac Chuyen and he had infiltrated a CIA/Green Beret project called Project Gamma. His betrayal cost the lives of many Special Forces men and their people. Entire teams had been compromised by Chuyen, decimated or disappeared altogether. The entire program was ultimately closed by the efforts of this one enemy agent.

But Chuyen, the painstakingly cloaked and embedded spy had been unmasked by a simple serendipitous photograph. It revealed him receiving an award of honor from the Viet Cong in a secret Communist base area. On this discovery, the berets tricked the spy into a new mission from which they captured him. He was interrogated by the Americans and given sodium pentothal, truth serum. His role was confirmed. "I will not work with you Americans," he shouted when he could no longer deny the evidence.

"What will we do with this spy?" the Special Forces leadership asked the CIA, as it was ultimately a CIA project. "Eliminate with extreme prejudice, of course," was the answer. But the task was given back to Special Forces. "You do it. Chuyen is no good to us." And when they did, the CIA threw the berets "under the bus."

The Green Berets injected Chuyen with drugs rendering him unconscious and stuffed him into a large burlap sack. It was a particularly dark night when they arrived at the harbor. Everything was still. The slightest ripple showed in the calm water. A water bug swam in circles on the inky surface, the top of its tiny wake etched from the glow of a window like a bullseye. Fog rolled in, obscuring and leaving the grey unpainted buildings in deep shadow. With the curfew, no one strolled on the planks of the wharf, not even a dog barked. Alternately dragging and carrying the body to the correct slip, they heard the squeak of their boots on the fog-wet dock. The mole was dumped into the bottom of their boat where his form in the burlap resembled a pile of rope. Like prowlers, the berets furtively looked around as they untied and started the outboard. They smelled gasoline and saw exhaust smoke rise in the low-watt streetlight as the motor choked and sputtered. For a moment they wondered if they would have to drag their prisoner back up the ramp. But the engine ceased to cough and ran more smoothly. They putted out of the harbor and made their way out to sea.

At a place, with the lights of the city over their shoulders, they hoisted the inert body of the double agent high enough in the skiff that placing two bullets from the silenced pistol would not put holes through the hull. They parted the sack's opening to expose the man's head. "Pffft. Pffft." Two shots into the temple, "terminated with extreme prejudice." They lifted him in the weighted bag, rolled him over the side, and he sank into the sea to the waiting sharks.

Story ended. Only for Mr. Chuyen. For several men of the Fifth Special Forces Group, it was only beginning. The charge was murder. It did not matter that the CIA had a unit called Project Phoenix, tasked to do pro forma the very act the Green Berets had done, which they themselves had told them to do, and for which the Geneva Convention offered no proscription. At the insistence of the commanding general of all forces in Vietnam, Creighton Abrams, they were arrested and imprisoned in Long Binh Jail to remain at the general's pleasure.

Deep into enemy-denied and controlled territory in Cambodia was base area 609, the sanctuary of the bloody 66th NVA regiment. It was a crack force, one of the most lethal and elite of Ho Chi Minh's army. At one time when General Vo Nguyen Giap, the military commander of both the Viet Minh and the People's Army, needed to send forces to a major battle, he said to an aid, "Well, I can send three regiments . . . or I can send one: the 66th NVA regiment." That regiment was involved in every major battle from Dien Bien Phu against the French, to Khe Sanh, then Dak To, and later at Ben Het when they made the initial assault on the camp with ten Soviet PT-76 tanks. That regiment claimed the finger of land which on a map lies where Laos, Vietnam, and Cambodia touch as their safe area. Centered in that sanctuary was a target that SOG designated as L-50, Lima Fifty.

August 24, 1969, Dak-To Launch Site: Recon Team Florida waited to perform our mission of infiltrating base area 609 to gather intelligence on target area Lima Fifty. It was mid-morning. Persistent rain squalls darkened the sky like a threat and caused us to lay about at the launch site. My people huddled under the eaves of the mortuary with their knees drawn up to avoid the drip that overflowed the gutters. It was not a front in which the whole sky was overcast with low clouds, and rain persisted so that after everything dripped for days. They arrived today with showers, broken at times, to be followed by patches of clear sky. Covey suggested that we mount up during one of these cloud bursts and follow it in. We could hang at the trailing end of it and drop into the opening we selected with the last drops of rain. Perhaps the 66th NVA regiment would be deceived thinking we could not arrive in the inopportune weather.

I had a close rapport with my people. I had been their leader before. Chin and Nhok had been certain before this mission to write their Chinese blessing on my back. When I looked in Ba's direction, he lifted his gold Buddha pendant so I could see it as we flew, "Me Buddha man," and he would smile, knowing I was a Christian.

We followed the grey before us, flying level, following that curtain of rain the bottom of which hung all the way to the tops of the highlands. I could barely see the contour of the ground below. A half hour. There was an abrupt change in the pitch sound of the Huey. I looked out the side door and saw a Cobra gunship nursing us alongside. We banked steeply. A vortex, really, like going down a toilet bowl. My throat caught in my mouth. I felt pressed into my seat. What little I could make of the trees was a blur.

The spin ended as abruptly as it had begun at the exact height to hop out and land on a piece of real estate which the Communists claimed as their sanctuary. Ken Worthley as the team leader, and I, with the radio, leaped from the strut of the first craft and ran to cover at the edge of the trees. The rest of the team with Robert Garcia was seconds behind and joined us at the security stop. Five minutes. At a nod from Worthley, I dismissed the air assets; "Team okay, good day."

Vegetation was thin and spindly and with the beginning monsoon rains, our feet deeply impressed their passage into the soft earth, leaving its trace for Ba, our tail gunner, and the challenge of erasing. For those crucial first minutes of our arrival, we had air cover lurking above the fog a valley or two away. We had the comfort of knowing it was there, available, waiting for our call. But with my "good day" call they departed the area and we were left to our own wits and training for the remainder of our time in Communist base area 609.

There was little cover at first. I felt exposed walking across a lighted stage but with the audience in shadow. Passing through a vulnerable area we could not avoid, we crossed a stream. The heavy rain of the previous days left it full to the banks and the grass along its sides bent in the direction of the flow. From there with all of the stealth and training we knew, we proceeded knowing the enemy was lurking, ready and waiting for us.

We crossed trails, several of them new and well-used.

Noi, at point, was crouched double, rifle pointed dead ahead as his fingers moved twigs and leaves to clear a space for his feet. Each step was a planned one, silent, perfectly placed. Every shadow, bush, and leaf was inspected for danger. At the opposite end of our column, Ba replaced those leaves.

Noi froze. His non-trigger hand inched back like a fist. "Stop!"

Worthley was at his side. Florida did not move. Every eye panned the area. Each ear demanded answers from its surroundings.

A high-speed trail.

We crossed it. It was wide enough for vehicles to drive. A glance above. The upper branches of the trees were tied into an arch hiding it from the air. Several soldiers could walk abreast or truckloads of troops and munitions could pass unseen.

A gunshot. The first.

It was slightly muffled and came from our backtrail, in the direction of the LZ.

We had trackers.

We crossed the road and maneuvered up a ridge. It was steep, to be climbed with rubbery legs. We made several security stops, listening, studying the vegetation, looking for the slightest clue of the enemy we were certain was there. It was morgue-quiet. So quickly, it seemed the wetness of the shower had disappeared. I imagined I could hear evaporation or the stealthy crawl of a leech. A flutter of bird wings was explosively loud as I sat there and watched. I even noticed when the last drop of moisture had disappeared from a leaf; its weight no longer held it down and it rose to its former place.

But there were enemy, and we were aware of it.

It was just then when one would think it so quiet it was

impossible to move even slightly; when it seemed one's own breath was inordinately loud, that it happened.

A gun fight. From the utter stillness, nearly next to my ear, Ba fired half a magazine into the shrubs only twenty feet away. I saw the place and joined in the shooting.

Ba turned to me and shouted, "Hanson, Hanson, VC come!"

His eyes were wide. I saw one soldier in khaki flat on the ground less than twenty feet away.

Ba pointed at the fallen enemy, "Hanson. VC, him die. Him die. Him VC tracker, him very good. Him die."

Ba and I were about to rush the enemy. He glanced at me and shouted again. "Him die. Him die very good. But I see two VC," he said holding up two fingers. "This man, him die, but no see other VC." His eyes glanced left and right. "Where him go?"

Our eyes pierced the bushes. Garcia joined us. "There's another one in there that we can't see," one of us said.

Garcia was at a different vantage point. He also studied the place. "There," he said after a few moments. "There, I see his feet under the bushes."

Garcia had an M-79. He sighted on the feet, raised the muzzle and shot. The canister round exploded and there was a thump sound and broken twigs as the body dropped to the ground.

The three of us sprang to the fallen enemy. At our feet were two highly skilled trackers. Not once had we heard them. One of them carried an SKS rifle, still over his shoulder perhaps so he, like our own point man, could remove twigs and debris as he moved on us.

Signal shots. Close by. Just over the first belt of bushes and trees. The initial shot seemed to signal all of them to shoot in our direction. Loud shouts erupted from several directions as the mass of enemy moved on us. The shouts were of command, not of anger, fear, or frenzy. An orderly movement was being made in our direction.

Ken hissed and pointed a direction he wanted the point man to lead and break contact to continue the mission. As rapidly as was prudent we proceeded in the direction he pointed to distance ourselves from the enemy. A solid ring of fire: a huge circle of enemy that had gathered around us began to attack our old position. Perhaps a hundred rifles were involved, mostly with the "pop, pop" of AK rifles.

Fifty hurried meters. We changed direction, taking care now to cover our passage and move silently. The speed of our team at that point was that at which our tail gunner could hide our trail.

Another change in direction. A fishhook change this time. We traveled at the speed of a glacier. Noi was crouched forward. He moved as one about to enter a thicket inhabited by cobras and mamba snakes.

We halted frozen in place. We were at a slight rise that overlooked the path we had just made. If the column of enemy trailed, we would ambush and take them out. A half hour. There was not the slightest sound or movement. My eyes were dry from not blinking. I shut them a moment and swallowed. To observe the area below us was to move only our eyes, not our heads. Leeches crawled unheeded. A bird, the first I saw since the helicopters, landed on a branch, scant feet from my face, cocked its head in wonder, and flew off.

The scene below us was that of a painting of the old days: a landscape, nothing more. Nothing moved in the frame of my eyes, no sound, no smell, no movement. I watched with every sense alert for anything living.

A dog barked.

It was less than a hundred meters distant, slightly muffled in the bushes, but deep and throaty. Its image flashed into my mind: a bloodhound. No other canine could mimic that woof. My mind conjured the hound in action—Baskerville or men of the south hunting coon with their lanterns; a sheriff in pursuit of an escaped prisoner; a half dozen dogs on the leash all but dragging the officer in the chase. This chase came from our own backtrail, the voices of the handlers followed us with their mummy-grey hounds, slobber dripping from their mouths.

Close behind the dogs, countless pantlegs pushed through the tall grass, the cloth rubbing against the stalks, shushing toward us on line like a breeze over a dry wheat field.

They were on us. Two enemies emerged from the shrubs at the front. Noi and Ken shot and put them down. They charged us on line, crashing through the last of the cover that had concealed them. With short bursts from my rifle, I engaged the enemy as they cleared the bushes. Off to one side, three others in mustard-colored uniforms sprang from the bushes and shot at me on full automatic. With the rounds left in my rifle, I half-turned and fired at them. Two of the three fell to the ground. My magazine was empty. The remaining soldier was still shooting at me.

His aim was slightly off, and some of the rounds hit my right hand. Bullets tore off my middle finger leaving it hanging by a piece of skin. Slugs hit the ends of all my remaining fingers tearing the ends and ripping all the fingernails back leaving them hanging on the backs of my fingers. The knuckle of my index finger was blown away. I felt it, but the business at hand was to end the threat.

I had practiced the immediate action drill of changing magazines a thousand times, but my middle finger swung freely from the piece of skin and caught between the magazine and the well. I had to look to see the problem. I tilted the weapon so the finger hung away, and using the tip of my little finger and thumb, slammed in the fresh magazine and shot. My tail gunner joined the fight and the third man dropped to the ground. "I think him die," Ba said.

The casualties we inflicted on them ended the fight. The enemy backed away and disappeared leaving several of them dead at our feet.

I lay my rifle in the crook of my arm on the wounded side, pulled an ace bandage from my harness, and tried to wrap my hand. My middle finger swung like a pendulum and got in the way of everything. I flipped it into the palm of my hand so I would not lose it and wrapped the bandage around the hand. I could not tie the knot. I grabbed one end with my teeth and tried to pull the bandage tight and tie it off but failed. Ken Worthley saw my struggle, rushed over and finished the knot for me. Blood continued to stream down my fingers and soak the bandage.

I heard the enemy breaking through the brush in their haste to get away and a few groans of their wounded as they receded into the woods. We used the short hiatus to evade and continue the mission. Garcia and I both spread CS powder on our backtrail to ruin the dogs when they sniffed it up their noses. Noi led us out to the north. The direction was of no great importance as we changed it often, avoided open areas, and took time to distance ourselves and hide our passage. We used every trick we knew to evade, even crossing the back trail of those who pursued us.

We made a security stop at a vantage point. My hand ached. I could not stop the bleeding. The bandage had soaked through leaving the outside red and sticky. I wished I could at least arrest the bleeding. I hooked my thumb in my harness so the hand was higher than my heart as we watched for enemy.

Two hours later it seemed we had evaded our pursuers. It least we neither heard nor saw any; but then, we did not hear the skillful trackers earlier in the day either. We maneuvered east this time. Here were numerous trails, all of them heavily used. Even where the slight elevation along the ridges left the soil less wet, the foot traffic on the paths mashed the earth to mud, at times the sides of the prints were still caving in to the center. It was in places like those I listened, thinking surely I would hear the movement of their passage farther down the path, perhaps even their feet pressing, even sloshing, into the wetness of the trail.

Our efforts failed. We heard the dogs. A new batch of them perhaps, for baying and barking joined the woofing of the hounds. There were shouts from several quarters. At a nod, Noi led us out again, to the northeast this time. Bob Garcia sprinkled out the last of his CS powder. He held the container up so I could see it. I nodded and signaled; I had one left. Soon, we could not arrest the following hounds.

It seemed that we had distanced ourselves and evaded the North Vietnamese, at least for a time. We sensed there were only a few hours of daylight left. We would need to prepare a sitrep for Covey should he fly over, eat our PIRs, then find a place to RON. With my thumb hooked on my harness I hung my hand up over my heart again, and I was pleased to see the bleeding at stopped. My red bandage was now a solid red cast, hard but usable. With the thumb and the tip of my little finger sticking out of the bandage I would be able to change magazines.

We heard the faint drone of the airplane and Ken transmitted the sitrep in code. He gave the particulars of the day, my wound, and that we would continue the mission. The covey rider was my friend Rich Ryan and he tipped his wings at the news. As he was unwounded and could use both hands for the dials, Garcia took the radio.

We found a place to remain the night on a shallow hill with a gully on one side. We slid in as light was fading and the enemy would not have time to fix our location exactly. I laced our passage with liberal amounts of CS powder. Perhaps it would be the howl of the tracker dog as he sniffed the powder up its nose that would alert us. The area around us was thick and an enemy moving in the dark would be sure to reveal himself.

We were touch close where we lay. I was near the rear with Ba to one side and Nhok on the other. It was overcast, dark, but did not rain and I was grateful. We would be hard pressed to get air support if we were being overrun. Light rain on the ground sounds like creeping enemy and masks their approach. I had no illusions about us being surrounded. We heard their presence the whole day. I found a firing place next to Ba and I lay on my belly in the dark without moving. The bay of the hounds was fresh in my memory, the shuffling and tapping of their feet in the leaves unforgotten. Our position was the best we could find, but I fully expected the shadowed enemy to burst upon us. So, I lay there on my belly with the detonators of four Claymore mines in my hands and waited for the Communists to come for us. Although my wounded hand was handicapped and I could not change magazines as quickly as before, it was functional. The bloody bandage that wrapped it had coagulated into a solid red cast and I could use the tip of the little finger and thumb for the functions of war. The four Claymore mines were set judiciously before our position and aimed at the most likely avenues of approach. To make up for the measured use of my wounded hand I braced the plungers on a firmness of earth and positioned the heels of my hands on the triggers.

My fingers on my good hand were nervous. "One, two, three, four, one, two, three, four," they counted over and over as they passed across the detonators, keeping them side by side.

With the mass of enemy around us, should they assault us up that hill, it could be our last battle, but with the first assault, I was confident: nothing would be living to my front after I pressed those detonators.

It was quiet, deathly silent. It was a night to hear the slightest movement: a mouse moving in its nest of hair, the sigh of a bird, the path of a wandering breeze below the hill, a trickle where yesterday's rain began its journey of a hundred miles to the sea. I heard a soft rub near the area we came to this place. Nhok, my scholar, anticipated my wonder and whispered, "Not VC. That is where the joints of two bamboo shoots slide back and forth."

I heard a soft pop below the rise where we lay. I felt Ba flinch. He inched over and whispered to me knowing that I heard it also, "No VC do. Bamboo do. Bamboo wet in daytime. Water fini. Bamboo pop. You hear."

And I understood.

Another hour. I heard the drone of an engine, faint and far away. I thought I heard Bob as he hovered over his radio just in case. We both thought it might be Covey making one last pass to check his chicks. But the sound did not pass, it droned on. It labored, and I heard a downshift perhaps for a change in grade.

Then over the low rise of the next hill I saw the faint glimmer of light, like a sliver of moon rising over the horizon. It continued in our direction, flickering, growing ever brighter. We were perched above a finger of the Ho Chi Minh Trail.

The engines stopped. I heard thumping sounds, the dropping of tail gates, and the grunts of soldiers as they leaped from the beds. There were shouts of command, faint on the other side of the rise of the ridge and its vegetation. It took nothing to imagine truckloads of soldiers lining the ditch, just waiting for the command to go.

Dogs barked, the flop-eared kind whose jowls hung below their mouths; the red, droopy-eyed slow-moving ones whose redeeming feature was their ability to smell and follow the faintest of trails. There were two or three of them.

I felt a slight tap on my shoulder, then his whole hand. "Han Son, Han Son," he whispered, "*Beaucoup* VC. *Beaucoup, beaucoup*! Many, many."

I tapped the back of his hand to let him know I heard it too. I heard him slide over and shift his weight over his weapon.

I turned to Nhok and tapped him with the back side of my wounded hand. I felt him nod in understanding and he slid himself over his M-79.

I aligned the four detonators side by side again, my fingers sliding over the detonators and counting, "One, two, three, four, one . . ."

None of us of Recon Team Florida moved. Although there were only seven of us, I was not sure those on the other side of our short line heard anything. But we were prepared on this side. For long anxious minutes we listened but heard nothing at all. We never saw a shadow slink to the side to get away from the advancing men in the yellow-mustard uniforms. We knew they were there. They were coming for us yet we did not hear a sound.

Perhaps they decided to wait at the bottom after all, thinking, "We will just get them in the morning when they come down to us."

Still nothing. A half hour. An hour. Nothing.

Then I heard the soft movement below. A shuffle in the moist leaves. A brush against the grass. A faint snapping of a twig. They were there. A disciplined and trained adversary.

And there were the dogs. As highly trained as were the enemy, so also would be their dogs, but muzzled perhaps just for this sweep.

I prayed, "Lord, please plug the noses of those dogs." My fingers slid across the detonators again, "One, two, three . . ."

Their passage was nearly inaudible but we heard the enemy creep. The clues were there, close in front of us, but at the last, they veered to the side. As a moving stream divides itself to pass around a large bolder in the center of its passage, so it seemed the advancing force did for us. "Please plug the noses of those dogs," I prayed again.

We were still frozen in place, listening. Once or twice, I thought I heard sounds of their passing on the other side. They were faint and receding. Hounds passed as if their noses were plugged.

An hour or two later darkness, shade by shade, surrendered to day. Thin stalks of bamboo at the fore showed first in the light leaving the shadowed interior to resemble a cage until full light showed it empty of men. There was no sign of those who passed through in the dark. I glanced to the rest of the team on the other side and it seemed they noticed nothing in the night. Ba, when I looked in his direction, was curled into a ball, exhausted from the ordeal and fast asleep, his cheek crumpled over his forearm.

We ate. There was a steady ache in my hand. I took pains to not bump it lest it bleed again and soften the blood-cast that made it more functional. Ken prepared a sitrep and we waited for Covey to pass in the vicinity. We left the RON to the north, ever mindful it was a dangerous time in a mission; for the adversary had an entire night to maneuver his people around the place and prepare an ambush.

Many trails crisscrossed the area, some of them sidewalk-hard and smooth. The area was city-thick with activity. There was but to see a high-rise or streetlight to express it all. The adage was always to stay off trails for you would be certain to bump into enemy. However, for us to maneuver in the thick vegetation was to move in an environment of swishing grass and breaking twigs, when a dozen feet to the side might be one of these hard clay trails on which the enemy moved quietly, unseen, and able to hear us a few meters away.

We determined to set up along one of those trails, perhaps to catch a prisoner as he pacifically strolled by feeling secure in his sanctuary. A glance left and right. A perfect place: sparse vegetation at the side of the packed earth gave us a great field of fire and visibility down the way. But serendipity picked the place for us. We had no time to further consider, no time to set up a Claymore or fully disperse as we might have liked. They appeared of a sudden. A magician pulling soldiers out of his hat one after another. There was no sound, no shuffling of feet, not a cough, or a whisper. They were mere yards in front of us.

We froze. Any soldier glancing to the side could not fail to see us. There were several of them! A full patrol. An escort fully armed and alert, in complete uniform. When they were abreast of us, we attacked. The quiet morning with its rays of sunlight shining through the boughs ended in a crescendo. In moments it was over. All of them lay dead on the wide path or thrown in death at the edge. One of them lay near my feet, eyes and mouth open wide, his arms hugging his rifle like a doll. Only one of them made it off the narrow road but was dispatched twenty feet into the foliage as he arrested his run and turned to shoot at us.

Our people assaulted through the column and took up positions on the far side of the trail. We three Americans assaulted the head of the column. Fire came from soldiers farther down the trail and I engaged them with my rifle and hand grenades, and discovered the difficulty of pulling the pins and throwing them with my bad hand.

Two enemy lay in front of us crumpled in a pile. They were in full uniform and by the insignia on their clothing, both were officers, full colonels. They were taller than the Vietnamese, well-groomed with short haircuts. A Tokarev pistol remained in the holster of the nearest man, and slung diagonally over the shoulder of the second officer was a large satchel. They were the highest-ranking enemy ever taken by a SOG team.

Noi, our point man, rushed over. "Chinese," he said. "Them be Chinese man. No be Vietnam man."

The two dead men were Chinese couriers. We willed our fingers to be calm as we opened the leather bag. Large sums of money filled much of the space: money to give to their agents. There was a paylist, as we later found, of every Communist agent in two corps of Vietnam. As the paymaster, he needed to know where to find his spies to pay them and collect their intelligence, so their locations were affixed to the names. Although we did not know it at the time, on the spy list was the name Thai Khac Chuyen—the double agent the Green Berets had eliminated and dumped into the ocean—and a warning: "All agents lie low as Chuyen has been captured."

Pages of top-secret orders were in individual folders which the paymasters were to personally deliver to various commanders. A list of fifty-two NVA soldiers who had wounded themselves during the siege of Ben Het so they would not be involved in the fight, was on a separate section. Discipline would be administered on the basis of the list. The information of that list prompted the headline in major newspapers: "Informed sources, Kontum Province show NVA soldiers wound themselves to avoid battle of Ben Het." Two underground factories and a field hospital were mentioned for commendation along with their locations. Also in the bag were two ID cards of American soldiers. In all, it was the largest intelligence trove ever captured by a small unit in the Vietnam War.

Shots came from different sectors. Rounds cracked over my head as they broke the sound barrier. I glanced up and saw bullets slapping the leaves in the trees. Twigs and parts of foliage sprayed to the ground. Shouts from up the trail! The three of us scrambled to undress the spies. We had no living prisoners but we could gather what intelligence we could from the dead.

The shirt came off the first colonel. He must have died instantly. There was very little blood, even at the bullet holes. As we tugged at the shirt, blood rose above the level of the skin, dowel-like and did not flow, and when his torso was freed of the shirt, the blood sank back into his body. We took everything. Clothing—our intelligence would know where it was made, where was the cotton grown, who made the uniform. Samples of hair—the officer's health before we killed him, his diet. Everything we could gather in two or three minutes. We pulled off his trousers. His heels made a thud sound when they fell back to the hard surface.

I am certain that I hear other thudding sounds too, perhaps running feet from where these men had come; Bata boots, the slapping of Ho Chi Minh sandals on the path—or was it my heart I heard in our scramble to collect these clues before we were overrun? We gathered the contents of their pockets turning them inside out into our hands. We steadied our hands and placed everything into our bags to be carried away.

Angry shouts from down the trail. Crashing in the brush. Bullets Swiss-cheesed the leaves above our heads. I tossed one more grenade. Without the use of my fingers, I palmed it and threw it with a grunt as far as I could. Mistake. The hand began to bleed again. One more burst from my rifle. Time to leave.

The bloodhounds again! More excited now that they once again had our spoor. A few of the bullets whizzed down the road as their aim is better directed.

Ken Worthley pointed a direction for Noi. Quickly we moved off the trail as I sprinkled CS powder at the edge and Ba tried to hide the signs of our leaving.

We did not get very far before it was apparent the North Vietnamese had arrived at the ambush site. Loud angry shouting filtered to us as they found their naked couriers and dead soldiers. For a hundred yards the length of road was filled with shouting men. They fired hundreds of rifles into the bushes hoping we hadn't gotten out of the kill zone. They are sending RPG rounds deeper into the woods and dozens of explosions fill our back trail.

At a nod from Worthley, Garcia got on the radio. He declared a Prairie Fire emergency.

Covey circles nearby and I recognize my friend Rich Ryan's voice. "Direct you, Lima Zulu, one hundred meters, zero nine five degrees. How copy?"

Garcia shouts into the mic. His voice cannot hide the angst. "Copy five by. Get here fast!"

Hundreds of them crashed through the brush of our back trail. Over the din of pursuit, trucks rumbled along the road, dumping fresh troops. Officers shouted. Sergeants steadied the pursuers. From other quarters, deeper down the road, others charged toward us.

For the next twenty minutes we fought our way to the LZ. When it appeared our enemy was closing on us, we set up hasty ambushes and fired them up.

As we grew near the very edge of the landing zone, they charged more quickly than we could evade. I shot two who made it a stone-throw away. One of them, the closest one to me was an officer who had a carbine rifle and I grabbed it along with a handful of magazines. I turned and at a near run joined the rest at a slight opening on the crest. Light machine guns and mortars arrived for the enemy attack. Green tracers ripped the air over my head. Mortar rounds joined the rockets of the RPG in the explosions around us.

Covey told us there were several hundred charging us up our slight slope and we were being flanked on one side. Ken yelled over the noise of the fight, "Dale, cover that side!"

I ran to the far edge of our stand as many of the enemy charged up that corner. I engaged them as fast as I could change magazines using that little finger. Rounds buzzed low over my head like green bees. I threw my rucksack down for cover and shot from behind it. Rich Ryan told me later three platoons had assaulted on my side. Over the explosions, I watched the grass in front of me being mowed down by the bullets and heard them hiss in their passage. Each time they advanced I put fire on the place.

One of my little people ran over to me crunched down and panting. His eyes showed his terror. Frantically, he shouted over the din of battle, "Sergeant Worthley tell me tell you give rifle to soldier in middle so him shoot. Use gun you capture."

I understood immediately but could not believe what I was hearing. Apparently one of the rifles needed to stave the attack in the middle was not functioning. They needed one for a soldier who was not handicapped as I was and could change and use the rifle more quickly. I glanced at the carbine. I had that and gave him my weapon.

Soldiers burst through the undergrowth in front of me, their shoulders shoving aside the bushes, weapons waving left and right as they sought targets, their mouths wide open as they shouted. Only I could not hear their shouts over the explosions. I conserved my ammunition, taking careful aim each time I shot: aim, shoot; aim, shoot. The carbine was at my face. I smelled the man that I had killed. The odor of the last seconds of his life was etched on the stock of the carbine. I smelled his sweat, his emotions, and his fear as clearly as if he spoke them to me in words. I aimed at a group clearing the bushes and prepared to fire. A bullet from someone on my left who I could not see slammed between the fingers of my left hand, my good hand, striking the weapon at the comb of the stock at my cheekbone. The wood prevented my wound but shattered the stock leaving the rifle splintered and flimsy, nearly falling apart.

One of our Vietnamese rapidly crawled over to me with another rifle, my third one, and a handful of magazines and handed them to me. "No need now," he simply said, and he scrambled away. I wondered if the previous shooter was dead.

There was intense fire. Masses of enemies charged toward us. They wanted to kill us and retrieve that satchel. If they lost all of their men in the process of getting it back, their efforts would be a success to them. They came on. Rich Ryan, monitoring the fight from the Bird Dog told me later a thousand PAVN troops were massed in the effort.

B-40 rockets exploded all around us. They used their mortars and the rounds exploded everywhere. Why was I not dead?

Covey directed the assets to fire at the enemy danger close to us. Mini guns firing 6,000 rounds a minute cut down bushes and small trees around me. The cannons and rockets of the Cobras slammed in the ranks of the charging forces. Debris from the explosions rained on me.

"Han Son, Han Son, Han Son!"

Although the gunfire and explosions were a steady roar to the extent that I could not hear individual shots but rather one long continuous explosion, in the middle of it all I heard my name.

"Han Son, Han Son."

It was Ba. He was standing straight up with tracers flying over his shoulders and around him. He had taken a few paces in my direction and stood straight as a pole, his arms hanging down with his weapon limply held his hand. He was distraught.

I ran to him. His face was a picture of anguish, fear, utter terror. "What?" I shouted.

"Han Son. Worthley, him die. Worthley, him die!"

## SOG: Missions to the Well

It took me a second for it to sink in. I glanced down. Worthley lay in a pile at Ba's feet. "Worthley, him die," Ba kept saying.

There was that moment in the maelstrom of war, when, as in the New Testament, "You are sifted as wheat," you are tossed in the tornado of pressure, when you misread it all. "What do you want me to do about it?" I shouted back. I thought Ba wanted me to bring him back to life, an impossible thing.

It hit me. Ba's world had just collapsed. Only he and I were left alive, apart from our team. Worthley was dead. "What do we do now?" his mind screamed.

A glance around me. Explosions impacted around us like raindrops hitting a puddle. Worthley was dead, shot through the neck.

I heard a helicopter. With Cobra gunships giving cover, the helicopter descended to the treetops and the gunner threw ropes down. Another one of our little people, still alive, ran to us.

I shook Ba by his shoulders and pointed at Ken. "Get him out of here. Save satchel."

It was immediately clear he was incapable of doing what I said. With my hands, I signaled Ba to make a loop in the rope so we could snap Ken's extraction rig into it. I grabbed the satchel and jammed it down Ken's shirt. Safely snapped in along with the intelligence we had captured, I signaled my people to snap in.

Ba stood a moment, not wanting to leave me. "Go!"

I needed to know the status of the rest of my people and did not want to leave. "I'll cover you," I shouted and backed away far enough the door gunner could see my sign. The pilot lifted off with Ken, the satchel, and two of my people hanging from the ropes. For more seconds than I should have I foolishly watched them ascend, my two Viets hanging on to each other, Ken limp, arms and head slumped down, chin to his chest.

I had miraculously not been struck down by bullets. I ducked and spun with my CAR-15 not sure of the best place to fight. They were everywhere. All around us. The explosions were a continuous roar, both theirs and ours. Our gunships fired 6,000 rounds a minute from

189

each gun plus 40 mm cannons. F-4 Phantom jets dropped 250-pound bombs around our perimeter trying to arrest the onslaught.

Sounds of their advancement came from the direction I had left and I dashed to the place and began to shoot. It didn't matter, really. They were everywhere and I thought I was the only one left.

"Dale! Dale!"

The voice seemed to emanate from a dream. I didn't know there was anyone left to call me. But I heard my name above it all. It was Bob Garcia.

"Where's Ken?" he screamed above the noise.

"He's dead," I shouted over the explosions as I ran a few paces toward him.

"What?" there was anguish and disbelief in his voice.

"He's dead, Bob. He was shot through the neck. I already sent him out."

He dropped to his knees and nearly collapsed into a heap. He screamed into the radio at the A-1 pilot. "I want 500-pound bombs fifty meters out."

I heard the pilot answer. "Are you crazy? You will be killed."

"I tell you; we are being overrun. I want it right now!"

"Are you sure?"

Bob rolled on his back and stared at the sky. "I said, fifty meters and I want it right now. That's an order."

"Good," I shouted. There was nothing left for us.

A prong of the attack began anew where I had just come from a couple dozen meters away. I ran to the spot with more magazines I had taken from Ken's harness and fought there. It seemed no matter what I did, nor how intense our air support, the numbers never lessened on the other side.

There was no mistaking the big bombs. The SPADs flew low over me. I saw the grey blur of the bombs leaving the plane then the massive explosions nearly on us. The blasts flattened my shirt to my back and my eyes were forced shut to a squint. Shrapnel angrily slapped the trees; turned some of them to stumps. Surely, nothing was alive under those bombs.

## SOG: Missions to the Well

Another bomb run. I opened my mouth this time to keep the air from being knocked out of me. I glanced up. None of my people seemed alive. I no longer heard shooting from our side.

I recalled from other occasions, how the enemy got as close to us as possible when we called in air strikes, thinking the safest place for them was right next to us, where we dared not drop our bombs.

Expecting that, I raised myself to take them out when they got close. I felt consigned to die. I would stay there. Shouting to no one in particular, but on the chance someone on the other side was alive I yelled, "You people get out, I can hold them off."

I could no longer pull the pins and throw my grenades. I had magazines for my rifle. This was it. I was certain Florida was finished.

But I was not alone. The sky was full of help if I could just harness it. But I had no radio. Garcia had it and he was probably dead and crumpled in the torn-up ground somewhere.

I remembered my handheld RT-10 radio. I pulled it out of the canteen cover and held it in my bloody hand and stared at it. I had no idea who to call. I had no call sign. I only knew that when I pressed the button, every airplane in south-east Asia would hear it.

With all of my nervousness and adrenaline I pressed the button and simply shouted, "Is there anybody there?"

My voice may have been high pitched and like a child's, but a calm voice came over the speaker. It was Rich Ryan's. "We got you Dale. We will get you out."

That reassuring voice was all I needed. A calm settled over me. The danger was still there. Green tracers yet crisscrossed over my head. B-40 rockets continued to shred everything around me.

"Han Son, Han Son!"

I heard it above the battle. "Han Son, Han Son!"

It was Noi. I glanced over. A Huey was hovering at the place. He and Bob Garcia were already strapped into two of the ropes which hung below. I ran to the place.

"Dale, hurry, hurry," Garcia shouted, "Hurry."

I ran to the place and looked up just as one of the ropes was shot through by green tracer bullets. It fell through the air wriggling like a wounded snake. One empty rope remained under the chopper. I grabbed it and realized I could not tie the knot with my hand. I grabbed the rope with as much hand as I had, made the biggest overhand loop I could and pulled it through itself since I could tie nothing else. I snapped in hoping my weight would cinch the knot.

Soldiers charged the open area to pull me off and I fired what was left in my magazine at them. A bullet hit me on the back of my head. It miraculously did not penetrate my skull. I did not lose consciousness, and I remember the sound that came from my mouth when it happened; "Nghaah."

I scraped my fingernails over the wound and shrapnel came from my skull.

The helicopter took heavy fire from the ground and lifted off with us hanging below on the ropes. But the pilot did not wait for us to clear the trees. He made a horizontal dash away from the firefight.

We were dragged through the trees, slamming against them, bouncing against the trunks having the air knocked from us, until finally our bodies caught in the limbs. We were about to be pulled apart.

The Huey felt it too. Perhaps the craft shuddered. Anxiously, the crew chief looked over the side and I knew they would cut the ropes and let us fall, rather than have the helicopter go down. I cradled my rifle and frantically chopped at the limbs with my knife. Perhaps at about the time the crew chief was about to use his own knife, the last tangle was cut and we sprang into the sky.

We burst into quiet and the surrealistic view of battle. Below us was a cauldron in which the 66th NVA Regiment was being mauled. Countless explosions in white, yellow and orange covered the area below us. Black and grey smoke rose and above it all. I watched the jets and planes make pass after pass over the site. In seconds we were thousands of feet into the air, shaky-cold, hanging by a half-inch of rope, hoping we would not fall five thousand feet back into Cambodia.

The Huey had been low on fuel after waiting for ordnance to suppress the enemy fire enough to pick us up. It was necessary to proceed directly to Ben Het on an azimuth. We passed directly through a storm; the icy rain hitting us like needles. It was painful. Crosswinds slammed us and I recalled watching the writhing rope as it fell when shot through. I hoped the ones that held us now had not been shot halfway through.

Norm Doney and Mike Buckland steadied our ropes as we descended at the helipad. They were hugging us even before we were unhooked. I walked like a drunk man on my battered legs. My words came out garbled and incoherent. I stumbled over to Noi, glad he was alive. I stared into his eyes and saw weariness, relief, and most of all, life. I hugged his shoulders.

I saw Buckland and Doney and turned to them. I asked about the satchel. I was looking at Norm Doney, my mentor, father figure, and first sergeant of Recon; looking into his eyes with all the earnestness of my being. "Did you get the satchel?" I wanted to ask but the words came out mispronounced and in an order of their own. It was the language of the ultra-weary. It took effort to say the words. Each word was a sandbag; too heavy for my tongue to lift to my mouth. Sentences arranged like the chaos of battle.

I knew the question did not come out correctly and I repeated them. I sounded drunk. Frustrated. Why can't I talk? I started again. "Did . . . you . . ." Even then I knew the words came out backward.

Again, "Did . . . did . . . ?"

But they knew what I tried to ask them. Both of them smiled at me like a brother, like a son. "Yes, we got the satchel, Dale. It's already on its way."

# CHAPTER EIGHT
*Arizona in Juliet Nine*

I was still in Japan. In the same ward, the same bed. It had been a month since I was admitted to this amputation ward. Others arrived during the month. Sometimes I would wake and hear someone come in on a gurney, pushed by an aid dressed in sage green, the patient barely seen among the sheets and bandages. A plastic pouch of solution hung above his head, the tube disappearing at a wrist I could not see under the sheets. Others shuffled in and were steered to a bed. They were all ward-quiet. And, over the weeks, beds emptied for a new destination. The one under the sheets and tubes left the same way he arrived.

All of us would remember amputation day, when the nurse and a surgeon worked their way down the rows and paused at each bed with a clipboard. "So, you are Sergeant Hanson, is that right?" And they confirmed that the sixth bed in that row was indeed the sixth person to be operated that morning. The nurse double-checked the clipboard and confirmed the part the scalpels would remove in a few hours. They looked at the bandaged hand and double checked the record. The two nodded to each other in confirmation, removed a felt pen from her lab coat pocket and marked the place they would cut. It was blue marker. She drew a dotted line around the place so there would be no mistake. My whole hand was bandaged and I reminded them, "It isn't the whole hand, now!" I affirmed the place and was sure in my mind they would not take a foot instead of part of my hand.

"Do not get out of line or change places with anyone."

A man in a lab coat came in and shaved my armpit.

It began promptly at eight o'clock. The first bed was rolled out the door behind the nurse's station then down the hall. They shoved us out in order, one after the one before. There were two operating rooms next to each other, with two beds in each and two set of surgeons at each bed. Four wounded soldiers were operated on at the same time. The rest of us were lined up in the hall and waited our turn. The lines grew shorter and the next beds in order would make the turn into the room and the waiting doctors.

I was not put fully out, only slightly looped. Earlier, the doctor, accompanied by the nurse with the clipboard, stopped at my bed and gave me a nerve block. The needle was large and was directed at a certain place in my armpit. When the point jabbed the nerve, a jolt of electricity shot up my arm. Shortly after, it seemed the limb was asleep, but when I reached across with my other hand and felt the skin, my wounded limb felt the tickle of my finger. I hoped the block would take more effect before it was my turn.

Movement. An aid rolled me another bed length down the hall.

I was awake. Fully awake. I would be the next to go in. There I was at the doorway peering inside and watching them work. Eight doctors cutting on four men. I was transfixed. Unable to turn my eyes away. They cut a part away. It was heavy. I knew that because the basket they tossed it in skidded on the floor.

Then, it was my turn. They started to work on my hand. It hurt. "That hurts, Doc, I can feel it."

The one I said it to looked across the table at the other. "He can't feel that, can he?"

## Dale Hanson

The second doctor lifted my hand into the air a couple of feet and dropped it. It plopped on my chest. "Nah, he can't feel it."

They continued their work, ignoring my interruption. "Doc, I feel that. I know what you are doing. You are scraping the gristle off my knuckles."

This time they looked across at each other in surprise and one of them shrugged, "We're almost there, soldier. Almost done."

But I knew what they were doing. I felt it, could see it in my mind like in a small shop where they made baseballs. A worker, tightly stitching the soft white skin around a string core.

So, we all had our stories.

The soldier to my left was a paratrooper who lost his left hand in the war and we became friends over the weeks. What we had in common was what we did not have in common: his injury was to his left hand, mine was to my right. Together we could tie the knots on our shoes. We tried out the hospital bowling alley, he, tying one side of the knot and me the other. He had been a professional bowler before the draft call, and before he enlisted to join the 173 Airborne Brigade. We perfected rolling gutter balls down the lane. He was transferred out and we waved each other off when they came for him that morning.

I never met the guy on the other side of me. Not with words. He was always asleep. He seemed to have many wounds. The most severe of them were under the sheet. That morning when I glanced over, the mattress was empty. The bed was made. The sheets were tight. The pillow was fluffed with no head press in the middle.

I was not badly wounded, ambulatory, and I often left the ward to get away. Sometimes the wounded would cry out. Nightmare perhaps. Or more likely from throbbing pain. Sometimes it would be the ghost hand or foot and the soldier would "walk" in a dream, causing the muscles to contract where the wound tried to heal. The worst time they would cry out was when they came to change our bandages. It hurt more than the initial wound at times. I knew medicine's demand for cleanliness, but it seemed to me that just as my wound created scab or tried to make skin, they would come down the ward with the cart and those clamps and scissors and pull off the bandages, with the fragile, new skin stuck to them. Blood would fuse to both wound and bandage and always the bandage won. Why could they not soak the bandages in something and just ease them off? It was then I would sneak from my bed and wander down the hall.

Grey walls lined the halls. They were empty and bare. I do not recall any pictures adorning the way. Surely there could be a Norman Rockwell print, perhaps the one of the old country doctor, his eyes rolled up toward the ceiling as though he were concentrating, a faint smile on his lips, with his stethoscope pressed to the little girl's teddy bear.

We could have used one with Holstein cows grazing on a summer field, a red barn in the background. Perhaps with a weather vane of a rooster, rusted but working. Even a simple painting of a city for the soldiers who came from such places. It might be a night scene in the rain, the reflected lights melting in the puddles. The downpour would make the red roofs glisten. Water runoff could make its way down the drainpipes and ripple across the sidewalk. A cat, calico and drenched, would be curled up in a doorway.

None of those were here. Grey walls. As I the ward to my right, I could walk forty-four steps. It was eighty-eight the other way. At one end, where the structure came to a bend was a single window. It faced Japan. I say it that way because everything else was our world, the field hospital. Some of us felt healthy and able to visit what lay beyond our confines, but any of us who had open wounds could not leave. I glanced out at my microcosmic view of our host country. Normally there was nothing to be seen—no bustle, no vendors in push carts, no restaurant that sold sushi, the real thing.

One day as I looked out that window I saw a funeral. A procession of mourners passed slowly by, dressed all in white, with white bill-less hats. It was followed by a horse-drawn carriage upon which was the white casket. The horses were white and there were large plumes, like ancient Roman centurions wore, and they were white. If there was music, I did not hear it, but I faintly recall a low, mellow drum.

Its beat was that of the pace of the mourners. And they all walked at that beat, as if their footsteps made the sound, for I did not see a drum. The cadence was that of a heartbeat.

The last ward on my left as I walked was the burn ward. If you knew it was there, you might smell it. The odor was that of char, but along with it was whatever it was they sprayed on the wounds. I felt a slight breeze when I came abreast of the door as if they tried to soothe the exposed flesh with moving air. Or perhaps, unseen angels sent their breaths across as they whispered, "There, there. We are here." The sign outside said, "BURN WARD NO ADMITTANCE." Below the sign, in smaller letters it stated that full gowns and masks were required to be worn at all times.

Another ward was for broken bones and other trauma wounds. Acute wounds such as those caused by explosions were addressed there. The last unit, the one closest to our solitary window, specialized in gunshot wounds. It was as I passed by on my strolling regimen, that I heard a voice I knew. Some voices you never forget, like an old acquaintance whose walk you know, and you recognize him at a distance in a crowd from his peculiar gait. And you smile even before you see his face.

The voice was that of Michael P. Wilson. I was certain of it. We had been together since Camp Crocket, through jump school and all the way through Special Forces training group. We were of the small bunch that made the trip to CCC at Kontum in April. I could not mistake the voice. He spoke from his chest, a resonant voice in an Eastern accent, Connecticut or something like that. Regardless of his audience, he spoke as if he were giving a lecture; always speaking with volume, like an orator who wanted to be sure the half-asleep guy in the back row heard. He was like the old settler I knew in the old folk's home when I asked about the old days. He thumbed his suspenders, rolled back his eyes in memory, and with a tone of nostalgia recited about blizzards of the north and how they used to see big black buffalo shoving through snow that was deeper than their chests.

An instant picture of Michael came to mind. A few of us had

been talking just outside our hooch when I last saw him. Then, he held his pipe in one hand as he addressed the topic at hand. His had been tilted slightly back and his eyes looked upward as if the notes he was reading from were up there. He seemed to gather his words from distant experience. Mike was slightly older than most of us, by six or eight years at least, with its added experience of life.

A thousand miles away. What were the odds?

That voice came from behind the door to the gunshot ward. I was at a dead stop and nearly placed my ear to the door. I was certain. It was Michael P. Wilson, sergeant, Special Forces.

I went through the door and stopped. I looked across the lines of beds.

"Can I help you?" asked a nurse.

"One of my people is here. Sergeant Wilson."

"You really can't be here. This is a trauma ward for gunshots. We cannot have visitors here."

"Just for a minute. He is one of my people. I just heard him talk."

The nurse was about to usher me out when I heard that familiar voice. "That's okay, Nurse. He is an old buddy of mine." Mike quickly added, "He is my minister."

She rolled her eyes and looked at me knowing our duplicity, "Just for a minute."

I went to his bedside. He smiled broadly, "Well, I. . . . What are you . . ." And he tried to reach to shake my hand. But it was his right hand and he had been shot in that shoulder, a severe wound. His face contorted in pain. He shut his eyes and webs of wrinkles shot to their sides. His mouth opened in a large O as he gasped for breath.

"Oh, oh, I better learn not to do that again."

"I am happy to see you, Mike, but not like this. What happened?"

"Shot in the shoulder. Nearly didn't make it out. It happened in Juliet Nine."

"Oh boy!"

"Yah, tell me about it. That is one of the worse targets. To make it even more dangerous, it was my first mission as a One-Zero. It gets worse from there." Mike realized his voice was carrying and lowered the volume.

I looked around at the nearby beds. None of the occupants were awake or seemed to care about our conversation. Or about anything, really.

"What about you, Dale? I remember you were hit."

"I've been here a month but they're going to send me stateside in a day or two. I think they were waiting for a bed to open up over there. I was wounded when we took out those Chinese couriers and Ken Worthley was killed. When did you get in?"

"Two or three days ago. They already operated on my shoulder. I still have to find out what the doctors decide."

The nurse gave me her warning eye.

"Mike, I will sneak in to see you as often as I can until I leave."

Mike began to breath more deeply. His eyes fluttered.

"Are you going to sleep?"

He smiled sheepishly. "Sorry. But I am awake now that I see you."

"Juliet Nine. Tell me what happened, how you were wounded."

He placed his good hand across his chest, lecture fashion and tilted his head back on the pillow. He lifted his eyes and began, glad to put into words the ordeal he had gone through.

"Juliet Nine," he began.

It was hot. Dry season. A gecko lizard panted on the window screen of the Arizona team room and pretended to not see a crawling fly. Two miles from the empty team room, down the asphalt road and its illusion of becoming water in the distance, Arizona was at the range honing their immediate action drills. They were moving on file across the open field with space between them as if they were in the jungle.

"Contact to the front!" the One-Zero shouted. The three SCU at the front of the column fired full-automatic at targets set up before them, and the team worked through the drill.

Sergeant Long walked to the targets and was satisfied. They had practiced marksmanship, and every possible battle drill in the open field. When the two Americans were satisfied with the results, they repeated the training in the woods next to the range. This was training SOG team always did, but they did it again, fine-tuning each detail. It was especially important they do it again. They had been tasked for a mission in Juliet Nine, a target known for eating teams alive. Most teams did not last the first day but were compromised or hit on the LZ.

No team could be prepared enough for any SOG target, let alone infamous Juliet Nine. Jim Young would be sure his team left nothing to chance. He wanted his people to be Spartans, warriors when the time came. He glanced at his next in command, Mike Wilson, raised his eyebrows in question. A hint of a smile. The gesture said, "I think we are ready. Do you agree?"

Mike, ever serious, said aloud, "We are."

Sergeant Long looked at Oi, his point man. A sheen of sweat was on the brow of the Montagnard. The challenge of maximum effort charging through the brush made even the people of those hills weary. "Oi, lead us home."

The tribesman smiled at the order and led the way to the waiting truck.

It was midafternoon when they passed through the gate of the FOB. The range was a few miles from CCC. It was through enemy country but otherwise pleasant as they rode in the open back and the passing air cooled the little people.

As the deuce-and-a-half truck came to a stop, Long said, "I think we are ready for our target. Let's give them the rest of the day off."

The two Americans were helping their people from the truck. Norm Doney joined them.

"Sergeant Long, let me talk with you a minute at the recon office."

Doney pointed to a chair. He took his own place and said, "Sergeant Long, we are short a few Covey Riders. If we are going to give the coverage we need, we need to add another rider. It requires someone with good judgment and considerable experience on the ground. Several of our people have suggested you. I agree with them. Would you be open to doing that?"

"Yes, anything I can do to help."

"Good. Settled then."

"When do you want me to start?"

"Now."

"Do you mean after this mission? Arizona is ready and just waiting to go in west of the bra. I already gave the brief-back and we are just waiting for the final word."

"I am aware of that, but Saigon wants this mission. What do you think of Sergeant Wilson taking over as the One-Zero? Do you think he is ready? Does he have the judgment and the experience to take over from you.?"

Long did not hesitate. "He is ready. He can do the job." Then, almost as an afterthought, "But wait! We are targeted for a mission, just waiting to go. Mike is the only American."

Doney smiled his Doney smile. "I knew you would say yes. Saigon is sending someone from up north the be the One-One on the team. He is a captain but knows that Mike will lead the team. He is going to arrive this afternoon."

"What about our mission to Juliet Nine?"

"It is still on. We will give him time to break in the new man. Go ahead and tell Sgt. Wilson what has happened and then send him in."

We'll call the captain Joe. He was in his late twenties, and slightly taken aback at Sergeant Mike Wilson's serious, pedagogical manner. "Captain, I don't know what they told you. The mission—to find a road or high-speed trail that Saigon swears is there but doesn't know for sure—is not a difficult task. The problem is where we are going. All of our cross-border operations are very dangerous, but this place is one of the worst. Everyone here knows about the "bra" area. On an intel map of the Ho Chi Minh Trail, it is those two bends in the road shaped like a woman's bra. It is so visible from the air that it's used as a landmark for navigation. It is saturated with enemy. It bristles with anti-aircraft batteries, 12.7 machine guns, and radar-guided 37 mm emplacements. It is the sanctuary area of several regiments. I know of only one team that completed its mission without a firefight."

Mike realized he was lecturing the captain and paused a moment to change his tone.

"We will take a few days to get you up to speed with our battle drills and meet the Yards." He put his hand on the officer's shoulder and steered him toward the team houses. "We can talk on the way."

"You will carry the radio. Take lots of ammo," he told him, pausing so his words lost no meaning. He looked down at the captain's web gear. The configuration did not appear to hold much. "If you need help setting that up, I can help you with your belt. Pack light. This is rough terrain to hump anything we do not need. And take a lot of water. We don't know about the availability in the AO." Mike looked up at the sky to make the point. "Many of the streams may have dried up."

Wilson lined his team in combat order along the edge of the CCC helipad. He faced his interpreter. "Given our target, I am going to go through our packs and check your weapons. They will be coming to pick us up soon. Put on your web gear, leave your pack at your feet." He looked at Lai the interpreter to be sure he understood, then nodded to his indigenous team leader, Not, to give the order to his people. Wilson went through every man's web gear to be sure ammunition was there and accessible. To Lai, he said, "You have a canteen in front. You need ammunition in front. Canteen is in back. Change it. You should know that."

When he was satisfied with everyone's weapons and web gear he turned to their backpacks. Two of his little people, Mui and Kai, carried Claymore mines in their packs. "I want them at the top of the pack where we can get to them quickly."

"Yes, *Trung Sĩ*," they replied.

"Now I want you to open them." They looked at him in surprise. The two men bent to the task and confidently presented the mines to their One-Zero. Both contained the full amount of C-4 explosive. The two Yards smiled. They had not removed any pieces of the C-4 to cook.

He proceeded down the line checking each man's pack for what they needed for the mission. Mike was diligent and the act conveyed the demands of the mission. He included everyone. Mike came to the officer's pack sack and looked. It bulged like a huge ballon about to burst. He could barely lift it. He opened the pack. There was a twenty-five-pound radio, a full five-quart water bladder, ammunition, more food than one could eat, more water, more ammunition and at least twenty more pounds of unnecessary items. Wilson wanted to shout! You could not waddle in the bush with all this stuff. You could not evade with all this equipment, much less attack. This was supposed to be a field-experienced soldier, someone who knew what it was like in combat. Mike doubted that the officer had ever been in the field. But he held his temper. He spoke in a tone that would not diminish the American before the tribesmen.

"Captain, you need to get rid of half of this stuff. Now. This is what you do not have to carry. You need to dump twenty pounds of this. Just give it to the first sergeant at the truck and he will get it to your hooch."

A burr of helicopters came from the west.

It was Monday, the 21st of September. Recon Team Arizona assembled on the helipad of Dak To launch site at mid-morning. The steel plates of the strip reflected the warmth of the day. The sky was without clouds. Wilson ushered his eight people under the eaves of the launch shed. Support helicopters would shortly arrive and fuel up before the final leg into Laos. Covey had picked out the entry place the day before and Wilson was glad there would be no hint of their coming.

He made a slow pass in front of his people to show himself to be calm and in control of the day. "This is the order I want you to remain in. You get off the chopper in the order you are in now." He paused before each of his little people and said their name and something about them. He stopped in front of Nui with his rifle leaning against his shoulder, and Oi, his point man, to Lai and Not and Kai and Le. To Lai he said, "Sometimes it is good there are clouds so they do not see us coming. But this is good too. If we have contact, there is no rain and black clouds to keep airplane and helicopter from coming to help *fini* VC and bring us home." Mike smiled and he knew the message would be passed to all of his people.

Two klicks west of the bra, Arizona poked itself into southeast Laos, a pin prick into the vast green fabric of the enemy sanctuary. The landing was quick, flawless, and, Wilson hoped, unexpected. The landing zone was empty of waiting enemy, as was the dash to the cover of the bushes which surrounded it. Nothing hinted that the Communists were aware of the team. The Kingbee slid into the small opening, their passengers leaped from the skids and disappeared into the tree line, and the craft angled away.

Although they seemed to be undetected where they were, the entry point was a place of danger as enemy usually rushed to the place and investigated the sounds of the landing helicopter. Wilson signaled Joe to release the aircraft and was pleased he could not hear the soft whisper into the radio.

Cautiously they moved north. The ground was dry and brittle and they picked where to place their feet. A half dozen steps, a dozen. They looked carefully around them as they paused and moved again. A half hour. They covered but thirty meters. Wilson heard heavy breathing.

He looked back. The captain struggled to breathe. He barely moved his feet as he struggled forward.

"What?" Wilson asked him when he went back to him.

"Huh, huh," he panted. "Just tired. I can barely move."

"What? We just started. You can't be tired."

"Huh. I just am."

"Get it together."

"Just give me a minute."

Wilson signaled his people to form a security stop.

"I'm okay now."

The team continued their slow deliberate pace. The tail gunner hid signs of their passage. Thirty more meters—the puffing again. The captain was leaned over, his hands around his rifle barrel like a cane.

"So, so tired," he breathed.

Wilson checked the safety of the officer's rifle.

Arizona waited again as the officer gathered strength to go on. Through the remainder of the morning the syndrome continued. The officer was acutely out of shape. Thirty meters, rest. Thirty meters, rest.

Wilson tried to process the unexpected handicap and somehow continue the mission. Finally, he said to himself, "Arizona will be the first team to ever do a security stop every thirty meters of an entire mission."

A few dozen steps later, the One-Zero looked back. The weary man steadied himself, one hand grasping a slender bamboo tree. Wilson looked up and saw the top branches of the tree jostled. A giveaway to anyone watching for movement. He scanned the bushes for enemy.

They moved on.

Twenty minutes. He heard the canteen cap tap the edge of the container. He turned just as the captain tipped the vessel straight into the air for the last swallow. Wilson looked for the reaction of his people. They looked away, monitoring the vegetation instead, to avoid the weak American.

So far, the Communists did not come for them. There were no signal shots. No breaking underbrush to drive them. They were there. Wilson knew it.

They changed direction and moved toward the area they hoped to find Saigon's high-speed trail.

Twice more, Officer Joe wheezed and halted. The team flinched. This might be heard by the enemy. This time he dropped to his knees, thrust down his pack and retrieved another canteen of water. He drank large gulps and swapped the vessel with the one in his belt.

Two hours. The tribesman could no longer hide their feelings. Now as Wilson looked back the Montagnards sought his eye. They rolled their eyes. Shook their heads.

Arizona gained a slight incline. Afternoon. A thump behind the One-Zero.

Joe was sitting on the ground, his back against a tree, feet splayed like a drunk in an alley leaning against a garbage can. He emptied his canteen.

Mike studied the man. Not a single time did he ever scan the area around him for enemy. He carried his weapon by the handle, not ready for combat. Mike looked through the tree leaves at the sky. At this rate he would need to think of a place to RON. He looked at his map and compared it to the incline beneath his feet.

Another hour. Three more times they waited for Joe to gather strength. Mike signaled for a security circle, and touched his mouth with his four closed fingers, "Eat." He composed a sitrep to give to Covey or Leghorn Relay Site. "Next time we stop," he thought.

They found an area near the crest of the rise where they had fields of fire and the enemy could not approach without making significant noise. Wilson pointed where he wanted the Claymores placed. It was the time of day when birds utter their last peep before dark, and slender lizards back into their holes. It was the time of the day too, when Pathet Lao and PAVN officers give the final instructions to their people. Wilson considered, "It is not possible they do not know we are here. They are waiting. Waiting."

The last glimpse of anything Michael Wilson saw as dusk turned to darkness, was of Joe as he fished into his sack and drank lustily from the depleted five-quart water bladder.

Morning arrived saffron-colored through the triple canopy forest. They listened without moving for twenty minutes before Mike gave the signal to eat. He prepared a sitrep in case Covey flew in the area, "Team okay, proceeding east toward the river. No contact during night."

Joe seemed rested and Mike hoped the day would not be the same.

It was.

Three times Arizona assumed security stops as Joe gathered his breath and pushed himself to his feet. This last stop, Wilson saw him tap the bottom of the canteen cover to gauge its emptiness. Perhaps a fairy had filled it on the way. Every drop was gone.

Fifty meters later, Oi, the point man, signaled "danger ahead." Wilson halted the team and they knelt to a stop, their weapons searching around them like antennae. Oi and Wilson slipped forward. Ahead, less than a hundred feet, a brook tumbled across gravel and polished stones. Along its bank, barely visible through the short grass was the high-speed trail they sought. He brought the team forward and they spread along its length and watched.

The stream was narrow, fast-moving, and shallow—about six inches deep. Along its edge lay the trail. It was not quite a road, but certainly troops could walk abreast on its surface. At best, a narrow jeep might use it. Wilson and Oi crossed to the road. It was hard packed clay, so packed and well-used it would not reveal a track. A dangerous place to be.

For a moment, Wilson considered trying for a prisoner. Then he remembered Captain Joe. It was out of the question to take a captive and have enemy in hot pursuit when one of his own who could not walk thirty yards without resting.

Joe stared at the stream.

Thick bushes lined their side of the creek and hid the team from the trail. He backed his people to the place and set them in ambush order. Two at a time, he allowed his soldiers fill their canteens while the remainder watched the trail. Nearly completed, the captain bent to his knees and drank lustily. Then he filled his canteens. Not finished, he took a canteen cup and proceeded to fill the bladder. Cup by cup he poured it into the small opening without spilling until it was full. Finished at last in the danger area. But unlike Gideon's warriors in the Bible who also drank from a pool but watched for enemy, Joe never looked up. With his containers full, he stood. Stood fully exposed above his concealment.

A North Vietnamese soldier appeared on the trail. On the hard surface, they did not hear his approach. He walked confidently, briskly—a point man of a larger element in his own territory. Six Montagnard fighters opened up on the enemy point man, the blast of so many threw him into a crumpled heap at the side of the small road.

A muffled shout in the distance along the path.

No time to check the body for intelligence.

Wilson clicked his tongue to his point man. He pointed a direction for him to lead. "Oi, move out."

They moved briskly. Although the officer knew the gravity of the situation, and proceeded quickly at first, thirty meters later he stopped. He was looking down at his legs, when Sergeant Wilson came to him. "Heavy. Heavy," he said. "Can't lift them. Can't. Can't."

Wilson grabbed him by the elbow. "You either move or you die here. Understand? Move."

Joe grimaced as in pain. He pulled at his legs as if they were stuck in deep mud.

Still grasping him by his arm, the sergeant said, "You either move or I am going to leave you here."

He nodded in understanding and stumbled ahead.

Another thirty meters. This time it was not a question of waiting for the weary soldier. Enemy soldiers were charging Arizona in the near distance. They heard them advance. Shrubs and bushes swayed at their approach. Arizona readied itself. The fight began at the first sight of them pushing through their concealment. Arizona opened fire. The North Vietnamese shot back. They heard movement from the flanks of the enemy position. They were about to be enveloped.

"Oi, break contact," and he pointed the direction.

The recon team moved away from the firefight. He motioned two of his people to help the American move and they each took a side under an arm. Fifty meters. They could not hear their pursuers.

With security out, Mike went over to Joe. "I am going to take the radio." He removed a few things from his own pack to make room and gave them to his people to carry. Wilson did not like to carry the radio as he positioned himself to the front, a place most prone to becoming a casualty. That took out the radio as well. But, he reasoned, perhaps taking the heavy radio from the exhausted man might help him keep up—especially now.

They changed direction. They moved with great stealth, expecting contact at any moment. They moved slowly, soundlessly. Surely, they were pursued. Perhaps the fire fight bought them time.

Joe was doing better. He slid over to Wilson, "I apologize," he said, "My poor condition has masked my training. I am doing better as we go."

With the crawling pace he kept up, and he peered into the shrubs for lurking foe, his weapon following his eyes.

They moved gradually north, halting frequently; the point man pausing to assess that which was before them, the rear gathering without meaning to as he did so. And so, they inch-wormed ahead until they reached the base of a ridgeline. The underbrush thinned slightly and they could make out the contour against the sky. Oi held out his hand in warning. The signal was passed down the line and they squatted in readiness. Oi did not know the cause of his alarm. He only knew with the thinning of the brush and an unidentified "something" before them, there was great danger. Perhaps this was the dreaded place of ambush they expected.

Wilson, although only a dozen feet behind the Montagnard, had not felt it.

"What?" he whispered as he gained his side.

Oi only panned his eyes around them before he answered. "*Tôi không biết,*" he said. "I don't know."

He did not take his eyes from the horizon. "Something number ten, Wilson." Then quickly, he held up his hand. "That!"

Both of the men felt it, saw it. As if the soundtrack of a movie had been shut off but returned to the screen in full force. The ridge before them was alive, bristling, a hive of activity.

A hum filled the air as if from a swarm of bees. A powerful generator's growl vibrated among the trees. It was powerful, the kind that could serve the needs of a large village or small city.

It was then they began to hear the other sounds of bustle. Along the entire ridgeline from left to right was a high-speed road. It could not be seen by the team, perhaps not even from the air. An unnatural line of trees was bent over to hide the road, but passing engines of trucks and smaller vehicles hummed as they drove by and told the secret.

There were shouts, loud talking, orders given, and worst of

all, the bark of dogs, perhaps tracker hounds. Deeper into the ridgeline—perhaps over the top where the site continued—came the muffled use of loudspeakers. This was a vast encampment. At a place where the movement of sunlight scanned the ridge along with the watchers, a silver, single spider thread weaved among the tree limbs: power lines.

Wilson wanted confirmation about what they were seeing. More than a battalion, this had to be a regimental-size headquarters. He looked to the side as the Montagnard team leader came to him. The Yard looked but a minute and, in a whisper, exclaimed, "*Beaucoup VC.*" Slowly he shook his head, "*Beaucoup, beaucoup.* Many, many enemies."

He needed to document the site clearly; record it without error in his notebook. With the rugged terrain, to be fifty meters off could place the bombs in the valley which hugged the camp, the destruction shielded by a steep ridge. He looked for landmarks to be sure. Surely there would be an airstrike used on this. "Kai," he said to the Zero-One, "Bring the captain to me. He needs to see this."

He briefed the officer on his conclusions and asked for his concurrence regarding the coordinates of the headquarters for later air strikes. Joe placed the dirty nail of his forefinger on a small landmark on the map, raised his eyes to the corresponding location on the ground, and with utter clarity said, "I fully concur sergeant."

"Captain Joe, put this in your notebook in case I don't make it through this."

"Copy," and he began to scrawl into his pad.

Wilson formed one of his rare smiles. The man was coming around.

An acute change in direction was needed and they moved southeast along the side of a ridge. They had no contact with their pursuers the remainder of the day. No tracker dogs. No signal shots. No worrisome sounds to be deciphered. With the ultra-slow pace as they evaded, the rest stops were fewer and as dusk placed the shadow of her hand over the forest and hid the team, they tucked into a thicket for the night. Security was vigilant. Most of the Montagnards were of the Sadang tribe, educated by missionaries. They bowed briefly in prayer as they held their weapons. Like Nehemiah of the Old Testament who said, "Everyone with one of his hands wrought in the work, and with the other hand held a weapon."

Joe was immediately asleep.

Wednesday and Thursday they maneuvered easterly. Mike drew the captain into the mission more. He would signal the officer over to him, consult him, study the map and have him indicate from it likely places they might be ambushed. They updated information not shown on their map. They thought they had found Saigon's road and mapped it for debriefing when they returned. Their pace was that of expecting to be ambushed at any moment. PAVN knew they were in their backyard. With no signs of pursuit, Wilson could only suspect at some point, some advantageous place for the enemy, a place where Arizona might lessen its guard, the enemy would strike. With those stops, they moved at a crawl pace, always expecting, deciphering the smallest sound, the smallest flick of a leaf. Joe required less stops, drank his water, watched for enemy.

Thursday night they tucked into a tight perimeter. It was bamboo with surrounding thicket. The undergrowth was dry, brittle dry. Nothing could approach without dragging the prisoner of sound with them. In a way, it was too perfect. The parched leaves were megaphones that made the smallest gecko lizard sound large, its shuffle in the weeds resembling a tracker's furtive crawl. Throughout Thursday night, dry bamboo knuckles stretched and popped in the changing humidity of the evening. The team did not relax, always listened. Alert.

With the arrival of dusk, the men leaned back against their packs, each in their position. They had planned an escape route if they were hit in the night. They chose one which would be the quietest considering the dry debris.

There was a sigh. It came from the dry lips of the captain. But for the quietness of the evening, the escape of air sounded loud. It carried. Wilson shuffled over to him. "Dry. No water." And he showed the empty bladder. "Gone."

## SOG: Missions to the Well

"Shhh," Wilson wanted him quiet. "We are all short, but we conserve it. We have seen no streams the last two days."

Wilson remembered something Norm Doney wrote in one of his weekly Tips of the Trade, Lessons Learned newsletter he printed and handed out to the men in Recon Company. "Joe, Doney used to say . . . but you don't know him, do you? Doney used to say, 'In times of thirst, put a little pebble under your tongue.'"

Wilson turned to go back to his position but stopped.

"Here, take my water," and he gave it to the thirsty man. "This has to last you."

It was Friday and Mike Wilson maneuvered the team to an area where he hoped to be exfiltrated. A place was found on the map, a small place, hopefully too small for the enemy to take notice. They remained at a distance where vegetation thinned and pale light showed before them. Such places were fraught with danger. He would wait until he was certain the FOB would come for them before they approached the edge of the opening. He placed the radio to his ear.

The air sparked with electricity. A Prairie Fire emergency had been declared. A Company Hatchet Force was in trouble. Somewhere in Laos, perhaps but a few miles from Arizona, all assets were being directed to their location. For only a moment Wilson wondered, "Is that the reason the Communists have not come for us? They were concentrating on the SOG company?"

A Company was commanded by Captain Ronald Goulet with Lieutenant Pool as the second in command. Both were struck down, perhaps dead. Goulet was a courageous, powerful-looking leader who ran recon missions, led a commando force with Robert Howard to rescue an overrun force in Laos, was the commander of Recon Company, and commanded the company at the Yard camp when it was attacked. Now he was down. They had fought the enemy for two days and discovered a large ammo dump. As the company brought in resources to destroy it, an enemy RPG round exploded near them and severely wounded the two officers. There were other casualties.

Mike Wilson listened. His people were in a protective circle.

Assets were on the way to put down the enemy fire around the stricken Goulet. The entire company was to be exfiltrated. Mike knew it would take numerous helicopters and attack aircraft to accomplish the task. There would be no getting out today.

With his people circled where they were, he was captivated and monitored the radio. They needed to find a nearby place to RON until they themselves would try the next day. He shuffled over the Captain Joe and brought him the news.

Saturday, 27 September. Wilson used the CAK code and requested exfiltration and gave the requested coordinates. FOB responded, approved, and confirmed assets would respond. ETA two hours.

Wilson assembled his people. To his Zero-One he said, "We go to LZ. Helicopter come two hours."

He slid over to the captain. "We are going out. Choppers are coming in two hours. We need to hustle. You need to go even if you are tired. We do not want to be left here." Wilson looked into his eyes until he read his understanding and resolve to maximum effort.

10:30 a.m. They arrived at the place they selected before and had to turn around where the trees thinned in girth and number. More sunlight shone through the gaps and shrubs, and tall elephant grass indicated an opening in the triple canopy. This was always a place of great danger. The North Vietnamese had not struck them thus far, but this could be the very place they planned to do so.

Approaching the very edge of the clearing, Wilson looked back. His people moved cautiously, their faces intent as they peered to the sides, their weapons following their eyes. They too were aware of the peril.

With a last glance to assure himself that his people were prepared, Oi and Wilson made the first step on the dry grass of the LZ. At that very moment the enemy opened fire and attacked the team. Thousands of small arms fires struck the eight men. One slug smashed into Wilson's shoulder. He heard himself utter a deep, "Uuhhh." With him, Oi, the point man, was also struck, but continued to fire. It was only when Mike tried to reload his rifle that the severity of his wound became apparent. His arm would not work.

Explosions joined the incoming fire and Kai received shrapnel wounds. But in moments the team recovered and returned fire. For the next hour Arizona fought back against a determined enemy. One of the Yards wrapped a hasty bandage around Wilson's wound, then rushed to the other wounded. Although they fought desperately, the incoming fire from the other side of the LZ did not diminish.

A rumble of helicopters came from over the treetops on the far side of the field. Wilson shouted into the set, "Contact, contact, we are under fire, have casualties. One-Zero is WIA."

But the choppers passed over the LZ and hovered a distance away.

"We do not have visual on you. Have smoke?"

Wilson realized the exfil was over the wrong LZ. "I hear your engines at azimuth one-seven-five, one hundred meters."

The choppers immediately adjusted.

Another glance back at his people. The captain seemed fully alert, invested in the situation.

"Joe," Wilson shouted, "Take the radio. I might pass out. You need this. You know what to do."

The two men shrugged off their packs. To make room for the radio, the officer pulled the bladder from the pack and tossed it aside.

"Give me that panel," Wilson shouted to one of the Yards. With bullets flying around him, he ran to the edge of the field, then realized with his one good arm, he could not fully unfold the panel or snap it to make it blink. "Tell Covey, I am at the edge of the field waving a panel."

"I copy, Palidan," Covey responded, addressing Wilson by his code name. "We will mark your position so gunships know where you are. Where are you taking most of your fire?"

He was puffing when he dashed back to the cover of the team. He pulled his compass from his shirt. His eyes misted with pain and adrenaline. "Zero-eight-five, east side of LZ," the captain shouted.

"Copy, heads down."

Cobra gunships raked the far perimeter with their ordnance. The runs were followed by a pair of A-1 Skyraiders with their 20 mm cannons.

"Choppers coming in for pickup."

A Huey sloped in between the canopy of trees, but before it descended below the uppermost limbs, massive small arms fire erupted from the far edge, driving the chopper away.

Aircraft swept in again and dropped their bombs. The far side flashed in explosions.

Twenty minutes. Hueys made a second pass. Wilson was in agony and losing blood but watched the craft descend again. Heavy fire. Wilson thought he could see the shudder as bullets impacted on the sides of the helicopter. And he watched as it also rose and flew away.

Again, SOG ordnance rained around the opening in the trees, trying to suppress the enemy. Arizona watched as slender trees were denuded of leaves, splintered, and exploded into pieces.

It had been an hour since help arrived. For a third time, help tried again. And again, they made it but to the second layer of canopy before the sides of the craft shuddered under the impact of bullets. And as before, the Americans dropped their bombs and fired their heavy machine guns. Surely, no enemy could survive this.

And the helicopters tried again only to be shot through and leave again.

Perhaps the enemy were in prepared bunkers or spider holes and had been waiting for this moment.

It had been three hours of firepower exchanged between the foe. Skyraiders dropped heavy bombs on the source of fire.

Huey helicopters tried a fifth time and for a fifth time were driven off.

Fast movers this time used napalm canisters and the helicopters came in on their heels. For the sixth time they were driven off with the withering small arms fire. It had been five hours of continuous fighting.

"Palidan, Covey." Wilson crawled to the officer and the radio.

"Palidan, choppers will try again but this might be the last of the day. They have reached the max of their fuel and ordnance. If we don't get you out this time, it will be tomorrow. Understand? Tomorrow. We will have Spooky around you all night. This time we will try get you out on strings. We will take the wounded out on the first chopper and the rest of the team on the second one. Understand? How copy?"

There was a moment of pause as Mike sorted out the implication of his words. Leaders went out last, but his one arm was useless and his loss of blood made him lightheaded enough to soon pass out. He shouted the instructions to the captain and his Zero-One.

"Copy," he said.

Wilson ran back to tell them they would be going out on strings and ensured that each had their McGuire rigs fully buckled. The captain joined him.

Wilson looked at his casualties. Three so far; himself and another gravely wounded. "I should stay for the last lift, but I can feel myself weak with this," he said pointing to his shoulder, I can feel myself passing out. I don't think I can saddle my people with dragging me around for the next lift. You have the radio and know what to do."

"Sergeant, you go out with the other wounded. I will take the next lift. I can handle it." Joe replied.

There was no more time to think. For the seventh time Cobra gunships passed just in front of the rescue helicopters, dealing lethality at the enemy. On its heels, a slick was sloping down. Gunfire met the craft as before and at the treetops the gun crew tossed out the long ropes.

Wilson and Oi, though both wounded, dragged the very seriously wounded Mui deep into the field and snapped into their McGuire rigs. He chose Kai, the interpreter of the team to assist with hooking into the ropes which swayed under the hovering aircraft. Wilson was dizzy and wanted to heave. He snapped in.

In seconds they were jerked above the treetops and rose higher into the air. Green tracer bullets arched around their feet. Mere seconds passed. They were a few hundred feet up. Brief terror of falling from great height. They were flying away from the maelstrom of bullets, and the sounds of combat faded below them. Bullets streamed from the trees directly at the slick. He looked up, half dizzy from the loss of blood. He watched as if from a silent film of the old days as the rescue vessel above them was slammed with gunfire. The engine stopped. Instantly. Dead, absolute, utter silence. There was a cry of fear—someone in the chopper? One of his strikers? His imagination? Or was the cry his own? For only a second they were dead in the air, before the plunge to earth began. The Huey was falling. In seconds the souls inside would slam to the ground with four soldiers hanging below on ropes. Helplessness. Sheer terror. The trees rising up to meet them became green teeth of grinning death. Above them was the belly of the stricken helicopter ready to crush them.

There was little the pilot could do in those seconds. The good pilots practiced for such a time. They would autorotate until they slammed to earth. Limited steerage. He would try to direct the descent to the river and hopefully lessen the impact on the wounded men below. Just as the hanging men were tree height, he pulled pitch to diminish the speed of the freefall.

They did not make the river. They crashed through the trees and slammed hard in a field of tall elephant grass. It flipped and burst into flames, killing the door gunner and the pilot. With the slight sideways drift, the men who had dangled from the ropes under the stricken craft slammed to earth alongside it and were not crushed. They landed hard, their bodies thudded to the earth, almost bounced. They were stunned, the air knocked out of them. Kai, the only one of the three not wounded at the time, moaned. His arm was fractured and lay at an angle which left him in shock. They felt broken, not yet able to process that they were alive.

Someone ran to the side of the Huey to pull the bodies from the wreck. The pilot was slumped over the controls, unmoving and lifeless in the white-hot flames. The white furnace drove the men away. For a moment they stared at the molten wreck. "We can't save him. Come away."

The speaker grabbed the would-be rescuer by the shoulder and turned him away from the inferno. He pointed up. An H-34 was coming in to rescue the survivors.

On his back in the elephant grass and hopelessly tangled in the ropes lay Wilson. He heard a crackling sound and a whoosh of combustion. He felt intense heat. Perhaps the dry grass was alight and coming toward him. With his good hand he grabbed his K-bar knife and sawed at the ropes and gasped painfully to recover his breath. The elephant grass was alight and eating its way toward him. But it was this same grass which cushioned the fall of the wounded men and let them live at all. And it was the selfless decision of the pilot who was charred behind this controls, who changed the pitch early to slow the fall of the wounded under him but made his own fall more severe.

A Kingbee chase ship followed the downed chopper to the crash site. Only seconds separated the two. On it was a Vietnamese doctor, Bác Sĩ Nhok, whose presence on such occasions seemed to be ubiquitous. He sprang from the rescue craft and ran to the nearest man. Wilson still lay on his back in the deep grass struggling against the web of rope which bound him and saw looking down at him the face of the doctor. In perfect English Nhok said, "You will be okay now. Soon you will be back at FOB."

Relieved that the face was not that of an NVA and that he was not a prisoner, Mike Wilson passed out.

Every able man dragged, carried and hoisted the fallen into the Kingbee. Bác Sĩ Nhok dragged the unconscious body of Mui, saw his wounds and sadly shook his head. It was only moments before they gathered all of the crew of the Huey and the wounded men that were tangled in the ropes next to the craft. Last to crawl into the Kingbee was the Vietnamese doctor. He backed away enough so the pilot could see him, gave the signal that all who could board were in, and sped to the door. The gunner grabbed his arm and hoisted him in.

They rose into the air as a few desultory rounds struck the skin of the chopper. Left below them lay the burning, molten-white helicopter. One dark shape, the pilot, remained, unrecovered. It continued faithfully at his duty station.

Mike Wilson remembered being pulled into the Kingbee. Just in time, for he passed out before his body slumped to the deck. Vaguely, as in a dream he felt the chopper lift from the ground. Briefly, he woke from the numbness of his mind when Special Forces men at Dak Pek helped get him into a dust-off helicopter for the next leg. He woke up next at 71st evacuation center in Pleiku. From there they flew him to Japan.

They were not able to get the second lift out that Saturday. The captain, with the need of the day, pulled himself together. It appeared to the North Vietnamese that all of Arizona had been taken out already and did not look for the rest of them. Captain Joe led his people away from the LZ and found a place to nest for the night. He had radio contact with Covey. Spooky was in the area if they were needed. He would only need to mark his place and the miniguns would keep the enemy at bay through the night and pave a path to an LZ. Arizona was lifted out Sunday morning.

The nurse gave me the final evil eye. "This patient needs to rest," she said.

I glanced over at Mike. I think it was good for him to tell me his story. There was a thin smile on his face as his eyes flickered and he dozed off.

In my role as Mike's alleged minister, I smiled at her and said, "Confession is good for the soul."

# CHAPTER NINE
*Maine and an Hour of Hell*

I scarcely remember the flight from the field hospital in Japan, so they must have drugged us up. I do recall we were packed into that airliner. Perhaps they thought limp soldiers packed better. Many of the wounded were unmoving and out of it already. They did not stir the whole trip and some, the amputees, did not take up much space anyway.

    The hours had been a migration, lemmings from the various wards led by aides with their clipboards, joining a larger stream in the hallways, becoming a surge as we joined the rest at the bottom floor and the sidewalk where buses and vans met us with their engines running. I had been in the hospital a month breathing the closed space's air, so I paused at the open outside door and filled my lungs with the night air. In addition to its cooling freshness, I imagined Japan and its culture—paintings, music, food, and haiku poetry attached to those molecules—to breathe it in and savor. I hoped to smell the ocean as its scent slipped across the land, bringing with it the odor of the morning's catch, starfish and seaweed at low tide, the perfume of Japanese girls who had dived for pearls and rested; of fishermen in shallow sampans with a lantern on the bow to bring fish to its glow and the cormorants in their laps, a metal ring around their necks so they could not swallow the catch all the way down. But that was just a thought, a pause as I left those doors.

Almost shyly, a young Japanese man was standing to the left of the door. I recognized him. He worked the counter of the snack bar of the store. He seemed to like Americans and I visited with him over the weeks. I think he came to see us off. I shook his hand with my left, as the other was still well-bandaged, and I thanked him. My father may have fought his father in the war before last, for Dad fought in some of the major battles in the Pacific.

My thoughts of drinking in this country with my nose ended at the buff-green bus that idled in front of the walk. Diesel fumes snaked from under its belly and erased my olfactory pondering as I waited to take my seat.

The boarding and the configuration of the jet was similar to that which brought us to this hospital in the first place. The wounds were more contained than when we arrived, the immediacy of care having been stabilized. It was now the trip to the States for prolonged care. As before, there were more seats squeezed into the fuselage than a normal airliner. Seats were narrower and could not be tilted back into the lap of the casualty immediately behind. If you slept, you did so sitting upright. When the last of us were unloaded from the buses, seated and strapped in, they brought in the stretcher wounded. The compartments above the seats for baggage had been removed and hooks hung in their place from the ceiling. Last to be loaded were the bed wounded. Aides carried them in on stretchers and snapped them in directly above our heads. There was no getting up from our seats after that point.

When loading was finished, someone squeezed down the aisle, glanced left and right confirming we were all buckled, and nodded to the crew in the main cabin. The jet hissed, then growled, and began to move. There was a rumble, and I imagined gravel on the pavement as we taxied to the active runway. In minutes we were off.

# SOG: Missions to the Well

I saw the lights of the city through the porthole, a city that went on and on and on.

The lights dimmed for the flight. They turned the heat up in the cabin to make us calm and sleepy.

They must have refueled somewhere halfway across the ocean. But I can't remember. Before I began to slumber, I recalled the nurse in my ward telling me, "You are going to Fitzimmons Hospital. Oh, you will like it there. It is a good hospital. It's where President Eisenhower went to stay when he had his heart attack. You will like it there."

The flight lasted forever. Those of us who were in seats sat upright, rigid, with nothing to read. The soldier next to me slept most of the way. When his eyes were open, he stared straight ahead as if the bulkhead were a screen and he was watching the event in the jungle that put him there, or the explosion on the firebase, or the drop of his helicopter as it landed on the tin roof of a Quonset hut. Or perhaps he was watching his future; life without a hand, healing time in a ward, the remainder of his life in his home town. No book, no conversation.

To pass the time I tried to remember the words of poems I had memorized, Bible verses, anything to pass the time: the seven churches of the book of Revelation; Ephesus, Smyrna, Pergamum, Thyatira, Sardis, Philadelphia, Laodicea. The eight Greek cases: nominative, genitive, ablative, dative, locative, vocative, accusative and instrumental. I composed lists: my ten favorite smells, ten favorite books, ten favorite musical pieces, on and on. I glanced over, my seat-mate was sleeping.

A stewardess shuffled down the aisle. Nearly everyone else was asleep. "Something to drink, soldier?"

I looked sideways in the direction of the toilet and wondered how I would ever make it to the place. "No, thank you ma'am."

I recited Rudyard Kipling's *If* poem to myself and got stuck halfway through.

I tried to quote Carl Sandburg's *Preludes of the Wind*.

## Dale Hanson

*The woman named Tomorrow*
*sits with a hairpin in her teeth*
*and takes her time*
*and does her hair the way she wants it*
*and fastens at last the last braid and coil*
*and puts the hairpin where it belongs*
*and turns and drawls: Well, what of it?*
*My grandmother, Yesterday, is gone.*
*What of it? Let the dead be dead.*

*The doors were cedar*
*and the panels strips of gold*
*and the girls were golden girls*
*and the panels read and the girls chanted:*
*We are the greatest city,*
*the greatest nation:*
*nothing like us ever was.*

The soldier next to me began to snore and I lost my place. It took a minute and I picked it up again.

*The doors are twisted on broken hinges,*
*Sheets of rain swish through on the wind*
*where the golden girls ran and the panels read:*
*We are the greatest city,*
*the greatest nation,*
*nothing like us ever was.*

I forgot where I was and missed a stanza or two and continued.

*And while the singers sang*
*and the strong men listened*
*and paid the singers well*
*and felt good about it all,*
*there were rats and lizards who listened*
*. . . and the only listeners left now*
*. . . are . . . the rats . . . and the lizards.*

I was stuck and gave up the rest of the poem.

## SOG: Missions to the Well

The stewardess squeezed by again. One of the cot patients hanging above us was moaning. I couldn't make out the words, but her comforting tone spoke clearly, like a mother to her sleeping child.

"How much longer?" I asked as she passed on her way back.

"Close now. Maybe an hour more."

I quoted the twenty-third Psalm to myself. "The Lord is my shepherd; I shall not want. He maketh me to lie down in green pastures: he leadeth me beside the still waters. He restoreth my soul: he leadeth me in the paths of righteousness for his name's sake. Yea, though I walk through the valley of the shadow of death, I will fear no evil: for thou art with me, thy rod and thy staff they comfort me. Thou preparest a table before me in the presence of mine enemies: thou anointest my head with oil: my cup runneth over. Surely goodness and mercy shall follow me all the days of my life and I will dwell in the house of the Lord forever."

The crew was making their way down the aisle in preparation for landing. Phrases of the passage clung to my soul. "Presence of mine enemies," was one of them. I had come from that. "The valley of the shadow of death," was another. SOG was assuredly such a place. A twitch of my ghost finger and the tightness of skin where a bullet burrowed on the back of my head placed an exclamation point on "surely mercy shall follow me." All my life I have felt God's presence and he had shown mercy to me.

Fitzimmons was a massive beehive. It covered 600 acres, nearly a square mile and 322 buildings. In the last world war, it became the largest hospital in the world and could bed 5,000 patients. The ward felt like I was on the sidewalk of a busy city with its frenzied activity. Rooms were filled with patients in pajamas and robes. They talked loudly, leaped from their beds, walked the halls, and returned to their beds to lie down again. A mania. Halls needed signal lights as nurses in white rushed from place to place; aides consulted their charts as they pushed their carts. A murmur of a hundred voices, the metallic sounds of trays and bed pans, the low sound of rolling plastic cart wheels, and the loud television programs: Ironside was playing on one of them, I Love Lucy on another. This was the cacophony of my ward. Not a place of rest.

I managed to get a place in one of the quieter rooms, a bed far back in the corner. My injuries did not require a bed; I was not ill, only wounded. The bed with the back raised and the chair beside were my respite from the chaos.

It was evening. The other patients in the room were sleeping. Johnny Carson ended his show with his last guest and they shut off the TV. A nurse came to my bed and stopped. I think it was because I was the only one awake. Slim lines of grey like the first pass of a spider making a web showed in the black of her hair. We talked.

"Were you there when Eisenhower was here?" I ventured.

"Oh, yes, that was something," she said with a smile. She looked above me as though looking into a memory that hung just over my bed. "I certainly was."

She looked down at me again, glad that of all the patients in the ward, someone was aware of those days. "He was a very loved president, don't ya know. Everyone loved that man."

I saw her name tag on her shirt. "You know Gladys, when I was a little boy only about five or six years old, I remember praying that he would win the election. It was one of the first real prayers that I remember praying for in earnest. I remember telling my dad, 'Dad, I am praying for Eisenhower that he will win.' He did not say anything to that; he was a working man and Eisenhower was a Republican, but he could not hide his surprise I was aware of such things so young. Anyway, I interrupted you. Tell me about it."

"Oh, he was a very loved man. He had a heart attack, you know, and they gave him the whole eighth floor, because the country was run from there. They had offices and secret service. People from all over the country sent flowers every day he was here and the halls were filled with them. He had his own room so he could rest."

"Were you there for that?"

"Oh yes. Such an honor. He was a grand man. He was very loved you know."

"I'm not keeping you, am I?"

"No, the floor is quiet now. Someone sent him a pair of red

pajamas with the words, 'I'm Doing Better, Thanks,' embroidered on them. He wore them for a press conference. He was that kind of man."

I smiled at her and her obvious fondness for the president.

"Oh, I remember another thing: his wife Mamie. She had the room next to him so she could be close. They asked her what she would like from their home so she could have it here. I think she was joking but she said, 'Just the pink toilet seat cover from our home.' And they brought it. The next day someone from the Secret Service came in with a pink toilet seat cover under his arm."

She shook her head and smiled at the memory.

"Oh," she said, "I have a letter for you. It came from Vietnam and was sent to you in Japan. It took a while for us to get it as they did not know where you were." She held it with both hands and presented it to me like a China plate, a precious thing.

"I'm on duty until morning so if you need anything let me know."

They gave me a thorough physical in the morning, parts of which continued through the day. A doctor came in and said I was healing fine. Regarding my legs and being nearly pulled apart when we were in the strings and caught in the trees, it was an uncertainty they would fully heal. He said, "But you have worms. Lots of them. We will take care of that today."

After breakfast a nurse came in. "Well sergeant, we'll take care of those worms." She held up a tiny paper cup with two red pills shaped like very large jelly beans. They usually give you one. Here's two. Take them. Don't go too far from the john. This doesn't kill the worms; it only gets them so drunk they forget to hold on."

She hovered over me to be sure I understood it all. Then she smiled. "Bottoms up Sarge." And she waited to be sure I swallowed them down.

She was young and pretty and she sashayed from the room, knowing that I was watching her.

I guess I was looped. I had been dozing and woke with the room gently turning around. I was sitting in my bed with the back rolled up in a sitting position. In one fist, still in the wrapper, was a cigar.

I don't smoke, much less in a hospital, and further, I do not recall how I got the cigar. On my chest with the pages open was the newest James Bond book. It was the first book written in the series after the death of Ian Fleming. It was called Colonel Sun and was written by Robert Markham.

I glanced at the cover. Just left of center was the full-color handsome face of James Bond. His brow was furrowed, a knight on a mission. To the left, facing upward was his pistol, held in his right hand, his finger on the trigger. To his left was a blond girl in a bikini. On the right side of the cover, painted all in pale, sinister green tones was Colonel Sun. M, the head of the Secret Service, had been kidnapped. Assisted by a Greek spy, they traced him to an Aegean island where a sinister plot of international dimensions unfolded. I know I was smiling as I looked, eager to read.

Inside the book, marking my page, was my letter from Mike. I opened it and read it again. I was surprised: On the very day I had been shot in the hand on our mission, Mike and RT Maine were in a life and death struggle of their own. I held the letter in the same esteem the nurse had and read it again.

Rain arrived. Just a few drops at first. Slim fingers tapping Morse code on the tin roof of the Quonset hut. Sergeant Dave Baker, the team leader of RT Maine, heard it and looked at the sky. Droplets struck his forehead. Would it be heavy with dark overcast, a preview of the coming days, or a passing shower? It mattered. Overcast and squalls could delay Maine's mission, or worse, prevent air support if they needed it. Accomplishing the mission was the first priority for any team, but he wanted every chance his people would survive them. There were breaks in the clouds. At the horizon the sky was not a blanket of mortuary-grey of a front moving in. There were patches of blue sky over the launch site, and a breeze came from the South China Sea to the east, carrying moisture. South of the control tower, sunlight reached her yellow arm through an opening in the mist and placed her hand on the far side of the runway leaving the concertina wire yellow and shining.

The SPAF pilot was standing next to him and saw him looking.

"Patchy but clearing, I think. It is better over the target. At least it was yesterday."

Dave Baker nodded in agreement. "I hope it stays for this mission. Let's go find us an LZ to get in there."

Baker walked over to the O2-Skymaster, his rifle in one hand and his web gear slung over the other shoulder. Baker was the average guy on the street: hair, build, demeanor, mannerisms. Everything about him blended in the crowd, a perfect spy if he so chose. He was quiet in temperament; as the Scripture says, "not puffed up." Under that veneer of commonness was a very brave, intelligent, experienced tactician, who was cool under fire. With Baker's leadership and that of his predecessor, Dave Kirschbaum, Maine became a highly skilled unit, a machine; the individuals in it thought as one mind. In the words of Michael Buckland, "We were an organism, not an organization."

Their target was deep into Communist-controlled territory, fifteen miles across the Laotian border. Somewhere in the thickness, tucked among the ridges and steep valleys, hidden under the canopy of trees was a suspected battalion or regimental size base camp of hard core NVA. Maine was tasked to find it.

The SOG men boarded the spotter plane and headed west into forbidden country.

Scattered showers and clouds lay between the launch site and the target and they dodged them en route. Coming out of especially dark squalls they found landmarks, reassessed their path and worked their way over the suspect area.

"I'm looking for an LZ, just big enough for a helicopter, but I do not want to go directly over it." Baker said.

Most of the One-Zeros wanted to fly over the actual LZ and see for themselves, but SPAF nodded to Baker, "Roger that. No point letting Charlie know you are coming."

They flew high enough it would not appear they were interested in the area, but low enough to make out subtle openings in the forest.

Off the cowling of the spotter plane, to the front-left lay an indentation in the earth.

"What is that over there?"

SPAF studied it for a minute. "Looks like a slash-burn, an old one. Someone long ago must have farmed there and abandoned it." They needed not to speculate the reason. The villagers may have fled the Communists, knowing their cruelty, made the long trek east, walking for days. Anything was better than to be impressed into the hands of slavery.

Dave used the binoculars and examined it for detail from his seat on the far side. "Doesn't look recent for sure." He looked carefully at the area around it. Baker resisted the urge to fly directly over for a closer look. "I don't see any sign anyone is around now. Just forest and thick brush right up to the edge. Let's use that one tomorrow."

"Will do," the pilot responded, "That should hold your helicopter, maybe even two or three of them. Thick stuff all the way to the edge."

Recon Team Maine—three Special Forces men and five Montagnard fighters—waited at the launch site. A shower was passing through. The sky was broken with patches of grey-blue cloud and scattered areas of blue. Their insert helicopters were en route, about to arrive; two H-34 Kingbees with their Vietnamese crews. Sherman Miller, who rarely spoke, found a dry place under the eaves and sat on his rucksack. Black hair showed under his flop hat. His brow was furrowed and intense. Miller had an even temperament; regardless of the situation he was the same: unruffled and solid.

Mike Buckland carried the radio and patrolled immediately behind Baker at the front. He too was unruffled under stress, intelligent and quick thinking. He was an intellectual, Christian, spoke several languages, never swore, drank, or smoked.

Next to them, five Montagnard tribesmen waited with their weapons. They, like their American leaders, were stoic and unruffled under pressure.

Covey dropped in and taxied to the group. "Looks good over the target area. The area is clear of clouds. We did not fly directly over the LZ. See you in Laos," he said and he returned to the plane and lifted off.

# SOG: Missions to the Well

The Kingbees landed in their camouflage paint, sterile of markings, set for the day. Maine boarded and headed west.

It was clear over the slash-burn and looked like just another day below. Until Maine in their helicopters arrived making a straight-in approach, the field below seemed pristine. Had there been deer or monkeys in the clear-cut eating the vegetables that came up of themselves when those farmers fled the land, their first indication of the arrival of the Americans would have been their descent into the opening. But there were no deer to jerk their heads upright and turn their large ears like antennae before bounding off, no animals of any kind. It was as empty as a stadium. The morning was quiet; no breeze brushed the leaves or stirred the grass. The lead H-34 flew in out of the sun with the sudden sound of engine, sloped in and hovered just long enough for the team to hop out onto the slash-burn. As quickly, the Kingbees rose into the air and arced away leaving only the faint image of their shape and color in the memory of anyone below.

For a moment, not much longer than a flinch, they stood alone in the center of the opening in their sterile uniforms. Teams always rushed from the LZ and headed for cover in the nearby brush to appraise the situation. They froze. It was only a few seconds, but they froze. There was no signal, no one spoke a command. Each soldier took in the information around them and as a single unit, they understood the state of affairs: there were no trees and undergrowth toward which to run. Instead, there were bunkers! Bunkers all around. They were sturdy structures, nearly bombproof, of heavy logs and earth and camouflaged to perfection. Even the old slash-burn on which they landed was not walked on—no trails, nothing to reveal what it really was from the air. Perfectly hidden until one were to drop in on it, a Venus fly trap. The men glanced around them. In every direction, the full circumference, were bunkers, enemy bunkers. They were in the exact center of a military complex. Here was the moment the gladiators of old must have felt in the Roman Colosseum, "We who are about to die salute you." Only floodlights on them could have made them more conspicuous.

The team's arrival out of the clear sky and the engine noise left the enemy in complete surprise. Soldiers poured from the bunkers. Two 12.7 heavy machine guns were permanently mounted on top of a pair of bunkers. The SOG men watched as crews of North Vietnamese scrambled to their place behind the guns. In small portions of a minute, one or two dozen armed soldiers in pith helmets stood gazing on each bunker. Perhaps a hundred if not two hundred filled the circle around the team.

But the enemy were perplexed, dazed at the spectacle in front of them. "Who were these people?" seemed to be their prevailing thought. They did not shoot.

Maine held their weapons, CAR-15 rifles, definitely American made, along their thighs out of sight.

From one end of the complex, six ranking PAVN officers strode quickly and deliberately toward the team. Their steps said, "We will get to the meaning of this." There was anger, irritation, and puzzlement in their approach.

Buckland had the radio. Like a prophet he could see the events unfold. He whispered into the radio handset, "Have inserted into a major unit. Not yet engaged. Standby for some serious stuff."

In moments the six were within twenty meters of the team. The officer in the lead seemed to be in charge. They were close enough that Mike Buckland read his rank on the shoulder boards, Lieutenant Colonel. He saw the Tokarev pistol tucked at his waist. He also read his face. The officer and those surrounding the team did not know who they were. But that would change in seconds.

Buckland appraised the quandary immediately. The Kingbees were unmarked and looked like the Russian MI-5 helicopters. The uniforms the team wore were sterile of patches and the men showed no aggression. The officer thought Maine was Russian Spetsnaz.

But the officer was angry, furious. The expression was, "What are you doing here. Why was I not informed?"

Before the enemy officer got closer and demanded answers, Mike stepped forward with Baker and the point man one step behind, raised one hand in greeting and said in a loud voice, "*Dobroye utro, tovarishch—eto doroga na Moskvu?*" (Good day, comrade. Is this the road to Moscow?)

The officer was startled. The serious stuff was about to happen. There was nothing left.

It was time to dance.

Without a word to the others, Buckland raised his CAR-15 and shot the colonel twice in the midsection. There was a moment of briefest surprise, before his eyes rolled back and he collapsed. Baker double-tapped the one he thought was number two. Kiep, the point man joined them and the three men proceeded to down the six officers.

Lifelessly, the officer element dropped to the grass with an audible thud. Two AK rifles cluttered together as they slid from lifeless fingers. There was a last, loud gasp of air from one of them; two seconds of silence had its time on the stage. In it, dominating the ear, was an unmistakable sound. A gunner on one of the bunkers pulled back the metal slide of his machinegun and prepared to shoot.

The heavy machine guns were their immediate danger. Buckland turned to the gun crew manning the 12.7 machine gun on the right as Baker did the one on the left. Two shots double-tapped each enemy of the gun crew. As though they could not miss, their rounds struck home. Death flung the enemy behind their guns to the grass-covered roof and silenced the weapons. But even as they did so more soldiers ran to take their place.

The enemy who lined the bunkers were stunned. They did not react for ten seconds, an eon of time in a battle. Their weapons remained at their sides, their mouths open in amazement.

They were numbed stiff, but that was changing. Those frozen soldiers were thawing into movement, waking, about to train and fire their weapons, hundreds of them, at the team. Maine could not survive that. They had to engage them now in the respite they had. The imperative was to eliminate every soldier in the compound, and they had to conserve their ammunition. There could be more soldiers than they had bullets. Discipline: two shots per target.

Sherman Miller and the tribesmen were clearing the stunned soldiers on the tops of the bunkers. Each SOG man made short bursts at the clusters of enemies, then went to two shots at each person. The M-79 man on the team sent his rifle grenades into the clusters of men on the roofs. Again, they practically could not miss. Twelve to eighteen enemy on each of several bunkers. Eliminated. Bodies lined the roofs. One lay dead on his back, his leg dangling over the side. One wounded man on a bunker lay on his back just out of sight. Only his arm was seen as it twitched and jerked in the air. The bunkers had no slots on the inside to engage an adversary. They only had them on the other side where they could expect an attack. To engage Maine, they had to climb to the top where they were cut down by the firepower of the recon team.

From the far side of the compound, 160–180 enemy moved in their direction, some taking position on the bunkers surrounding the slash-burn.

Heavy machine guns again. Buckland de-manned them. Baker pointed to a depression in the slash-burn. "There! Go there."

The dip in the field was slight, but enough for limited cover. Maine flung off their rucksacks and shielded behind them for cover. Incoming fire grew. The bunkers around them were re-manned by enemy. Incoming fire increased.

The 12.7 was fully manned again. A khakied soldier hovered behind the sights as his assistant gunner held the belt of ammunition and fed it into the receiver. The heavy machine gun fired on the team fully automatic. But the rounds went high, skimming over the heads of the team. The machine gun had been fixed to fend off attack from the outside and from air attack. They could not depress the barrel low enough to engage the team, instead the rounds were hitting their own people on the opposite side of the circle.

Someone was screaming in Vietnamese. It came from the opposite side of the field where the 12.7 rounds impacted. The interpreter ran to Baker. "Man, him say, 'No shoot, no shoot. You hit us!'"

Baker glanced across. NVA were wildly waving and screaming unheard across the field.

The communists brought in 60 mm mortars. Maine heard the,

"whumff, whumff," as the rounds left the tubes and expected the worse when they fell. Seconds later the rounds exploded—on their own bunkers. Soldiers were tossed into the air. There were shouts of pain. Anger. Shouting went up the line of bunkers until it reached the mortar crews and the incoming ceased.

The Communists discovered the mortars and firepower were not dislodging the team. They began a new thing: human wave attacks.

About eighteen North Vietnamese charged the group in the depression. Maine had seconds before the enemy would be among them, if the team remained alive. They maintained their discipline, aimed center of mass, and double-tapped the charging force. Many fell to the rifle fire. Not enough. Buckland rose high enough to throw and began to heft the M-26 hand grenades and the more powerful M-33 baseball grenades. Maine ceased their fire on the charge. The bodies lay from where the charge began and ended nearly at their feet.

Miller directed fire on the bunkers as shooters continued to arrive and engage the team from the tops.

Air support arrived. Buckland directed the Cobras to fire their rockets and 20 mm cannons on the bunkers. Explosions erupted along the perimeter and the 20 mm cannons left their lethality in their wake.

Heavy RPG rounds exploded among the team. Small arms fire increased toward the team.

Shouting from the north, the side from which the six officers came. Were they providing an endless supply of men from another compound? Another human wave attack began.

They charged, their bodies leaned forward under their pith helmets, rifles thrust forward, a poster for a North Vietnamese recruiter. They screamed out their rage as they ran.

Baker, Buckland, and the little people closest to them engaged the enemy. "Bang, bang. Bang, bang," double tapping the enemy, watching them fall, but not fast enough.

Buckland half-stood again, tossing grenades among the thickest part of the onslaught. Three explosions among the enemy. Two more sets of double taps. The charge ended.

Baker reached for his RT-10 radio. A bullet went through it, smashing it as he spoke.

Buckland continued to direct the air. A1-E dropped their heavy bombs on the bunkers as directed.

Another human wave attack.

As before, they charged, intent on destroying the team. Their screaming was a PAVN version of "Banzai" nearly as loud as the weapons they fired. Passing bullets whizzed above the team. B-40 rockets exploded around them. Green tracers raced toward them, and again the team fired with discipline. Aim, two shots. Aim, two shots. The front ranks were falling, but a mass was yet behind them to destroy the team.

Buckland rose again and threw the last of his grenades. With that, the third charge was broken. The team inserted fresh magazines anticipating another charge.

It was about to happen. Loud shouting from the endless source of attackers. Officers, sergeants, brave men among them shouted to encourage the rest. They seemed to gather a larger contingent of soldiers.

Baker took the radio and talked with control.

He shouted to Buckland. "Covey says they could try to come in and get us, but I don't think the helicopters could survive the landing. What do you think? I told them, 'No.'"

A loud shout. At least two dozen bunched for the next assault on the team. "I agree, they wouldn't be able to live through it."

Baker got back on the radio just as the fourth charge began. "That's a negative on the extract. They've got heavy machine guns still. We'll hold our ground and keep pounding them with tac air before any extraction attempts are made."

The charge began. More severe than before. It began with B-40 rocket explosions and the determined "pop, pop" of rapid AK-47 fire. Incoming was intense. The last charge was stopped only yards from the depression, close enough to see the expressions on the faces of the last to fall. If this were to be stopped, they needed more grenades.

Buckland, ever polite, turned to Miller, "Sherm, could I borrow one or two of your grenades, please?"

He was surprised at Buckland's anomalous words and shuffled over to him with an armful.

Maine offered their disciplined fire to the enemy and the ranks fell, some stumbled over the bodies of those who died before. Among the press, Buckland heaved grenades and for a fourth time the assault failed.

A-4 jets arrived. Baker directed heavy bombs and cluster bombs on the enemy. They kept coming.

A fifth assault. As before, the mass was ginned up by shouts and orders from the other side of the compound. Two dozen or more soldiers with **RPD** machine guns, RPG rockets and assault rifles. Maine administered their disciplined firepower. The NVA stumbled over the piles of their own dead but continued to advance. Buckland stepped forward and threw the last of his grenades. This time the jets were there and dropped their cluster bombs.

A pile of dead lay before the depression. At a place or two, a slight movement of a sleeve or pant leg among them.

Baker was bleeding. A stream of blood coursed into his eye and along his cheek. A piece of shrapnel had struck him on the forehead. Irritating, not debilitating. He continued with the handset.

The area around the team smoked. Orders were shouted from among the broken bunkers. Men ran to ordered positions in their khaki uniforms carrying bandoleers and backpacks of ammunition. A crew was trying to re-set the heavy weapons that had been blown off the bunker. From the far corner it was clear: another human wave was about to begin.

A-1E fighter planes were overhead.

Baker: "About to be overrun. Bring napalm. Bring it close, danger close."

"Confirm, danger close?"

"Affirm. Do it now. Do it now or there will be none of us to care."

"Roger. Heads down."

The plane passed overhead. A 750-pound canister dropped like a giant capsule. To anyone who watched it, the fall of napalm was a thing of slow motion, and the eight men who stood little chance of holding off this sixth human assault watched its descent. It took all of the resolve of each soldier to force himself to aim-shoot, aim-shoot, when there was a certitude it would not be enough this time. A glance up said, "relief is coming," but they doubted they would be alive to see it.

The napalm canister was falling . . . was falling . . . was falling.

They continued to squeeze the triggers of their rifles. Aim-shoot. Always take the nearest one; the most dangerous one.

Was falling.

And it struck. It seemed effete at first, no loud boom, no crack of explosion, no molten metal shards flew to slice a wound. Instead, there was a loud "poof." It landed in front of the team, danger close. A flash. White matter sprayed the area, a black angry cloud of death. Air was sucked out of the area as it ignited, even the breaths of the living. Twelve to sixteen soldiers briefly turned into flame. They were still upright holding their weapons, in a stance of a running charge, but frozen in place like those of Pompei under the ash of Vesuvius. Buckland watched as the last of the attackers tuned black and cindered to the ground only thirty feet away.

Fragments of the napalm splattered the team. Perhaps someone had prayed for them for the splatters that struck the team did not ignite as it did among the Communists. Napalm landed on their hands and shirts and did not ignite. Rucksacks were set afire but were quickly flipped over and smothered. One piece landed on the stock of a Montagnard's rifle and it began to burn and melt, but they rolled it over and smothered it in the dirt.

The team took stock. The back of the battalion had been broken. Maine was yet alive. They looked around the depression. Mere yards in front of the team the enemy lay in heaps, piles. Napalm still smoldered. They virtually had no casualties themselves. They glanced in the direction from which there seemed to be an inexhaustible supply of enemy. Nothing moved in their direction.

## SOG: Missions to the Well

They still took fire from the bunker line. It was desultory, poorly aimed. A look above showed a gun crew setting up another 12.7 machine gun. It would easily take out a helicopter.

Mike removed a partly empty magazine from his weapon and replaced it with a full one. He slid the half empty one into his shirt. Those would be his final rounds. He reached back into his rucksack and retrieved three or four magazines and one grenade he carried which would not fit into his web gear and prepared for the next wave. His people observed it and followed suit.

The radio crackled.

"We still have the bunkers to worry about. There is anti-aircraft capability there. Put in one more napalm on that, then come and get us."

This time the men in the depression watched the slow, very slow, canister leave the plane, followed it with their eyes, saw it utterly to the end. They saw it erupt, heard the whoomph, tracked its billow under the black cloud.

Then they heard the Kingbee over the hill, the engines muted by the vegetation, a low rumble, and they watched it hover and wait for them as the Scripture says, "as a hen gathers her chicks."

In this battle was ample time to age, to grow old, to be a seasoned veteran.

It lasted forty-three minutes.

# CHAPTER TEN
*New York's Christmas Eve Mission*

It was nearly Christmas in my hometown in northern Minnesota. With the runoff of the wet summer and attending strong current, Rainy River, the border between the United States and Canada had not frozen. Steam drifted across and frosted the trees along the bank. Most of the shop windows in town were outlined with the new trend: strings of all-white lights instead of red and green. Minneapolis said traditional red and green was associated with Christmas and was deemed too religious. Even the oak trees along the street dazzled in white, the strings reflecting themselves in the crystal of the snow.

Mr. Olsen of Olsen's Meat Market, "Fresh From Friendly Farms," was "having nothing to do with that nonsense," and stuck with red and green to frame his windows. Besides, he liked the colors. His world was red and green, fresh, red meat on sheets of green paper. Mr. Melville, the art teacher in the school told him the two colors were on the opposite sides of the color wheel. Together, the presence of one magnified the color of the other. Green paper, more attractive beef. He admired the colors in his window. "Matched the colors of my trade," he thought, scratching his chin as he examined the case from the sidewalk.

Woolworth's Five and Dime, and a few other gift stores stayed open for late shoppers but were closing their doors for the night. Mr. Ericksen in his wool trench coat was the last merchant. He was tight fisted and paused on the sidewalk deciding if he should leave the lights on in his window case. "All that electricity." He faced the door with his key and set the lock. The turn of the bolt sounded loud down the silent street.

Outside the main door of Woolworth's, the Salvation Army lady behind the red donation kettle ceased to ring her bell. She was old. Except for greyness under her eyes and her red nose, her skin was white, the color of old snow. A thick wool scarf was wrapped over her hair and tightly tied under her chin. Almost reverently, she closed the lid and waited for her ride. She was frail and shifted her weight from foot to foot. Swaying back and forth with her hands in her pockets, she tucked her face into her coat for her warm breath. As the Salvation Army van drew to the curb she looked up. Her breath steamed from her coat.

In the park off main street, teenagers hung a wreath around the huge statue of Smokey the Bear. Having no ladder, they did it by making a living, laughing, human pyramid. But even standing two levels high on the shoulders of those below, they could reach only to his waist where they tossed the wreath until it finally caught on Smokey's shovel. They stood back and shrugged. "Looks like Smokey shoveling a fire break."

I was on convalescent leave from hot and humid Vietnam. Skating. I was almost at the end of my leave, healing from wounds to my head, legs, and hand. It was cold, northern Minnesota cold. The month I spent in hospital in the Dakotas with its own cold and blizzard-wind shrieking across the prairie was scant acclimation for International Falls, "the cold spot of the nation." But stars filled the sky, bright and clear. Somewhere above, there must have been thin whisps of cloud, for the stars twinkled. All was still, a silent night with no wind to blow the stars around. Perhaps it was on a night like this that Vincent Van Gogh in his freckles and red hair took off his ice skates and said to himself, "I need to go home and paint this."

We were in the heating shed of the ice rink next to Smokey the Bear, my girlfriend and me. It was referred to as the band shell rink. When I was a boy, musicians performed outdoor concerts at the band shell in the summer. The back of the stage was in the shape of a giant shell that thrust the music toward the audience. Bands played as folks sat on folding chairs and fanned themselves with their programs. Sometimes bagpipers came from Canada and extra chairs were filled with listeners from "across the river." Inside the heating shed, the electric heater blew warm air from the ceiling. Under the heater, astride a sturdy plank bench sat the caretaker. He didn't look up from his cribbage game as we entered. He was grizzled and unshaven, with messy black hair and a toothpick in his mouth. He slapped his cards down as he counted. He mouthed the toothpick like a cigar.

I had trouble tying my hockey skates. My wounded hand still ached when I used it. But with Robyn helping with the knot, we got them tight enough to be firm on my feet with no slop. She was pretty and smiled as she waited for me on her white skates. Her red hair streamed from under her stocking cap and hung over her shoulders.

Our skates clopped on the plank floor as we went to the door. The caretaker never looked up, but as I waited, holding the door open for Robyn. He shouted as he slapped down his cards, "Shut the door. I'm freezing."

The ice was brittle-cold, and the moon laid its arm across the rink to show us the way. I held her gloved hand and we skated around the edge. For a time, a couple dozen people skated around us, mostly children who called to each other and laughed when they fell. One child was so bundled his legs could not bend and when he tumbled to the ice, he could not rise without help.

Northern lights swayed on a darker part of the sky and I remembered writing a poem referring to them as God's curtains. The aurora was crisp and clear and I imagined I heard them rustle, but that might have just been this pristine and pacific evening in which I skated with pretty Robyn. The children had left the ice and we skated alone. Neither of us talked. There was only the sound of our skates.

We stopped at a corner of the rink as the moon looked away and I kissed her. There was a sadness as we kissed. In a few days I would be going back to the war. What chance was there that I would live to return again when my unit received nearly 100% casualties every year? I remembered opening a small box I found in Grandma Hecker's closet. It was from my Uncle Herb, sent home from the Battle of the Bulge. It was full of shrapnel and bullets he had taken from the battle field. There were bullets in the box with bullet holes in them; the fierceness of the battle when bullets struck bullets in mid-air. Before Grandma even got the box in the mail, he was killed in that same battle. Robyn and I smiled, but we could not hide the sadness of parting.

Another emotion lay its shadow upon my soul. I felt guilty. Guilty for enjoying this pacific night. Eight thousand miles away my brothers were engaged in hairy missions deep behind enemy lines. In days, I would be back with them. Even as I thought this, my brothers were surely in peril.

The rink manager blinked the lights then dimmed them. "Time to leave," they said. We put on our boots, tied our skates together by the laces, thrust them over our shoulders, and hand in hand made our way to the door.

The caretaker was folding his cards into the pack.

\* \* \* \* \*

Reconnaissance Team New York was airborne—8,330 miles from Smokey the Bear and the ice rink—en route to a SOG mission in Southeastern Laos. It was a mission of peril in which ultimately, they would be hard pressed and hunted by a skilled enemy. The target was Tango-7, assigned by the Seventh Air Force and SOG headquarters in Saigon. Wolcoff's eight-man team was tasked to infiltrate and maneuver in enemy controlled lands, set up a road watch along Laotian Route 110, and monitor enemy traffic. It would be the third time the team leader would be in the area.

That area of Laos was sanctuary for several elite regiments of PAVN. It was deemed to be saturated with highly skilled and motivated enemy. Weeks before, only two miles from New York's target, Recon Team Hawaii under Glenn Uemura had their harrowing mission in which Dennis Bingham had been killed.

Wolcoff's first encounter in Tango-7 was to reconnoiter this same road. It was a major support route, a highly protected section of the Ho Chi Minh Trail network which funneled troops and material to the war. Somewhere, within the gullies and ridges of Tango-7, and well camouflaged under a canopy of trees, lay a headquarters; hidden like an African tick unseen in the folds of a rhino's hide. These bounds marked the sanctuary of the elite 66th NVA regiment, their support, and their command.

For three days New York conducted reconnaissance in that backyard without detection. On the fourth day as the team exited a bamboo forest, the point man heard voices in Vietnamese, in the dialect of the north. They crept forward. Before them was a large, cleared area with four permanent structures made of logs. A canopy of camouflage was stretched over the entire complex. It seemed certain they had found the tick in the rhino's hide—a major Communist headquarters, at least a regiment in size, perhaps the 66th. The One-Zero of the team, Sergeant John St. Martin, decided to call in a very large airstrike, after which New York would immediately assault on what remained of the headquarters, try for a prisoner, and gather what items of intelligence they could find in the buildings. The plan was authorized by Kontum and as assets arrived on station, St. Martin marked his position and that of the target. The attack from the air began utilizing numerous 500-pound bombs and CBU bomblets. The base area erupted into an unsurvivable mass of fire and explosions. The team readied themselves as near the base as they dared, danger-close, and waited for word the last bomb had fallen. Word came. "Last bomb." Sergeants St. Martin, Wolcoff, Blaauw, and the rest of the team charged, firing their weapons full-automatic, tossing grenades, and unleashed all the firepower of the team.

It might have been hoped that everything living had been eliminated but was not the case. As they assaulted the base, a group of soldiers were running their way. A fire fight ensued in which several enemies were immediately cutdown by the team. The fight grew in intensity as enemy poured from the buildings which were yet standing. In the ensuing fight, John St. Martin received massive injuries. An AK bullet struck his thigh, one foot was nearly blown off and hung backwards by strings of flesh; his intestines poured from his stomach. The fight quickly grew larger than they could handle. Wolcoff took over the team and as heavy firepower was directed at the recon team, made contact with Davis who rode Covey that day. The small plane flew over the pressed team and directed them to the nearest LZ. It was a running fight for survival in which Wolcoff alternately returned fire on the advancing foe, communicated with the assets on the radio and struggled to drag the wounded team leader to the LZ. St. Martin outweighed Wolcoff by forty pounds and he could barely budge him on the uneven floor of the forest. He pointed to a striker, "You. Help drag St. Martin." The Montagnards loved St. Martin and the tribesman slung his weapon and eagerly helped to tow his leader the remaining 75 meters to the sought-for opening in the trees. With his men suppressing fire, along with the air assets, Wolcoff better wrapped St. Martin's stomach in his shirt and web gear to contain his intestines and prepared him for extraction by Swiss seat.

A glance around him showed his team accounted for, suspended from the ropes which hung below the helicopter. As they lifted off and ascended above the trees, Cobra gunships swooped below them bringing their lethal pass of death to the LZ. Moments later they were high above seeing the land below in shades of green, with a lighter green which marked the place of death they had just left. He watched as white flashes of napalm and billowing grey smoke poured from the place of their escape.

It was late in the day. Had assets not been nearby, the team would not have made it out. St. Martin, strong and hard to kill, was evacuated to Japan for the care of his wounds. He never healed enough to return to the war.

Wolcoff's second mission to Tango-7 was to do a bomb damage assessment. Such BDA missions were tasked to send a team in just after one of the huge B-52 bomb strikes and tabulate the effects of the bomb run. Often, when teams arrived at the place of destruction, they encountered formations of enemy that were doing the same thing. Those investigating troops rushed to the scene only to halt in amazement and utter shock at the moonscape that had been their base. They were dazed as they walked, looking left and right, not so much for the SOG team as the great effects of the bombs. They might discover a boot and leg, a crumpled torso of a man in torn fatigues, or passing by a tree shred of leaves see a body part hanging from a limb. Shock and amazement would quickly turn to unbridled anger as they sought the team to vent their fury. Often the BDA mission would be anticipated and great effort was made to intercept those teams en route and annihilate them. For this mission, Wolcoff informed the Operations section that he wanted to go in right after the bomb drop, land directly on the site in the morning, do the assessment, and be lifted off the same day. His request was approved.

Smoke still seeped from the ruins and shredded trees and structures as the team landed directly on the site of the bomb run. They smelled the acrid smoke and fresh-turned soil. Slight sounds of earth and debris settling to their new stasis were faintly heard. Moving cautiously across the site, they discovered a large tunnel complex. It was large and significant. Was it a place for storage, an underground headquarters, or even a place where prisoners might be held? The fearful Montagnards would not venture into the cave, so Wolcoff, with a pistol and penlight, began an exploration of the tunnels. He made it only a short distance into the depths when he noticed the sides showed signs of crumbling and imminent collapse because of the explosions. He retraced his steps and as he emerged from the network, saw panic in the faces of some of his Montagnard strikers. Large forces were on the far side of the impact area and were rapidly approaching. By the look in his strikers' eyes, it seemed they had been discovered. Having accomplished their mission, New York radioed Covey circling in the next valley and requested an immediate extraction. A quick pass-over and the Covey rider steered the team to the nearest LZ that could accommodate an incoming Kingbee.

Expeditiously, with regard to the fast-approaching enemy, they hustled toward the pick-up location. They nearly did not make it. Perhaps what saved them was the black fatigues Wolcoff always wore and the modified version of the Communist RPD machine gun in his hands. At first glance he appeared to be a North Vietnamese regular or Russian advisor. As the team hustled toward the opening in the trees, his people moved wide-eyed and trance-like, looking fearfully about like children rushing through a graveyard. Unknown to Wolcoff, they had just passed through a large enemy ambush position. This he learned only later from his strikers. Perhaps the trap had not been sprung because New York was dressed similarly as the uniforms of the NVA and Wolcoff and his team may have been mistaken for their own. That, coupled with the circling aircraft above may have saved them.

The tension among the Indig was severe, a taut string about to snap. Their bodies were stiff in apprehension, backs bent, shoulders thrust forward as they approached the pick-up area and the thinning of the vegetation. His people sensed the LZ and its offered escape. They heard the oncoming engines. At the last, as the Kingbee sloped to a hover, the point man lost his nerve, sprang from cover, and dashed for the safety of the approaching helicopter, leaving his teammates behind.

It may have been too many missions, too many close calls, too many friends lost in faraway targets, but this was the last one for the point man on New York.

War often has its anomalies. Like the Christmas truce of a past world war in which soldiers in a trench of one side of the fight, lit candles and sang Silent Night. Some, as they sang, recalled the deep meaning of the words, "Christ has come." Some men, sitting on their helmets, actually sang to the enemy on the other side of the field. On this one day the enemy in the grey coat was someone like themselves, just a soldier, far from home. From the trenches across "no man's land," where uniforms emptied themselves of those who wore them and fell, yet remained on the field, those words drifted over:

*Stille Nacht, heilige Nacht*
*Alles schläft, einsam wacht*
*Nur das traute, hochheilige Paar*
*Holder Knabe im lockigen Haar*
*Schlaf in himmlischer Ruh*
*Schlaf in himmlischer Ruh*

*Silent night, holy night*
*All is calm, all is bright*
*Round yon Virgin Mother and Child*
*Holy Infant so tender and mild*
*Sleep in heavenly peace*
*Sleep in heavenly peace*

New York prepared to slip into Tango-7 and its grave lethality for the third time. Even as they shuffled to the airfield to do so, cargo planes rumbled in to Kontum airfield, heavy with post office bags: packages for soldiers from home, presents—canned peaches, wool socks from grandma, even fruit cake to be passed from hand to hand. In two or three days it would be Christmas.

The sides of the conflict in Vietnam agreed to a truce in which each side would not fire on the other over the holiday. There was hope the tidings bore truth, but it was a time of suspicion. The utter deceit of the Tet Offensive had not been forgotten. True, some holiday agreements in the past had held. The tick bird of truce in its paper-white plumage and rubber feet strutted inside the alligator's wide-open mouth, safe because it cleaned its teeth. It was in those times of hiatus, under the dark and starry sky of the holy night, the Communists used the lull to safely move their material of war to position itself for the next day.

In preparation for the holiday, cargo planes carried massive amounts of frozen turkey, dressing, cranberries, and all that that went with it. There was pumpkin pie and whipped cream, dill pickles, even Christmas candy. Plans were made that dinners would even be flown to the most remote Special Forces A camps. Bing Crosby's White Christmas would be played on AFVN, the radio station broadcast across the war-torn land.

It was in this period of time that RT New York "came from the east."

They flew high, well above anti-aircraft fire. With the altitude, it was cold in the open H-34 Kingbee helicopter but Wolcoff was asleep on his back. Around him five Montagnard tribesmen and two other Americans readied themselves in their thoughts. A Montagnard drummed his fingers on the stock of his rifle.

As they approached the target, the rotor blades altered pitch and the team felt the change of movement. The choppers dipped for descent. Wolcoff was instantly awake. His team straightened for the quick leap to the ground and the unknown that awaited them. A glance from the helicopter confirmed Wolcoff's memory from his previous missions in the area: the tall bamboo and dense hardwood trees were taller than any reach of ladders or length of rappelling ropes. It was necessary to use an opening in the canopy to infiltrate. They picked the smallest break in the trees that would not strike the rotor blades and hoped with its small size, it had not attracted the attention of those who tried to monitor every opening in the Central Highlands.

Thousands of North Vietnamese were committed to watch every break in the trees large enough for a helicopter to land and discharge a SOG team. From the elite of their own army, their own Special Forces, Hanoi created highly skilled hunter-killer teams whose primary purpose was to eliminate Special Ops teams. They used every subterfuge and resource to kill or capture SOG personal. In addition, PAVN utilized 40,000 line-soldiers to monitor infiltration and protect their support system.

Wolcoff had chosen a place near the primary entry point and the Kingbee dipped and squeezed in, the rotor blades slapping the upper leaves and limbs. Leaves rained down and were tossed by the wind of the blades. New York leaped from the craft and rushed into the nearby cover. In moments the pilot lifted off and sped to multiple false insertions in other areas. New York made a brief security stop to appraise the situation. It was often at the landing zone where many teams were shot out or destroyed along with the helicopters. On other occasions, teams became overrun after the support aircraft were dismissed and enemy rushed to the LZ and annihilated them.

The vegetation was dense. Watching enemy could be anywhere; in thick, low bushes, from leafy boughs of a tree. These were some of the most crucial moments of a recon team. They remained in tactical formation. Watched. Listened. The engines of the insertion craft had long gone. No sign of enemy watchers.

A shot.

It came from the northeast up a stream valley. More shots. The enemy was aware of the team and had signaled a pursuit. New York's road watch mission had just begun but it was already compromised. It would have been easy to call Covey, bring back the helicopters, and have Christmas dinner in the mess hall. But the team had been given a mission and Wolcoff would not be deterred at the first sign of enemy. The mantra—which was even on one of Doney's cards on the mess hall tables—was clear among seasoned Special Forces men: Break contact, continue mission.

The area of operations, Tango-7, was surrounded by hills and valleys. A significant stream lay in a valley to the east, from which the signal shots came. Wolcoff would evade and continue to his objective, the road watch of highway 110. He would complete the mission.

More shots from the valley to the east. Wolcoff signaled his point man to evade to the west. Hga, a Sadang Montagnard, nodded and pushed through the thickness. The team moved with stealth while attempting to distance itself from the pursuing enemy in the east. They crossed a small hill 200 meters away and encountered a network of well-used high-speed trails. The trails were oriented north-south, were well hidden, and parallelled the Dak Lay River to the west of the team.

More signal shots. Closer now

It appeared the North Vietnamese were massing from the east, fanning out as they grouped and closing rapidly toward the team. The indications were that additional forces would shortly approach from the high-speed trail system from both the north and the south and trap the team against the anvil of the river where they would be hammered out of existence

Signal shots became more frequent, closer now. They were being pushed and pressed against the river. The opportunity to make a decision of any kind was diminishing. He could contact Covey and declare a tactical emergency and abort the mission, if help could even get to them in time. He could perhaps set up and assault through the advancing forces from where they were and continue the mission from there. But there was one other option, a risky one. They would wade fully exposed across the Dak Lay River, set up an ambush on the other side and eliminate the enemy when they attempted to cross in their pursuit.

He rushed his people across the high-speed trail and paused at the river bank. He gazed across. There seemed to be no structures or signs of people on the other bank. The river was wide, mocha colored, and slow moving with no eddies or signs of a current. It was late in the dry season and the depth was at its lowest. At any other time, a venture across the exposed area would have been impossible. They would be in full display in the crossing, if they could do so at all and not drown or be ambushed halfway over. "The decision," he would say, "was fraught with danger."

He looked to the sides at his people as he hoisted his RPD over his shoulder, "Cross."

Another shot. This time slightly more to the northeast. It was followed by an answering shot from the southeast. The enemy was on line coming in their direction.

"Now," he ordered.

They stepped into the edge of the slow-moving current and proceeded across. They held their weapons high above the water. The little people were shocked. Amazed. A janitor who accidentally stumbled on the stage in the middle of a performance, caught in the flood lights. Some of them looked fearfully about. Others gazed before them at the deepening waters and the distance yet to go to the other side. The tail gunner, with his M-79 cradled over his shoulder, twisted his body around at the shore they had just left, expecting enemy to burst from the shrubs and fire on the team.

They tapped the river bottom with the toes of their boots before placing their feet. At any moment they expected to step into a hole and go over their heads. The level rose above the waists of the Americans, the chests of the tribesmen. Wolcoff did not look behind at the shore they had left, only the one before them.

Halfway. They held their weapons high in the air. The level was up to the chests of the Americans, to the chins of the tribesmen. Shorter tribesmen tilted their heads back, thrusting their chins and mouths as far as they could from the water. Fear and near-panic marked the faces of the little people. Would the next step be over their heads, and as they were weighted down with their gear? Americans placed their hands under the armpits of their men and buoyed them along. Some of the men bounced on the bottom, there was no purchase to wade.

The waters shallowed as they neared the far shore. The Yards sensed it and moved more quickly and soon scrambled to solid ground. Water poured from their ammo pouches. Silt-filled river water drained noisily from the small holes in their rucksacks.

No time could be lost. They needed to scramble to cover and prepare to ambush the trackers as they crossed mid-river.

"Go!" the One-Zero pointed up the bank and they rushed across the narrow belt of vegetation. The point man froze. He glanced back at Wolcoff, his mouth open in surprise. Before them was a road.

They were unaware there was such a road. It did not appear in aerial photos and was not on any map. It was well-used, hidden from view, and parallelled the river they had crossed. New York was in even greater danger than before. Perhaps even now truckloads of PAVN were en route on the very road they stood. Ambush on the pursuers from here was out of the question. They must cross and get off the road. They looked for a way. The road had been incised along a steep ridge and the sides had been cut into the ridge making steep cliffs along the way, cliffs they could not climb. They could not get off the road.

The decision to be made was an obvious one, and one to be made immediately. Wolcoff caught the eye of his point man and pointed down the road. "Go," and using hand signs signaled, "Hurry."

"Down the road!" he signaled to the rest of his people. Water still ran from their pouches and drained from their soaked fatigues and splashed on the road. Their soggy boots shushed with each step. They moved southward at speed looking for the first place they could exit the roadway.

Wolcoff glanced back where his people joined the road. The surface was wet with the runoff from the soldiers. Surely the trackers would know which way they had gone. He could only hope the sun would dry away the telltale trace of the team.

New York was fully exposed in the hard gravel and felt it. The faces of the team scanned like radar antennae on a ship, expecting opposing forces to rush in their direction. With the speed they moved they soon found themselves beyond the no bomb lines of their target, where even friendly firepower might be encountered. Enough distance had been covered that Wolcoff made the next decision. "At first opportunity we will re-cross the river to the other side where we will be beyond the flanks of their pursuers, evade to the east, then turn north again toward our objective and continue our mission."

They continued their rapid tactical march down the road until they passed a bend that was hidden from view of their first crossing. A place was in a thicket that edged the flow and they assembled for the crossing. Water no longer stained the road with their drip to betray their intentions. The tail gunner erased the signs of leaving the road and the team proceeded across. Although as exposed as at the first crossing, they were more confident this river would not be their grave.

Back on the east side of the Dak Lay, the reconnaissance force reasoned they had skirted the flank of the sweeping force. They continued a distance to the east, then proceeded to the north, the direction of their objective. It was again a time for stealth as they edged deeper into the sanctuary.

One hour into the team's skirting movement, they heard a signal shot. It came from the west side of the river, the location New York slogged out of the slow current, soaked and with river water pouring from their equipment. Skilled trackers had found the place they passed over and exited on the other side.

The team continued north toward their objective of Laotian Route 110, leaving behind the area of the broad sweep of the North Vietnamese force.

An hour later, another shot. This time from the area of the east side of the river where they had recrossed back into their target area. Whatever the elite force was that was following the team, it had found the place in the thicket they had crossed and deciphered the tail gunner's attempt to hide their spoor. The enemy was back on their trail. Each time New York changed direction, regardless of the effort made to hide their passage, a signal shot.

An elite force was in pursuit of the team. Perhaps one of the rare hunter-killer teams specifically trained to eliminate SOG recon teams. It seemed the trackers and the organized pursuit could not be shaken. Like hounds on the chase, they would surely sniff their presence. Using the utmost care and skill of the tail gunner to hide any sign of the team's passage, Wolcoff steered his team to the west again, and to the Dak Lay. The One-Zero perused his map. The steep ridgeline seemed to gentle to the north. Perhaps the cliff that lined the road would no longer be an issue. Somehow the force behind them must be evaded.

They crossed the river again. A third time.

The map bore true. They road marched north until the cliff side gave way into a narrow valley. They left the road on the far side of the narrow valley and proceeded west.

Shots from the river.

They were unable to shake their pursuers.

New York maneuvered 200 meters up the valley as dusk approached then fish-hooked to a low ridge for an RON. Teams did not normally transmit from the overnight position but with the dogged chase behind, it was imperative to give a status report to alert the FOB and adjust the no bomb lines, lest American bombers hit them in the night.

The team was exhausted, nearly panting when they circled in tactical position. They leaned back against the bases of trees and their packs, their weapons ready across their legs. It was the time of day when the creatures of the forest ceased to forage, grey birds settled into their nests, but before the hunters emerged from their dens. There was that utter quiet when daylight slides its shoulders from the leaves, barely causing them to rustle. It was then, just as darkness joined shadow to form, the strikers' weary heads snapped up. They sought the source of their alarm. Not the flutter of a bird. No lizard eased from its burrow. They heard it again. This time, it was clear in their minds. The enemy was moving across from them in the narrow valley. Tomorrow! Tomorrow.

They moved north at dawn, as soon as they could maneuver without brushing against the grass. They placed their feet in the tracks of the one before them, and the Montagnard at the end hid the impression, straightened the errant blade of grass, then placed a leaf or two into the deception. They used all of their skill, changed direction often, fish-hooked to no avail. Each time they changed direction the trackers learned the secret and fired a shot to alert the others. They coursed up and down ridges and deep vegetation, yet they were followed. At a place, they maneuvered through a low area with elephant grass and waited in ambush on the other side. But the skilled adversary sensed the danger area and skirted around it

At a tactical stop Wolcoff contacted the FOB, declared a tactical emergency, and requested close air support. From there the team climbed a low ridge, crossed over a small low area and made their way up the next ridge where they could monitor their back trail. From there they took up defensive position and waited.

The Montagnards nearest the backtrail signaled. They looked

back at Wolcoff, "VC come!" the enemy were approaching. Their press in the grass was less than that of a soft breeze, but it was there. They heard their movement in the vegetation.

Another striker signaled, "Close now. Very close."

The support aircraft arrived on scene. "Mark your position."

The team leader knew that to do so from their location would pinpoint it to the Communists and initiate an attack on the team. With one other striker he slipped from the team position and made his way toward the enemy. As the tail gunner pointed out the exact enemy location, Wolcoff fired a white phosphorous grenade at the site and the two of them turned to join the team.

At that moment the tail gunner saw three NVA, the lead element of an attacking force. In the group was the squad leader, a rifleman, and a soldier carrying an RPG launcher over his shoulder. Behind the three, closer to the team, were six more of the squad. The nine soldiers were very close and were the lead element of a much larger group maneuvering toward New York.

The tail gunner opened fire on the three enemies killing them instantly. Six others had been responding to the phosphorus grenade shot and although they were very near the team had not seen them. The team engaged the six and dispatched them. As per the team battle drill, they fired two magazines on full-automatic into the vegetation from which the nine men had come.

As New York expended their two magazines FAC directed the team over the ridge top and down the reverse slope to a bomb crater. It would be their LZ. As the recon team vacated the position, A-1 bombers dropped cluster bombs on the known location of the enemy. Other aircraft paved the way before the team with 20 mm gunfire.

The eight men arrived at the crater, flopped in, and faced the hunter-killers with their weapons. Attack helicopters and an A-1 Skyraider fighter airplane expended their ordnance on the attacking enemy. Under the withering firepower of the fighter craft, a UH-1D helicopter sloped in to lift off the team. New York covered each other as one by one they climbed the Doney ladder into the chopper. They lifted off as Cobras passed below and covered the Hueys. As they cleared the LZ Wolcoff looked over the side to watch the exploding ordnance below. He looked again. Only twenty meters from the bomb crater from which they were taken was the pale ribbon of a road. They were within twenty meters from their goal.

The team released a sigh of relief, and, exhausted, lay back against the side of the chopper for the ride back to Kontum.

It was Christmas Eve, 1969.

# CHAPTER ELEVEN
## *Cambodia and Ford Drum*

Staff Sergeant Michael Buckland knocked twice, two raps on the frame of the open doorway, and entered the S-3 office where the officer in charge sat behind his desk. Although the major was aware of him, he did not look up. The officer had a way of ignoring his people for a time before giving them his attention. When he raised his eyes, he saw a soldier in slightly baggy fatigues. Only one patch was displayed on the uniform, that of the 219th Aviation company on his left shoulder. The officer was annoyed. Buckland was a Green Beret, a SOG operative. When in proper uniform, he should wear his rank, parachute wings, combat infantry badge, Special Forces tab on his shoulder, and the red SOG patch over his pocket. The soldier standing in front of him should at least appear to be in some regard professional.

Buckland read his mind.

"Sir, as you recall, I am flying on the Ford Drum missions. It is behind enemy lines and we are required to be sterile. My cover is that I am a poor, slovenly mechanic on one of those planes, looking for a lost airplane. If we get shot down, the Communists will not expect to get much of anything useful from me."

"Huumh. Yes, I guess I haven't seen you dressed for the field."

"Yes, sir. It would not have been good to go in completely sterile with no patches either. They would surely guess I was from SOG."

"Shut the door."

Buckland turned and eased the door shut.

"Well, Sergeant Buckland, I have a significant and sensitive mission that must be flown today. This mission comes from SOG headquarters, from much higher up than that in fact. I am certain that the CIA and the State Department are the source of this mission. Do you understand, Buckland?"

"Yes sir."

Major Kerby Smith stared at the man in front of his desk. He expelled a long breath out of his nose, a bull behind a fence. He could not hide his misgivings that the man in the baggy fatigues could accomplish the task. He finally consoled himself in that every man in CCC was highly skilled and prepared, regardless of his appearance.

"All right Buckland. This is it. This is a non-standard mission and it must at any cost be accomplished today at a certain place and time. The document is personally signed by the Secretary of State, and the President of the United States. The mission is of national if not international importance. Your mission, Buckland, involves the enemies of the United States."

He paused to be certain that the sergeant was getting the importance of the task.

"As you know, Buckland, Cambodia is a core part of the Communist drive to take over South Vietnam. Laos is important because most of the supply routes go through there via the Ho Chi Minh Trail. But Cambodia is where most of the supply dumps and base areas are located. COSVN, the headquarters of it all is somewhere in Cambodia. Their government has allowed them there.

"Prince Norodom Sihanouk is the current monarch of the Cambodian dynasty going back twelve hundred years. But either for compelling reasons or his personal leanings, he had been falling more and more into the Communist camp. He has leased the eastern part of his country to the North Vietnamese to send in supplies and has allowed them to create huge base areas away from the border."

Again, he stared at the sergeant to be sure the compelling nature of current events were grasped. Staff Sergeant Buckland missed none of the details of the monologue but could only wait quietly before the officer.

"Sergeant Buckland," the officer continued from a full chest of air, "This is your mission. Sihanouk is in the process of wholly selling out to the Communists. Our intelligence people—CIA, NASA, whatever—are absolutely certain that Prince Sihanouk is meeting with high level North Vietnamese officials and generals today at which time he will be allowing them to increase their control of a much wider swath of eastern Cambodia, beyond the reach of President Nixon's bombing campaign.

"Sergeant Buckland, we know exactly," he paused, "exactly where that meeting will be held and the exact time. It will take place a few hours from now. I will give you a map with the exact location, even a photo of the building. It is a private dacha away from towns for security and privacy. It will not be mistaken for the wrong place."

Buckland waited. He had not yet received the exact mission.

"We want you to fly over that dacha during the meeting. I mean low over it. We want you to buzz the meeting so there is no question Sihanouk knows we are aware of what he is doing. He needs to know if we can buzz him, we can do more than that. We want you down on it, roof level if you can. If the door is open and you can do it, get a picture of him at the meeting. Do you understand that?"

"Yes, sir."

The major may have been reciting the patrol order in his mind, situation, mission, execution, admin and logistics, command and signal. "This is the rest of it," he said, "how you will do it. This is top secret. You will have no backup, no second Ford Drum plane to accompany you. There will be no air support. You are not to fire on the meeting place or shoot a single round except in self-defense. Do you understand?"

"Yes sir," Buckland answered in a tone that conveyed, "Of course, it is clear."

"One last thing, Sergeant," he said as he slid the map and photo across his desk, "I said this is top secret, endorsed by the President of the United States. You will not even tell your pilot the mission until you are airborne and en route to the target. Understood?"

"Yes sir."

This time the S-3 officer did not look at the uniform, but the man in it. "Good luck to you, Sergeant."

I met Mike as he was leaving S-3. I was flying Ford Drum missions also, often in the second airplane with Mike. There were not many of us in the program—Mike, Ted Wicorek, Armstrong, and me. Armstrong had been killed on a mission earlier in the week. That left three of us.

I was about to ask him if we were flying together that day when I saw his eyes. They were focused in the distance—perhaps eternity. I had seen that look in the eyes of someone who was about to die, knew it, and was already departing the body.

"Mike?" I spoke.

He nearly walked past me.

"Mike, are we flying together today?"

There was a slight hesitation in his walk as he noticed me in front of him. Mike and I had been together since Camp Crocket days. His eyes still retained the far-off focus, but he quietly said, "No. Just me and SPAF-2. I can't even tell my pilot about it until we are airborne and on the way." That was it. He walked past me, slipped into the jeep, and drove out the gate.

\* \* \* \* \*

Cambodia. They were the Khmer civilization, the smiling people. There was a time they were the dominant empire of that part of the world, the most prosperous and sophisticated of all. The Khmer boundaries included all of present-day Cambodia, the Malay peninsula, half of Thailand, and a huge swath of the full length of Vietnam. Some of their roots were in India with its Hindu religion and architecture. Huge temples rivaling the wonders of the world dotted the country. One of them, Angkor Wat, covered four hundred acres of land and one thousand stone edifices, a gigantic place of jewels, art, and opulence. Later in history, Buddhism added their influence and there were times of great conflict between the two religions.

A dynasty of Khmer kings began and lasted 1,200 years to the time of Prince Norodom Sihanouk in 1970. About 1150 AD, Angkor Wat was built with its massive sculptures and bas relief. The faces that adorned the temples and wats across the country always smiled. Anyone who ever met the Cambodians of the land saw first their infectious smiles and left thinking they were a sweet and gentle people. A smile would be the lasting image they recalled, be it the farmer behind the sweating ox in the field, an old woman sweeping her hut with a grass broom, a new mother washing clothes in a tub, or the small boy bathing his water buffalo and petting its velvety nose. The carved frescoes on the ancient walls also smiled.

Over the centuries the civilization shrank to its present boundaries. The huge wats which were built in the jungles and forests across the land were abandoned. In part, they were reclaimed by verdant trees and vines. "Ashes to ashes, dust to dust." As a child in school, I saw the pictures in the books. I hovered over those pages, my nose just above the paper. The wood pulp that made those pages were cut from the trees around my home town. I smelled the paper as I was studying the long-empty ruins. It became in my imagination the odor of the dust I imagined in the old temples. I was awestruck. It would not occur to a small boy that those ancient stones would not have the odor of paper but rather, of monsoon rains and verdant trees in the jungle. Even then I imagined the people that lived there sought eternity within those grey stones and carvings. But the answers were not there and the glue that held them failed and I wondered how the people of an entire civilization could disappear, then and nearly again at a later time. Nor would it ever enter my mind that in a war in the future I would be wounded three times in that very country whose architecture I so marveled at when I was a child.

Later when I was older, when I discovered the Carl Sandburg poem Preludes of the Wind. I wondered if the author had been sitting next to one of the ruins in that country, gazing at Angkor Wat, perhaps awestruck as I was as a little boy looking at those same images in a book. I tried to recall from memory the words on an airplane flying to hospital, the last of those lines were:

> *It has happened before.*
> *Strong men put up a city and got*
> *A nation together,*
> *And paid singers to sing and women*
> *To warble: We are the greatest city,*
> *The greatest nation,*
> *Nothing like us ever was.*
>
> *And while the singers sang*
> *And the strong men listened*
> *And paid the singers well*
> *And felt good about it all,*
> *There were rats and lizards who listened*
> *. . . and the only listeners left now*
> *. . . are . . . the rats . . . and the lizards.*
>
> *And there are black crows*
> *Crying, "Caw, caw,"*
> *Bringing mud and sticks*
> *Building a nest*
> *Over the words carved*
> *On the doors where the panels were cedar*
> *And the strips on the panels were gold*
> *And the golden girls came singing*
> *We are the greatest city,*
> *The greatest nation:*
> *Nothing like us ever was.*
>
> *The only singers now are crows crying, "Caw, caw,"*
> *And the sheets of rain whine in the wind and doorways.*

## Dale Hanson

*And the only listeners now are . . . the rats . . . and the lizards.*

*The feet of the rats*
*Scribble on the door sills;*
*The hieroglyphs of the rat footprints*
*Chatter the pedigrees of the rats*
*And babble of the blood*
*And gabble of the breed*
*Of the grandfathers and the great-grandfathers*
*Of the rats.*

*And the wind shifts*
*And the dust on a door sill shifts*
*And even the writing of the rat footprints*
*Tells us nothing, nothing at all*
*About the greatest city, the greatest nation*
*Where the strong men listened*
*And the women warbled: Nothing like us ever was.*

Now that I am old, much older than my years because of war, my impression of the ruins is perhaps a parable, a metaphor, perhaps even an epitaph. The ruins are as grey as death. That which may have been of value since those pictures I studied as a small boy are gone. Much which remains and could not be carried away by looters or defaced by vandals has been eroded by weather and time. Perhaps Sandburg's first lines well said it:

*The woman named Tomorrow*
*Sits with a hairpin in her teeth*
*And takes her time*
*And does her hair the way she wants it*
*And fastens at last the last braid and coil*
*And puts the hairpin where it belongs*
*And turns and drawls: Well, what of it?*
*My grandmother, Yesterday, is gone.*
*What of it? Let the dead be dead.*

I studied the newest images of the area. Jungle had crept to the edge of the stone wats. Monkeys mostly, lived there and thrived in their thousands. And there were the bats. Lizards and snakes sunning on the rocks. Vines grew across the faces of passive, unmoving, lifeless Buddhas. There were no chanting monks; only monkeys shrieked down the empty halls now, their echoes magnifying their importance. Giant baobab trees grew on the roofs of temples, their long grey roots crawling down in every direction to the ground, clinging to the rock walls like tentacles of an octopus on rocks. Grey vines and baobab roots lined the corpse of Angkor Wat like raised grey veins on the skin of an exposed mummy.

A green vine grew from a nostril of a large smiling stone face.

Faces carved high up on the wat, too heavy and beyond the reach of looters, remained, still smiling.

\* \* \* \* \*

COSVN was the main headquarters of the Communist in the war. Referred to as the "bamboo pentagon," it had overall command of all aspects of the war of Communism in Vietnam and Southeast Asia. The People's Revolutionary Party, the National Liberation Front, the Provisional Revolutionary Government of the Republic of Vietnam, and PAVN received direction and supplies from it. It was hidden in the jungles of Cambodia and moved at various times. It was a huge complex, believed to possibly be secreted in Angkor Wat, tucked away in the green jungle within the spreading, sprawling complex of a thousand buildings.

Ted Wicorek, who flew back seat in the Ford Drum missions was tasked to do a photo-reconnaissance of Angkor Wat. He was told, "This is one that you and the SPAF pilot will have to do by yourselves. No backup plane. You will not have air cover either. You are not to fire on the target, just photographs."

On a calm morning, he and the SPAF pilot flew west with the sunrise. The mission was at the extreme distance they could fly and make it back to Kontum. The mission was at significant risk because they could not zig-zag or change course and have enough fuel to return to base. Any headwind in either direction, they would not make it back.

They were tense. Surely any enemy who followed their straight course knew their destination. Anti-aircraft fire could take them out easily, anticipating their arrival.

They flew west. They flew low at times making themselves less visible to spotters, watching the shadow of the plane brush the trees before them. As they grew nearer to the target, they climbed to better see landmarks. From time to time as they grew closer, the pointed peaks of ancient ruins poked through the forest canopy. The pilot watched the fuel gauge. Not quite half and they were only partway there.

They continued west. The shadow of the SPAF plane was nearly below them "Below our vulnerable belly," thought Wicorek.

Farther west. The gauge hovered near half. The pilot shook his head. "I hope we find it soon," he radioed back to Ted. To himself, he thought, "Much farther and we will have to land in Thailand or on some remote road."

They passed areas of cultivation, breaks in the green below. In places they saw dark squares of cultivation, and a few hamlets, but they could not skirt around them. The pilot tapped the gauge and looked back at Wicorek.

Then they saw it. The vastness of Angkor Wat.

"We have to get down there. We gotta get low enough to see if COSVN is in there and take pictures."

"They can knock us down with a stick," the pilot answered.

They buzzed the ancient city of the smiling people. It seemed an empty place. There were no trucks or flags. No soldiers dashed into the ruins to hide themselves from the observation of the small airplane.

But there was no fire either. They made it without event to the edge of the complex. There was no sign of activity. They did not see a human. What they did see, were many paths, all well used. Whatever occurred inside the structures was a carefully kept secret. If the headquarters were there they were disciplined in their activities. The enemy well knew about photographs from satellites.

## SOG: Missions to the Well

They received no fire from the enemy, to do so was to reveal their presence.

Wicorek snapped as many pictures as he could in one pass. They breathed easier. No 12.7 anti-aircraft fire knocked them from the sky. No squads of infantry ran into the opening to empty their rifles as they passed. Perhaps officers held them back by their collars lest they expose themselves.

As they completed the circle over the ruins the pilot glanced at the fuel gauge. "Kontum or Thailand?" He wondered. His maps did not cover the area in that direction. One last glance. He banked east. The tank was less than half full. They would try for gas at Dak To or one of the A teams. But they picked up a modest tailwind, perhaps a prayer of a white-haired lady who prayed on her knees beside her bed for "her soldiers."

It was on fumes and moisture in the tank with which they made it back to Kontum. Saigon would make the decision. Was the complex being used as the main headquarters? A thought crossed the sergeant's mind, "We did not see a single person. But we never saw any of the monkeys they say are everywhere in the place either. Does that mean there are people living in those temples who have chased away the gibbons? Oh, well, Saigon will figure it out."

\* \* \* \* \*

Saigon was indeed still figuring it out when Mike pulled into the airfield on the far side of Kontum, the section where the SPAF pilots and their planes were maintained. A mechanic, on hearing the approach of the jeep stepped down from one of the airplanes with a wrench in one hand and announced, "All done, good to go."

Captain Phil Philips had been looking at the damage on his Bird Dog. The last time Philips flew in the airplane was when SFC Armstrong had been killed in the back seat. He joined the others meeting the jeep.

Mike usually flew with Captain Frank Doherty, call sign SPAF Two. Doherty walked to the jeep with a coffee in one hand.

"Good morning, Michael," he said.

Mike's good morning was barely a mumble as he approached the officer. A glance told the officer something was up. Mike seemed remote. His eyes were dark, nearly black. Doherty needed no other clues. Something significant was coming down.

"What is it?" There was a hint of anxiety in his voice. Had something happen at the FOB?

Mike wondered at the words of the S-3, "You cannot even tell the pilot until you are airborne."

They had flown together long enough, knew and trusted each other with their lives. In the plane, Doherty with his rank and skill, called all of the shots; shot down and on the ground, having to fight and evade, it was left to Mike to lead. They were an integral team and when alone called each other by their first names.

"Frank, we have a mission, just you and me. No other planes with us. We have to go right away and I am sorry, but I can't even tell you the mission until we are airborne."

Doherty was slightly taken back at the information.

"I am sorry, Frank." Mike's voice was low. It was not that he was speaking so the others would not hear, but from a sadness in his heart that he could not tell him all.

"When?"

"Now."

Buckland knew the question he would ask next would hint at the nature of the task, but he must ask it. "Are we topped off?"

Doherty knew from the question they would be flying a significant distance, perhaps much deeper than Ford Drum normally flew. "Yes, Mike. Tanks are topped off."

The other pilots waited at a discrete distance.

"I have to tell them something."

"Of course. They need to know too."

Doherty and Buckland gave the others all of the information Mike was free to give.

"Let's do it, then," Frank said.

Mike nodded. "I have to get something from the jeep."

He returned with the map and photo in his hand, as the pilot untied the plane. "I will explain it all up there," said pointing at the sky.

They climbed and leveled off heading west as usual, for their missions were always in denied areas in that direction.

Mike pressed the button to talk and leaned forward. "Frank, you and I have been given a mission which has been signed by the Secretary of State and the President. The Ops officer said the mission is of national importance and involves perhaps the direction of the war. What happens today because of us might have a major impact on the war."

Doherty did not answer in words, but tilted his head back to let Mike know he was following it.

Buckland slid the map over Doherty's shoulder in the cramped cockpit where he could get it. He knew that regardless of the risk, this pilot would perform the mission. He was a courageous man but Mike wanted him to see the entire picture and see its importance, as he himself did. "See that dot I made over there to the west?" Mike said, as he reached over the pilot's shoulder and touched the map with his forefinger, "There is a dacha there along that small road all by itself. I have a picture of it here. There are no towns or anything around it."

Frank nodded his head.

"Prince Norodom Sihanouk, the king of Cambodia, will be in that dacha. Several diplomats and generals from North Vietnam and perhaps even Russia will be meeting with him there. At that meeting, the CIA and NASA believe he will be leasing perhaps the eastern half of Cambodia to the NVA. There will be ample space for base areas such as COSVN and much of the infiltration routes can be placed farther west beyond Nixon's bombing campaign. The fear is Sihanouk is becoming more embedded with the Communists."

"And what is it they want us to do?"

"They want us to buzz the dacha while he is in it. I mean low. Roof top level." Mike paused a second. "Actually, lower than that. If the door is open in the dacha, they want me to get a picture of him inside."

Mike heard Frank's breath as he spoke. "That is really low, just above ground along those single-story buildings. Nothing around the dacha you say?"

"Nothing that I can tell. It is more like a cottage along the lake where people go for a weekend, only no lake of course."

Frank nodded his head again as he thought.

"They want us to buzz him. Our people want him to know that we know about the meeting and what he is doing. I assume if I get a good picture they will send him a copy."

Mike could not see his friend's face as the observer seat in the small Bird Dog sits directly behind the pilot, but he knew he was digesting the information so far. Mike gave him time.

Frank finally spoke. "We have the obvious considerations: Our fuel. We will be at the max. We might not make it back; perhaps we might have to try for Thailand, but we will get to that later.

"The task now," he continued almost to himself is to time it so we get there at the correct time without being seen. With fuel considerations, I am not sure we can make any course changes to confuse them as to our purpose."

There was another pause as he thought, "I need to compute airspeed, time, and distance to arrive at the right time."

Mike did not interfere with the pilot's calculations but looked at the terrain around their flightpath. Typical tree-covered Cambodian mountains. Who knew how many PAVN eyes watched them through the leaves, tracked them, radioed their presence, and tried to determine their destination. He looked for new roads in the breaks of the trees evidenced by freshly plowed red-brown earth, shines on windshields of vehicles in a camouflaged truck park, marching troops caught on a road before they could dive into a ditch, or even a line of grey vapor as an over-anxious soldier shot a shoulder-fired rocket toward the plane.

"Got it," Frank said into the handpiece. "We are good," and there was a pause before he continued, "At least halfway."

Nearly a half hour passed as neither man spoke, both absorbed in their thoughts and the dangers of the mission. The engine hummed as they passed through the still air. The pilot pressed the talk button of the radio.

"Mike," Frank said. The tone of his voice conveyed something which pressed on his mind, a thing his friend needed to know.

"Mike, I want to tell you a story, an incident that I had with Major Smith." He paused as if he wondered if he should go on and finish what he had started to say.

"He gave me one of those missions one time, like the one we are flying today. The target was way out there. He gave me the map and pointed to a place on it and said 'That is where I want you to go.' Smith never seemed to care about us, never seemed to care if we got back. He gave me the mission, not a really important thing; more like he just pulled it out of his hat to give us something to do.

"When he was finished with that, he slid the map across his desk to me and I told him, 'Major, that is at the very limits of our fuel tanks. Any deviation we have to make, any wind the wrong way, anything at all and we can't make it back.'

"He just looked at me as cold as a fish. 'That's your mission, Captain.' And I told him, 'Then we will either have to land somewhere in the jungle or in Thailand.'

"You know what that major did, Mike? He pulled the map back and laid the map over the edge of his desk and tore off the entire half of the map that had the route to Thailand. He handed it back to me and said, 'You have your mission, Captain.'

"I just blew it. I shouted at him. 'Major, do you want us killed?' I was at the point of a court martial. I was so mad. I just turned and walked away. I did not salute or anything. That man does not care if we live or die, Mike."

They droned on toward the target using their compass and terrain features to give precise guidance. As they grew close, they found the exact break between the mountains to the valley. Doherty began to lower their altitude and position themselves to find the dacha and make one pass just above ground level. In the distance they saw the shape and color of the dacha. They aligned themselves with the gravel road in front of the structure.

"What if they have wires across the road to the house, electrical wires?" Doherty asked as he dropped to a height just above the road's surface.

"We hit them," Mike answered.

Mike was already at the window, the camera held just outside the fuselage.

"Get ready!" Frank shouted needlessly, "Now!"

No power lines sliced across the window to cut them off at their necks. No electric wires grabbed the prop to hold them in place like a web waiting for spiders clad in olive drab uniforms to finish them. No cable grabbed their wheels and flipped them over. It was a smooth glide a few feet above the earthen road at the level of the porch.

The door was wide open. He could not see into the interior. He pressed the button on the Leica camera, two photos one after the other. The first was of the dacha in its entirety, the second of the front and porch with one wide-open door.

Frank shoved the throttle full and pulled the stick toward his chest. They arced upward. They were pressed into their seats as they climbed, scraping just over the trees that lined a bend in the road. Frank was tense with the demands of the moment and did not ask, but Mike quietly said as they left the country cottage in the center of Cambodia, "Got it."

He peered down as they edged over the trees, the wheels brushing the higher leaves,

"Well, Captain Doherty, I suppose that you want to go home now."

Their "wing and a prayer" mission ended as Captain Frank Doherty sloped his small airplane to the runway at Kontum, his tires softly touching down on the hot pavement with the squeak of a perfect landing. They taxied to the revetment and shut down. Neither of the two men leaped from the plane. Without speaking a word, they decompressed. They heard the engine cool and make its ticking sounds and felt the quiet. Gravel crunched under running feet. Anxious fingers opened the door. Smiling, friendly, concerned faces greeted them back.

Doherty stepped from the airplane. His legs were like rubber but he quickly felt his strength return. He turned and slid the seat forward so Mike could get out.

"You two need a steak," one of the other pilots said, and there were hugs all around. There was laughter. "Tell us about it," said another, and they looked over at Mike Buckland.

"They didn't say anything about after the mission," he said, "But I need to get back," and he excused himself

Two hours later, Mike Buckland finished the prints of the photo mission. He was still in his quasi-sterile fatigues. The pictures were crystal-clear. Although he could not see into the interior, there was no question that Norodom Sihanouk would know that we knew.

History would relate that Sihanouk got the message. His cage was indeed rattled. There was no question that Nixon's bombers could pinpoint him and eliminate him if he chose. As demonstrated, they knew where he was at that minute. With the pass of that single engine airplane, and that squint-eyed guy pointing the camera out the window, even a king could take a hint.

He needed to get out of the country to think about it. He flew to Moscow.

For a few days, the king basked in the receptions due a head of state. His uniforms were white with gold trim and the medals of state resplendent on his chest. An orchestra played the national anthem of his country, and even the dignitaries of Russia stood at attention.

In the evening, Russia honored him with a banquet, its splendor in the finest of settings under chandeliers from the time of the Tsars. From cellars across the globe, they served the choicest of wines in cut-crystal vessels which caught and sparkled in the light. Waiters with white towels neatly folded over their arms stood behind each guest to attend to his personal desires. On a raised dais at one end of the banquet hall, the orchestra played the compositions of Russia and Cambodia. They ate pheasant and the finest dishes from around the world. Toasts were proclaimed and they felt good about themselves.

But at the end of it all, after the Russian heads of departments bid them good night, a Cambodian aid in a somber face edged to the ear of the king and solemnly whispered the essence of the writing on the wall which Belshazzar in the Scriptures saw: "Your majesty. There has been a coup. Your highness, your kingdom is lost. You have been deposed."

An angry, hurt, and confused monarch flew next to Beijing, China. He felt betrayed. Was he not the Father of Independence for gaining his people's independence from the French? Did they not love him? Did they not owe him something? How could his people, his smiling people, do this to him?

China counseled him, "Resist the coup. Join China and North Vietnam in the fight against the Americans." And he did. To regain his own power, he allied with the Communists who actively fought South Vietnam and the Americans. The day before he was non-communist; that day he joined them. His duplicity, and riding the fence cost him his country.

His actions grew to their logical outcome. The seeds of Communism matured and bore fruit. Lon Nol, who replaced the king, ensured the dictates of the system were carried to their climax. They were known as the Khmer Rouge. Both Russia and the cultural Revolution of Mao in China were already erasing every vestige in their countries that was not purely Communist in nature. Perhaps 140,000,000 citizens would be brutally murdered by the regimes.

It was deemed that cities were tainted and impure because of the influence commerce and comfort afforded. Entire cities were turned out into the countryside where citizens languished and perished; entire valleys and fields were knee-deep in half-decomposed bodies.

If one of the laughing people wore glasses or had a watch or spoke a foreign language, he was executed. Teachers, and anyone who went to school were killed. A person caught looking for a missing relative was terminated. If one were to be seen weeping at an execution, they also were executed. If someone was arrested, his whole family suffered his fate.

Money was abolished. Private property was confiscated. Schools were closed, as were hospitals, shops, and stores. The right to travel was over.

At checkpoints, the Communists forced passersby to show their hands. If there were no callouses on them, that person was shot.

Anyone who could read was executed thinking they might have been contaminated with thoughts of the West. A trick of the regime was to present a book to a citizen and say, "Read this." It was not long before everyone realized to do so was the kiss of death, so they would say, "I don't know how." The Pol Pot people began to trick the people by handing the book with the print upside down. If the person made any movement to turn it so the words were right side up, they were executed, dragged outside, shot, their bodies left in the street as an illustration.

There came a time when it was determined that using a bullet cost more than the victim was worth, so pickaxes and clubs were chosen as a cheaper way to go. Starvation worked well when entire populations were considered not Communist enough.

They discovered that starvation, as a method of eliminating large numbers of people at a time, left many of them too weak to dig their own graves deep enough. They often died with a shovel in their hands but with the thinnest layer of soil to be kicked over their bodies. But the method did not abate. After months, even years of Communism murdering the smiling people, filling once-fertile fields and valleys with corpses only partly buried, and empty cities and towns, one half of the population of Cambodia perished.

If a person could stand it today, he might find one of those places and look across one of those killing fields and see the white bones exhumed by the monsoons of the years. Thousands and thousands of them, mostly in the positions in which they fell, and here and there a fleshless hand and arm raised from the dirt. "See, I am here. See what they have done."

An important thing to remember: The killing fields and those more hidden fields that exist in the other Communist countries are not the anomaly, incidents out of the norm. They are the natural and expected branch and fruit that grows from the root of that wicked philosophy.

*Dave Kirshbaum with silenced Swedish K*

*Recon team Florida at a wedding Norm Doney in back center*

*Norman Doney*

*Dale Hanson on a training group mission*

*Dale Hanson new in-country*

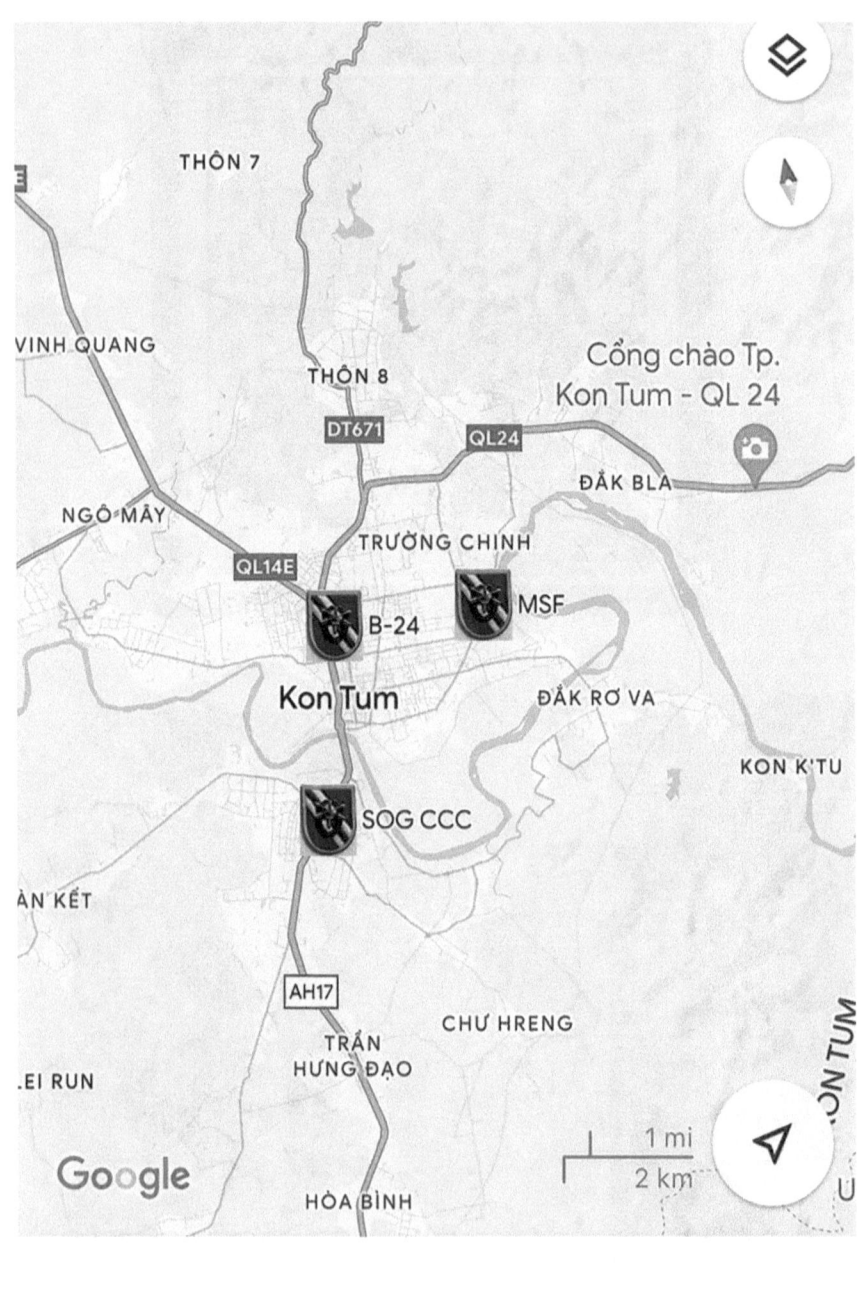

*RT Arizona/ Sgt Wilson top right*

*King Bee Sikorsky H-34 helicopter*

*RT New York*
*Ed Wolcoff front, Peter Wilson in sunglasses, Harold Wilson, Don Benesh in rear*

*RT Maine, Mike Buckland standing, Dave Baker and Steve Sherman in front*

*Michael Buckland*

*Michael Buckland in photo lab*

*RT Hawaii; Uhmera, Delema, and Ripanti in back*

*Glenn Umera of RT Hawaii. He got a pure-bred Alaska malamute as a mascot. The Montagnards ate it.*

*Dennis Bingham. He was KIA on RT Hawaii mission.*

*Kenneth Worthley, KIA on RT Florida mission*

*The two photos of a building were taken by Ford Drum of Norodom Sihanouk's secret dacha and meeting with foreign Communist heads of state negotiating them using the east half of Cambodia. Taken at the time of the meeting.*

*Secret dacha of Norodom Sihanouk where he met with North Vietnamese diplomats to yield them the east half of Cambodia*

*Dale Hanson in SPAF plane (Ford Drum)*

# CHAPTER TWELVE
*Delaware and a Downed Jet*

I was talking with Homer; not speaking into the air as I read *The Iliad* and *The Odyssey* explaining to the author how I would have better written those two books, but to Homer Hungerford. The old staff sergeant in my hooch might have been a passable model for that old Greek; he was slightly grey at his temples and in the stubble that grew since his morning shave. My Homer did not orate in classical Greek but spoke softly and slowly in a drawl, usually with a toothpick in his mouth. Homer was one of those old soldiers in CCC who was a father figure to me. There were a few of them in SOG whose exploits would have paled that author of centuries past.

I do not know what it was about me which left me so blessed with the attention of those first Green Berets, now long in the tooth. I can only say I was honored and grateful to be in their presence. There was Jan Novey for example. The disguise of his humble greatness was that he was the old dark-haired man in baggy fatigues who ran the camp motor pool. I described the appearance of this aging soldier in another book as a man in baggy pants who had been caught in the rain and was hung on a line in his uniform to dry. His exploits began in World War Two in the resistance against the Nazis. He fought throughout the war, was wounded several times, captured, and escaped. He would never have dirty fingernails. He had none. They had been peeled off under torture. He continued to fight not only against Nazism but Communism over the world: Europe, South America, Cuba, and now Southeast Asia. I was privileged to chat, the two of us leaning against the side of a jeep, to talk at length, learn, share, talk about philosophy, life and, my relationship with Jesus Christ. He gave me one of his books: poetry.

Does a warrior read poetry? The Japanese required their samurai warriors to paint flowers and compose verse as a balance to their training in violence to leave them tempered for society. I had memorized one of the poems in Jan's book and shared it with him when he was in hospital in Pleiku. He had been wounded in an ambush, the sole survivor. A bullet creased his forehead leaving him momentarily paralyzed with his back against a tree, his eyes wide-open and blood covering nearly all his face. The Viet Cong shot the two other wounded Americans and one of them approached Novey to ensure he also was dead. He saw the ring on Novey's finger and tried in vain to pull it off. Failing this, the Viet Cong sawed the ring finger off his hand with the back of Novey's K-bar knife. As he played dead, he saw them cut through the flesh, then snapped the bone; watched as the enemy soldier slid off the ring and threw the finger into the bushes, saw him blow the blood off the ring and with the fingers of both hands held it in the air so the light would catch the shine of the stone. The Viet Cong's eyes glistened in the light like diamonds.

Jan Novey reminded me of Epaphroditus in the Book of Philippians in the Bible. The people thought of him as just a messenger carrying a letter, a mail man. But the Apostle Paul described him as "my brother and companion in labor, and fellow soldier, but your messenger." The text goes on to say, "he labored nigh unto death."

Jan Novey was far more than just the aging sergeant who ran the motor pool.

And there was master sergeant Norman Doney, my team leader and mentor, and father away from home. In addition to all else, he made it a point to find and introduce me to all the old hands, the legends in Special Forces. I never had the impression as he did so, that I was of a lesser caliber than they.

Homer Hungerford. This was his third war. He fought in the second World War as an officer, then in Korea. He told me one time when he didn't agree with something that was going on, "I think I will petition for my rank back as a major."

But Vietnam and the spread of Communism was becoming a flood, and Homer Hungerford, the owner of the largest hotel in Hawaii, left it all and enlisted to fight in the war. He joined as a private, went through the ranks, joined Special Forces, volunteered for SOG and ran on Recon Team Delaware into enemy controlled territory.

"I think things are heating up a trifle over here," Homer said as he leaned back on my bunk with his hands interlaced behind his neck. "Heating up, gettin' ready to boil."

I waited for him to continue but saw him gazing at eternity on the other wall. Thoughts, sentences even, were digested and hashed in his mind before he said them aloud. The toothpick changed sides in his mouth. "Have you been following what has been happening around us, young fellow?"

It was rhetorical, and I did not answer.

"Just this week the communists gave up on their siege at our Special Forces Camp at Dak Seang. It was a big 'un," he drawled. "Lasted six weeks. One of our boys got the medal of honor out of that one. Sergeant Beikirch was the name, I think." He looked over at me. "Got wounded a passel of times. At the end he couldn't walk or even stand up, so he had a couple of his little people rush him around on a stretcher so he could take care of the wounded under fire.

"Then there was Dak Pek. That one has been going on for a month. Still goin' on," he said after a slight pause to be sure he was keeping all the incidents straight.

I interrupted Homer. "I was there on one of our Ford Drum missions," I said. "We were flying over Dak Pek in the bird dogs. Dak Pek had nine hills, and the Communists had taken eight of them. There was a buck sergeant on the radio talking to the A-1 planes. The bombers asked him, 'Where do you want us to drop the next load?' The sergeant on the radio answered in the calmest voice ever, 'Put it along the wire on my west perimeter.'

"I watched the plane pass over and the whole side of the perimeter lit up in a napalm run—brilliant white-light explosion and black smoke rising, and the sergeant answers back to the bombers, 'Well,' only he drawls like you, Homer, 'Waall,' he says, 'you got about a hundred of 'em that time. Now put it . . .' and he went on to the next target."

Homer was thinking about that. The toothpick centered in his mouth not moving. When it seems that what I had just said was permanently recorded in his mind, he went on.

"Have you been following the big assault we are making into Cambodia lately? It has been going on only a few weeks now, mostly in the sanctuaries like the fishhook and parrot's beak areas. Americans and Vietnamese. A big push to find COSVN, their big headquarters and supply center to break the back of the enemy.

"By the way, do you know the other name for the Ho Chi Minh Trail system? It's called the Sihanouk Trail and it runs alongside of the Ho. Our ole buddy the king of Cambodia who is supposed to be our friend. Anyway, the communists got the heads up that we were coming from a mole and our people say they moved out most of their supplies before we got there.

"But," he raised a finger as he loudly repeated, "But!" He removed the toothpick from his mouth, set the pick on the bed cover, and pulled a slip of paper from his shirt pocket and unfolded it. "I still have a few higher up friends from when I was an officer. Listen, Dale, to what we've gotten so far. Bear in mind they claim eighty percent of everything was moved farther west out of our reach. 11,369 enemy killed, 2,300 captured, 20,000 individual weapons captured and 2,500 crew served weapons."

He looked over at me to be sure I was following his numbers. "There's more," he said, "things are happening, Dale. I was in the other big wars. I have nearly eight years in combat all told. I have a feel for what goes on in war. Charlie isn't Charlie anymore. He is Mr. Charles. They are ready for conventional war. We are underestimating them. Listen," he said.

"Our people destroyed 435 vehicles. 140,000 rockets and artillery shells were captured with 7,000 tons of rice, 800 tons of munitions, 199,552 anti-aircraft rounds, 55 tons of medical supplies, and 29 tons of commo equipment. And remember, Dale, they think eighty per cent of everything was removed before we got there."

I was awestruck. The concept that the war in Vietnam was merely an unconventional war must surely be revised after this, I thought.

"Homer," I said, "What about the rice?"

"What about the rice?"

"Anything else we can destroy in place, but you can't blow up rice. If you try to burn it, only the top burns. Blowing it up just scatters it around. Seven thousand tons. That is fourteen million pounds of rice. Can you imagine what it would take to transport that much rice to South Vietnam, how many helicopters?"

Homer was just looking at me.

"Just wondering," I said.

The door to my hooch opened and Jim "Jonesy" Jones thrust his head in. "Oh, there you are!" Jonesy was the One-Zero of Delaware. He had red hair and freckles, and his code name was Wild Carrot. "Ah, Homer, they want us to do a Bright Light at Dak To. We're changing out with the other team a little early. They want us to go in an hour." His movements were quick and hurried, always moving, unlike Hungerford's deliberate migrations to a task.

On hearing the information, Homer slid his fingers over the blanket to find and retrieve his toothpick and placed it back into his mouth. "Right there," he said as he rose to leave.

The door shut and Homer waved me goodbye.

A minute later the door was thrust open again and Jonesy poked his head in. I saw only his red hair, bright eyes, and rosy cheeks. "Oh, sorry to burst in and take him away so quickly. Were you solving the problems of the world?"

"Matter of fact," I started to say, but I did not get to finish. Jonesy was gone.

Recon Team Delaware, two Americans and five Montagnard tribesmen landed at the launch site at Dak To and streamed off the choppers. They passed the line of men of the team they were replacing, laughing, joking, patting shoulders. Homer led his people to the mortuary where the team would billet until they were relieved while Jonesy checked with the leader of the other team regarding activities around the area and information about teams on the ground then joined his people in the old mortuary.

From the doorway, the One-Zero told Delaware to take everything out of their packs not needed for a mission. "Have your packs ready to go into the field, straps out, weapons across the top." These were needless instructions. The team understood their purpose for being at the launch site.

"Homer, let's go to the control tower and find out what is happening on the ground."

He nodded.

They climbed the wood stairs to the small space where two Green Berets sat behind a bank of radios and maps. "Just wanted to get a feel for what is going on in the field," Jones said as they entered the space. Homer took a seat in an office chair slightly in the shadows. The bank of radio lights brought out the grey in the stubble of his whiskers.

One of the men behind one of the radios thrust up a hand like a policeman, "Stop," it said. The second Special Forces man faced the men from Delaware with the same gesture and placed a finger over his mouth in the "quiet" gesture.

Something was coming down.

The first soldier strained to hear; his face close to the radio and the hissing static.

# SOG: Missions to the Well

They waited for more communication. The room grew silent as the background noise from the radios diminished. Homer sat upright. He listened as intently as the radioman. A thing of significance was occurring.

The second sergeant at the radios motioned the two men of Delaware to the far side of the room where they could quietly talk.

"You boys may need to get your people ready to go in. Here is the situation. We had two F-4 Phantom jets making a bomb run on a bridge on the Ho Chi Minh Trail. That is hill country as you know. The first Phantom, call sign Cobra-84, made a bomb run on the target, but heavy machine gun fire hit it and knocked out the hydraulics. According to the second Phantom, it hit the top of one hill and burst into a ball of flame, then bounced over a second hill, and crashed to the top of a third hill.

"I thought we would get the call right away, but the Air Force tried to send in their own people. Unfortunately, they got pushed out by heavy ground fire. I do not think, from listening to this, there are any survivors but who knows."

The first man behind the radios turned toward the Delaware Americans. "I expect word to come down to send you guys in to the site. FOB is already sending in Hueys with ladders and support although we have not gotten the official word we are going in."

"We will be ready when they get here just in case," Jones said.

"What do we have for daylight?" Homer asked.

The radio man looked at the clock. "Now, about five hours. But they are not even here yet."

SSG Jones gave a warning order to his team and got them ready for insert. He explained the nature of the probable mission and its location centered in a concentration of enemy in Cambodia. The Montagnards received the information quietly and stoically knowing that a force capable of shooting down an American jet would be a formidable adversary.

"It's a go!" shouted one of the Dak To sergeants from the top of the stairs. "Choppers on the way."

Homer Hungerford quietly left the mortuary, climbed the stairs to the tower, and solemnly returned with two body bags over one shoulder.

Two Hueys received the team; Hungerford and two Yards in the second one, and Jones and three Yards in the lead. They stepped over the rolled-up Doney ladders in the doorway and sat on the deck with their weapons hugged in their arms. "The choppers will put you guys in on the first hill where the jet struck," Covey told them. "The vegetation is torn away and burned. It is a starting point you cannot miss."

Although it would be clear to the North Vietnamese what the destination of the choppers was considering the downing of the jet, the SOG group of aircraft zig zagged anyway. Cambodian highlands and fast-moving rivers passed below Recon Team Delaware, unwatched by the men whose present thoughts could be their last. That which could shoot down a jet would have no problem destroying a helicopter.

Jones glanced out the door. A hundred meters to the side, short segments of the Ho Chi Minh Trail, which had not been fully camouflaged, lay exposed like lengths of tapeworm. In most places the road was hidden with a net of interlaced bamboo and leaves.

The pilot chose not to descend along the flight path of the jet and the anti-aircraft fire which took it down, but from the side, turning the last seconds to a hover ladder height above the ground. The crew chief left his machine gun for only the time it took to kick out the ladder letting it unroll of its own weight.

In less than a minute, the first half of the team scrambled down and spread in a half circle around the landing. The second craft dropped to a similar hover where the first had descended and in seconds the two halves joined.

Delaware waited for the sounds of the choppers to abate and glanced about. The hilltop was burned, a place of cinders. Bamboo was broken and snapped into shards. Sharp ends tore Jones' pants and sliced his skin. The area smelled of smoke. Soil that had been dry at impact steamed and thin whisps of smoke escaped the ground like prisoners from a jail.

## SOG: Missions to the Well

Delaware waited at the landing site making a security stop in place. There was popping and snapping like people moving through the brush. The team faced the sounds, ready for the engagement. They waited, but the enemy did not show its face nor close upon the team. Another popping and snapping sound, closer now. One of the Montagnards saw the place, turned, and smiled. It was the sound of vegetation heating and cooling under the ash.

Jones nodded to his point man and pointed at the burned path which the jet made in its passage. He clicked his tongue once. "Go."

Their goal was to follow the course of the aircraft to its final place and retrieve the two Americans. They moved in stealth, ever in that direction, over the crest toward the second hill.

The point man froze. He raised his weapon and prepared to shoot. There were three NVA soldiers, two partially hidden in the foliage, the other in plain view. For a reason which was difficult for Jones to explain, the team did not engage and kill them. Jones thought of them as simple trail watchers. He said in Vietnamese, "*Dung lai, di di.*" (Stop, go away.) The enemy froze, slowly turned, and walked away. Jones could not explain, even to himself why he did not shoot; only, that to engage the enemy now, so far from the stricken jet, could prevent their arrival at all.

Intelligence had relayed to the team the jet had been hit, struck a hilltop and burst into a fireball, bounced over a second hill, and landed on the top of a third. Delaware proceeded along the crest of the second hill, moving along the swath the A-1 cut through the vegetation. Along the way they found pieces of the jet, then what may have been abandoned bunkers, one with an unexploded CBU inside. At the site the team walked abreast to not miss any signs of the crash.

Delaware continued; eyes scanning back and forth into the trees looking for lurking, waiting enemy, as they similarly studied the ground for clues. They followed the eerie swath of destruction where the stricken jet plowed its way through the vegetation. Places were sheared level to the ground. Within that boundary, slim splinters of broken-off bamboo yet stood erect like punji stakes, snapped, yellow, earthen bayonets.

A short distance farther the point man froze. Without turning his head, he slowly raised his hand in a "halt" signal. The Montagnard lowered himself, bending his knees, his eyes never leaving the anomaly before him. His mind was on death, those of two airmen, but he had found evidence of other death in front of him. He cast his eyes around the site, watching for that which caused his heart to quicken its beat. Jones slid forward.

"What?" he whispered.

The tribesman nodded in the direction of concern.

It was a graveyard. There were seven graves, slight mounds of soil not yet settled level with the earth. They were not old graves. The site was enclosed with a double bamboo fence. Affixed above the entrance was the communist red star. Their inspection of the site was brief and cursory. A very slight breath of air passed over the mounds of men, then over the team. Other fallen men were their concern.

The team maneuvered on. Each tribesman glanced to the side at the site as they passed; each soldier with his own thoughts carried not in their heads, but their breasts.

Jones tried to pick up the pace while not giving up security; he bore in mind they had only a few hours of daylight.

"Click, click." A Montagnard in the middle of the column made the sound with his tongue. The One-Zero was too far ahead to hear it. He glanced back at Hungerford and with the barrel of his rifle, pointed to a place on the ground next to a small area of disturbed soil. The men in front of him had missed it.

Nearly invisible in the dirt, half-hidden by fallen debris, grass, and twigs, was a boot. An American boot. The tribesman had fought the enemy for many years and was aware of those the VC might use. He arrested his desire to rush forward and pick up the boot. He was careful that it was not a booby trap. It took only seconds of time. He glanced at the fresh-plowed soil near the boot. Such signs of disturbed dirt often indicated places Viet Cong saboteurs slide mines under a road. There were no wires, no sign of a pressure plate or trigger. He was satisfied. The boot was indeed American, black leather with the green cloth sides. He turned it with his own foot and picked it up by the top. It was heavy for an empty boot. A glance. There was a foot inside.

He wanted to let the Americans know of his find. Perhaps the rest of the body was nearby. He glanced at the front. The column was proceeding ahead, he was lagging. He glanced back toward the other Green Beret, but he and the tail gunner were looking into the bushes to the rear. His mind returned to the boot. Fresh blood; not coagulated, barely covered in the dirt and grime of explosion. Quickly he slid off his backpack and shoved the boot inside. He would show them later. He cinched the pack, slipped it on his back, and rushed to catch up. Carefully as he continued, he cast his eyes about, ever expecting a body part lying under the new dust.

The ground leveled to a small plateau. Centered in it was a large bamboo structure on stilts, perhaps the command element, twenty feet on a side. Nearby were fifteen smaller hooches where an enemy unit was billeted. Among the smaller structures was a swath where part of the stricken jet had fallen, skidded, and tore out four of the buildings. Near that, lying like a sleeping smooth-skinned monster among the hooches, probably broken free as the jet was going down, was an unexploded 750-pound bomb.

Delaware swept the small compound and returned to examine the position. They were time-conscious knowing they had to find the crash before dark but glanced inside the structures for intelligence. They were not sterile. The enemy had been there. In one corner, covering a significant portion of the structure was a large quantity of bandages, crumpled, bloody, cast off to be replaced for new, or, as it has been known in war, washed to be used again. There was ample sign of occupation and hasty leaving. Uniforms, mostly used and old lay about. Some bore a metal tag on the shirt pockets, perhaps for an award or belonging to a specific unit.

Homer looked over at Jones, willed him to look up, and when he did, he tapped his watch. "Time!" the gesture said.

Wild Carrot recalled the task and signaled the point man. "*Đi*.

Đi. Go. Go."

Delaware arrived at the far side of the second hill and gazed across. Clearly the wreckage of Cobra 84 lay like a giant black cinder on the crest. The fireball, which it was as it fell through the sky, burned and scorched all around it and left everything black, a still smoldering ash. The area around the jet was bare of trees and shrubs leaving the wreck conspicuous and bare. The wings were gone. What was left was crumpled and burned. There was no sign of life. It was clearly impossible anyone could survive the crash, yet Jones wanted to see for himself, crawl into the cockpit, carry what might remain back home.

They looked at the slope before them which they must climb to arrive at the site. Jones slumped to his knees. Hungerford joined him. To scale it was impossible for many of his tribesmen and could not be completed in the time they had.

"Homer," he said in a voice which expressed both disappointment and conviction. "We can't get up there. Even if we had a couple of days and ropes, our little people could not climb it."

Homer did not have a toothpick in his mouth, but he drawled the obvious, "They will just have to take a helicopter and land right on it, that's all."

Homer took a final look at the steep sides. "And there are no alternative routes up that hill that I can see." He looked at his watch. "And we can't make it up there in time either."

They stood. Their people were standing in a semi-circle around them, their weapons covering their rear.

"That's it," Homer said, making Wild Carrot's decision for him.

The warriors of Delaware had moved swiftly and silently, hearing only the soft sweeping of grass against the sides of their boots, or the real or imagined popping of the burning wreck. That quietude ended in one second. The world around them erupted in massive and repeated explosions and the whine of miniguns. Without a word of command, the team dropped to their knees and faced the firefight. The explosions came from behind them, from their back trail and the Ho Chi Minh Trail.

Jones heard aircraft pass overhead and called Covey, "What's going on?"

The team had no time to get a formal call sign before proceeding on this mission and Covey used Jones' code name. "Wild Carrot, this is Covey. Be advised that we are working your back trail. Six truckloads of troops and two armored personnel carriers just pulled up on the trail and are in pursuit of you. Many foot soldiers were following the trucks on foot also. Estimate three hundred enemy on your trail."

There was a short pause as Covey relayed information to another unit.

"Wild Carrot, we need to get you out. I am working on it."

The explosions and mini gun fire were at a crescendo. The impact seemed very near to Delaware.

Covey again. "Enemy units are pursuing up your hill. We are hitting them hard. The road is full of wrecked vehicles. Enemy has many casualties laying on the road."

Another pause.

Covey again. "Estimate two hundred enemy KIA. More have joined them and are pursuing."

Jim motioned Homer over to monitor the radio with him. They heard jets pass overhead. Cobra gunships passed between the team and the road, with the ripping sounds of their miniguns spewing six thousand rounds a minute at the enemy near the road. They heard the drone of the birddog over them.

"Wild Carrot, I have assets on the way for an exfil. I need your position and I will lead you to an LZ."

They were in an area of single canopy. "We hear you zero two zero degrees, one half mile, sending smoke." Jones nodded to his point man, and he pulled the pin and threw out a smoke.

Covey: "Roger. I see red smoke."

"Good copy."

Covey circled a minute to find a good location to extricate the team.

"Roger Carrot. Despite our firepower on the enemy, they are

closing on you. Head zero six zero, one hundred meters. Expect ladder exfil ETA twenty minutes."

"Copy."

The impact on the North Vietnamese was a crescendo, a roar of miniguns and explosions. There seemed to be no break between rounds.

Covey came back. "Wild Carrot. New location for you. Choppers on the way. Make way to the ridge top you came in on. Will pick you up on the swath the jet made."

"Copy."

Jones turned to his point man and shoved his index finger toward the hill they just left. "*Đi! Đi!*" he shouted.

They scrambled, rushed toward the place, and crested. The top of the hill seemed smaller than they remembered and quickly found themselves on the far side. The conflict below the slope grew louder as NVA attempted to shoot down the gunships which rained death on them.

Explosions and enemy shouts grew louder as the advance closed the distance with the team. They themselves would be directly involved in the firefight. They dove for cover and prepared to shoot.

Covey: "Choppers coming in. Two Hueys. Ladder exfil. Two minutes. How copy?"

"Homer!" Jones shouted as the roar of the first helicopter approached. "You and your two, first lift, coming in."

At that very moment the first helicopter sloped in and the three climbed the ladders.

Jones glanced back as the last SOG man disappeared inside and the craft rose and sped away.

It was less than a minute before the second Huey with the ladders unrolled began their descent. At that moment the lead element of the enemy assault force cleared the trees and charged with their high-pitched voices and engaged the remainder of the team. The four SOG men emptied their magazines at the force. A B-40 rocket exploded among the team sending small shards of shrapnel into Jim Jones' wrist, forearm, and chest.

But the Huey helicopter did not arrive alone. Cobra gunships flew in on both sides of the Slick like shields, sending minigun fire on the attacking force as they descended. The opening in the trees was less than they recalled. To get low enough for the ladders to reach the ground, the chopper had to descend below the treetops. The rotor blades slapped against the upper branches cutting through them. But the cost was two feet of the rotor blade ends were broken away. The pilot felt it in the shudder of his craft, saw the pieces of the blades fly like arrows. He held it steady, steady enough the ladders did not sway away from the Montagnards who desperately reached for the rungs. Jones and the three remaining Yards snapped into the rungs of the ladders where they hung below all the way to the launch site.

A glance sideways out his window revealed the faithful Cobra gunships. A word from the crew chief, all were safe and aboard. The pilot willed his craft above the trees, banked east and steered his wounded helicopter toward home.

Air assets estimate three hundred enemies were eliminated in retrieving the team. The remains of the men of the jet were never recovered. Saigon did not appraise the men of Delaware of the contents of the boot.

# CHAPTER THIRTEEN
*Ziobron Leghorn Hatchet Force
Montana Kentucky Alabama*

The Green Beret lay on his stomach at a gap between two sandbags and waited. He had made his way to the place well before daylight, long before North Vietnamese watchers could decern shadow from form or make out the lines of his sniper rifle. As on other occasions, he tried to discern the moment when greyness took on color, but that magic time slipped past him again as when he was a child, he waited to catch the sandman when he slipped into his room. But the day had taken on its colors and it was already hot and still. Far down the steep slope, a monkey shifted in its sleep with one black arm dangling from a tree limb. The movement of the leaves was slight but the soldier saw it and located the spider monkey hundreds of feet below in a grove of trees where long fingers of bamboo crossed and held fast among its knuckles. He was satisfied that any movement of an enemy soldier would betray his presence in the thickness. A twitch of a small bird in the leaves caught his eye as it flitted from limb to limb to a nest of mud suspended in the air by vines. Its tiny feet dislodged a piece of thin, dry bark which bounced branch to branch to the ground. Like ants carrying leaves, the silence of the morning carried the brittle sounds up the slope to the listening soldier. He searched the thickness for sign of enemy; any movement, any sound, a color or shape that did not belong.

He looked without moving his head, his hand resting on a sandbag next to his binoculars. Sweat blackened his bandana and a drop gathered at the tip below the knot and dropped on his skin. A small lizard darted to the drop expecting an insect. It cocked its head left and right. Edward Ziobron saw himself reflected in the lizard's eyes as it studied the unmoving soldier, its stomach moving in and out with its breathing. Long rubbery fingers took purchase on the back of Ziobron's hand.

Only eight feet away, a thick snake, the color of the sandbags, sunned full length on the row. It appeared bloated for its length, its long, forked tongue darting like flames from its jaws. Its eyes were pale, the whites spotted like speckled eggs with cruel black slits for pupils. Slowly the viper turned its head toward the lizard on Ziobron's hand. It raised its head from the canvas cloth and coiled its body forward to attack.

Not seeing the viper, the lizard rested on the sergeant's hand. It was certain that the snake would strike. Ziobron dared not move. Would the bite be true and only take the lizard? "Which of us will walk only three paces after that venom?"

Moving only his mouth, he blew a puff of air at the lizard. It froze, surprised, then in blinding speed darted toward waiting death, but changed course and vanished over the edge of the wall. The adder struck with fully open jaws catching only air behind the disappearing lizard. Ziobron had an impression of long dripping fangs in the black interior of the mouth. He heard a loud hiss and dry scales scraping across the sandbag. The snake slid off the line of bags, first the head and searching tongue, followed by its length. The serpent's scales reflected in the sun like jewels slowly seeping from a sack.

He exhaled, long and audibly. How long had he not breathed?

Adrenaline released its grip and he felt himself shake. His heart beat visibly in the veins on the back of his hand. Had he been bit, tri-pacer snake or not, he would not get help in time. Granted, he was on the SOG radio relay site, with immediate communication with the FOB at Kontum, but he would be dead before the pilots made it to the helicopters. There would be intense pain and he would swell up in minutes as venom coursed through his body. He would convulse on this Laotian mountain top with his eyes bulging, perhaps die with his hands around his throat as he choked and his lungs begged for air. He took a long breath, but this time it was to settle his mind. "What just happened was of the past," he told himself. He was in command of his body. He faced the jungle again but glanced at the sandbag mere feet away. "I still smell that snake."

He renewed his search of the steep slope below Leghorn. Ed Ziobron would give it one more hour, another attempt to discover the enemy he was certain maneuvered under the thick canopy of trees. Most of the approach to the site was clifflike. He recalled Dale Hanson saying that that part of the approach reminded him of Jonathan's commando raid in the Bible where the pinnacle was so steep the prince had to climb on his hands and knees to attack the Philistines. "But then," Ziobron thought, "If Jonathan could succeed by crawling up the cliff, the Communists could do it too." He would ensure that was not being done this morning, after all there were only a few of us and Charlie wanted us gone.

Leghorn was a top-secret radio relay site situated on a near-impregnable mountaintop in fiercely controlled enemy territory in Laos. SOG teams operated deep into Communist sanctuaries, often beyond the range of their radios and could only communicate when Covey flew over. Often that interval of time was fatal to the teams, and bad weather frequently left them without help for days. Leghorn was the sought-for answer. This thousand-meter pinnacle of rock bristled with antennae and was manned by only two or three Green Berets and a platoon of Montagnard tribesmen.

Ziobron made a macro view of the green below, a snapshot of the whole, looking for any anomaly, a single fraudulent bush or shrub that would betray the presence of lurking death. At a place just before the contours began its steep upward slope, a strip of green foliage rustled as if a breeze was passing over. But there was no breeze, only a dry heat in which nothing moved. The line of movement in the bushes moved and twisted like a stream of water, nothing any movement of air could do. He imagined columns of North Vietnamese soldiers passing through with branches affixed in their pith helmets.

He made a final pass, this time dividing up the scene below into grids and examining each with a forensic eye.

A flash!

It was brief, only enough time for him to locate the proximity. He willed every leaf to part and peered between them to the ground below. Keeping his eyes on the place, he reached for his binoculars and slid them to his eyes. Another flash of light, twice this time. He studied the opening in the shrubs. He saw a dark shape and another flash. It was not the diamond-colored flash of sun on water. This flash was cobalt-blue. It was the reflection of light in a binocular lens or a rifle scope. Was a sniper looking for a target?

Without moving the rest of his body, he grasped his rifle and slid it forward to his shoulder searching for the place through the scope. The flash came from a grove of bamboo beside a dead hardwood tree with peeling bark. He found the place in the scope and moved the crosshairs down the trunk. The dark spot in the break between the shrubs was gone.

Ziobron was certain that watchers could not see reflection from his own scope to betray his presence. He slid back from his concealment on the perimeter, slung his rifle, and stood to a crouch. Leghorn had not taken sniper fire in his memory. Any such move would have brought mortar or recoilless rifle fire from the Montagnards, or worse, a bombing or strafing run by aircraft brought in by the SOG men at the top. He stretched and strolled to the commo bunker stopping first to peer over the cliff approach to the top. King Saul's son could not climb this face even with modern climbing gear.

Ziobron dipped his head and entered the dimness of the bunker.

Over the years the various fortifications had added comfort to the protection and resilience needed to keep the site secure, for the soldiers were committed for a month each time. The two Green Berets who manned the radios and commanded the platoon of tribesmen on the site were inside.

"Hey, you guys like ribs?"

Homer turned from his radio set and smiled. There had to be a catch. "Love ribs," he said.

"Well, there is a huge snake on the west side—that is if you guys haven't already eaten."

Homer lowered his eyes and moved his toothpick to the other side. He spoke with a quiet measured drawl. "I know that old snake. He is a bad one. It is getting so I can't get any of the Yards to do guard duty there. Anyway, we have no barbecue sauce and the last one I 'et had too much venom to suit me. Don't like the taste."

"Aren't you getting particular in your old age, Homer."

Homer ran his hand over the grey stubble of his cheeks. "I like my meat like me, aged and tender."

Rich Ryan was the other Green Beret doing his month on Leghorn. "I guess you can be a bit particular, Homer, since this is your third war."

Homer slowly nodded.

Ziobron laid his rifle flat on the floor, a habit he learned in recon. A weapon laying on the ground cannot be knocked down creating sound that could alert the enemy.

"See anything down there?"

It was Rich Ryan who asked, always alert for lurking enemy. He had endured hair-raising missions in recon before flying Covey as the lifeline to recon teams from the air. Ryan knew first-hand the extreme peril of being on the ground. On one mission Ryan had been shot point blank in the chest with three AK-47 bullets, all of which pierced the cloth of his shirt but stopped at his skin. Heavy small arms fire, exploding grenades, and RPGs detonating in the trees sounded clearly over Ryan's radio when the team called for support. It was doubtful that any of the team would survive.

# SOG: Missions to the Well

His small recon team had been split up and chased in the fight and they had multiple casualties. It seemed a miracle then, when Covey announced that all of the team had been extracted from the field and were on their way in to base. Every American of CCC stood around the edge of the pad and waited. Some prayed. Medics rushed to the landing strip with their three-quarter trucks, thrust open the doors and waited with stretchers and aid kits. At the back of the truck bed in a crumpled heap, lay a half dozen olive-drab body bags under a tarp. We were prepared to see the bloody, mutilated bodies of our friends sprawled on the deck of the chopper. We watched the helicopter settle through the raised dust and were troubled that it did not go straight through to Pleiku and the emergency hospital. We thought the worst, that it was too late, and no emergency ward could avail. But as we looked, Rich Ryan and Charlie Bliss were sitting upright with their feet on the skids. As the Huey touched down, the two Green Berets hopped out, turned toward the open door, and helped their little people step off the craft.

I was one of the first to get to Ryan and stared in unbelief. No blood soaked his shirt. He showed no effects of being shot multiple times. He was not in critical condition. Rich saw my worried look and smiled at me. "I guess you were praying for me." He opened his shirt to show three angry, raised, red welts on his chest where the bullets struck. "God had to have saved us. The bullets went through the cloth and stopped right at our skin. They shot Charlie too. Same thing."

With his experience in the field, Rich was asked if he would consider being a Covey rider coordinating communications and air support for the teams on their missions. He reasoned that he could only walk through the rain so long before the drops hit him if he stayed in recon. It was time.

He flew Covey until he became short. Rich Ryan was flying Covey when I had been wounded in Lima Fifty, and Ken Worthley was killed. I thought I had sent the rest of the team out on the helicopter and that I was the only one left on the ground, still under horrendous fire. It was Rich's calm voice that came over the radio and said, "We have you, Dale. We will get you out." When his tour was nearly over, he took his place behind the radios of Leghorn until the Blackbird came to take him home.

"Anything unusual?"

"They are watching us that is for sure. I saw the glint of a scope. At least that's what I think I saw. I know I saw movement down there."

Homer digested the information. Despite his age, he also went to the field on the demanding and dangerous recon missions. Like Rich Ryan, he chose to finish his tour on Leghorn. His voice was always low, slow and unexcitable—a perfect person to answer the radio from a recon team in desperate state. "Oh, they are there all right," he said, "They are very aware of what we are doing here. They attacked us several times before and they used to harass us with rockets and artillery. Oh, they are watching us. We are right in the middle of their sanctuaries and their roadway to the war in 'Nam."

The toothpick in Homer's mouth flicked to the other side of his mouth and he stared into the shadow of the bunker. "We used to launch some of our recon teams out of here. The NVA had watchers at nearly every opening in the jungle big enough for a chopper to insert teams, so they tried it from this place. Worked," Homer said softly, as though he were recalling the events from the yellowed parchment of the past. He continued in his slow drawl, "We are a boil on their backside. It irritates them to no end, and they can't reach us to get rid of us."

Ziobron sat on a wooden 5.56 ammo crate as he listened. "I've been thinking. The FOB added me and my five-man recon team to the regular platoon doing its month. My team is extra. You won't miss me on the perimeter. I am going down there and have a look."

Homer raised his gaze from the corner shadows and turned turtle-like to look at the young sergeant. "That is something that you do not need to do. We will manage here without you risking your team." The toothpick hung on his lower lip.

Ryan studied the younger sergeant. "You are quite serious about this, aren't you?"

Ziobron filled his lungs and raised his head in final decision. "Yes."

He looked at the two men. "If you can give me the layout of the minefield and guide me as to how the teams went down in the past, I will lay out a compass course I can follow in the dark. I will get my people ready and we can go in the morning before daylight." He looked at Homer, "I will need the radio frequencies and call signs. I will plan to be back before dark tomorrow. Just a short recon."

Ryan considered clearing it with Kontum. "Maybe we could think of it as doing a patrol around the perimeter and leave it at that."

"Maps?"

"Got what you need."

"One other thing. I will need to know where all the mines are so I can navigate them in the dark with just my compass. And we need to know where the wires are so we don't set off any trip flares."

Homer nodded. "I can get you the maps for sure but with all of that down there we need to be very sure when we change them from true north to magnetic, we even put in variation and any local changes. I'm getting too old to go down there looking for missing feet."

A sound, like hacking up phlegm, followed by a loud voice speaking Vietnamese halted their conversation. The hacking sound was static and the words following had a tone of a commander giving orders. "Oh," Homer continued, "That is your enemy down the hill. We are intercepting their traffic on the NSA radios. We listen in on their conversations. Amazing what we hear. Someone in Washington is probably plugging that into their intelligence assessment."

Homer smiled at Ziobron. "Well, at least we didn't hear them say your name in that conversation, Sergeant."

"Gee, no one to welcome us!"

Ryan studied the handsome young sergeant. Ziobron was fearless and full of energy. "I will let the guards on perimeter know when you leave so you do not get shot up going through the line. You will have to let us know when you are coming back up here so we can let the little people know. When the Yards hear anything down the hill they tend to throw a grenade down at it. A grenade goes a long way from up here."

Ziobron picked up his rifle and cradled it in the crook of his arm. "That's it then. I am going to alert my team and then figure out how to navigate the mine fields down the mountain in the dark."

The sliver of moon on the back side of Leghorn's pinnacle barely produced a shadow as the six men slipped over the perimeter wall. That hint of light hardly demarked the sky from the ground and were it not for the stars constrained in their constellations, they would have had to maneuver by braille. Ed Ziobron eased over the wall, his foot touching down on a clod of dirt. He shuddered to think he may have placed his foot squarely on the coiled snake of the morning. He proceeded on the route memorized from the map, relying on his compass and counting his steps. Something touched the front of his lower leg. He stopped mid-stride. Was it the brush of reeds or a taut trip wire? He reached down and felt blades of stiff weeds. Before setting his foot, he felt the soil for anything that could betray their presence. Black tape covered anything that could shine even in the near dark. Their faces and the backs of their hands were blackened and they edged their way at the speed of shadows that advanced before the faint moon.

Ziobron slid his foot to the side to confirm the path and felt something solid, unlike dirt clogs or tufts of grass. Keeping his foot in place, he sank to his knees. His fingers brushed the place, like a blind man reading a page. The object was small and round and smooth, perhaps exposed by past rain. His first thoughts were a toe popper mine or a bouncing Betty, the dreaded one that flew into the air at groin height before exploding. Either of those mines could destroy a foot or spring into the air and shred a torso with shrapnel. Had he veered off course?

He turned and whispered to Nhet, his point man, "Mine."

His heart quickened. He glanced around for clues to fix his position. Even a few feet from the path he memorized could be fatal. He looked to the constellations and the grade before him. Before they began the descent, he had placed his grenades in a pouch and slung his rifle to distance the metal from his compass. He knew the knife on his harness was not enough to throw off the compass needle. He adjusted his course a few degrees and moved on.

For three hours, they groped ahead, moving, stopping and listening, moving again. He glanced back. The sharp peak of Leghorn loomed, barely discernable against the dark grey sky. The steepness of the mountain lessened as they descended and he sensed the thickness of the hardwood forest as shrubs pressed his legs. Even the air felt denser. He filled his lungs with the fecund odor of dense foliage and noticed the humidity rising from the leaves. He glanced skyward and gauged the waning of the night. It was imperative they be off the hill and deep into cover before daylight left them exposed. They listened in their security stop.

In the fullness of a tall tree was a single peep. He fancied a sleeping bird having a nightmare. Team Ziobron barely breathed as they listened. Silence. A silence so complete he thought he could hear evaporation as it steamed from the undergrowth.

Another chirp. Three times, soft muffled chirps, "chirp, chirp, chirp." He was sure it did not originate from the throat of a trail watcher. He imagined a small yellow bird in a nest, encircled in its down, eyes closed, its chest moving in and out in sleep.

They rose to their feet. The brush of their clothing seemed loud. They were well past the mines and trip flares and tin cans which hung in the wire with stone pebbles inside ready to rattle when bumped to alert the sleepiest guard. A hundred or more feet to the side, sounds of thrashing erupted in the grass. Weapons ready, they faced the struggle. Small twigs snapped like lady finger fireworks. The team coiled to a crouch, expecting advancing enemy. Eyes pierced the shadows for targets. Their brains computed the disturbance. It came from a single location. Two creatures were in mortal struggle. The sergeant reached back and tapped the arm of the closest Montagnard twice. "Go! Go!" the signal said. They rushed, using the rustling of the animal and prey to mask their own movement. A dozen yards away, with the diminishing struggle, he slowed the pace. Ziobron wished he could continue more quickly and find concealment in a defendable location before light exposed them. From there they could assess the presence of the North Vietnamese. He motioned for his lead man, Nhet, to take point. In the poor visibility, smell and hearing were more important than sight, and the Yards were more attuned to the jungle than he.

They crept west a hundred yards where the ground sloped abruptly upward. He recalled from his map study how the contour lines formed a circle and were close together to show a small hill. It could be a natural defense assuming the enemy had not considered the same thing and formed their own RON at the place. Even now, they might be challenged by a sentry on duty. Nearing the top they stopped even more frequently. He sensed Nhet bent over, looking side to side and listening. All was as still as a tomb, and they moved with the stealth of death as it creeps to the foot of a sick-bed. They listened for Death breathing in the dark.

At the military crest he halted the team. It was becoming increasingly more difficult to move quietly in the poor light as the vegetation grew thicker. They formed a tight circle, each facing outward, touch-close, and waited for the day.

Like spectators at the start of a play waiting for the murmur of the crowd to cease and the stage lights to brighten degree by degree, they remained. A muffled cough covered by a sleeve of vegetation startled them with its nearness. A half hour later an engine labored to start. It turned over reluctantly a few times before it caught and hummed in the distance.

People chopped wood close by, and nearer yet, they heard the clattering of mess kits and muffled speech, perhaps cooks in preparation. The speakers were careless, unaware there could be listeners in the bushes.

The sky lightened revealing the contour of the ground but color had not arrived. Birds awakened to a new day and fluttered low over their heads.

More coughing beyond the bushes. It was rasping and sickly. Ziobron recalled Dale Hanson talking about the cough of an emaciated rickshaw driver in Kontum. He was slumped over the handlebars, trying to catch his breath. He said the ribs of his chest were like flimsy slats of a birdcage and he wondered if the gasping sick man secretly hoped that he would not get a fare. Hanson said, "The soul of the man was like a caged bird ready to fly into the sky when the door of life opened. And his mouth was opened wide like a door, big enough for his soul to squeeze through anyway."

Ziobron had that image in his mind as he listened to the sickly man on the other side of the bushes. Perhaps he had taken sick along the long journey from Hanoi, through Laos, and on into Cambodia. Or were the Communists filling its ranks with villagers impressed along the way? Ziobron thought, "Could I be listening to a slave laborer, to be used and then discarded along the trail when he could no longer carry a load?" Ziobron would write these thoughts in his notebook.

Ziobron saw his machine gunner flinch, when, even more close, there was moaning as of someone stretching in sleep. It was followed by rustling and the stirring of many people. The camp was waking. More coughing and muted conversation. A raised voice.

A couple of the tribesmen looked up nervously and glanced at Ziobron to be sure he was aware of the danger. It could be only minutes before they were discovered. In their stealth the team had passed by an enemy encampment, passed their outposts and sentries, perhaps even as it had happened to other teams, they had stopped inside the perimeter of a large force and in their stealth encircled themselves. Ziobron held his breath. He glanced to the side. His people leaned forward, stiff and as ready as the viper of the morning. Their eyes never left the bushes. No command would need to be given to fire. The least wide-awake enemy soldier could see the team when he left the perimeter to relieve himself.

Ziobron softly clicked his tongue and pointed a direction with his chin to a place deeper into the brush. They rose, erased all trace of where they had been, and stole deeper into the undergrowth. The tail gunner walked backwards and lifted the grass of their backtrail. Y Lap stood over his form and covered him with his rifle.

They found an area of bamboo and thick brush to conceal themselves and from which they could put up a strong defense. Ziobron gave the sign to circle. At a signal, Hiep crawled forward and placed a Claymore on the enemy side of a tree.

The same bushes and shrubs which hid the encampment from view only forty or fifty yards away now revealed it, as vegetation swayed and shivered from motion on the other side. Three or four times, branches parted as uniformed men emerged and relieved themselves. Although they were only a dozen yards from the ready Montagnards, they never raised their eyes and discover the recon team.

Ziobron's people prepared to fight. Thil Bae, a Rhade tribesman removed his rucksack and propped his M-60 machine gun on its bulk, then lay on his stomach behind it. Phui Don lay next to him with his M-79 grenade launcher with a canister round of lead pellets to deal with the mass of enemy, to be followed with a CS tear gas round to confuse the North Vietnamese. The others readied their rifles.

At least a company was before them. Camp noise of a group confident they were safe in their own backyard said as much. At a muffled command, the company prepared to leave. A few soldiers groaned as they hefted heavy packs to their backs. Thumping of half-empty canteens, metal tapping against wooden rifle stocks, and canvas straps rubbing against uniform cloth accompanied trudging foot falls as the unit peeled from the area. Their feet trampled weeds and dry things and in minutes there was complete silence when the force joined a hard-packed trail and traveled to an appointed destination.

The recon team remained in place. Silence enveloped them. They listened for a stay-behind unit, or possibility of an ambush. Twenty minutes. Ziobron pointed to Nhet, his Rhade tribesman in an NVA uniform and AK-47 and signaled him to check out the RON site of the enemy. "Go slow. Be very careful," he signed. "We will follow you at a distance."

Nhet understood. Dressed as an NVA it would be perfectly

normal for him to approach the site. He slipped from the circle.

A dozen paces from the others, he straightened. With his rifle slung over his shoulder he moved with the confident air of a person who belonged, but he held the strap of the weapon in a way he could slide to shoot in a flash of time. At the edge of the campsite, he stopped and listened for movement. He heard rustling in the grass. His AK-47 rolled from his shoulder to the ready. He looked back at the team, signaled his concern, then parted the leaves and stepped into the edge of the opening.

A dozen birds strutted in the clearing, scratching and pecking at rice grains and food left with the passing. He scanned the shrubs looking for a waiting enemy, then entered the clearing. It was empty of men.

The recon team joined Nhet. Ziobron pointed to Thil Bae with the M-60 machine gun and signaled him to watch the trail the enemy had left, then positioned Y Lap with his M-16 to the opposite side. The opening was a danger area, but he would risk exposure to gain information about the enemy. Phui-Don was standing next to him clearly guarding his safety.

"Phui-Don, run quick and see places where *Cong Sahn* lay. Look. Look see if they *fini* anything. Count how many soldiers here. *Biet? Di! Di!*" he whispered. "Go! Go!"

They ranged across the area, looking for anything left by the enemy.

Phui-Don, his M-79 man, shuffled to Ziobron and placed his mouth close to his ear. "Think maybe one hundred *Cong Sahn* stay here."

The tribesman was troubled. His brow was wrinkled. Ziobron had never seen a Montagnard wrinkle his forehead. "VC maybe him go, but him smell still here. This place still have smell him, like maybe him not all go *fini* yet."

Ziobron understood. "Yes, I smell VC too. I know what you are thinking."

"Yes, I smell him stink. Him sweat *beaucoup*. Him not take bath long time."

Ziobron knew the Montagnard was concerned the enemy had left in body but his spirit stayed behind to watch the camp. They had not been in the campsite two minutes but Ziobron was uneasy that even that was too long and wanted to button things up.

"How many VC sleep here last night? Did you *fini* counting places matted on ground?"

The Montagnard looked at his fingers, thinking how to say ten tens. When he came up with the word, his eyes lifted from his fingers and he said, "One hundred. One hundred VC sleep here last night."

"Did you find anything on the ground that VC left?"

"Nothing. VC *fini* everything." Then he added as running brown birds bobbed their heads in the grass. "Except what birds find now."

He was surprised they had found nothing of intelligence value left behind by a careless soldier. He only learned that they moved with a confidence of being in their own territory. Although they policed the RON before they left it, they seemed not have outposts around their perimeter nor practice noise discipline. They had not cooked here and Ziobron wondered if there was a staging area farther on. These were things he would enter in his notebook

Ziobron pointed a compass heading to the point man and they proceeded west.

They reconned for nearly two hours, stopping often for security, and passing through a grove of bamboo with shrieking white-faced monkeys in the tops which scolded and threw moist brown pellets at them. Skirting a marshy area, they entered a grove of hardwood trees surrounded by tall grass. The point man froze. Ziobron was close behind and did not move even to signal to the Yard behind to stop. Danger was palpable but neither of them discerned the source. Acute danger was nearby.

Nhet sunk lower down and faced the American. A slight breeze brushed their faces. There was a half-smile on his face as he slowly brought his hands up to his nose. He need not have done so, for Ziobron smelled it at the same time. Someone was smoking not too far away. He knew the smell. It came from the French cigarettes the Viets so loved.

Ziobron slowly faced his people, brought his hand to his nose, then to the back of his head in the sign for, "enemy, danger, we smell something."

They crouched, ready for their leader's command. Ziobron had determined before they left the radio relay site, that this would be a mission to gather information, not to engage the enemy. They could easily take out this soldier, perhaps even capture him, but that would just be the beginning. He had no assets on standby and many North Vietnamese between him and Leghorn.

A voice speaking Vietnamese joined the smoker, "Hey, hey, so there you are hiding. Where did you get those good French cigarettes?"

The response was quiet and sullen and muffled in the leaves.

"Hey, I only have these."

"Hey, remember, I covered for you when you fell asleep on guard. You remember that, huh?"

There was a pause as the smoker realized that he had no choice. "Yah, yah. But that's all I got."

"What are buddies for anyway, huh?"

There was a pause as the soldier lit his cigarette. "The captain sent me to get you. We are moving out in twenty minutes." The team heard him as he made a place in the grass to finish his cigarette. A few minutes later he stood and warned, "Twenty minutes!"

"Yah, yah."

The soldier grunted and stood and shuffled off into the bushes.

He had called the captain *"dai úy,"* which meant he commanded a company of soldiers—too many for a small recon team. They waited as the force assembled and passed across their flank and disappeared.

They probed west ever deeper into the sanctuary crossing overgrown trails and found an abandoned bunker with caved-in sides edged by a row of six grave-like mounds. They skirted open areas keeping to thick undergrowth and discovered a recent trail where the tree limbs above were bowed across and tied into an arch. At a bend in the trail where they could see down both axes, they set up to monitor movement. Twice, company sized units passed by moving inexorably to the southeast and the war in Vietnam. Ziobron counted the men and noted the discipline with which they moved. No point element scouted before them for security. They moved at a brisk pace for their appointment of war. He wanted a better view to see the uniforms, weapons, the condition of the troops, and if possible, even the rank and patches of their unit. They crept closer to the trail and hid in the elephant grass and vines. His Yards looked at his face to be certain he wanted to be this near.

He smelled garlic!

Hanson once told him that he discovered an ambush by being close enough to smell an enemy's breath. Well, he did so now. He smelled garlic. He glanced sideways at Nhet, his point man. He wrinkled his nose and gravely nodded in agreement, "I smell it too."

His people squatted on their heels, hiding in the sawgrass. Ziobron lowered himself to one knee, thankful the tendons gave no popping sound. The Yards peered through the greenery like owls searching for mice among the stalks. Nhet edged forward then stopped. The corners of his eyes wrinkled. He faced his team leader and smiled, a full smile that revealed his toothless gums. An enemy soldier was fast asleep in the bushes. He lay on his back with his mouth fully open, his head resting on his flop hat on a mound of grass and his weapon in the dirt by his feet. His sleep was deep with his eyelids tightly shut over his eyes. The breaths were deep, filling his rising chest. His inhale paused at the full like a timid skier at the top of a run before he exhaled down the run as the strong odor of garlic leaped into space.

Ziobron made a calculation of taking this man prisoner. They were in the center of enemy controlled territory with occasional troops passing by. No air support stood by if they needed it. He considered the risk and the value of this enemy private who was asleep on guard duty. What could he know that would be of value? But taking this man prisoner could be done in a minute; just tap him on the head, drag him from the trail where they would tie and gag him, and be off. It would be done quickly and quietly-knocked out he would not even need to be tied next to the trail. They would be certain that the trail was clear, do the job, and be gone.

He signaled his intention and what he wanted his people to do. He needed a sap. The back of his combat knife would do. One glance to be sure his people were in place and that the trail was clear, and he made a rush to the hibernate man.

He was two steps from him with his arm raised to strike, when a loud voice came from the other side of the bushes. Ziobron had just enough time to spring back but saw the heavy turtle-like eyelids slowly raise.

Had the waking sleeper time to take in his image? The team expected instant combat.

"Tran," the voice called in Vietnamese, "Tran. Are you sleeping? Why didn't you see me coming?"

"Huh? Huh?" The voice of the waking sleeper was puzzled and afraid.

They heard the bushes part and the voice standing over the prostrate form on the ground.

"Huh? Aaugh!" The waking soldier cried in fear, his fingers clawing the air. "Ah, it's you, it's you." His voice was high pitched.

"Of course, it's me. Why are you happy at that? You have been asleep again. I caught you."

"No. I thought you . . . I saw a green man over me. He was there. He was right here where you are standing now." Tran said.

"You were dreaming. Tell the captain your dream."

"No, it was real. His face was green and his eyes and teeth were white. He was green like mold and slime from *Thu Huon*."

The man stared at him, wondering what to do. "You can see me standing here, that it was me. Maybe you have a bad dream that is all."

The team was still close enough in their silent get away to hear the sleeper sit up on his nest.

"I see him for sure and I blink my eyes and then I see you. But green man was real. You know story of Thu Huon, same me. One day every year there is the gate in the Yin Yang marketplace when living people can visit dead relatives. There is very bad hell. Sometimes very bad people sneak out of gate from hell and walk around. They have mold and green slime on them. One come to take me. I see him!"

There was silence as the man pondered what do for his friend. Tran was utterly convinced at what he saw.

"Okay. I say I believe you. When our people come, we will look for trail of Thu Huon. You okay now?"

The sleeper did not answer. Ziobron imagined the scene—him lying there, his terrified eyes boring between each stalk of vegetation for lurking green men.

"Here, I'll help you up."

He imagined him extending one hand and pulling on his arm. There was a grunt as he stood.

"We have to go. *Đai úy* send me. Let's go."

Another pause.

"Hey, get your rifle."

The team drew back and became one with the vegetation. Im Nei Ksor, the interpreter, edged over and translated the conversation for Ziobron in a whisper. He added, "Him tell other VC. For sure, if VC come back, they find our trail."

"Thank you, Ksor. It's time for us to go back to Leghorn anyway. I want to be through the perimeter before dark." He patted the tribesman on the shoulder.

"Nhet, we go to Leghorn now."

They patrolled east to the promontory that was Leghorn. Twice they heard breaking twigs and sounds of large formations moving, but the direction was toward the war in the south, and they waited for them to pass. With only hours left in the day they arrived at the steep ascent to the radio relay site. The last of the thick forest was giving way to bushes when Nhet held up his hand. The team dropped to the ready. A high-speed trail that had been hidden in the thickness barred their way. The sound of enemy on the move confirmed its presence; the shuffling of a hundred pairs of boots and heavy breathing of burdened men on the march. Scant yards before them, a column of North Vietnamese regulars appeared in full uniform and web gear. RPD machine guns and AK-47 rifles were slung over their shoulders. A few balanced B-40 rockets across their backs. Had any of them looked to the side it would have been impossible not to see the team along the trail. One look would signal the start of a firefight.

They passed across their front left to right, unspeaking, moving at a fast pace. How could they not see the team? Ziobron studied their faces as they passed, waiting for that fatal glance from the enemy. It never came. Every passing soldier was looking upward as they marched, at Leghorn.

They disappeared down the trail, the sounds of the passing unit lagging behind like a rear guard. The team gave it five minutes, crossed the enemy path, and climbed the pinnacle to the relay site.

"Glad to see you boys," Homer said, spitting out his toothpick. His drawl hid his apprehension for the team. "We watched you climb back. Even though you radioed you were coming in, it was hard to see you. We looked to see if Charlie was watching but didn't see 'em."

Rich Ryan patted the shoulders of the weary little people. "Don't let that old buzzard act like he didn't worry about you. He spent half the day at the sandbags with his binoculars watching for you. He made you guys a C ration stew if you want some."

Ziobron glanced at his Montagnards to see if they were interested. "We could eat as much as a water buffalo does. That is if there are no ribs in it."

Homer smiled at the young sergeant. "Trust me."

Six times over the next ten days Ziobron repeated his foray into Indian country. Each day as dusk sent monkeys to their safe place in the trees with their babes necklaced by slender arms, and the rare tiger to wait at the watering hole with striped sides matching the tall grass along the banks, the six men stumbled back to the safe side of the sandbags. They arrived exhausted from the near-vertical climb, and spent from the tension of being spit-close to the enemy. He fed his people and rested as he archived his findings, mapped enemy trails and filled his notebook with the locations of bunkers and staging areas. When his notations were to his satisfaction in six-digit coordinates and there was still light enough to see, he made his vigil to a certain crag on the cliff overlooking the Communist sanctuary below and sought out that which deserved a closer look. He would go to the bunker where his people cooked around a fire of C-4, duck his head as he entered the low opening, his body a shadow against the fading light, and quietly say into the dim interior, "Get some sleep. We are going in before daylight."

They never groaned aloud with the order but looked into each other's faces in disbelief. "Again!" they thought. But they faithfully prepared for each mission, and followed their sergeant, and as darkness surrendered to the first rays of morning, found themselves at a new point of danger.

"Our intel will be very happy with what you learned. We knew PAVN was thick as flees on a hound below us, but not their units and equipment," Rich Ryan said. He added Tabasco sauce to the concoction he was stirring. "Oh. Before I forget, FOB reminded us, you and your people are due to go back to the FOB tomorrow. It won't be the same here, Ed. You did a great job down there."

"It is just what we Green Berets do, Rich."

Ziobron was seated by himself in the mess hall, the farthest table away from the side door with his back to the wall—a habit all of us would carry after the war. But his head was down as he ate, for he was among his own in the FOB. He ate hungrily but he seemed weary as I noticed him across the room. Eating, a shower, and a soft bed were on his mind. His jungle fatigues were dark with sweat. Circles of salt stained his arm pits. Even his bandana was limp and dark, almost black, along the side of his face.

I joined him with my tray of food. "Nice costume," I said, "Reminds me of a soldier who just came from the field."

He looked up. A bright smile. His voice summoned up energy to talk. "Hey, Dale. If I look like I feel, I should win first prize."

"Just get in? I didn't hear the choppers."

"Couple of hours ago. Had to take care of my people first. I'm starved for real food."

"Glad you are back. Missed our workouts."

Ziobron nodded. The last thing on his mind was a speed run to the Dak Bla River and back.

"Anything happen while I was gone?"

Out of habit I glanced around before I answered. The hum of conversation at the other tables and the clatter of plates and utensils tented our conversation. "Our recon teams have been using the good weather and have had several missions. So far all have made it back with good intel." I looked around to be sure the Vietnamese helper was not in earshot as she cleaned tables. "I think we have people going in shortly."

"What else," I thought. "Oh, while you were gone, Cambodia booted their king after about twelve hundred years of dynasty and appointed a guy named Lon Nol as president. The thought was that the king made so many deals with the Communists and would not go in even with all of the equipment the US gave him, that PAVN has the east half of the country for a sanctuary. We will see how that goes with the new guy."

"I would like to have been behind the scenes on that one," Ziobron said. "I remember you telling me about the phony war on the Plain of Jars when Laos set up all of those fake tanks and wood artillery pieces where they could be seen by our spy planes and claimed that they were being invaded. So, Uncle Sam gave them all that money and military help and sent advisors."

"Let's see. What else happened while you were gone? President Ky of Vietnam spoke to the class at West Point and warned about giving in to the anti-war bunch. He obviously was well aware of how Vietnamization was being pushed in the States. He cautioned about withdrawing American troops too fast. He said Cambodia would fall in twenty-four hours if the US left and South Vietnam had to go it alone."

"Good for him," Ziobron said slapping the tabletop. "Good for him. I liked him. He was a fighter and a pilot, not quite like some of the others."

"What else? Oh, the left-wing national news they listen to at home. This week the trial of Lieutenant William Calley was the big story. Remember, he and his men went into a friendly village and torched it and murdered over a hundred women and children. They tell me that the newspapers and magazines and television show burned bodies of little children. Obviously the pinko bunch are emphasizing it to paint us all as monsters."

Ziobron's hands grasped the edge of the table. "Are kidding me?" He looked around him and lowered his voice. "Are you kidding me?"

"Not kidding. I cannot express in words my hatred for Calley's criminal behavior and cowardness. Nothing can excuse that atrocity, but I also find it strange when the Communists do that over here all the time and you don't hear a peep in the papers."

He slammed the table with his fist.

"There's more, Ed. CBS went to great lengths to show troopers of the First Cav Division over here smoking pot through the barrel of a shotgun. The Communists do not need to do propaganda; our press does it for them."

Ziobron slid the salt shaker back and forth between his hands on the table. "I am so mad I can't talk. Calley should be executed, the dope heads belong in a stockade, and the press should be charged with collaborating with the enemy!"

"I agree." I pointed. "Your food is getting cold. I better tell you some good things that happened before you explode. Our SEAL friends hit a POW camp in the delta area and freed nineteen Vietnamese who were captive in those cages. They were scrawny and dazed at being freed. Their eyes looked like someone in a dark room when they turn on the bright lights Their mouths were open as if they could not express their thoughts in words. I saw the pictures.

"More! I don't have all of the information yet, but last week while you were at Leghorn, Special Forces pulled off a huge raid on a POW camp only twenty miles from Hanoi. Get that? Only twenty miles from the capital of North Vietnam. The place was called Son Tay. It was right under their noses. I wish the general staff of North Vietnam were having breakfast on the veranda and could have heard the shots. They did it right in the face of Ho Chi Minh or whoever else was around. Gutsy! There was an enemy base only five miles from the target with twelve thousand soldiers. They could have made it to Son Tay in a half hour.

"About fifty of our Special Forces guys made the landing into the compound and strategic points. They had choreographed air support and diversions. It went with precision and without a casualty. The only problem was that PAVN had moved the prisoners to another location just before they assaulted the base.

"The newspapers jumped on that one. They said the mission was 'poorly planned' and our 'intelligence was sloppy.'"

"Of course."

"I hope somehow that the POWs hear about it and know that they are not forgotten."

We were eating, engrossed in our thoughts when I uttered what nagged on my mind. "I have heard from someone, that the upper echelon planners picked Son Tay because they knew there were no prisoners. But I don't even want to think about that one."

The mess hall was thinning out and conversation from the other tables diminished. I heard lunch plates being scraped over the slop barrel at the other end of the hall and dinnerware being dropped into the tubs of water. Both of us had been thinking of our people held in bamboo cages or slave labor. "Ed, this idea of ever becoming a prisoner, you know getting wounded and captured on one of our missions. One of the guys told me that he wears no socks and he puts a little bit of coarse sand and pebbles in his jungle boots to harden his feet. He said that the North Vietnamese take prisoners' boots first thing and make them go barefooted. They know our feet are tender and we would have a hard time escaping."

Ziobron slid his plate away. "It is getting more possible."

"I tried the sand thing but gave it up after one day. I choose to die fighting."

Dessert was a low cake smothered in peaches and we were finishing ours when two of our people in sterile fatigues entered the mess hall and looked around the room. One of them spotted Ziobron and pointed. Without looking to the side, they walked briskly to our table.

"Hey, Sundance," one of them said, using his code name, "We heard you were back. Boy we are glad to find you."

Ziobron pointed to the empty chairs at our table.

"Glad to see you guys too. Do I owe you money?"

"Nah. Nothing like that. Worse!"

"Uh oh! I don't like the sound of that." And he turned to me. "These guys are in A Company with me, same platoon. That one is Chester Zaborowski, our medic and this is Clyde Conkin. This is Dale Hanson."

We shook hands but they barely noticed me. "And you are about to go into the field," I said.

"Huh!"

"You are sterile. You are ready to go in."

Conkin glanced down at his fatigues. "Yes. It's why we are here looking for you, Ed. We are going in in the morning." He sighed deeply wondering if he should go on. "We want you to come with us."

"I just got out of the field. I haven't even showered."

Zaborowski glanced over the table for my reaction.

Conkin leaned forward in his chair and lowered his voice. "We really need you on this one."

He removed his glasses and held them in his hands. He looked down and seemed to speak at the lenses. "Ed, I know that you just came off Leghorn and are not looking to go back in the field so soon, but here is the story. It is just our platoon going in: Clyde and me and two new people just assigned. The target is across the fence in bad country; search and destroy, recon, and maybe a POW camp, that kind of thing. The kind of mission we might survive with good leadership."

Zaborowski took over the narrative. "Ed, Clyde and I are dreading this one. Our little people are up to the mission, no problem. The concern is the new people they assigned to lead us. Somebody sent us this second lieutenant who, as far as we know, has never been in combat. He came from the marines. Can you imagine that—the marines! Probably one of Abram's people. Ran him through the officer's Q course and sent him to us. He has no idea how to do a SOG mission. He has not done a single training session with the SCU, and has not spent a minute getting to know the Montagnards. He is extremely out of shape and at least forty pounds overweight. He waddles across the compound as if he were Napoleon. Our little people don't know what to make of him. I cannot imagine what they were thinking letting him lead a mission on a dangerous target. Are they trying to get us killed?"

The dining hall was nearly empty. The mess sergeant slapped the metal slop can with a heavy spoon to remind us that he was there and wanted to close up and clean. The two sergeants continued to talk, heedless of the urging to finish and leave.

"As the medic on the platoon," Conkin said, "I will tell you that the man is so out of shape he will not be able to keep up with the regular movement of our people."

"Oh boy," I said hearing the dread in my voice.

"There's more," Zaborowski said. They assigned us a platoon sergeant who is new to SOG. He has never been on one of our operations either. We don't know where he has been before, but he is a bundle of nerves about to crack. All of that leaves the two of us with the platoon. We have been in the field before but we don't have the experience to lead the team if it all goes south."

"We need you on this one."

I glanced at Ziobron. I knew my friend. The need itself was his decision. He would always be there for his people.

"You are going in in the morning? How could you get me assigned that quickly? Would that lieutenant want me to strap hang? I would have to spend all night to get ready to insert in the morning."

"Ed, I think the team sergeant is so nervous he would be glad to have you. We could tell him that you are the recon element of the company and could scout ahead for security. Captain Krupa will go for that. We will do all of that and get you on the roster."

"Have either of you guys been to any of the briefings on the mission? What did you learn?"

"We haven't had any briefings on the mission. The lieutenant has not told us anything."

"Maps?"

Zaborowski had his head down and looked over the top of his glasses. "I guess he thinks because I am the medic, I don't need one."

Conkin said, "I don't have one either. We also have not had an inspection of our people to be sure they are ready nor had any training with the new leaders."

"If my recon people go in tomorrow, I want maps or I don't go."

"We will get them."

"Okay. I will round up my little people and get us ready for the morning. It might take us all night."

The mess sergeant sent a Vietnamese dish washer to our table to collect our trays. She was old and waddled over to us. Her hair was tied in a bun with a pair of chopsticks holding it in place. When she smiled her teeth were black like rows of raisins.

"*Tôi xin lỗi,*" (I am sorry) she said, for she knew she was there to hurry our conversation and leave the mess hall.

"*Cam on ban bà,*" I said to her. (Thank you, ma'am.)

We stood. I reached back and ate the rest of my peach. "All right! Let's do it!" Ziobron said.

Ziobron skipped the steak he had dreamed of for the last week, with mushrooms and onions and melted fat sliding off the top. He ate instead with his little people in the Montagnard mess hall. The fare was that which tribesman have eaten for centuries in steamy jungles: portions of rice and brined pork, raw vegetables seasoned with the pungent fish water collected from carcasses of fish left hanging from the rafters, and brown fermented eggs shelled and eaten with a spoon, the consistency of yogurt. Phui-Don was across from Ziobron with both cheeks chipmunked with egg. He stopped mid chew. "You no eat. You no like?"

Ziobron realized that he was not eating, gazing instead at the joyful way his people devoured their meal. "No, just watching you." He swallowed to prepare himself and spooned month-old egg into his mouth.

Finished, they drew supplies for the operation, then isolated themselves in a hooch on the back side of the compound. It was an empty one room affair just behind the Huckleberry Inn, Muffled music from the reel-to-reel tape deck filtered inside. Base notes of the songs were nearly felt. The team worked into the night cleaning weapons, preparing rations and configuring their gear.

I tapped lightly on the door.

"Come in little fella," drawled one of the Montagnards, imitating John Wayne.

I opened the door and the moon rushed in and lay on the floor like a yellow dog. Fresh air slipped in among the sweating men. "I brought you a case of cold pop. Do you have anything I can do? I could help you load magazines," but even as I said it, I knew they, like me, would want to configure their own gear. Behind me, a soldier stood in the open back door of the club taking in the night air. Simon and Garfunkel played on the tape deck inside the Huckleberry Inn. The Yards did not know the lyrics but hummed the melody as they added spices and anchovies to their rice rations.

*When you're weary*
*Feeling small*
*When tears are in your eyes*
*I will dry them all*
*I'm on your side*
*Oh, when times get tough*
*And friends just can't be found*

*Like a bridge over troubled water*
*I will lay me down*
*Like a bridge over troubled water*
*I will lay me down*

"What can I do, Ed?"

He looked around at his people. "Nothing really. Anything left to do we have to do ourselves. But I think we will be at it all night."

"I will check on you during the night. Got your maps and things?"

"Got the maps. I went to the TOC myself and got them. Clyde and Chet took care of everything else. Still haven't met the lieutenant or team sergeant."

"Figured," I said. "I know that you haven't been informed about that target so I did some sneaky Pete. From the map they gave you I found teams that had been in that area before. None of them have been able to stay very long without getting shot out. I guess that is why they call them target areas. The consensus is that there is a heavy enemy presence, and lots of activity."

I wondered if I should have said all of that. I did not want to add stress but I wanted him to be fully aware of the situation on the ground. My friend did not look up. He sat on the floor with his back against the wall. He breathed slowly and deeply, his normal exuberance abated. I glanced at his people to gauge the extent they were following remarks I meant only for him, trusting the language barrier to block my nuance.

"I was able to learn from some of my recon friends and a friend in intelligence something else."

I glanced again at his people. They were engrossed in their preparation for the mission and conversing in low tones.

"Ed, you are going smack into the Communist Base Area 609. That is the home of the 28th NVA Regiment. You may need to be the main person who is calm and wise in the platoon."

He slowly nodded. Almost with ceremony, he pressed each bullet into his rifle magazines, as one would who writes a note on an artillery round, and signs it before it is launched, "For Charlie, from Ed."

"I will be praying for you as I always do."

I hoped I was not communicating dread and foreboding instead of useful information.

Ziobron smiled. It was a weary one, but a smile. "You always do and I know it."

I rose to go. Two of the little people hummed in guttural tones, the genesis of which were hundreds of years old, from the other side of the morning mists, always one hill away. But the tune was only minutes old, from Bridge Over Troubled Water. I patted them on their shoulders and left the building. The air was fresh with the night but the compound was dark, and it seemed that the moon no longer shined.

Three deuce-and-a-half trucks noised into the compound and fish-hooked to a stop beside the waiting platoon. "Load up," the platoon sergeant barked. The lieutenant stood beside the flag pole and watched them file to the trucks. His eyes were small black beads in the folds of his flesh as he monitored the boarding soldiers. Loading complete, he nodded for the drivers to proceed to the waiting helicopters. Grunting, he hoisted himself into the cab.

Seven Huey helicopters waited at the airport with the rotor blades turning slowly and the soldiers rushed aboard holding their flop hats and squinting against the dust. They skirted the city and the eyes which watched for signs of impending missions. They flew high, above small arms fire, and twice changed direction from the direct course to Dak To, descending finally at the launch site. Covey reported the target socked-in with night fog and it was necessary to wait for it to burn off. The lieutenant faced forward and remained on the canvass seat without replying. When it was clear that all would remain where they were, Ziobron, remembering the chain of command, approached the platoon sergeant.

"Sergeant, you probably thought of this already, but we usually get the men off and away from the aircraft when we have to wait like this. Enemy spotters on the ridges can see the choppers on the runway and might send rockets and heavy mortars on such tempting targets. You probably saw the flash on the ridge. It might have been from binoculars."

The platoon sergeant was startled and his eyes flicked in the direction of the hills that bordered the helipad. "I'll tell him." He grabbed his rifle and hustled to the officer.

The lieutenant was mopping his forehead with his cravat when the sergeant relayed the information. He looked at his wrist watch and blew away sweat that rolled along his cheek and furrowed into his mouth. He looked at the sky in irritation, then upward at the control tower. The platoon sergeant remained at the helicopter door and waited for the order to deplane but the officer looked away without answering. The platoon sergeant looked toward Ziobron and slowly shook his head and returned to his own people.

Ziobron glanced up at the row of hills. Certainly, by now, PAVN had counted the helicopters and guessed how many soldiers were in them. He imagined men under straw conical hats with mortars suspended over the tubes just waiting for the order. Ziobron and his people were in the third chopper in the string of aircraft. It occurred to him this was the order of landing on the LZ. Perhaps the lieutenant had not noticed the mistake. He jumped from the strut and strode over to the perspiring officer.

"Sir, I noticed that you have me on the third lift. We are your recon element. Shouldn't we be the first to go in?"

"Sergeant, I am in charge of this operation and I say what goes. Is that clear?"

Ziobron was surprised at the tone and paused to be sure he heard correctly. "As you say, sir."

A half hour later, the control tower shouted down at the assembled group, "Covey says the target is clear and assets are in the air."

The Hueys started with a hiss and slow circuit of rotor blades. As the craft made full RPM, the Bright Light team on the ground faced away and held their flop hats against the blast of air and debris.

They lifted off in unison—a string of helicopters with lethal Cobra gunships on either flank. Covey circled nearby ready to marshal attack aircraft should the need arise.

Forty-five minutes. Covey directed the first lift to a break in the canopy where they would glide to a hover and let the soldiers jump off. When the pilot was certain of the location, he placed the opening at a spot on his windshield and ensured it moved neither up nor down on the glass to remain on the glide slope. Before him, a Charlie model crossed his bow and made a low pass over the opening to draw fire and, drawing none, was followed by the choppers carrying troops. It was hoped that the enemy would think choppers would not be able to land in the confined space and leave it unguarded. The pilot held his breath as he slid into the opening—a metal letter opener sliding into an envelope. "Here we go then, air mail," he thought. He must have said it aloud for his co-pilot added, "Special delivery." Thin branches of overhanging trees that were clipped by the rotor blades swirled in the air as they settled to a hover above the blowing grass. Both door gunners bent mantis-like over their machine guns, ready to shoot. The co-pilot leaned back and shouted, "Go. Go. Go," as burdened soldiers thumped heavily to the ground and rushed toward the tree line and cover. Seven Montagnards from the first lift hastened across the open area to make room for the next helicopter moments behind. But an eighth person, the lieutenant lumbered behind in the landing zone.

Seeing him, the second aircraft hovered to keep from landing on the halting officer. The pilot shouted effetely through the windshield. His helicopter was left motionless and exposed—a tempting target. The next half minute seemed eternal as he waited above the opening until he saw the officer bent over and panting next to a broken trunk of a bamboo tree.

The remainder of the helicopters descended in turn, seconds apart. Heavily laden tribesmen pushed from the struts, dropped heavily into the tall grass with loud grunts, and rushed under their packs to the cover of the underbrush. Their loads discharged, the fleet circled in readiness on the far side of the next ridgeline until they received the "Good day" from the team, and then turned toward their home base leaving thirty-seven men in a remote jungle in enemy-controlled territory.

The men pushed into the foliage and circled into a perimeter as they had been taught and waited for the order to move. Around them was deep forest and moderate undergrowth veined by well-used trails. Ziobron noticed platoon sergeant Smith (not his real name) staring, his eyes fixed at a particularly wide path that was worn bare of vegetation. Indentations of countless boots showed in the pale light, resembling the scales of a very long and dangerous snake. Ziobron read the tension in Smith's face and walked, bent over to the older sergeant.

"Real fresh. I think if you put your hand on the path, you could still feel the heat from all those feet that just passed by."

The sergeant saw no humor in the remark. Ziobron nodded toward the path and its relevance. "I am surprised that we were not hit on the landing zone. For sure we are in their backyard. I don't know how they missed guarding this one." Ziobron considered a moment then added, "Unless they did have watchers here and they went to get help. We will need to be vigilant."

The sergeant did not answer. He continued to stare as if Ziobron were not there.

When Smith did not respond, Ziobron shuffled over to the lieutenant and whispered, "Want me to start reconning ahead of you? It looks like the trails all lead up this hill. I will try stay ahead of you by a couple hundred meters and keep you informed."

The lieutenant nodded.

Ziobron clicked his tongue at his point man and nodded at the main trail leading up the slope most likely to reveal enemy activity. They advanced on it, ready with each step to encounter an ambush or an unwary patrol. They moved a few meters, stopped, listened, and scanned every leaf. Insects that buzzed in the shrubs ahead abruptly ceased as they approached, and they hoped the sudden silence of bugs would not give them away. Twice they heard the brush of leaves in the bushes. They froze until the point man saw deer passing by. Once Ziobron had a start when he saw a pale, round face in the shrubs that mockingly nodded as if to say, "Yes, yes, I see you, I see you," but it was a palm frond that had died and yellowed and nodded with the lifting of a small bird. The ground rose steeply, at times forty-five degrees, with thick vegetation. They stopped to listen, studied the bushes and trails, moved, stopped again. In the utter stillness stalks of tall grass spread apart as if enemy fingers parted them and peered through, and spied a crawling green caterpillar on the blades. The 28th NVA Regiment whose sanctuary this was, was battle wise and hardened. They would not be careless.

They continued on, anticipating contact at any moment. At

times, Ziobron searched the faces of his people for clues as he did the bushes. There would be as much to learn in their seasoned eyes as in the disturbed soil.

His point man froze and eased to a crouch. Although Ziobron could not see his face, he knew his eyes were bouncing left and right, pinballing in his skull, seeking that which was amiss. Other tribesmen sensed it too and did not move. Nhet, edged to Ziobron's side and tapped his arm. "There. There," he whispered, pointing.

There was a slight leveling of the grade and sunlight shouldered through the trees. Ziobron looked in the direction of the finger. Mounds. Rows of them. Mound after mound. "Place where man die. *Fini* man," he whispered.

It was a graveyard. No white picket fence lined this place, but it was a burial site nonetheless. It did not resemble the cemetery in Kontum with crosses and cement slabs bearing names of fallen French soldiers, nor temporary rows of recent fallen of a camp under siege, hastily dragged under the eaves of a still-standing building, where olive-drab ponchos covered the slain, but here were rectangles of dirt on which grass chose not to live. Twenty-five mounds in two rows marked where people had been buried. On a few, where it was rocky and tombs could not be deeply dug, and bodies were near the surface, stones and rocks were piled to keep scavengers at bay. Some had stakes to mark their place. Others were simple bare mounds of dirt. In a remote place in the central highlands, far from home, two dozen humans were entombed. Ziobron glanced about. There seemed to be no sign of battle nearby where men may have been covered where they fell. Nor were there signs of an ancient bomb run with shattered trees above and broken limbs. Were these perished soldiers—far from home, buried in an unmarked graveyard in a remote jungle—known only to God? Perhaps they were slaves, worked until freed by death and left without a marker. "Or even prisoners of war," considered Ziobron, "Perhaps an American was among them."

The Montagnards were nervous. Many of the people believe spirits of the dead hover near their graves. There was a rustle in the leaves. Ziobron saw the flutter of wings but the Yards heard only the rustling and they imagined the restless departed moving just above their heads. The point man looked into Ziobron's eyes—did he hear it too? Phui-Don, the M-79 man, licked his lips. The stock of his weapon was wet under his sweating palms.

Ziobron turned to his indigenous team leader. "We need to make a perimeter and you and I need to look, look graves, see what we can learn. Understand?"

Im Nei Ksor swallowed and nodded. But his eyes were wide and he squeezed his weapon as he did so, his thumbs moving the safety on and off, on and off.

There was not much they learned from the earthen graves, only that it was an established site. There was recent use, for one of them was still embossed by the marks of a spade in the dirt indicating that that burial was after the last rain. On the chest of another grave was a small wood carving of a water buffalo with its legs pressed into the soil to keep it in place. It had not been finished and they wondered if the artist had died before he could complete the work for the eyes had not been carved and it remained, like the artist, without life. Sunlight, which had poked through the trees over time, had colored the sculpture, painting it with the thin brush of its rays, bleaching it to the color of the living creature.

Faint static, like the last breath before one becomes a corpse came from the radio. Ziobron raised the volume just enough to hear without being heard. He breathed his call sign into the handpiece.

"Return ASAP for an administrative emergency. Repeat, ASAP."

"Roger," he whispered. "Alert your people that I will be coming through and not to shoot me up."

"Administrative emergency," he thought. "Administrative? What does that mean?" He could only respond quickly if he went alone. The platoon, if they were following as they planned, should be at most one or two hundred meters behind him, almost earshot. He would leave his recon team in place.

"Hiep, I must go for message and come back. Stay here. Face that way, ambush VC if they come before I get back. I come back soon."

Hiep glanced at the mounds, then at his leader, and nodded solemnly.

Ziobron positioned his people for ambush. The hard-packed path from the ridge was his first concern. If the North Vietnamese heard them land, they would respond the quickest way: down this path. He positioned three of his people facing the length of the trail. "Ksor, watch. I think VC come down trail. Watch here." With a final glance to ensure that his people were in place and concealed behind cover, he turned and made a half-jog down the grade.

He didn't know what to expect. What could require that he "return immediately?" He proceeded on the route they had come, tracing in reverse the shrubs that had been deemed to be clear of enemy, trying nonetheless to move quietly. His pace was a near jog when he was certain that there were no persons in caterpillar-green awaiting his approach. Still, he stopped often and listened but heard only his own breathing. He had gone two hundred meters; surely the platoon would be nearby. His eyes pierced the foliage, this time not for the enemy, but for his own people. But there was no sign of the platoon. He continued on another hundred meters, then two hundred, still no sign of his people. Another hundred and he wondered if the unit had missed the spoor of his team's passing and were sidetracked. At six hundred meters, far behind that of a unit which was supposed to be following behind his advance element, he heard the murmur of voices.

He moved cautiously. The voices could be enemy. He clicked the handpiece of his radio and received two in return then whispered into the handset, "Coming in. Be sure your people don't shoot me."

"Copy. Waiting."

A dozen steps further he parted a thickness of shrubs and found a smiling tribesman. "I could *fini* you," he teased. Chester "Chet" Zaborowski was a few paces behind the tribesman. "Glad you're here Ed. We are having problems with our lieutenant. He cannot keep up with you, can hardly move in fact. When he moves at all, it is barely a trudge."

"I can tell. I expected the platoon to be only about one or two hundred meters behind me. I had to leave my people there but you are about six hundred meters behind."

"He just cannot keep up. It is all that he can do to pick up his feet. You will see."

At the center of the perimeter the lieutenant sat with his back against a tree, his legs splayed, his eyes closed, his mouth slack and open. Conkin, the medic, was giving him water, his own, and Ziobron wondered if there would be enough to last the mission. Profuse sweating left him soaked in his uniform; a pile of wet laundry with a pink face showing through.

Zaborowski whispered, "You see how it is. He's heat exhausted and grossly out of shape. I don't think he is capable of doing this."

Ziobron slowly shook his head in disbelief. He approached the prostrate man. "Lieutenant Jones." (Not his real name) "Lieutenant Jones."

The eyes slowly opened in his flushed and glistening face. Ziobron would not have been surprised if Jones said, "Leave me alone."

"Sir I had to leave my recon element farther up the trail. What is your situation. What are you going to do? Should I pull my people in?"

Jones took a long breath and struggled to his feet.

"Are you able to continue this mission?" Ziobron asked.

Jones swayed as he stood. He gathered his thoughts like flies pulled from a cobweb.

The platoon sergeant appeared in the circle of men and Ziobron faced him. "Sergeant Smith, I gotta know something now. I left my people up the hill thinking you were right behind us. I cannot leave them alone. What does the lieutenant plan to do?"

Clyde Conkin spoke. "His condition is not a true medical emergency . . . yet, but that might happen. So, the lieutenant is still in charge."

The officer's soundless mouth opened and closed like a guppy fish.

"What are your orders. Do I continue on ahead? Are you able

to continue?"

There was a flash of anger in the lieutenant's face. He straightened himself and after a deep breath said, "Ziobron, continue your recon. Sergeant Smith, prepare the men to move out. Zaborowski, your squad is in the lead."

"Lieutenant, I need to get back to my people. We will wait for you to catch up."

He rushed along the path. This was the third time he passed this way, but he did not forget that this was still Indian Country, the sanctuary of an elite enemy that might have squeezed in behind his people and waited behind any tree or bush. Knowing by now many SOG tactics, they may have chosen to wait for the Americans to release their air assets before they struck. Nevertheless, he rushed, and it was only the steepness of the hill that slowed his progress. The way was rugged and he puffed with the exertion and wondered if the lieutenant would be able to negotiate it. He recognized landmarks; the twisted vine shaped like a snake, the slanting bamboo with an entrance hole of a small animal above one knuckle, increased light where the forest thinned before the opening. The graveyard was nearby. He slowed and used more stealth lest the ambush he left behind fire on him.

He clicked his tongue.

He skirted around a familiar pile of dry, brittle bamboo leaves and twigs keeping to the path for stealth. He clicked his tongue again.

An answering click

His tail gunner stepped from concealment and smiled, relaxed in part because Ziobron was with them among the hovering ghosts.

Relief was apparent in the Montagnard's face. His shoulders relaxed as stiffness flowed from his body but that changed in an instant. New danger placed its cold boney hand on his shoulder. One moment he was hearing spirits in the trees, but that soft whisper of ghosts was replaced by the whisper of uniforms brushing against leaves. The rapid beating of his heart and the thudding of hearts he imagined in the empty chests under the piles of dirt, morphed into beating, running feet on the path. Imagined tapping sounds from bones of dancing skeletons were realized as the tapping of weapons and harness of fast approaching men. Pressure filled the air, as that moment before a tornado strikes in its fury. The tail gunner flinched. Ice water of grave danger poured into his soul. His shoulders jolted in his shirt. He ducked to avoid an invisible projectile. A glance at the other little people showed a similar jolt as they spun to their weapons and faced the trail. Nhet's eyes left the sights of his AK-47 and glanced at Ziobron, his eyes wide. His mouth gaped. He nodded once at Ziobron, a nod that said, "Yes, yes, you felt it too," and he sprang again to face the unseen specter.

Similarly in the utter quiet, Ziobron heard the soft rustle of fabric when the tail gunner rose from concealment and whispering smiled, "I could *fini* you." That stillness ended. Tapping sounds like rain-drops striking tree leaves filled his ears: Bata boots of dozens of running men slapped the clay surface of the trail as North Vietnamese regulars rushed down the slope to fight the Americans. Leather harnesses squeaked farther up the trail. Metal clasps struck wood rifle stocks. Puffing, running North Vietnamese were seconds from the waiting recon team. A shout of command from deeper in the thicket urged the rushing soldiers on. Ziobron's people trained their weapons at the place the trail entered the clearing. The first enemy emerged from the shadow of the forest and entered the opening. The soldier's chest heaved. He froze in place and glanced left and right. Beams of light from above placed the man's eyes in shadow and paled the skin around them, empty sockets in a skull-white face.

Not knowing if those spectral creatures were flesh and blood and would fall, the team emptied their weapons into the advancing group and down the length of the path. The M-79 man sent rifle grenades at the mass and beyond to those following close at their heels. Riflemen shot into each bush which could conceal a foe.

The front rank of enemy fell in a heap before the team. Moaning came from the wounded in the undergrowth. PAVN was well trained and disciplined. Soldiers rushed forward and took the place of the fallen and also fell. Shouts of command came from the rear of the force and the enemy pushed through the bushes to the sides and formed a skirmish line. They returned a massive fire at the team with AK-47 rifles, B-40 rockets and grenades. Orders were screamed from the rear of the advancing enemy and in response, a force charged the recon team from their left flank. More shouts came from the rear of the attacking force.

The interpreter shouted, "Sergeant Ed, Sergeant Ed. Enemy, him say, 'Kill American. Kill American. Shoot American!'"

The NVA were advancing on the left side of the trail and Ziobron charged to the left and into the undergrowth. As he cleared the first tangle of green, three soldiers were directly in front of him. He fired a burst of his CAR-15 and the three went down in a heap.

He shouted to his Montagnard, "Charge forward go, go!"

Ziobron sensed his people followed his order and he advanced with his rifle throwing grenades one after another. There was moaning after the explosions. He received heavy automatic rifle fire in return and B-40 rockets exploded nearby.

"Charge them," he shouted to his men.

Knowing his location, the enemy directed the bulk of their fire in his direction.

A rocket went off near him. Something slammed him in the face. Shrapnel pierced his jaw, spun his head around, and knocked him to the ground. He stood and continued to shoot and throw grenades.

Another rocket exploded.

This time shrapnel went into his arm and his leg.

"Keep shooting, keep going," he urged his people, knowing that only taking the initiative could save his tiny force. "Go! Go!"

He sensed that the enemy were running from the fight, smashing through the undergrowth. At least seven or eight enemy soldiers lay dead around him. To his right, one of his little people stumbled to his side. Lap glanced at Ziobron and smiled, his ubiquitous smile. He had been shot in the side. He held his hand to the place as dark-red blood oozed from the site.

"Me okay, Sergeant Ed. Wound not number ten. No *fini* Montagnard. Be okay soon," and he tore a piece from his undershirt and poked it into the hole. "We go *fini* VC now," and he faced the hill.

Ziobron got on the radio and gave the call sign of the rest of the platoon. Surely, they heard the firefight. Where were they? They should be close by now. He heard only static in the handpiece.

He heard the North Vietnamese regulars crashing through the tangle at his left and fired several bursts into the leaves. He tried his radio again but could not raise the platoon. He faced down the slope and shouted, "Hey, hey, where are you? Get over here."

Nothing on the radio. No answers to his shouts.

Shouts of command from the enemy rear ordered them and they regrouped and assaulted on line. There was a roar of incoming fire. Ed's people fiercely returned fire. Ziobron tried the radio again and shouted down the slope.

Nothing.

He got on the frequency for Covey and was relieved when they immediately answered.

"I am in heavy contact and need immediate support. Can you help?"

"Roger, I have Cobra gunships standing by from another mission. Mark your position."

"Smoke out. Identify."

He threw a red smoke and a white phosphorous grenade next to it so the smoke would make it through the trees.

Covey answered, "I see red with white smoke."

"Good copy. I am in heavy contact and moving up the hill. Rest of the platoon is still down the hill about six hundred meters. Enemy immediately to my front up the slope."

"Copy. Cobras will send their ordnance across your path up the hill from you."

"Roger. Heads down."

Moments later the first Cobra helicopter passed left to right fifty meters up the hill. They heard the "whoosh, whoosh," as the forty-millimeter cannons left the gun barrels and the crashing and exploding among the enemy. A second chopper followed, this time expending twenty-millimeter rounds which tore a swath ahead of the team. The first Cobra made a second swath firing its mini-gun. Debris and broken parts of trees and shrubs rained down on the team from the explosions.

"Perfect," he shouted to Covey on the handset. "Work it again and walk it up the slope. I intend to assault them when you're finished."

The slick shark-like gunships worked the way before the recon team. There were shouts and cries farther up the ridge. The shooting on the team diminished as the helicopters' ordnance took effect.

Ziobron knew that when the runs were completed, the enemy would emerge from their holes and regather for another assault. He shouted to his Montagnard team leader. "As soon as the helicopter finishes its run, we will assault the hill. Understand?"

"Yes."

Covey came back over the radio. "Sundance," he said, using Ziobron's code name, "Assets have only time on station and ordnance for one more run. Where do you want it?"

"We are going to assault the hill before they can regroup. I think they are running. Put it a little farther up the slope. We are going to begin our assault after the next run."

"Copy."

"Get ready!" Ziobron shouted to his tiny group. "Attack and fire them up."

The last run dropped cannon fire and minigun fire ahead of the team, and they heard the crashing explosions and "brrrr" of the minigun.

"Now!"

The six men burst from their cover and charged up the slope. Several enemies who stood from cover and fought were shot. Ziobron charged from the left flank and soon outdistanced his people. He fired magazine after magazine from his rifle and threw grenades into every defilade. Twice, he saw Lap stop, bend over, and grasp his side as he caught his breath, then run again after the fleeing enemy.

Fifty meters farther up the hill another B-40 rocket struck a tree near him sending splinters of metal into his leg, but the wounds were small and barely noticed. He heard a muffled cry of pain to his right. Nhet took a bullet which went through his deltoid, out his bicep and struck his weapon. The impact spun him to the ground but he was immediately on his feet. He examined his weapon to be sure it functioned and continued after the fleeing enemy.

Ahead of the small charging knot of men, the NVA were in full flight. Brush cracked and bushes swayed and broke in their flight. There were cries of fear. A voice of command shouted for order and to stop and turn to fight but was unheeded. Clearly the force ahead thought they were being pursued by a much larger force. Crew-served weapons were dropped and discarded. Those who were dead were left where they fell, nearly thirty of them.

The recon team continued after the enemy force. Lap dropped to his knees holding his side and gasped for breath but stood again and stumbled forward. Although their bodies were exhausted, adrenaline kept them moving. Ziobron's mouth was desert-dry and he felt the pain of the shrapnel embedded in his jawbone.

They fought their way up the slope and sensed that they neared the crest of the ridge. There was fierce firing from the top by an estimated thirty men armed with rifles and rockets. The little people and Ziobron continued to fight their way up the slope until the ground leveled and more daylight made its way through the foliage. Nhet could not hold his weapon against his wounded shoulder so was firing off-hand. A dozen more paces and they could see across the top: silhouettes of enemy against the sky ready to shoot his people when they cleared the undergrowth. Y Mop appeared at his side. He was the first to come up from the platoon below. Ziobron saw that he held an M-60 machine gun.

"Give me that," Ziobron shouted, and he strapped his CAR-15 over his shoulder and closed with the silhouettes on the ridgetop. "Go, go," he shouted at his men. "A little farther."

He burst from cover and engaged the enemy on the crest. He took aim with the machine gun and squeezed the trigger. Nothing. He pulled the bolt back again and squeezed the trigger. Nothing happened. He quickly looked at the weapon. There was no firing pin. He threw the weapon to the ground and finished the charge with his rifle, directing it at the last of the silhouettes on the top. Survivors in pith helmets threw down their weapons and packs and disappeared over the crest either wounded or assisting the wounded.

Ziobron's people charged into the clearing. There were numerous fighting positions and spider holes, and they cleared each one of lurking enemy as the lead elements of the platoon below arrived at the top. They found numerous blood trails of the wounded. Grass was matted and red where others had been dragged from the fight.

The rest of the platoon arrived along with the lieutenant who gasped out orders for two squads to sweep and secure the area and the third to assess the enemy dead and weapons. Nearly thirty enemy lay around the site. Most were in full NVA uniform with chest pouches. They were thin but otherwise healthy. Scattered among the corpses were their weapons. Most carried the standard AK-47 issue of the regular army of the north, but there were SKS rifles among them. In their flight, the NVA left one heavy anti-aircraft machine gun and rocket launchers. The B-40 launchers themselves had been smashed during the fight. Three cooking stations were set into pits dug into the ground so as not to be observed from the air. They found old, decomposed clothing and empty bags for carrying rice.

Sergeant Zaborowski tended to the wounded as Ziobron watched. "Y Lap, you did good plugging that hole with your shirt. We will have to get you a new one." He looked up at Ziobron, "I can't get that out of your jaw, but I could get you out on the medevac when it happens. It is too late to get anyone out today."

"I'll stay."

The lieutenant walked over to the group.

"Sergeant Ziobron, that was a remarkable job you did. I am going to put you in for the silver star."

Ziobron nodded to the officer. "Thank you," was all he could say.

"Tomorrow I'm going to put your people at the end of the column about a hundred yards out as rear security to give them a rest. We will RON here with two listening posts to the flanks."

"I will take one of them. It's what my people do."

The officer nodded.

Leaving his two wounded in the RON site with the medic, the four unwounded of the recon team found a small bump in the terrain a distance from the RON, with thick, noisy approaches and settled in for the night. The night was still, with no breeze to imitate the stealth of man. Ziobron and the Yards were bone tired. Their last real sleep was on Leghorn and even that was brief. They fought to remain alert and awake. Their only aid was the real enemy they knew lurked around them. Twice bats fluttered above their heads, the shoosh sound a bullet makes when it passes just over one's head, but in all, there was nothing to alarm the outpost.

The chill of the highlands woke the platoon about the time that greyness toned the sky. A thin haze shrouded nearby ridges and the Americans of the platoon gazed upward and wondered if they could get air support should it be needed. Many of the soldiers had slept near the spider holes where they could dive for shelter if they were mortared or received rockets during the night. The soldiers ate and prepared to move out.

They moved out in file by squads, following the ridge line, a reconnaissance in force. A halt was called mid-day for rest and meal. Ziobron and his people remained a short distance to the rear of the platoon for security. Zaborowski sought him out. "We have to stop often to rest. The lieutenant has to rest. He can't keep up even with the wounded."

"How are my wounded doing? Will we be able to get them out soon?"

"I hope so," Zaborowski said as he turned to go.

"Hey," Ziobron said, "know what I ate for dinner yesterday?"

"No."

"I had C-Ration canned turkey processed during the Korean War."

There was a puzzled look on Zab's face.

"Know what yesterday was?"

"No."

"It was Thanksgiving."

The platoon descended to a connecting ridge, moving at glacial speed and stopping frequently. Jones' face was flushed. Under the profuse sweat was a thick sheen. He looked up into the sky, swayed, staggered and fell in a heap. His last thought on the way down was to grab something to stop his fall. That something was a broken stock of standing bamboo, but he did not notice it had been broken at an angle into a sharp shard. Dagger-like, it sliced his hand to the bone. Conkin ran to the cry and examined the wound. The laceration was severe and could not be addressed adequately in the field. The platoon halted in place and the Americans gathered to assess the situation. Jones moaned. He no longer seemed to notice his surroundings. He was clearly no longer in control.

Sergeant Zaborowski looked up from his bandaging. "You can see how it is. We have to get this man out. We have other wounded also who need to go."

Smith considered the overall situation. His voice was quiet, nearly a whisper. "Agreed. The lieutenant is no longer able to command. I will assume command. Conkin, see who you can get on the radio, give them a sitrep and ask for an exfil."

"Copy," Conkin said.

Smith looked around him. "Set up a perimeter here for now. We will see what the FOB wants to do."

Minutes later, Conkin rejoined the group with the handset in his hand. I got Leghorn Relay Site. "Tomorrow!"

Smith's face paled. Horror marked his visage. "Tomorrow?"

"It's late in the day and a recon team has declared a Prairie Fire emergency. We are on our own. Tomorrow is the earliest they can get to us."

Smith was a blow-up figure whose air was fast escaping. He bowed his head and croaked, "Tomorrow, tomorrow."

### *RT Montana*

Miles to the north of the platoon sergeant who slumped on his rucksack and rocked himself mumbling, "Tomorrow, tomorrow," was another recon team on a separate mission. RT Montana's six SOG men did not believe they would live until tomorrow. They were deep into communist controlled territory, somewhere in a sprawling, remote and secure enemy base area. From the air it appeared to be a rusticated, slow-moving place of no importance. It was distant from many of the battle zones, logistics routes, and major base camps. The few structures which could be seen among the broadleaf trees were dacha-like and peaceful dwellings having no relationship to war. One would not have been surprised in past years to find a painter of landscapes bent over his easel, searching his repertoire of paints for the one marked pastoral to use on a shadowed wall. But, hidden with great skill among the flowered yards and vines, were sophisticated defenses; like the slow, gentle porcupine moves without threat but is ready to resist the stroking hand and raise its painful quills. So also, the base area was ready to raise its quills of rocket tubes, anti-aircraft gun barrels, and screens of sniffing radar. That the peaceful area was prepared for intrusion was discovered when the One-Zero of Montana, Mike Shepherd, made a visual reconnaissance over the target in a bird-dog airplane only to have the windshield shot out of the plane before he even got above the field.

Structures which housed the many soldiers stationed there, and there were very many, could not be seen from the air. That many soldiers secreted themselves in the foliage was a given to the intelligence people in Saigon or Langley, for this strip of remote land was believed to be the chief R&R area for Communist leaders, commissars, and generals who carried on and directed the war in the south. Two features marked the area on a topographical map. One was a large grassy field known to SOG as "the golf course." Nearby was a round blue circle on the map referred to as Dollar Lake. Higher ups in the Communist hierarchy used the area as a private resort to fish, swim, stroll on the field, hold major strategy sessions, or just relax in a private dacha. RT Montana's mission was to parachute onto the golf course and capture one of those high-value targets.

## SOG: Missions to the Well

RT Montana—three Special Forces sergeants and three Montagnards—trained in a top-secret location for the static-line jump behind enemy lines. The tribesmen had never parachuted before and had to be taught from the ground up, learning every nuance needed for the mission. On the target day they were flown to a secret base from which to launch and boarded a C-130 Blackbird airplane. In utter darkness, the team boarded the shuddering, growling four-engine airplane, and to the tribesmen it seemed they were entering the very bowels of a living beast.

The persistent haze and rain which the platoon was enduring miles away, was much worse for the tiny recon team farther to the north. Here, they flew low level, contouring just above the mountains and valleys to avoid radar and were buffeted by gusts that funneled through the gaps. When it was apparent that radar discovered the airplane, they dodged and evaded by abrupt, violent maneuvers which jolted the men out of the canvas seats. They approached the target in a torrent of rain and wind gusts which threw the aircraft about. Nearing the drop zone, the pilot dropped the tail gate and freezing air and deluge sprayed in. Staff Sergeant Harry Waddell was to be the first to jump and hobbled down the ramp in the turbulence. He grabbed an overhead cable to keep from falling. The plane bounced like a rodeo bronco. What he could see as he looked into the night was blackness and swirling rain. He looked back at his team leader as if to say, "Are you sure about this?"

Sheppard shouted, "affirmative," but the wind tore the words from his lips.

The team jumped into the cauldron of air; first Waddell, then the Yards, then Paul Boyd, the One-One, with the team leader last to jump. They were thrown into the blackness and deluge, both by the prop blast and the hard wind. The jump was at a low altitude, less than eight hundred feet, and they touched ground mere seconds after their chute opened. What the team did not know was at the last minute the colonel in charge changed the drop zone from the spacious field that they had planned for and could easily assemble on and perhaps complete their mission in short order. Instead, he chose a place in the forest several miles from the designated drop zone without considering the tribesmen had not been trained to land in trees. They were miles from the target, with no idea where they were and the place where they landed was off their maps. Further, the officer had not informed Covey or the FOB of the change in the drop zone.

Their chutes opened with a hard jolt as they prepared to roll in the grass, but instead, tree limbs struck the bottom of their boots, each tap becoming stronger as the limbs were larger toward the bottom. There was an abrupt stop and sway as they were caught up and hung in the air by their parachutes. In the utter darkness they did not know if they were suspended one foot or a hundred feet above the ground. One American dropped his steel helmet to gauge the height but did not hear it hit the ground.

Waddell crashed through the tree limbs of a very tall tree until his harness brought him up with a jolt and a large grunt high above the ground. Directly below him burned a large campfire, A voice cried out as he crashed through the tree top. Sparks billowed upward and he smelled smoke. Dimly in the fire light, the shapes of many men in shadow scurried away from the campfire and ran into the night, some of them shouting in fear. "It's a tiger jumping from the tree to get us!" screamed one of the terrified men.

The team was not together but scattered into three locations. One American, Harry Waddell, only had a pistol, none of his gear, and was alone trying to evade a searching enemy. He had slipped from his pack and rifle, let go and dropped to earth intending to roll and retrieve his gear. But the tree limb, released of his weight, sprang back and out of his reach. Another Special Forces man, Paul Boyd, was also separated from the team and holed up to avoid the ever-present searchers. He shivered in the rain and wind then wrapped himself in large leaves against the cold and wind. Harry hid in his concealment until a grey dawn revealed searching enemy pass and watched as they found his pack suspended high in the tree. He watched as they pulled it from the limbs and gathered silently around the pack's opening as they examined the contents. Boyd considered briefly taking the group out with his rifle, but they were only one group of several which passed by. To shoot them before he would be able to link up with the team would be certainly fatal. There was no longer any question in the minds of the enemy that the SOG men were among them, and the search intensified.

The third group included the team leader, Mike Shepherd. He too had landed in the trees and found himself alone. His first task, he decided, was to locate his people, and as dawn allowed, reconned down a slight grade and managed to locate his three scattered Montagnards. The four of them huddled near a slight opening in the trees which for a time could be an exfil site. Pursuit of the team was intense and organized. As the SOG men crept among the trees using all of their senses to avoid death or capture, PAVN broadcasted from loudspeakers hung in the trees martialing their units to find the invaders. Prospects of survival were grave. Heavy highland rain soaked the men and brisk wind chilled them. Hypothermia numbed their senses, hunched their backs, and made their teeth chatter. The deluge masked sounds of enemy movement in the bush. Throughout the day they avoided enemy patrols, often watching them pass pistol-close through the undergrowth. With low fog snaking in and searchers with it, they risked walking into the coils of their patrols.

Shepherd and his three strikers made a short recon and found a firing range in what appeared to be the fringe of an enemy base area. They entered an empty hooch, captured documents and took photos of the site.

At a time when it appeared that no enemy patrol lurked around him, Paul Boyd whispered the situation on the PRC-25 radio. Hillsborough acknowledged the split team message and returned for a fix of the split team. "We have been looking for you on the golf course making wider and wider circles where we thought you would be. No wonder we couldn't find you. We need a fix on you." Both Boyd and Waddell, from their locations dared to shoot pen flare signals and fixed their locations.

"No wonder we couldn't find you" he said again almost to

himself. "Got you now."

Shepherd was able, finally, to make radio contact with his other Americans on the ground via survival radio, and then with Hillsboro. "Covey, we need immediate extraction. We are a split team and the place is teeming with Charlie. This is Prairie Fire emergency. Repeat, Prairie Fire. How copy?" They were in great danger of capture or annihilation.

"Montana. Earliest is tomorrow with distance, rain, and overcast. We can try link you with your people. Copy?"

"Copy. If we have to wait for tomorrow, we will all be dead men. Place crawling with enemy and we just popped a pen flare to give our location. Now they know where we are too. Repeat. If we wait for tomorrow, we will all be dead men."

There was a pause as Covey reflected on a course of action.

Montana continued. "We have a split team. We are frozen and surrounded."

Lloyd O'Daniel, the Covey rider came on. "Weather is closing in but we will make it happen, Montana. Stand by."

As promised, support arrived. Only the courageous would fly in the maelstrom. They felt their way through the thick fog almost finding their way by touch between the ridges and valleys before setting down between the jaws of terrain until each trooper was on the highest ground they could find. They looked alternately upward at the descending helicopter then to the sides, constantly scanning for advancing enemy.

Waddell was the first to be lifted out. Huey helicopters located him, dropped a STABO rig, and hoisted him from the closing enemy. He was pelted and thrown about under the chopper until they landed in the first open area they found where they dragged his shivering, hypothermic body inside. It was days before he felt any warmth in his body. Boyd was the next to be pulled out, also shivering to his core.

Last, Sheppard and the three tribesmen were lifted from a gap in the trees. The Huey slid in between threads of fog and weaved through a sky that was a blanket of grey. Nothing made sense to him of this mission. They were not certain where they had been. There was no large field, or small round lake, and if they found anything of relevance, he would not be able to show it on a debriefer's map. As he shivered beside the portside door he looked down through the breaks in the fog and then saw a broad green "golf course" and to the side, just a few klicks away, the grey sky reflected on a small dollar-shaped lake with pristine and peaceful dachas tucked in the trees at the edge of the shore—miles from where a half dozen American parachutes hung in the trees.

* * * * *

Chester Zaborowski looked at his wounded patients in their blood-soaked bandages and at the lieutenant with his bandaged hand and squinting porcine eyes who only trudged when he moved at all. "Sergeant Smith, we really can't be moving very far with our wounded and the lieutenant. What about remaining in place where we are?"

Smith seemed relieved that the situation suggested its own solution. "Alright. We will RON here. Sergeant Ziobron, I leave it to you to place the people. And set up fighting positions."

"Got it. My people also need an ammo resupply. I would also like to have our M-72 LAWs in the center with me. If we get mortar or RPG fire from that high ground there, I can hit them from here."

"See to it. And Conkin, take four people and do a listening post at that higher ground." He paused and looked at his three sergeants so see if there was other input. "That's it then. We stay for the night."

The Green Berets turned to their tasks. Smith was not aware that his hands shook and his heart pounded. But things were happening. Perhaps FOB would pull the whole platoon.

Everyone stood-to by 0600. Leghorn reported the dust-off was a go. There would be just enough time to prepare the LZ for arrival and resupply. The mission would continue with Smith in command. Smith blanched at the news. They would proceed with the original plan of moving north for 500 meters, then follow a stream to the east where it would converge with a river and hopefully, an active POW camp. Ziobron's recon element would scout 50 meters ahead of the main element.

Ziobron and several Montagnards prepared the LZ for the helicopters' arrival, cutting away tall bushes and one or two small trees. As Ziobron labored next to the perimeter, Communist soldiers brought heavy automatic fire from two 12.7 mm anti-aircraft machine guns. The air was filled with green tracers on the platoon's position. SCU dove to cover and spider holes. The large caliber bullets struck and seriously wounded two of the little people. One of the Yards who stood next to Ziobron took a round through a buttock, tearing the cheek nearly in two. Another one of the powerful rounds went through the side of the other Yard, passing between two ribs throwing him to the ground where he lay facing skyward, with both eyes open and gasping for air. Ziobron directed his people to suppress fire on the two positions on the ridge 300 meters away as he and Clyde Conkin dragged the casualties to cover. Ziobron directed his people to increase their firepower on the enemy sites as he dove to his LAW position. Waiting for a flash to give away the first enemy position, he stood and carefully aimed at the muzzle flash. Buzzing bullets passed his face and tore up the soil around him. He was a magnet for lead but forced himself to remain upright and make careful aim. He sighted, held his breath, and slowly squeezed the trigger. Before the first round impacted, he remained standing and carefully aimed and fired two more rounds. His determined resolve was rewarded because one after the other the three rounds struck home. A huge secondary explosion threw parts of a tripod and portions of the anti-aircraft weapon high into the air. Loud cheers erupted from the Montagnards.

But thick streams of green tracer fire continued from the second heavy machine gun, this time directed mainly at him. He stood and, like the first, carefully aimed at the source and fired three more rounds. Impacts were on target and his people cheered again at the secondary explosion. Enemy fire appeared to be suppressed, but with the clearing of the site for the dust-off, he was not certain that more forces did not wait to attack the coming helicopters. A situation report was sent to the relay site informing them of the additional casualties and possible hostile fire from the ridgeline.

Leghorn responded with a calm reassuring drawl and Ziobron wondered if the speaker was Homer Hungerford. "Dust-off confirmed and on the way along with appropriate assets. Stand by."

Ziobron was relieved with the news. Hungerford spoke in his most calming and matter-of-fact voice ever, "We ate that snake you recommended, young fellow."

Ziobron felt the adrenaline erode from his body. Weakness coursed through him for a moment as the danger subsided. He collected his thoughts and spoke into the handpiece, "Cooked or raw?"

They placed the wounded in a row at the edge of the clearing and waited for the dust-off. The rumble of helicopters arrived first, seconds ahead of the first descending craft. The platoon was in readiness around the ridge top facing outward as instructed. A "Charlie" model gunship made its pass across the site and drew no fire and was followed by the first slick. It glided to a hover and descended for the wounded. Tribesmen ran to the platform and unloaded the resupply.

"Hurry, hurry," shouted the door gunner with his hands glued to his machine gun as the first two wounded were carried by soldiers who ran with them slung on their ponchos. The second wounded man had not been even dragged fully into the craft by the chase medic before the chopper lifted and sped away.

A dozen breaths later the next slick landed for the remaining wounded and captured weapons. Tribesmen dumped the ordnance on the deck as the chase medic shoved it to the side to make room for more wounded men. Nhet struggled to board with his only usable arm until the gunner grabbed him by his harness and pulled him aboard. The enemy began to fire on the team and green tracers buzzed and whistled over their heads. The crew chief's head bobbed back and forth as he sought the source of the shooting. The lieutenant had insisted he go without help but staggered and stumbled halfway to the helicopter. Compton and one of the tribesmen ran to him and each with one of his arms over their shoulders dragged him the rest of the way.

Near the edge of the clearing Smith stood by himself, looking longingly at the escape of the wounded men. He held his stomach with both hands and rocked back and forth and were it not for the engines of the Hueys and the incoming explosions, one could hear him moaning.

Zaborowski noticed Ziobron with his blood-covered clothes and swollen jaw. "You could go out on that too, you know."

Ziobron glanced at the departing officer, then at Smith, the ranking officer who rocked back and forth, oblivious to the incoming around him. "No, Chet. If I go you all will die."

With all of the immediate power around him, it had not sunk in and Ziobron repeated it, "If I go, you die!"

Incoming fire from the ridges was becoming intense. They were receiving heavy anti-aircraft fire from the east and rockets were landing among the men. The platoon sergeant was still standing erect and watching the receding helicopters. Heavy small arms fire came from the ridge to the east. Tribesmen dove into spider holes and other cover.

"Hey!" Ziobron shouted to a tribesman, "Get him into a hole."

The Yard ran with his head ducked and grabbed the sergeant by the sleeve and led him to a spider hole.

The platoon opened up at the east ridge. Covey was given the azimuth and location of the enemy positions on the ridges and the forward air control worked bombs and ordnance on the enemy locations using Cobra gunships and Skyraiders. The North Vietnamese probed and attacked the perimeter until they were beaten off by the platoon or air support. By 1015 all incoming ceased. Tribesmen eased from the holes and trenches.

Zaborowski and Conkin approached Ziobron. One of them pointed over his shoulder at Smith who was just emerging from his spider hole. "Are we going to continue with this mission?"

Conkin said, "It's just us. Maybe we should ask FOB about this."

"We can do this. We have our mission, and that includes looking for a POW site. We have most of our people. We can do this," Ziobron said.

Conkin lowered his voice and said, "Not with him. He never got out of the hole the entire fight. He can't lead."

Ziobron studied the man as he approached the group. "They are right," he thought. "He will get everyone killed." The sergeant's eyes seemed glazed.

Smith strode to the group. He seemed smaller now. Lost. "I guess we better get going," he said.

Sergeant Ziobron spoke. "We will but we need to make a change. I will need to lead the platoon the rest of this mission. You will need to take a rest. I think you have seen too much combat. You are very tired and shouldn't have to make decisions for a while."

"You can't tell me what to do. I am in charge. You are not. I wear the stripes."

Conkin spoke. "No, you are not in charge. Ziobron is. He is the only one with experience doing these missions. We decided to let you rest."

"I am going to let the FOB know now. Give me your radio Chet." Ziobron stepped away from the group and called Leghorn. "Homer, I have taken command of the platoon and will continue the mission. I think Smith is shell shocked and cannot command. Can you relay this to Captain Krupa. He is the commander of A Company and he can forward this to FOB if he wants. I will stand by."

"Copy. Stand by."

Fifteen minutes later Krupa came on the secure line. "I copy and concur. Do you want me to join you and take command?"

"No sir. I am fully ready and we can continue the mission within the hour."

"Copy. It is all yours. I will be standing by and will come out and join you whenever you need me. I will also get a small Bright Light ready just in case. I have confidence in you and know you will do just fine."

"Copy, sir. Out."

Ziobron did not like having all of the Americans gathered in one place, especially with the nearness of the enemy. But to remain in place was dangerous, and more so if time were given to the unseen regiments to coil about them, constrict them, until the final fangs of charging commandos consumed them. He used a depression to secret their assembly and called the sergeants to join him.

"FOB concurs that I assume leadership for the remainder of this mission. Krupa will be standing by in case we need him to join us. He will also augment the Bright Light team if we get into something we cannot handle. We will continue the mission as we planned: maneuver down to the stream and follow it to the river and where we hope we find a POW camp with Americans. I would like to free some of them from those bamboo cages." He looked for questions in the four sets of eyes in front of him.

"We have the resupply from the dust off. I want it distributed within one half hour and then we leave. They were good enough to resupply our ammunition already in magazines. Doc, do you have all the medical things you need?"

"I think so. I will take everything they sent."

"Although I am in charge, I am going to go with the recon element ahead of the team instead of embedded in the platoon. This is because I have more experience in recon. To make up for not being inside the main group, I want the lead squad to follow closely, fifty to a hundred meters. Sergeant Compton, I want you to lead with the first squad. Sergeant Zaborowski, I want you with the second and any wounded we get. Sergeant Smith, I want you to follow with the third squad and rear security. Be careful of trackers on our tail. We move out in a half hour, Questions?"

The two young sergeants looked at each other, then at Smith, who listened with his head down.

"Okay then. Let's do it."

Ziobron, his recon people, and his interpreter peeled from the edge of the perimeter and descended down the saddle of the hilltop, followed by the rest of his people twenty minutes later. They kept to cover, moving as silently as possible while avoiding trails, ever vigilant for ambush or discovery. Their presence on the ridge top in the morning, the dust off and the deadly airstrikes on the NVA erased all pretext they had been there. They could only hope the Communists believed they were exfiltrated. But they moved with the caution that every movement was known by the enemy and they were ready to spring.

Twice, they found a suspect area and gave it wide birth. The descent was steep and made it difficult to not have a heavy foot and create a loud footfall. The air became heavy and humid as they descended, and they heard a soft burble of the stream. Ziobron halted and made a listening stop before creeping the last meters to its edge.

It was ten meters across, slow moving, and opaque-brown. Thick bushes lined the edge as was often the case along a stream. The vegetation was capable of hiding a sizeable ambush and the stream crossing would leave his people exposed. Although it was unlikely the foe could anticipate the arrival of the SOG people at this exact place, he would take full precaution before their crossing. Leaving the bulk of his recon element, he took his interpreter, retraced his steps, and joined the platoon fifty meters to the rear.

"Okay, Clyde. The stream is just below. My people will cross and clear the area around the crossing. I want your people to wait at the bank for my signal that it is secure. I want your people to cross four or five abreast stepping in each other's tracks. I don't want Charlie to be able to count us by our foot prints. I want the tail gunners to erase the signs of our crossing."

"Got it."

Ziobron pointed to the interpreter. "Go to the end of column and tell tail gunners to *fini* tracks at stream. Tell Sergeant Smith what I say, then come back."

The interpreter spun about to the task and worked his way down the line.

Five minutes later he returned. "Sergeant Ziobron, I tell Montagnard and they will do. I talk Sergeant Smith too, but he no talk me. He just look down."

"Give me ten minutes across the stream and wait for my signal."

"See anything number ten?" Ziobron asked his people when he returned to the edge of the stream.

"All number one. No VC."

Ziobron nodded. Weapons followed their eyes as they waded through the mocha-colored water, penetrated the undergrowth, and fish-hooked around the crossing. They were surprised to find no trails along the length nor sign of recent activity. Leaving his people in an arc around the site for security, he returned to the opening in the brush and signaled his people to cross. He put his finger to his mouth then pointed to their feet, signaling them not to make noise, to slide their boots through the water.

Once across, Ziobron moved his people eastward following the stream. He again moved with his recon element several dozen meters ahead of the main group as a recon strike force. If he encountered a target and engaged, the main body was to charge ahead and join him. They used caution following the water course, as enemy encampments often went to the streams for their source of water. They watched for cross-trails and paths which could hug the stream using it as their east-west compass. Twice they found paths leading to the stream bank but they could not tell if they were made from soft pads of animals or were old and lightly used by humans.

Twice over the two thousand meters to the river, Ziobron sensed the tangle had thinned on his flank farther up the grade and halted his force. He and his point man left the platoon and investigated, finding large, cultivated areas able to produce vegetables for a very large force. They were clearly in an established sanctuary.

Fast-moving water rippled before them, drowning out any sounds of hostile movement in the undergrowth. A small knoll lay ahead. He halted his people and along with his interpreter, climbed to the top. It was grassy, clear of trees, and uncomfortably open. Making their way to the edge, they peered down and discovered the junction of the stream with the sought-for river. The terrain was steep with a very large rock-like cliff to the north. As they studied the scene, five North Vietnamese regulars appeared, ambling in single file along the river bank. They were fully uniformed with helmets, bandoleers bulging with ammunition, and rifles slung over their shoulders. They walked without caution, looking straight ahead, then turned and disappeared on a trail hidden among the thick trees next to the rock outcropping. Ziobron returned to his force and secured his recon element intending to stalk the five enemy and determine their activity. Slowly descending to the river bank, they discovered a very large sand bar. It bore the footprints of many hundreds of men, perhaps a thousand sets of various boots and sandals. They gazed in wonder at the myriad prints and at the thick greenery capable of hiding any lurking enemy. "Something very large is in this area," Ziobron thought.

He brought his people to the site, placing one squad to the rear for security and sending four men to secure a crossing point. He had his sergeants place their people on line and wait, cautioning his people to not walk on the sandbar and thus leave traces of their presence. Ziobron moved ahead with his interpreter, Im Nei Ksor. They had only gone twenty-five meters when the interpreter clicked his tongue. Before them was an NVA compound. The two men studied the site. Five men had passed this way but there was no sign of them. The camp appeared to be abandoned. "Did the NVA just pass through here on their way? Perhaps they were aware of us and waited on the far side."

He brought up his two sergeants. "I want you to take your squads and make a perimeter around this camp. Zab, you go around the right side; Chet, you go around the left side. When you are in place, I will check it out." When they were in position, the recon element made a pass through for lurking ambush. He received a nod from Ksor that all was ready and Ziobron entered the enclosure.

The camp was large with many trenches and fighting holes. "This is where intel said there could be a POW camp," he recalled, and he studied the compound for any sign that that was the case. Four large structures in derelict condition were on the near side, barracks capable of housing many soldiers. There was a large podium where instructors and commissars could train or indoctrinate. Ziobron imagined a North Vietnamese doctrinaire lecturing beaten and chained prisoners about the utopia of Communism, and cadre beating prisoners who were too exhausted to remain upright. "Sit!" they would scream, as splattered spit slid unnoticed down their faces. "Sit, listen! Chinese friend speak you, for own good."

The guard would troll in front of the row of prisoners, pausing in front of each one and look into their empty hopeless eyes, all the time slapping his club in the palm of his hand. "Ah yes, this is all good for you. Learn about utopia."

To the side of the podium, a dozen meters away were six cages, each of which could hold a man in a fetal position. They were pig-sized, cramped, and exposed to the elements, "but good enough for imperialist soldier."

There were two posts also with a tether line attached, and Ziobron thought a stubborn prisoner who failed to understand the glories of Socialism might find this to be his home. Nearby he found a piece of old, nearly decomposed cloth similar to the material of a pilot's jacket. There were no markings or patches but he put it in his pack to bring back for intelligence. He remembered what Dale Hanson said about Sergeant Novey's hands from interrogation by Communists, all broken, twisted and without any nails.

Two cooking pits were near the cages and prisoners would be able to smell the meals as they were prepared for their keepers.

It was 1500 hours, still mid-afternoon with hours left in the day to further investigate the area yet have time to call in airstrikes in the event they got into trouble. The image of emaciated prisoners laying cramped in the mud in those cages welled in his mind.

He brought his interpreter and met with his sergeants to give them a situation report. Ksor would be able to inform the Yards as to the status of the mission. Smith sat among them with his elbows on his knees, his head propped on his hands, oblivious to the situation. Finding themselves centered among a vastly superior enemy force with imminent combat expected, his two other sergeants suggested an immediate extraction.

"We have not completed our mission," Ziobron said, "We have actually just found the thing we came to investigate. We don't go home now."

"Yes, but what we found is way too big for us. We are just a platoon," Zaborowski said.

"We won't leave the mission unfinished, then expect someone else to come in here to do what we left. We have not finished the mission they sent us to do. Besides, the thought of some of our people all beaten up and laying in the mud in those cages or tethered to a post like that one over there is more than I want to think about. We are going on. We can think of an extraction tomorrow, got it?"

The Conkin and Zaborowski nodded solemnly. Smith scratched a spot of dirt on his knee with one dirty fingernail.

The group forded the fast-moving river at the place he had left the four Yards an hour before. It was chest-deep and the current seemed to lift the smaller Montagnards and pulled them downstream. They looped their web gear over their shoulders and propped their weapons over it all. One of the shorter Yards bounced his way across, springing on tip toes, and he smiled as he caught Ziobron watching him.

Across, they began the ascent of a very steep grade. A half hour later the platoon was exhausted with the climb and Ziobron called a halt. Ziobron and the recon element scouted ahead with Ksor in the lead. The Montagnard observed a high-speed trail dead ahead at least two meters wide, smooth, hard-packed, and well used. Ksor watched one direction as Ziobron looked in the direction of the hill.

Ziobron caught movement.

He studied the length of the path. Six NVA, fully armed and in complete uniform moved briskly in their direction. Four of them carried AK-47 rifles and two carried B-40 rockets. Contact was inevitable. In a minute a fire fight was inescapable.

Ziobron motioned to Ksor about the enemy and they prepared for contact. When they were close enough they could not miss, Ziobron opened fire with his CAR-15, killing the first four enemy. Shouting, "Clear!" as he reloaded. Ksor shot and took out the last two in the trail. The recon element rushed forward and took up position beyond the location as Ksor searched the bodies. Ziobron radioed the platoon to rush forward and join him at the fight.

One of the recon team members ran to Ziobron. "Sergeant Ed, little bit down trail, trail have another trail that go…" He hesitated, not knowing the word for uphill. He pointed in the direction. "Trail number two go," and he pointed up the hill. "Have big building, big house, maybe VC camp."

The two sergeants joined him. "We need to sweep the site. For sure there is a long house just like the Montagnards have on stilts. I want two squads to sweep on line and one to watch the trail that we are on."

"Got it."

Sergeant Smith stumbled with his squad at the rear and Ziobron knew it would be fruitless to give him instruction. "Ksor, tell Montagnards I want five Montagnards to watch trail up hill and five to watch down the hill. Make ambush. Do now, Ksor."

Captured weapons were distributed among the Yards and the platoon swept to the long house. The site had been hastily abandoned, perhaps minutes before they arrived. A cook fire smoldered near the long house. The force had apparently fled, not knowing the size of Ziobron's force—or they were preparing to assault. Conkin and Ziobron inspected the interior of the long house and found it full of loose rice, perhaps thirty tons of it. The structure was ten by thirty feet long and was a major supply area for an enemy regiment.

"So much rice," said one striker in wonder. "So much rice."

Ksor appeared at Ziobron's side. "Look inside rice. I know what VC sometimes do. Move rice." Several of the Yards not on security duty began to paw and sift through the loose pile of rice. Items of war began to appear. Their hands moved faster and faster as the treasure was revealed. Under their fast-moving hands, piles of rockets for the B-40, and fifty 122 mm rockets emerged. At one corner a tribesman threw up his arms and exclaimed, "Wooah!" Under his shaking hands was a pile of a hundred RPG-2 rounds and next to them were hundreds of Chicom grenades still in their packing boxes. On the other side of the rice pile, a soldier called in disbelief, "Sergeant! Sergeant. Come quick. Look." In his hands, he lifted the first of six

RPD machine guns. There were 10,000 rounds of 7.62 ammunition for standard-issue AK-47 rifles. At the far side of the shed, under a pile of Chinese made hammocks, they discovered bicycles used to transport supplies, indicating that all of this was linked to an established base serviced by high-speed trails or road.

Ziobron thought of the bicycles and the high-speed trail network and knew that Charlie could arrive in force at any moment.

He composed an encrypted message to Leghorn regarding the discovery and requested instructions. It only took minutes for the reply to come back from the FOB at CCC. "Destroy everything in place and move to an LZ for extraction. Force far too large for unit of your size. Exfil will be tomorrow due to late hour."

"Copy."

He turned to Conkin. "I want every available block of C-4 and thermite grenades now. Quick."

They made a large well in the center of the rice and placed the C-4 and thermite grenade in the void. On that they placed all of the explosives they found in the cache, then tamped it with hands full of rice. The tribesmen were cleared to the edge of the clearing as det chord was strung to the outer edge of the opening.

"Heads down," Ziobron shouted and pressed the detonator.

They could not have guessed the magnitude of the explosion. It was massive. Even individual grains of the thirty tons of rice became projectiles making holes through the roof of the building and piercing tree leaves a distance away. The blast was deafening, not only exploding but imploding. Billows of flame filled the space followed by numerous secondary explosions as rockets and grenades cooked off. Rifle ammunition sounded like popcorn. Pieces of the building flew through the air as shrapnel, and shards of wood became arrows.

Tribesmen slowly lifted their heads from cover when the last secondary cook-off occurred, gazed at the depression which was all that remained of the enemy inventory, and smiled at each other.

Ziobron met with his sergeants along with his Montagnard leaders and interpreter. "We are going to run out of daylight if we don't move right away. The closest suitable place is the top of that ridge," and he pointed. "It is about five hundred meters away."

They nodded their understanding.

"Every PAVN knows we are here, especially with the explosion we just made. We just have to move up the ridge to the top and set up for the night. I want us on line, two meters apart. We move briskly, but with caution. They know we are here and will want to talk with us. We just destroyed someone's bicycle. My recon element will go slightly ahead of you and to the right. Everyone understand what we are doing?"

"Got it," answered Zaborowski and Conkin. Smith merely looked to his sides, left and right.

"Let's do it. I need five minutes' head start and I will give you the 'start' on the secure radio. We need to go now."

Five minutes later, Ksor and Ziobron joined the rest of the recon element who had been left in place for security. They had not been there to see the booty hidden in the rice nor were they warned about the detonation, so they smiled about the mystery as Ziobron joined them. At that exact moment, Hiep, the point man, shouted out, "VC!" and opened fire with his AK-47. A platoon sized element of 35–45 North Vietnamese regulars attacked the team, charging, shouting, and shooting on full-automatic. Hiep's opening salvo killed the front two NVA outright; however the heavy incoming rounds struck him in the stomach nearly cutting him in two, and he collapsed in instant death. The burst of fire also struck Nhet in the chest throwing him back with the impact where he died in a heap. Ziobron attacked the oncoming enemy, shooting with his rifle and throwing grenades, killing several.

The platoon arrived nearby and added their fire power as Ziobron charged ahead of the group, throwing grenades into the knots of enemy and shooting. In his attack as he leaped over several dead soldiers, a B-40 rocket exploded on a tree, the blast knocking him down. The air was sucked from his lungs, stunning him. He was dazed and came to only when his body screamed for air. His eyes opened, rimmed in dirt and he blinked to clear them and glanced about. He found himself twenty-five meters ahead of his own people and nearly in the midst of the Communists. Trying not to expose himself he rolled behind a tree, threw grenades, and shot into the oncoming mass of men. The charge was diminishing but he could sense more enemy units were joining the initial attack. His rifle was empty.

He glanced back. His own people had stopped in place and lay on their stomachs. They had not continued forward to overcome the attack. "Hey! What are you people doing? Get up here. Get into this thing! Get up!"

As he shouted this, two NVA attacked him at very close range. Before he could reload, they were on him. Ziobron drew and fired his .45 caliber pistol into the head of the first attacker and struggled to his feet just in time to deflect the barrel of the SKS rifle of the second attacker causing his shot to go wide. Ziobron grabbed the SKS by the barrel, ripped it from the Vietnamese' hands, and beat him to death with it.

Muffled shouts came from more enemy as they charged down the trails and crashed through the thick brush. He glanced back. Ksor, only a few yards away, and one other man were the only ones left of his recon element. Beyond him, the platoon had not advanced at all nor made any preparations either to join him or defend in place against the Communist attack. He dug into his rucksack and pulled two Claymore mines and placed them behind a fallen log toward the oncoming NVA.

Heavy fire was directed at the three men as the next wave of PAVN charged from the slope. A B-40 rocket exploded beside him tearing apart his gaiter leggings and boot and creating a massive laceration. It tore his Achilles tendon in two leaving the ends hanging out of his boot. White fatty flesh and blood filled his boot and poured down his legs. Almost at the same moment a burst from a machine gun hit Ziobron in the other leg rolling him over and down the slope where his descent was stopped by brush. Intense burning pain kept him from passing out. He glanced down at his wounds. Blood and tissue covered his legs. He was bleeding fast. As the shock of the wounds abated, he noted, "If I do not get the platoon pulled together, we will all die here."

He attempted to stand but fell. More RPG rounds exploded in the trees and incoming rounds tore through the leaves. He could only imagine what was happening a few feet above him on the slope. Two more rockets exploded above him but all shrapnel missed him. He tried to stand again but fell.

"Ksor, Ksor. I can't walk. Can you help?"

But Ksor was pinned down under makeshift cover and could not rise to help.

Ziobron rose, hobbled toward the Montagnard, fell, rose, hobbled again, over and over. His bleeding was unabated but he continued on. He fell over small logs, pushed himself upright and hobbled on. He fell again. He struggled up, hopped over small obstacles, fell, rose, and used his rifle for a crutch, finally making his way to Ksor.

Heavy fire came from one side, pinning them down. He crawled toward the enemy fire, his leg leaving a red swath behind his wounds. Were it not for the muzzle flashes, the bunker would not have been seen, camouflaged in the ferns and leaves. He pulled himself forward with his elbows and when he knew he could not miss, pulled the pin of a grenade with one blood-slippery index finger and tossed it into the window slot where four to six soldiers continued to shoot. Nearby, he discovered a second hidden bunker and crawled toward it and its incoming fire. Perhaps it was because he had to crawl, he was not shot, for the machine gunner did not suppress the bullets into him where he hugged the ground. He shot toward the flashes suppressing the fire until he was able to hurl a second grenade, ending the threat.

"Ksor, platoon is not moving. I must go and get them moving. I will send SCU to come help you, but you must hold until they get there. Here are two Claymores," and he handed him the detonators.

"Yes, Ksor will hold."

With a last view at his tribesman friend, he turned and hobbled to the platoon, grabbing for things to break his fall. At the end, he crawled the last steps to Smith's position and confronted him.

"Get your people up and move forward. Get up! Move. I have

only two men holding the whole front. Get up!"

Ziobron called Leghorn. "I need support immediately. Our situation is critical. We are assaulted by overwhelming force and have heavy casualties. Need help now."

"Roger. Copy. Sundance, hold in place and hang on. Will get to you ASAP. Assets committed to a smaller unit in Prairie Fire emergency extraction. Understand your situation. Will get to you as soon as we can. Copy?"

Ziobron sighed and bowed his head at the news. Could they survive that long? "Copy."

### *RT Kentucky*

Recon Team Kentucky was about to die. Their case was beyond critical or desperate. It remained only it seemed for the undertaker to roll out the caskets and give the flowers away. They began as a tiny recon team of five men: two Special Forces troopers and three tribesmen. They faced a hardened company of North Vietnamese regulars, fully armed and uniformed in boa constrictor green as they encircled Kentucky. The head of the enemy element, which numbered more than a hundred soldiers, struck with blinding speed and fury, and as the team responded there, the length of enemy coiled itself on the other side. The circle of soldiers ever tightened around the team and the end was near.

John Roberts, the team One-Zero was changing magazines and when he found the pouch empty, he looked down and saw the two next to it were likewise empty. He reached to the opposite side of his web gear. Three left. Fifty-seven more bullets. He had been using his rucksack as a shield as they lay and fought off the attacks. He fumbled inside. Not a single frag grenade left, not a spare bullet. Only one grenade remained and that was a smoke, the only way that remained to show his people where they were in the maelstrom. And that smoke was green and nearly invisible in the lush vegetation and was hard to see from the air.

The situation could not be more desperate. The assistant team leader lay dead somewhere on their backtrail. Two of his three

Montagnard fighters were wounded and bleeding. One lay on his back and his breath gurgled as he gasped for air, air that was pink and frothy where it showed through the large tear in his shirt. The other wounded Montagnard was trying to knot a cravat he had wrapped around an angry wound on the other arm. He held one end of it with his teeth as he looped and pulled with his other hand. But the closing enemy pressure took all of Robert's attention and he could not tend to the wounded men. If they just got a quick break from the fighting, he would attend to them.

He studied the edge of the tree line for movement and solid shades of green, revealing soldiers. His head throbbed. Splitting pain. He gingerly touched the place. The wound was significant, long and wide, but the blood seemed stanched by matted debris from the ground through which his people had dragged him to this place. He had no idea how long he had been unconscious. He woke up on his back as green tracers buzzed mere inches over his face. He rolled over and pressed himself upward and saw two of his people firing their rifles at charging regulars. He pulled himself to his knees and added his firepower until the charge abated.

Last thing he remembered before the bullet, or was it a frag from a B-40 rocket that knocked him down and out, was blowing up the enemy's source of water and the world coming down on them.

"What a dumb move I made—blowing up a simple water pipe—something they could repair in just hours. The move gave us away and got us to this point. And we had to leave Ron Smith's body somewhere out there." Those thoughts were in the wings of his mind as the fight before him was on center stage.

Kentucky was on a reconnaissance mission to gather intelligence and was certainly far too small to do anything else. With just five of them, they could maneuver and hide easier than a larger force, but on the other hand, they were poorly equipped to grab a prisoner or do real damage in this sanctuary. SOG suspected a new regiment or staging area hidden among the ridges and ravines. "We should have just gathered intelligence and brought it home."

But it became clear on the second day that something big was afoot. Perhaps new units and new roads and supply points were nestled in the contours of the highland's hideaway. With stealth, glacially slow-moving stealth, they proceeded, barely overtaking the shadows which crawled ahead of the sun. There were loud voices, wood chopping and movement of security patrols. Smoke rose from the depressions between thick forest knolls and ravines.

They moved at a crawl pace, keeping to cover. In contrast, enemy patrols moved by on shrub-hidden trails, always moving as on a schedule or with a destination in mind. Twice they remained in place near a well-used path trying to get a glimpse of uniform patches and equipment. At a low place, at the foot of a long ridge were camp sounds. A generator hummed and they thought they heard an announcement from a loudspeaker, but it was muffled with the intervening undergrowth. Roberts looked to his Montagnard counterpart to see if he could discern what the speaker said, but he slowly shook his head.

They moved along the military crest of the ridge line hoping to intercept trails or indications of the size of the installation.

The point man froze and slowly clinched one fist behind his back. "Danger, enemy."

Roberts closed with him. The tribesman nodded to his front-left and kept his weapon trained on the spot. Roberts saw it too. A long pipe lay on the ground oriented from the top of the ridge toward the area at its base where it appeared the bulk of enemy activity lay.

Roberts glanced back at Ronald Smith, his One-One, and motioned, "Come with me." His three SCU remained on guard as they slipped down to the pipe.

Smith whispered, "That's a water pipe. There must be a lake or something on the top of the ridge and this feeds the force down below. There must be a permanent base, at least a battalion down there for them to go to this much trouble to bring them water."

Roberts was silent for a minute. "I'm going to blow it up!"

"What!"

"I'm going to blow it up."

"Why? It's made of bamboo. They will just make a new one."

With resolve this time, Roberts said, "I am going to blow that thing up. Let's get with the team."

They gathered a distance away where Roberts collected all the C-4 in their rucksacks. "Cover me," he said as he slid down to the offending water system.

In less than fifteen minutes he placed C-4 at several joints of the piping, joined them with debt cord, and scuttled back to the rest of the team. Roberts glanced at his strikers and pressed the detonator.

A loud explosion blasted the sides of the small ravine which housed the piping. Shards of bamboo and water sprayed into the air.

Roberts looked at the team as if to say, "Did ya see that!" But his excitement was short lived as the response was immediate. The encampment was not as far down the slope as they thought. The shouting was clear and near. Roberts did not need to signal the point man that it was time to move out. Orders of enemy command were loud and repeated as were the calls of obeying men and tramping feet coming their way.

Ronald Smith was second to last in the tiny column as he covered for the tail gunner who tried to remove the clues of their passing. The PAVN troops must have responded at a run for their voices grew louder as they closed with the escaping recon team.

Scores of North Vietnamese charged up the slope and found the destruction of the water system. Joining them, clearly shouting from farther up the slope were more forces. No effort was made to hide their coming.

"Oh boy! Oh boy, we're in for it," Ronald Smith said aloud. "Forget that!" he shouted to the tail gunner who was trying to erase traces of their passing on the ground. "They are almost on us. Go, go!"

The small force determined to put distance between them and their pursuers and moved at a fast pace, caring only that noise of their flight did not betray their direction off the trail. There was a loud shout at the site of the explosion as the trackers found where they left the scene in their escape into the woods. Roberts halted the team as they listened to their back trail.

Yes! The voices followed like tracker hounds on the track. Several of the pursuers shouted from time to time as they found new prints and signs of the direction the team had gone. Crashing in the brush from farther up the ridge announced regulars from above had joined in the search for RT Kentucky.

Roberts faced his team. He held both hands in front of him and pressed them slowly downward. Time to move slowly and be vigilant. He pointed to his point man and gave him a direction to move, then to the tail gunner. "Watch back trail, cover tracks."

They moved with caution along the contour of the ridge. He recalled a small opening in the trees which could make for an exfil if they could make it. He tried to get covey on the radio. Either they were not in range or the terrain blocked the signal.

Signs of pursuit were closing on them. The enemy was neither moving with caution nor covering their passage as Kentucky was. Contact was becoming inevitable. They would have to fight them at some point. Whoever the trackers were, they were very good for Kentucky had covered their tracks very well yet they could not shake them.

Roberts looked back and saw the diligence of his tail gunner and shuffled back to him. "Trackers are very good. Maybe Montagnard?"

The tail gunner had a worried look about his face. "Yes, trackers very good. I do number one hide but tracker him still follow."

Roberts looked at Smith. "We are going to have to ambush them and give them a reason to not follow us. Maybe we can kill the trackers."

Smith acknowledged the reasoning and gravely nodded. "Commo?"

"Not yet. Maybe when we get to the top of this, we can get line of sight." He glanced at the back trail and the signs of pursuit. "First we have to get there."

Fifteen minutes later they found a small knoll on their way to the top. "Walk along the front of this and we will fishhook back to this knoll," he said to the point man. He walked over to the tail gunner. "Leave some track so VC will follow us here. We will ambush VC from there."

The tribesman nodded in full understanding.

Ten minutes later they were in position on the rise above the level ground. With frantic fingers he pulled one of only two Claymores from his back and propped it twenty meters below them and rushed back to the team unrolling the det cord as he hid what he could in the dirt. He barely had time to plop down on his belly and slide behind his rucksack, when they saw movement below them: the shiver of small leaves, then the sway of bushes, and finally uniformed men emerging into the thinness of the opening. One Montagnard tracker was moving, bent over studying the spore the tail gunner had left deliberately behind to guide their movement.

They were twenty feet into the kill zone when the tracker halted and held up his hand for those following to stop. An officer rushed to him and in Vietnamese demanded to know what was wrong, "Why are you stopping?"

"I no like. Before enemy cover tracks very good. Now I see them plain."

"Go!" the officer ordered. "Go. I want to catch them. Go"

"Captain. I think they want us follow. See tracks them plain."

"Go, I tell you. Go."

The tracker continued ahead following the spoor of Kentucky, but he no longer looked on the ground but cast his eyes into the foliage around him for the attack he fully expected.

Roberts waited until the kill zone was full of enemy before he set off the mine. Even as the explosion sent its 730 lead pellets through the thin cloth uniforms of a dozen men and his people poured their ordnance into those left standing, Roberts sought for the tracker to be sure he did not live. He was not there.

"Move out." He said to his people and they rose to continue to evade. Smith took one glance to the rear. Shouting came from farther back and the low shrubs violently shook as more enemy entered the scene of battle. A few of the fallen moaned or slowly got to their knees. To the left, one Montagnard staggered up and retrieved his SKS rifle. He walked a half dozen steps to where his captain had fallen and spat.

Again, the five men of Recon Team Kentucky evaded, first moving at speed to gain distance, changed direction, then slowed to stealth, moving without leaving signs of passage.

Twice more they ambushed the rear causing casualties to the Communists, giving them pause and reason not to pursue. They contoured around the ridge to the east side and Roberts tried to contact either Leghorn or Covey again.

"This is Leghorn," was the reply.

"Leghorn. We are in very heavy contact and being pursued. Need support and exfil."

"Roger copy. Covey en route. Assets standing by."

Roberts glanced back. Smith and the tail gunner were breathing heavily, their shoulders and heads bobbing with the struggle to catch their breaths.

"Coming again. Right behind us!" B-40 rockets exploded in the trees. Automatic rifle-fire buzzed above them and stripped bushes of their leaves. Disturbed monkeys shrieked and ran full speed along the ground.

"Let's go! Hurry," the team leader shouted and they ran deeper into the contour of the hill. Smith glanced back. He heard the enemy crashing behind them, but then also heard crashing coming toward them from another quarter.

"John, they are coming from that way too."

They all but ran along the slope but still the pursuers closed from at least two directions. They were no longer able to outrun them.

There was a slight rise where there were natural firing lanes below.

"Here!" Roberts shouted. "Here. Make a stand here. Maybe we can slow them up."

They threw off their packs and barely had time to flop down behind them when the first of the enemy came into view. The team shot full-automatic as the vanguard burst through the bushes. The rank stumbled and dropped with the impact of the bullets. Roberts made a fast crawl toward the group approaching from above and jammed his last Claymore on its pegs to a place behind a tree. The last two yards of his return was a desperate lunge to his rucksack just as a continuous roar of rifle fire and rockets filled the air. Enemy charged them from above the Claymore and he depressed the trigger. The blast tore away everything before it but many more soldiers filled the space. Roberts fired into the gap.

He heard a cry and a moan behind them. The company of soldiers were making a full charge, shouting as they came. Smith and the tail gunner half rose to shoot and change magazines as a half dozen enemies fired their automatic rifles directly at them. Both Ronald Smith and the tail gunner dropped to the ground. Smith's wounds were fatal: one to the head, one to the chest and another to his side. The tail gunner lay on his back with his mouth and eyes open. Already as Roberts glanced at him his flesh turned pale in death.

The remainder of the team fired on full-automatic at the advancing force, but as they fell, the team heard the movement of many others who ran forward to take their place.

It was clear they were being overrun. "Move out! Move out!"

As quickly as they put a few enemies down, others leaped over their bodies and closed with the team. Kentucky emptied their magazines of ammo on the adversary, turned and ran, changing magazines as they did. They gained distance briefly but heard them advance again. Roberts set up another hasty ambush whose lethality brought down the front rank. Soldiers behind them fired rockets over the prostrate forms. A B-40 exploded near Roberts striking him in the head and knocking him unconscious.

He woke on his back seeing the thickness of the tree tops sliding across his vision, for he was being dragged by his two remaining tribesmen, and the trees were blurry in his dizziness. The world spun around him. His head swooned and everything was a fog and bile drew up from inside and filled his mouth. He threw his face to the side and gagged and spilled it all on the ground and on his shoulder. He was dizzy, more so than he could recall ever having experienced. Sharp pain invaded his skull like a tormenter would cause by sliding thorns under a prisoner's fingernails. "Ahhh," he moaned.

"Sshh! Sshh," cautioned his point man as he bent over Roberts. "Sshh. VC hear you."

The tribesman saw the confusion on Robert's face. "You be wounded. But you no die. We drag you maybe ten minutes. You be okay now. We must go now. VC come soon."

It took only a minute for everything to sink in. "Where . . . ?"

"Smith, him die. Montagnard him die too. We have to leave him. Too many VC."

Roberts pondered the information for a moment. "Yes," he said. He glanced to see that he still had his rifle. "VC?"

"VC come again for sure. Think many die but more come. We need helicopter, go FOB."

Roberts rolled to one side and struggled to his feet. A wave of dizziness swept over him and he swayed for a minute. "I am okay now. How long I am number ten?"

"You sleep only maybe fifteen minutes. We drag you maybe fifty meters."

He glanced at the way they had come; two deep furrows revealed where his heels dragged to this place.

The three of them found a small piece of high ground where a few spindly trees lined the edges and was just open enough for an extraction, if only by strings. Roberts made contact with Covey just as the three SOG men heard crashing in the brush all around them. "This is Kentucky," he nearly screamed into the set. "This is a Prairie Fire emergency. Need immediate extraction. Surrounded. One soap bubble (code name for American} KIA, one straw hat, (code name for indigenous person) KIA, One-Zero WIA. Copy?"

"Copy. Assets en route."

Roberts saw the first of the new batch of enemy clear the vegetation, their rifles moving like insect antennae seeking prey. At the fore was the bandaged Montagnard tracker, whose eyes inspected it all and found the suspect place where Roberts waited and looked directly into his eyes.

"Copy. Hurry!"

He remembered how few rounds remained for his weapon. He took careful aim at the chest of the man with the SKS and squeezed the trigger one time. Roberts saw the bullet hit. The cloth of the fatigue shirt quivered where it entered and the soldier flew backward with both arms raised skyward as he fell, the SKS rifle raised banner-like in his right hand. Roberts watched the place for he believed in his heart the man would get up, that he would not die.

His people, for he had only two left, engaged the enemy. They were nearly back-to-back in their very small perimeter, each facing a different direction. "Aim, shoot one at a time," Roberts called to his people, but it was not a loud shout they were so close, and he did not want the enemy to know they had not much ammunition.

The bulk of the attack came from his part of the circle. They came nearly at him and at a narrow front, imposed in part by the contour of the ground and impassable thickets and vines which funneled them. He was able to choose a target, aim and fire, over and over. When he dared, for he feared an assault from another way, his Montagnard added to his lethality. "Be sure to carefully aim before you shoot or we *fini* ammo,'" he cautioned again. In this manner they held off what was left of a company of North Vietnamese regulars.

A half hour of continued contact elapsed. The number of infantry enemy diminished and was replaced by a deluge of B-40 rockets and mortar fire. What was left of Kentucky had no shelter, no hole in which to dive, and, surrounded as they were, could not evade the barrage. The Kentucky One-Zero rolled to his back and pulled out his last magazine of bullets from the holder. Twenty-nine more bullets. Perhaps twenty-nine more attackers will fall. Like many SOG men he never put the full thirty rounds in the magazine to not weaken the spring which fed rounds into the weapon. How he wished for that one extra bullet in his rifle. He looked over to his remaining fighters. The point man's arm hung limp and loose from his wounded shoulder; the other could barely breathe. Roberts heard the air in the man's lungs as it fought to make its way through the blood. He gasped and desperately pulled the life-giving air into his body. There was desperation and fear in the soldier's eyes.

Engine noise.

"Kentucky, this is Covey. Have assets, mainly Cobra gunships. Mark location."

"Roger. Have only one smoke left and it is green. Sorry. You are half mile at 180 degrees."

"Throw smoke."

"Smoke out."

"Got it."

The enemy heard the airplane also and began a concerted attempt to annihilate the team before help arrived. They attacked from both sides at once, risking hitting each other as they fired across the opening. The North Vietnamese charged and were in the open without concealment. Kentucky made deliberate firing at the attackers. Robert's heart thudded and sounded to him as loud as the shots he was taking. He had used his last bullet. He had nothing left—nothing! He looked across at his SCU to find him also empty. The American drew his knife.

"Cobra coming in. Heads down, Kentucky."

The first helicopter passed low overhead and unleashed its ordnance laying everything flat around the team. The second followed in its wake with a swath of explosive ordnance. For the next ten minutes the Cobras flooded the area with all they had, working the swath farther and farther out. On their heels a Huey descended for the team, deeming the shrub tops thin enough that the propeller could work through. All three of the recon men were wounded but stumbled to the chopper, the two least wounded dragging their comrade. A chase medic took charge of the seriously wounded tribesman as they lifted off and sped toward Kontum.

Roberts sat in the doorway next to the crew chief and looked down at the ruins below. Prop planes dropped their ordnance and explosions flashed between the bamboo around the site. Prostrate forms lay along the route the team had taken and where they had briefly held off one company of regulars. Some bodies one the ground crawled or stood upright and made for any cover to shield them from the revenge of the aircraft. At a place, next to the opening, a short, stocky, dark-skinned man slowly stood to his feet. He did not run. He was bandaged and held one hand to his wounded chest and with the other raised an SKS rifle in salute. The lone soldier seemed to stare toward the helicopter, and it seemed, although Roberts may have only imagined it, that he looked directly into his eyes.

* * * * *

Ziobron looked up. It was 1800 hours and greyness lay its shroud across the sky. He turned to the platoon who yet remained on their bellies and were not engaging.

"I said get up!" he shouted. Ziobron tried to stand upright and leaned on his rifle. "Sergeant Smith, get your people moving."

Smith responded in a sing song, wistful voice, "I will no longer follow orders because this platoon should be extracted now . . . right now!" And he folded his arms across his chest in finality.

Ziobron looked at the shrunken man. Smith was clearly shell-shocked and had decided that he wanted to go home. He no longer seemed aware of the situation. Ziobron turned to the Yards. It was imperative to get them into the fight or the platoon was lost.

"Get up and move," he shouted at the strikers. "Get up."

The Yards looked at Smith. Never before had they seen an American stricken and frozen. They heard the firefight to the front and incoming rockets and balked at the order. Ziobron grabbed his strikers, one at a time and stood them upright, pushed and shoved them. "Move, move, go!"

One by one they stood. "Let's go," Ziobron shouted and led the way, using his CAR-15 as a crutch. With his example they became a cohesive core again and rushed to the battle. As they joined with the forward recon element at the front, a new burst of fire struck another recon man in the chest killing him instantly. The incoming abated slightly and Ziobron contacted Leghorn again as Conkin and Zaborowski consolidated a perimeter to hold off the enemy.

"Anything new regarding support for me? I have several dead and wounded and am in constant heavy contact."

"I am having Covey go your way as soon as possible."

# SOG: Missions to the Well

"Copy."

As they waited for Covey and further prepared their defenses, Zaborowski applied field dressings to Ziobron's profusely bleeding wounds; not only to the bullet wound and rocket shards, but to his lacerated knees and hands from falling repeatedly. "I'm going to give you Demerol and morphine for the pain."

"No. No. I have to be able to think."

Conkin joined the two sergeants and Ziobron apprised them. "We will hopefully get air support shortly, but the LZ I had hoped for was up that ridge. We must have the whole enemy regiment between us and that extraction site. We are going to have to evade the other way to a different one."

The two men before him digested the information and waited.

"When I was getting ready to come on this mission with you, Dale Hanson came to my hooch and gave me the intel about this area. We are in Communist Base Area 609. That is the 66th NVA regiment, one of the ones that fought at Dien Bien Phu. They are hardcore, but we have bloodied them. They are the ones above us, blocking us from our way out of here.

"Here's what we're going to do: We are going to make a withdrawal from here and evade down this hill to the ravine below us. We are going to go down the ravine so no stragglers get lost. We will follow it to the river and we will cross it and go to the top of the knoll on the other side where we will be picked up tomorrow.

"Covey should arrive soon and we will use air support to cover us the whole way back. If we need to, Spooky will be on station and can put fire all around us all night. I am going to take ten strikers to hold them off while you make your way to the river.

"Chester, you will go with the wounded. You will be in the lead and the wounded are your responsibility. Go as quickly as you can considering their condition. Since you are in front, you might encounter enemy, so be alert. Copy?"

Zaborowski nodded. "I understand. Nearly everyone is wounded in some way, but we will do it."

"Clyde, you will have the platoon until I catch up with my

withdrawal force. Keep everyone together as a fighting unit. I want you to cross the river and wait for me. Find a place close by to support us coming across. If my blocking force doesn't make it, you must take what is left to the knoll and coordinate with Covey."

"When do we go?" Clyde Conkin asked.

Ziobron looked up. "We will be losing our daylight if we don't go soon. If Covey doesn't come with assets, I want you to start in one half hour."

He nodded.

"Okay, I am going to pick eight or ten men to take with me—ones that can move quickly so we can catch up with you at the river."

That the enemy was massing for a major assault could not be hidden, for the noise of shouted orders mere dozens of meters up the slope, the trampling of batta boots on the path, the sliding of bolts in weapons to seat the next bullet, even the hiss in the woods as hundreds of soldiers drew their collective breath said as much. Ziobron positioned three more Claymore mines to augment the three already in place and the dozen men of the stay-behind force waited behind fallen logs and rucksacks. The assault came as an explosion of violence.

A massive barrage of RPG rockets landed in the trees and among the strikers. So heavy was the incoming that individual explosions became a continuous roar. Every tribesman was injured by shrapnel. Ziobron was thrown to the ground by a blast. He regained his knees, grabbed an M-79 grenade launcher from a fallen striker, and began a salvo at a wall of charging enemy. Thousands of muzzle flashes shone through gaps in the undergrowth. As fast as he could, he shot, broke the action, and inserted another canister, firing at least ten rounds into the attacking force. Dozens of enemies fell wounded or were killed from his barrage.

Incoming was heavy among the platoon as well. A blast landed near Zaborowski hitting one of the Montagnards and throwing him in a heap. Zaborowski ran to the bleeding man as rockets exploded around him and tried to hold him long enough to check his wounds. The soldier writhed in pain. "*Bác Sĩ!* Montagnard, him hurt, him hurt."

Enormous amounts of blood poured from both pant legs. Zaborowski tried to straighten his legs by gently pulling his boot, but it separated from the pant leg with the foot inside. A cursory look revealed massive tearing of his flesh from foot to knee. The soldier's legs were shredded. Zaborowski placed tourniquets above both knees. He dressed the wounds as incoming rockets threw dirt on the stub ends. He turned his back to block the falling debris and completed the dressing, then dragged the striker to cover.

"Gas!"

It came from the attackers. CS gas floated across the defenders as a heavy impenetrable fog, burning exposed skin and eyes, and constricting their breathing. Ziobron donned his gas mask and rushed to his people, many of whom did not know how to put them on. On the heels of the shout, twenty to thirty enemy emerged from the cloud of gas and charged from the right only fifteen meters away. Ziobron blew two of the six Claymore mines and the fifteen hundred lead pellets dropped the inexorably moving force.

Another barrage of RPG rockets landed among the men knocking Ziobron to the ground and out of his position, exposing him to incoming fire. With the extreme pain of his previous wounds and concussion of the near rocket blast, he could not move. Ksor saw this, leaped from his cover and ran to Ziobron pulling him to safety as a rocket exploded nearby, mortally wounding him. Ksor collapsed, drawing ragged breaths and moaning. It appeared that the two of them would die together side by side. Ziobron rolled himself upright, drew his pistol and while shooting at the oncoming force, dragged Ksor to safety.

"Keep shooting," he yelled to his wounded defenders and to the platoon below. "Firepower!" Most incoming rounds focused on the forward element, but the platoon was also under fire. Shrapnel hit Zaborowski's shoulder. He felt hot burning and the blood run down the wound, but he continued on.

Bursts of RPD fire came from the right flank and with the now familiar muffled sound, Ziobron knew it came from a nearby bunker.

For a third time he crawled forward with his rifle and grenades. This time, fire was suppressed at a level that tore up the soil around him throwing dirt into his face. He continued on, rolled to his left side and managed two grenades into the slot. There was a muffled "whuumph" as they exploded inside. The position became silent. He dragged himself back to his position, gasping for breath.

Ziobron looked at Ksor and slapped bandages on his wounds as a voice came across his radio.

"Sundance, this is Covey. Assets are on station. I have cream puffs (the prop-driven Skyraider airplanes that many men on the ground preferred) with today's menu ready for you."

"What about a dust off?" Ziobron urged in return.

There was a very long pause before Covey answered. "Sundance. Covey. Bad news. We have another Prairie Fire from a recon team. We have to respond to that one first. We will get to you when we can. How copy?"

"Copy," Ziobron said quietly into the handpiece.

Covey could tell by the tone of his voice he might never hear him again.

"We are coming back for you. Hunker down. We are coming back."

"Copy," Ziobron said, but there was no confidence in his voice that they would be alive when the dust off did arrive.

He switched frequency. "Zab, start your exfil now. Start with the most seriously wounded first and get Smith to help you."

"Copy."

"Conkin, start moving out now. I am going to start the air support."

Switching to Covey's frequency he confirmed, "Ready for ordnance."

"Mark position." Covey made a fly by. "I see orange."

"Good copy. Heavy concentration of enemy at . . ." and he gave the azimuth and distance.

"Rolling over and coming in hot, boys. Heads down." The Skyraider—which flew slower than the jets—had more visual time over the target, passed low and seconds later four rockets exploded on the enemy concentrations.

As Covey directed the airstrikes on the target, an unexpected attack came from the front of Ziobron's small, wounded group. It was both an attempt to overrun and kill them and get as close as possible so air support would not dare to drop more ordnance. The last two Claymores brought down the mass of attackers but more made it to the holding force. One got directly above Ziobron and he pulled him down, tore off his gas mask and beat him with his fist. Another ran at him firing an SKS rifle as Ziobron grabbed the M-79 and shot him with a cannister round. Two more appeared and he drew his pistol and dispatched them.

A brief respite occurred as the attack was broken. Covey called and asked for corrections.

"You are on target. Hit them there even harder."

Conkin radioed. "All of our people are either in the ravine or already at the river."

Another intense attack began and the Green Beret realized that with all Claymores expended they could no longer hold the position. "Time to leave. Go to the ravine and go to the river. Go now quickly."

He called Covey. "Have the Skyraider drop their load on my position in thirty seconds. We are abandoning this location."

"That is not enough time for you to get a safe distance. It will be on you."

"It's on me. Drop it!"

With that, he hoisted the radio to his back and lugged the unconscious Ksor over his shoulder. He labored, having no sound legs, and using the help of the last remaining SCU, hobbling toward the ravine, stumbling, falling, crawling, and hobbling again. With each step he heard Ksor's rasping breath as blood filled his lungs. The three of them stumbled and fell just as the ordnance landed scant yards behind them and exploded throwing shrapnel through the bushes just above their heads. They crawled into the ravine and joined the rear of the platoon.

"Bombs too close! Bombs too close," shouted two Yards. "Bombs will hit Montagnard."

Ziobron contacted Covey. "Lift the bomb run one hundred meters and hit them hard."

Seconds later at that knot of enemy, the highlands erupted with cluster bombs, 750-pound bombs, gun runs, and rockets.

"Sundance, Sundance. Be advised that Skyraiders are low on fuel and out of ordnance. You have Spectre standing by."

"Copy. We are crossing the river and Sergeant Conkin is working to find a night perimeter. We have several dead and nearly all of us are wounded."

"Fix your position."

"Strobe out."

"Affirm. Copy."

"Good copy."

Chet Zaborowski had been carrying the wounded striker with the shredded legs in a fireman's carry. He was exhausted in the poor light as he stumbled over the uneven ground, moving out of breath. If they could just get him to a hospital in time, they might save his life. He gasped, out of breath, and as he stepped, he heard also the faint breath of the stricken man whose head lolled over his shoulder next to his cheek. "I don't know how long I can keep on with this," he thought just as he tripped and fell into the beginning of the ravine. He fell hard to the ground with the wind knocked out of him. As a medic he checked on his patient who lay sprawled on the ground before him. There was no sign of life. He felt for pulse, placed his hand to his chest, used every trick to ascertain breath. The fighter was dead.

He turned to the nearest strikers. "Help me bring his body back."

But the strikers, superstitious and frightened around the dead, refused to touch the body. "*Bác Sĩ*, we no do. You come me. You come me. Leave Montagnard now."

The river was waist- to chest-deep with a swift current. The shorter Yards were frightened at the crossing but were helped along by the sergeants. Ziobron still carried Ksor on his shoulders, air snorting through the Montagnard's nose with each step. Ziobron glanced about at the progress and noticed Smith on the other side. He was hatless and had left his pack and rifle along the way and hovered under the outcropping of the far bank. For now, the little platoon was hidden under the over-bank as what was left of the 28th enemy regiment searched for them, moving on line toward the river, and enemy patrols scouted along the river edge for the platoon. The current was swift and some of the weaker, wounded men struggled to keep their footing.

His eyes passed again across his line of men along the river edge. Smith was gone!

Ziobron looked again to be certain. Smith was gone. Washed down stream.

"Covey to Sundance."

"Sundance."

"Spectre wants to speak to Sundance on secure voice." Moments later Spectre was on line. "Sundance, I want to assure you that I will be here all night for you. I have flares that can make it bright as day if you want it. I have unlimited rounds in my minigun to make it miserable for Victor Charles. You can use the flashing strobe light with the filter and I can pinpoint your location at all times. It is invisible to the VC. Turn it on for a few seconds every hour and we can make it hot all around you."

"Copy."

Ziobron turned on the strobe so Spectre had him fixed.

Voices came from across the river and deeper in the woods as hundreds of enemies with lanterns and flares searched for the team. It would be a matter of time before they found where they had crossed the river. Ziobron gave the situation, azimuth and distance to the enemy.

"Heads down boys, enjoy the show."

Tracers from "Puff the Magic Dragon" appeared in the sky like northern lights, curtains of red fire from mini guns firing 6,000 rounds a minute. It was followed by 20 mm cannon fire and flares to light up the enemy. Enemy activity ceased.

After hours of being submerged in the water and the knowledge that daylight would leave them exposed, they moved inland to a pond area that Sergeant Conkin had found. They lay out a secure defensive perimeter deciding to continue to an extraction point just before daylight. Zaborowski tended Ziobron's wounds and those of nearly thirty strikers.

In the middle of the night, Smith walked into the RON. He simply strode in, walking upright as if he had been on a long stroll and knew where the platoon had stopped for the night. He had only his clothing; no weapons, pack, nothing to support his survival. He arrived like a truant, never uttering a word. He found a shallow place, plopped himself down and sat. In the semi darkness they could not see his features but knew he simply stared ahead.

Ziobron was in excruciating pain and he was glad for that because it kept him awake. He crawled the circumference of the perimeter over and over keeping his people alert. It was only 2230 and more hours to go before they would move out. In his rounds he tapped each shoulder that held a nodding head and whispered, "Stay awake. I want you to live and be a grandfather." And he would see the strikers' white teeth surrounded by a smile in the night.

"Hey, Sergeant Ziobron," softly called a Montagnard, "you *kahtong rahmong*." (Crazy tiger.)

Smith still sat upright in a shallow portion of the pool, his arms wrapped around his knees as he rocked back and forth and mumbled to himself.

At 0430 on a circuit which took him painfully past the most seriously wounded, Zaborowski informed him that Im Nei Ksor, a hero of men, had died. Ziobron halted on his hands and knees in sorrow for his friend, but duty propelled him on his course.

The enemy were beating the bush en masse looking for the platoon. Making no attempt to hide their presence, they shouted as they moved on line from ridge to river. Lights shined everywhere. Their thin beams were spears jabbing the darkness for SOG men. At the river edge, entire companies of the 66th NVA Regiment fired across the river, probing for response. Units of searchers scoured the river bank seeking traces of passage, and when they did not find clear tracks, they began again.

It rained. They were already wounded and shivering, most of them waist-deep in the water of the pool, and it rained without letup. It was unrelenting and miserable. Chills added their own pain to wounds. Was this deluge and fog a death shroud ending all chance of an exfil? Could the strobe, which Ziobron held in his hand, pierce the opaque sky and allow air support to know their location so they could drop their ordnance? Was the enemy at this minute using the downpour to mask their stealthy approach?

0530 Ziobron spoke with the sergeants. "We need to leave here for the top of that knoll now. We need to be underway before daylight. I want us to be in place as soon as they can get assets here. Check with your people and get them ready."

Ziobron turned on the handset. "Sundance to Spectre. Do you copy? Sundance to Spectre."

The response was immediate. "Spectre to Sundance. Are we glad to hear from you!"

"You can't imagine. I have 90% casualties plus KIA and we are critically low on ammunition. We are going to proceed to the knoll for exfil now if the rain does not prevent us."

"Sundance, we will make it happen."

The wounded platoon moved cautiously, as quickly as their injuries would allow, each hampered by wounds and weariness. Thick fog and rain kept visibility to just a few meters, but the goal was the knoll, always upward, wearily up hill, and they clambered on.

"Hey, hey." It was a husky whisper from Zaborowski, "Hey, Smith, get back, get back. You don't have a gun. Get back."

"Leave me alone. Leave me alone."

Smith pulled away and left the column. Zaborowski was propping up badly wounded men and could not pursue. In a moment Smith was swallowed by the rain and fog.

Conkin made his way to Ziobron. "Want me to go after him?"

Ziobron paused as he looked at the struggling men and at the haze which would preclude finding the sergeant. He considered the chance of losing others in the search. "No, stay with your people. I don't want any more to stray."

But they listened for Smith; for his puffing breath, for his footfalls as he crashed through the brush, even for a voice saying, "I'm going home, I'm going home." Zaborowski made his way to Ziobron as he pushed himself upright on his feet using his rifle as a crutch. "He just said, 'I am going home,' and he was gone. I couldn't stop him."

To the flank, about seventy-five meters away, automatic rifle fire erupted. It was an RPD machine gun. One burst, a long burst of thirty rounds, then deathly silence.

The people knew in their hearts what transpired, but could only wonder if he were still alive, that the bullets missed him, and he was yet wandering through the tangle muttering, "I'm going home."

Ziobron picked three strikers to be a small flank to move alongside of the platoon. He whispered to them, "Be very careful. VC that way. Maybe they *fini* Sergeant Smith. Maybe you find body."

They straightened. "Montagnard do."

"Move out," he whispered the order. "Move out."

They were nearing the crest. Trees thinned slightly. Underbrush lessened around their legs. Even the rain slightly diminished. The three Montagnards he had assigned to the flank and were slightly ahead of them, returned, rushing to Ziobron. "Sergeant Ed, Sergeant Ed, we find Sergeant Smith. He dead."

"You see him?"

"Yes, him dead."

"You are sure?"

There was a tinge of hurt in their voices to think they were doubted.

"Yes, him Sergeant Smith. VC shoot him many times in face and head, but it is him."

"Montagnard go now and stay with him until I come and take him away. I will come for you. I do not forget you. You believe this?"

There was just enough light to know that the tribesmen nodded.

Fifteen minutes later Ziobron stumbled in his halting, falling progress, mostly walking on his knees and arrived at the knoll. As if the Communists could see through fog and the rain, they opened up with withering fire from three sides with machine gun, rockets and small arms. It came both from the next ridge and from close range. A round hit Conkin in the head knocking him into a heap in nearby bushes.

"Conkin him die, him die," shouted a SCU next to Ziobron. "Him die, shot in head!"

Ziobron hobbled and fell toward the sergeant. He lay on his back with an entrance wound on his forehead just below his hairline and an exit on the back of his head. Massive amounts of blood pooled in the dirt. Conkin did not move. Surely he was dead. It was pure agony to see what could only be evidence of a bullet passing completely through his head and taking his life just as help was arriving and they hoped to be exfiltrated. Ziobron was on his knees and he cupped Conkin's head in his hands. There was a cough! Ziobron stared, amazed. Conkin's chest moved up and down. Breath! His body moved. It was no more than a shiver, but he moved.

Ziobron could not believe what he was seeing. But even if the choppers got to them and he made it to a hospital, he doubted he could live with such a wound. But people pray. Moments later Conkin's eyes fluttered, opened, and fixed on Ziobron. This could only be the miracle bullet. It entered his forehead at his hairline but did not pierce his skull. The bullet did not go in a straight line. Instead, it contoured the outside of his skull traveling just under his scalp and exited at the back of his head, leaving a large flap the size of a silver dollar.

"Ahhh!" Conkin groaned. He placed his hand where the pain was most acute, then pulled it away fully drenched with blood.

"I think you just got a miracle wound. God was looking out for you."

Zaborowski rushed to him and got a field dressing from his pouch. "My last one."

Conkin seemed to be coming out of it as from a deep sleep. "Are you going to be okay? Are you going to be okay?" Ziobron asked.

"Why?" he answered as if he did not know why he was being asked such a question. "I'm fine. I need to get up."

Ziobron looked one last time at his friend and pushed himself up using his rifle. "He's all yours, Zab. I have a lot to tend to before we can ever get out of this."

The platoon left the cover of the forest and arrived at the top of the knoll at 0745, a place the enemy had at one time occupied. At least twenty-five spider holes and trenches lay around the perimeter and the strikers immediately occupied them.

"Spectre to Sundance."

"Sundance."

"I am going to make a pass over you for location. I need an exact fix."

"Copy." The sky was thinning and he tried smoke. "Smoke out."

"Have visual. Smoke is red."

"Good copy."

"Situation report. What is your situation?"

"Sundance to Spectre. All Americans are KIA or WIA. Have ninety percent casualties with my little people. Critically low on ammunition. Surrounded on three sides and taking fire. How copy?"

"Good copy. If possible, draw all of your people in for recovery. I have fixed wing aircraft and helicopter gunships en route."

"Roger, give me fifteen minutes. I need to recover some of my people a little down the hill first."

"Roger, hurry."

Heavy rocket and machine gun fire erupted from the ridges, augmented by small arms fire around the knoll.

"Zab, Conkin. I have to go and retrieve my little people down the hill and try to bring back Smith's body. We are critically low on ammunition. We might run out if the assets don't get to us soon. Tell the SCU to aim and only shoot at enemy that they can see. Tell them not to shoot on automatic. Do it now.

"Conkin, I'm going to leave you my radio in case I don't make it back. You are more in the middle with the wounded so the radio is more protected. It will be up to you to work the air support."

B-40 rockets fell like rain nearby and Ziobron could not hear the response. Small arms fire buzzed in the air above their heads. "Remember, only shoot at what you can see and hit."

Ziobron slipped out of the spider hole and crawled down the slope to link up with his three tribesmen and Smith's body. The ground was wet with the rain and he slid across more easily. He still bled and was getting weaker with the passing minutes. On his belly as he was, he wanted to pause and rest, catch just a little sleep, just a minute. Even weariness was painful. The North Vietnamese fired through the bushes, the rounds raking the ground at knee and chest height. They shouted as much to draw fire as to keep their own men on line as they swept the forest looking for the platoon. Several times bullets slapped through the foliage and tore bark from the trees nearby. Twice he stopped when he saw passing enemy part the fingers of ferns and peer through them. Ziobron told himself, "Do not shoot. You promised the Montagnards that you would come for them."

He crawled as quickly as he could knowing the assets could drop their ordnance at any moment. "This has to be the place," he thought, as he studied the area. "They must be nearby." Then, next to a large hardwood tree, poking from a bed of ferns, he saw a boot. It was shiny from the rain. From the acute angle of the boot, he knew it was not on a foot of a live man. He clicked his tongue.

The answering click was immediate and very close. He clicked his tongue again, and three tribesmen emerged from hiding, relief evident on their faces. Days before they were in the graveyard among the ghosts there, and now they guarded a man with no face.

"We glad you are here."

"Me too. I never forget you. Airplane come. Helicopter come. *Fini* mission. But we must take Sergeant Smith. You must pull now. I am too wounded, too tired to pull anymore."

The Yards suppressed their superstitions, wrapped their arms around Smith's wrists and grabbed the cloth of his shirt and dragged. It took longer than Ziobron had hoped, but he could no longer stand to help. "I hope they do not begin air support before we get to the knoll," he thought.

Exhausted but alive, they crawled into the knoll dragging Smith's body just as the enemy began a concerted attack on the position. Along with the heavy incoming fire the force was shouting and yelling to gin up courage for the final assault.

Ziobron took the secure radio. "Spectre, we are all inside the perimeter. Feel free to shoot. We are under heavy attack."

"Roger, Sundance. Coming in hot. Prepare for the show."

Spectre unleashed his miniguns on the attacking enemy, firing six thousand rounds a minute at the charging force. Pass after pass decimated the assault as the platoon for once was able to keep their heads down during the fight.

"Spectre to Sundance."

"Sundance."

"That's it. I am about to run out of fuel and ammunition, so I will bid you good day. You will be glad to know that I have a squadron of A-1 Skyraiders and four F-4 Phantoms coming in to take over. Perhaps we will see you at the club."

"Sundance to Spectre. Thank you. You have been a lifesaver."

"Anytime."

"Break. Break. Sundance this is Covey."

Ziobron had just turned to prepare his people for the Phantom airstrike to come when he heard his call sign. "Covey, this is Sundance."

"Sundance, hunker down and use the assets. We have another Prairie Fire to deal with first. Be with you when we can. Copy?"

He looked about him at his ragged wounded force. At least they had some cover, and he was getting air support. "This is Sundance. I copy."

An A-1 Skyraider streaked low over the beleaguered platoon; a sudden pass, low enough to shiver leaves feet below its wings and suck out air above the blood-spattered soil. Charging soldiers hurled themselves to the ground. The pass was sudden, loud, and fast, and the enemy did not have time to raise their weapons to shoot before the plane was gone. The Skyraider did not drop ordnance. This flyover was a message. To the beleaguered men on the ground, it said with an exclamation point, "We are here and will defend you against your attackers!" To the 28th NVA Regiment it said, "The calvary has arrived, you should think of getting out of Dodge. Our next meeting will be with lethality." Even the most illiterate soldier got the message.

But the enemy regiment remained unrelenting in its mission; it would destroy utterly the encircled SOG platoon. Political commissars at the rear of the halting force pushed them ahead with their loaded weapons, shooting anyone who failed to advance. Throughout the day the airplanes dropped their ordnance on the regiment thinning them and sending them to cover but before the planes angled far above the shredded trees, the regiment tide continued on. They surrounded the knoll, fired rockets and mortars throughout the day, attacked from new avenues, used snipers, tried to infiltrate on their bellies, and when they were able, they made frontal attacks. They sensed a growing weakness in the platoon as their numbers lessened and firepower diminished and so continued their attack.

But the little group on the knoll was also steadfast. Their sergeant, badly wounded and exhausted, crawled around the perimeter moving from tribesman to tribesman with words of encouragement and sometimes a fistful of bullets. Had he a moment when which he was not involved with some aspect of keeping his people alive, he might have thought of King Ahab in the Bible, surrounded by vast multitudes of Syrian soldiers, who looked at his own force and saw them as a just a little flock of goats.

Ziobron looked up. In addition to the light rain, the day was passing. Shadows deepened and he wondered if they would survive the night.

\* \* \* \*

Sergeant Larry Predmore was on the radio at the launch site and got the call.

"Assemble the Bright Light team and prepare to insert and augment the surrounded platoon."

"What a week this has been," he thought. Was this the third or fourth time they had been given the alert? Every one of the previous alerts were cause to worry. There was RT Montana, the split team that parachuted somewhere around the golf course and were missing. They were all there on the helipad ready to board when they called that one off. Then it was RT Kentucky when Ronald Smith was killed. They were going to put Predmore and his team in to find and retrieve Smith's body, right in the middle of the firefight. That one was aborted only because Roberts could not give a good location of the body. Now this! Ziobron had been in continuous contact for three days already. Predmore knew in his bones that this would be a very bad one. The platoon had lots of dead and wounded. The adrenaline of death ran his icy hand down the back of his neck. He could nearly smell Death's breath of the tombs and hear his hoarse whisper, "I am waiting for you."

Predmore shouted to his seven Montagnards, "Get ready. Time to go," as he scooped up two full boxes of Claymore mines, one under each arm and headed for the door. Seeing the extra Claymores, the Yards looked at each other and knew that this would be an extremely dangerous mission.

As he cleared the door, Sergeants Steven Keever, the One-Zero and Phil "Woody" Wood, the One-Two met him.

"What's up?"

"We're going in."

"Where?"

Predmore stopped and hoisted the two cases of heavy Claymores farther up in his arms. "They are going to land us a few hundred meters from where Ziobron is surrounded. They want us to fight our way through the enemy forces and get into the perimeter to reinforce the platoon. John Plaster is flying Covey and found a place for the Hueys to put us in."

The two sergeants did not have to glance down at the Claymore mines to grasp the likelihood that this could be their last mission, perhaps their last day on earth. They swallowed and their faces blanched at the news.

"I already told our people. They should be coming out in a minute."

"Thanks," Keever said. "We will need to take all the grenades and ammo that we can carry."

"Yes," Predmore added, "and look at the sky. It might get dark before we can even land. We might have to do this . . . you know."

The Yards streamed out of the building ready to go. "Drop your packs," Keever told them. "We just need one canteen and ammo to fight with."

The Yards looked at each other and dropped their packs on the ground. They did not need to be told the peril.

The choppers landed and waited as RT Illinois climbed aboard. Keever, Predmore with the radio, and three strikers boarded the lead chopper as Woody and the remaining four strikers boarded the second. Predmore looked toward the commo shack of the launch site. Dusk already diminished detail and the sign on the shack was no longer legible. It would be full-dark within the hour.

No one spoke en route. Keever thought to himself, "We are going to die tonight."

Forty minutes later the group arrived over the knoll. It was not completely dark; that would occur about the time Illinois leaped from the skids a few hundred yards away. The contours of the land could still just barely be made out. But the drama below them was plain and desperate. The little knot of defenders was clearly demarcated as they fought off those who besieged them; red tracers outlined their perimeter. Around them in a complete circle were the attacking NVA. Curtains of green tracers streamed toward the inner circle of men. White explosions burst from B-40 rockets and mortars. The demarcation of the two forces could not have been more clearly marked on a map than Illinois was able to see in green and red.

The choppers banked left and Predmore heard over his radio, "Your place is coming up over here . . . somewhere. . . . I can't see it in this light."

Keever thought, "My point man has an SKS which fires green tracers. Woody carries an RPD, also green tracers. Even if we can fight our way through those guys in the dark, our own people will not be able to know that we are not the enemy."

Illinois looked at each other's faces and knew that they were facing certain death. They were going to die in the next hour. Keever felt the terror of the moment and thought, "I have never been so afraid in my entire life as in this minute."

One of the Montagnards sat with his rifle cradled like a baby. His eyes were clinched tightly. The point man swallowed over and over as he sat next to the crew chief and stared out of the opening. One tribesman seemed to pray.

"Were they going to prep this LZ or were they going to put us in cold and hope there's no one there to ambush us. I am sure they will prep it," Wood kept saying to himself.

Predmore glanced ahead to see what could be learned by looking forward through the pilot's window. There was a gesture as he abruptly placed the craft in a climbing attitude. He looked back at Predmore and drew his hand across his throat in a "that's it, finish" gesture. Predmore glanced at the door gunner who caught his eye in the near-dark. He also moved his hand in the same gesture. The mission was aborted.

Predmore grinned with an open mouth.

He looked at his team leader. "Mission aborted," he shouted.

The Bright Light team had been tense and unmoving, barely breathing, but with the news, their limbs unfroze, their chests moved visibly under their belts of ammunition, and they exhaled great sighs of relief. They might live to see another day.

The choppers passed over the platoon. Red tracers that shot outward were sporadic and deliberate as they conserved for the final push of the enemy when perhaps they themselves would not survive the night.

\* \* \* \*

On the ground, they could only hold on. Ziobron worked the gun runs and bombs and kept his people in the fight. The medic cared for the wounded as Zaborowski directed his side of the little circle. "Just hold on until morning. They will surely come for us in the morning."

### ***RT Alabama***

"Contact, contact, contact. This is Alabama. Contact, contact, contact. We have heavy contact, being chased. One-Zero may be KIA/MIA. Prairie Fire, repeat, Prairie Fire emergency!"

The voice was that of Sam Helland. It was fast-clipped and charged with adrenaline. "Repeat, Prairie Fire."

John Plaster was on the radio, one of his first flights as Covey, but with many SOG missions under his belt, he knew the tension of being near death on the ground. He recognized the voice. "We got you Sam. I have assets nearby. What is your situation?"

"Heavy contact. Chased. One-Zero is KIA and we had to leave the body. Very heavy pressure."

"Roger. Coming your way. What is your location? How do you hear us?"

"Wait one."

Plaster could tell in the pause that it was a crisis moment SOG men often experienced. "Where am I?" Plaster imagined the tension charging through Sam's brain, blurring his vision and challenging his ability to think clearly. From his own experience, he pictured Sam with deliberation pulling his compass from where he had it clipped it between the two top buttons of his shirt and laying it flat until the needle ceased to swing as green tracers zipped over his head. He would want to be actively returning fire, but disciplined himself to read the numbers. He would blink to clear his vision to see the needle and read the dial. He would locate the airplane again by the engine noise, line it up with the compass, ("Keep your head down!") and learn the numbers. And Plaster knew that although Sam Helland was a seasoned recon man, he would order himself, "Speak slowly, clearly, and accurately."

Sam cleared his throat. "I hear you at my 240 degrees."

"Copy, two four zero. Searching."

Plaster flew 060 degrees, the reciprocal, scouring the trees and ridges for signs of Alabama.

"I can't find you. Can you pop smoke?"

"Smoke out."

The birddog circled and tipped its wings to better see. Nothing showed through the thick forest.

"I cannot find you. The canopy is too thick. There is a slash-burn area part way up the slope where I think you are. Can you make that?"

"Have to. Out."

Helland relayed the information to the One-One of the team, Captain Kent Marshall. "There is a slash-burn up this ridge. They want us to make our way there. They can't find us under this canopy."

Marshall called to his point man and pointed out the direction, with Sam in the lead. "*Đi Đi.* Go. Go."

Alabama had not been on the ground long. Three times they sat on the tarmac at Dak To waiting to insert, only to find the LZ to be compromised or bad weather prevented insertion. It was a small recon team lead by the experienced One-Zero, Jim "Fred" Morse tasked to infiltrate a suspected base area. The mission was to do a wiretap and record enemy communication on existing cable strung along a high-speed trail or road. In addition to Marshall and Helland, rounding out the team were three Montagnard tribesmen. When heavy enemy activity seemed likely at larger breaks in the forest, Morse elected to rappel into a small, hopefully unmonitored opening in the trees.

The "slick" glided in to a slight gap among a tangle of bamboo, and Alabama smoothly rappelled into enemy-controlled territory. In seconds, certainly not a long enough time it would take to hover to a landing, the slick was gone. They hustled dozens of meters away from where they infiltrated and listened for movement to indicate they were compromised. Only chirping insects and dry cellophaned wings of dragonflies, and a brief flutter of a single bird in a tree disturbing a dead, dry twig, indicated life at all. But life did abound: human life, enemy life. The noise of helicopters, however brief it was, could not be hidden entirely, and the North Vietnamese began a concerted, although routine, search of the vicinity. Disturbed twigs were no longer that of sparrows or ground lizards, but searchers. The movement was not lost on Alabama. They maneuvered west avoiding enemy patrols and danger areas, pausing often to watch and listen. At length they found a high-speed trail that promised a communications cable and took up position along the path.

They waited like statues, unmoving bronze statues that had been tarnished green. They remained frozen taking care to not shiver the vegetation behind which they were concealed. Large drops of sweat gathered and rolled down their necks like many-legged bugs but they did not stir. Jim Morse let his mind wander a moment trusting his senses to alert him away from his thoughts. "What was it that Henry Waddell said to him before this mission that evaded his mind now?" Henry was on the parachute jump that was supposed to land on the golf course to capture an enemy general. He almost did not make it out alive; he just got out two days ago in fact, and was all shaken up. Waddell said they dropped the team nearly ten miles from the target and they got hung up in the trees. He spent the night fifty feet in the air, suspended from a limb with enemy all around him. When he managed to get down, the limb sprang back up and he lost his pack and rifle in the tree.

Waddell came to Morse's hooch as he was getting ready for the wiretap mission and sat on the only chair they had because Morse had all of his gear laid out on my bunk and the other chair getting ready for the mission. Waddell sat there with his legs and knees together and just watched Morse shove rounds into the magazines. Finally, he spoke. His voice had been quiet and Morse nearly did not hear him at first.

Morse glanced down the high-speed trail to where it disappeared in the greenery. "The sound—cicadas? Sounds like cicadas. Do they have them in Laos? I thought they did that sound only every seventeen years." Morse set aside his thoughts about insects and recalled again Waddell that afternoon in his room, pale and not quite out of his nightmare.

"Jim," he said, "You never carry pen flares, do you? I know you don't because we talked about it once. I always took them."

"Never did. Don't know why. Just never did."

"I want you to carry mine. Here. There are three left on this one. I had to use the other ones on our mission to the golf course."

Morse took the flares. "I just never carried them. They sound like a pistol when you shoot them off. Charlie knows where you are when you use them."

"Yes, I know but listen to me. I just want you to take these. You don't have to use them. If I did not have these on that last mission I would not be here today. Take these for me, okay? I mean it."

"All right, I will."

"Good. They go right there in that side pocket. Not in your pack or web gear, your pocket."

"Okay."

"Okay nothing. I'm watching you. Put them in."

Morse continued to listen for movement and the slightest indication of anything coming down the trail. He heard wood cutters several times in various locations but no other hints of activity. He glanced to the place where they had placed the Claymores. He recalled stories of enemy commandos sneaking up to the perimeter turning the Claymores around to face the teams so they would fire on themselves. "Hard to imagine an enemy sneaking up like that and the team not hearing them," he thought. Morse strained his ears. There were no longer animal sounds of any kind. Distant alarms become near and loud in his mind. The bugs are nervous!

A Montagnard called out. "Look! Look! Look! Shoot!"

North Vietnamese commandos had gotten grenade-close without betraying their movement. The line of SOG men was engulfed in a mass of explosions as a score of grenades was thrown among them followed by a mass charge of PAVN regulars firing on full-automatic. A grenade exploded next to Morse causing massive injuries over his whole body. A bullet struck him in the orb of his eye just under the brow and exited his upper forehead leaving a massive wound that exposed his brain. The orbs of his eyes filled with blood as if he wore red eye patches. He lay on his back, his mouth open, unmoving.

Shards of metal made gaping wounds in his chest, legs and wrist. A glance showed him to be dead as the charging force began to overrun the team, forcing them to retreat with numerous wounds. The team fired desperately as they walked backward trying to stop the onslaught. Someone fired the Claymores laying the first rank of soldiers flat, giving Alabama just enough respite to break contact. The man on point lead away from the pursuing North Vietnamese as the tail gunners engaged the enemy. In their haste to catch and destroy the SOG team, North Vietnamese soldiers merely glanced at the prostrate and bleeding Morse as they jumped over him and continued their pursuit. When they could do so, Alabama changed direction, and tried to distance themselves as death gave chase.

Nearly everyone was wounded. They moved east hoping to evade until they could make communication with Covey. The trackers were persistent and skilled and the team was not able to shake them. Alabama ambushed, broke contact, evaded, and looked for a defendable position, the repeated syndrome of a hunted team behind lines. The communication with Plaster gave them hope and a course of action. Over the next hour and several contacts with the trackers, daylight penetrated the trees as the forest thinned.

An airplane hummed nearby. The recon team froze and the men looked into the sky.

"Tossing smoke," Helland said.

Plaster's eyes scoured the area around the slash-burn. Was there more than one smoke signal out there? He saw more than one plume. Was the enemy monitoring the radios and throwing their own smoke to lure the helicopters into ambush? Perhaps it was just night fog reluctantly rising from the recesses of the ground.

"What color did you throw, Sam?"

"Banana! I threw banana."

Plaster smiled to himself. "Copy, I see yellow. I have Cobra gunships and A-1 on the way."

Alabama was taking fire on the LZ. "From my two seven zero, fifty meters," Helland said as the first gunships appeared. The suspect area erupted in explosions and the impact of the Cobras' miniguns.

A-1s arrived and added their payload on the enemy as the first slicks rumbled toward the waiting team.

"Sam," Plaster said over the radio. "Your slash-burn is on a steep slope of the ridge and the Hueys can't land without their rotors hitting the uphill side. We will need to pull you out on strings. Copy?"

Helland glanced at his people. They all wore STABO extraction harnesses. "Copy. We are ready."

A Huey slid in to a hover above the team and threw down the ropes, Alabama sped from their cover and snapped in to the several ropes and were lifted into the air. A dozen feet off the ground, heavy automatic fire was directed at the helicopter. Hearing the thudding impact of rounds slamming into the fuselage, the pilot accelerated from the LZ at a climb but failed to wait for the men hanging under the belly to clear the trees. They were helpless and dragged through the bamboo, bounced against trunks and wedged between limbs until they broke free.

Like a dream unfolding itself, they were soon high in the air looking down at the scene of their drama. They saw the flash of explosions and billowing white smoke, and presently as they rose ever higher, and saw an A-1 Skyraider pass above the slash-burn. It seemed small, not much larger than a child's toy.

There was always a great sense of relief being pulled from near death in this manner. The cacophony of war—explosions, the buzz of bullets flying near your head, the shouts and crashing through the brush, even the pounding of one's own heart which you were certain everyone near you could hear—was instantly replaced by the utter silence of being suspended in the air. There was a new fear however, for you were a mile high in the sky where the pilots felt they were above small arms fire. They flew at speed and the wind was cold and hard against your legs with only a thin rope between you and a terrifying fall.

Staff Sergeant Sam Helland felt those thoughts in real time as he clung to his rope, his very thin rope. He wanted to link with the others dangling on the nearby ropes and cling to them, for the unspoken thought was that if his line broke perhaps the other ropes would hold the men. As the helicopter banked for the turn to Ben Het and the lines neared each other, he grabbed the chest of one of the tribesmen. He found his face next to the bevy of grenades clipped to the harness. For the remainder of the perilous journey, every movement of the chopper, every twist in the wake, each shift of the tribesman, rammed his face against the grenades which tenuously hung from his chest.

Sergeant Jim Morse was not dead. Excruciating pain and a buzzing sound like steam escaping from a pipe brought him to consciousness. It felt like his head was exploding; indeed, that had nearly been the case. He felt himself squirming side to side and felt his body move but could not see and attach himself to the reality of here and now. He tried to see. He knew his eyes were open, but he could not see. He blinked and tried to wipe his eyes with his left hand but it seemed asleep and the fingers were full and sticky with blood. He used the knuckle of the other hand and pushed the well of blood from the orb. He turned his face to the side and emptied the well of blood, blinked and using his good knuckle saw once again. He lay in dirt and twigs and a pool of his own blood. "I am alive. I am alive but I am really messed up."

He propped himself on his good elbow and looked down his length. His shirt and trousers were red, soaked with blood. But the blood was shiny and not dried brown so he had not lain there very long. Blood ran from his crown and streamed down his face, some into his eyes again, and he cleared them with his index knuckle.

He saw no one. His team was gone. He was separated and alone. At least the enemy was not there to shoot or otherwise abuse him. He would have to move from there before they returned. He pushed himself up. The backpacks of the team were still on the ground in a neat row. They must have run and left them. Perhaps the enemy were in hot chase or they would have taken them. They will be back. He pushed himself upright and stood on splayed and shaky legs. He was dizzy, very dizzy. Everything spun around him. He must get away from this place.

"Perhaps I can follow the team through all of this," he thought as he looked to the east and the thick brush. He straightened himself to go and swayed back and forth with the effort. He reached for his rifle and pack and heard shots. A furious but brief firefight was taking place in the direction he chose to go. The distinctive rounds of American rifles and the "pop, pop" of AK rounds sounded to the east, muffled by the terrain. Near the end of the fight was the thump of grenades and the impact of RPG rounds.

"I can't go that way. I will be on the back side of the NVA, alone, and in no condition to fight."

He faced the trail. "We never walk trails but I need to risk it for a while, just long enough to distance myself from here. Then, I will head east."

He took a half dozen uncertain steps. "So tired. So weak. Want to sleep."

He stopped dead on the trail as dizziness again made his world to swirl. And he remembered, "I forgot to take the wiretap with me."

He turned to retrace his steps. "So tired. Just want to sleep."

Morse staggered to the site of the ambush, stooped for the device, placed it into his pack, and shouldered it again. "Don't stop. Go, or they will find you here."

Once again, he staggered down the path. One pantleg glistening red as fresh blood coursed down his leg. He glanced back on the path. "Am I dripping on the ground? Will they follow my blood trail? Time to go east," he decided and as carefully as he could without leaving sign of his passage, he plunged himself east, east, ever east, even to the next country if necessary. Ever east.

Twice more he heard firefights followed by the sounds of airplanes. "Hope. If I can just make it somewhere where they can see me."

He stumbled often and each time it was harder for him to rise. He had lost so much blood. "Keep going."

Morse was at a crawl now. The ground sloped upward and thinned to a small clearing. Staying awake and conscious was torture. He clung to a trunk of bamboo to keep from falling. He heard an airplane. "Covey?"

He stumbled and fell. He crawled the rest of the way over the crest to the edge of the field. Darkness was overtaking him. "Don't pass out now." He warned himself.

He saw it. It was Covey. How to signal? No radio. He wanted to weep. So close. So close.

The pen flares!

Morse reached into the side pocket and pulled them out. He inserted one into the device. "Hurry. The plane is leaving the area. Hurry."

He pulled the spring back and let it go and watched the white streak fly into the sky ahead of the flight path.

"Did you see that?" John Plaster asked the pilot.

"Are we taking fire?" the pilot asked.

"I don't think so. Their tracers are green. I know this was white."

Morse no longer had the strength to stand or wave. He screwed a second flare into the device, pulled the spring and watched the streak rise into the air toward the plane.

"It is a flare for sure," Plaster said with excitement. "There! Over there. Got him. I see him."

The pilot tipped his wings so Morse could see. In moments, assets were in the area, then a Huey helicopter. Having pulled the rest of the team, they knew that Morse wore a STABO rig.

A chopper, attended by nearby Cobra gunships, descended and dropped a rope. Jim Morse was weak beyond anything he had ever experienced. It took all of his resources to hook into the rig and when he heard the final snap, rolled back completely spent. He hugged his weapon to his chest as blood from his wound seeped between his fingers and over his rifle.

At Ben Het, where they pulled him off the string, they were astonished at his wounds; astonished mainly that he had received them and lived. His brain was exposed from the massive wound in his skull, his chest wound could have been fatal and he was wounded in his leg and arm. For a time, it appeared that he had died just as he made it to the camp. His eyes rolled back showing only the whites, his mouth gaped open, and they found no pulse, but the medic took charge and soon he breathed and his heart continued to function. Morse was medevac'd and spent a year in hospital recuperating.

But Covey still had another Prairie Fire to administer. They would refuel and rearm and return to the tiny place Ed Ziobron still held for four days against constant enemy attack—as Bernard Fall would say in his book, it was "hell in a very small place."

\* \* \* \* \*

The enemy sensed the break in the air support and chose the lull to make a concerted assault hoping to destroy the SOG people before more help arrived. They came in a mass of men with rockets and small arms. Clearly, it would take overwhelming firepower to break the attack.

Ziobron shouted. "I want one minute on full-automatic. Full concentration of fire. Do it now."

The men in the spider holes opened up on the wall of enemy as Ziobron crawled toward the oncoming force firing his rifle and tossing the last of his grenades. More pieces of rockets struck him but they were small and ignored. The mass of enemy fell like grass before a sickle. A minute later there was complete silence around them. There was a groan from somewhere among the enemy. Rain tapped in the trees, and errant drops sizzled on hot gun barrels. Someone with a chest wound coughed.

Ziobron called to tribesmen in nearby spider holes. "Run to wounded men who cannot fight and bring back their ammo and grenades. Give to Montagnard who can still fight. Do now."

They returned in moments. "They already give. Not much left."

Ziobron counted his own magazines. When he saw how few he had, he turned to his little people who waited for further orders. "Go tell Montagnard, shoot only man he can see. Do one shot, one man. Understand?"

"Montagnard understand."

He watched them as they rushed from hole to hole with the order even as the ceiling lifted slightly, enough for him to see swaying and rustling among the bushes farther up the slope. He watched and it was apparent that a new wave of troops was descending on his position. "In your holes," he shouted to the Yards spreading his instruction. They are coming again.

The SOG people leaned forward from their holes and sighted toward the shouts and swaying vegetation and waited for targets to appear and Ziobron's order to fire. Covey came on the radio. "Sundance, we have air support: four Phantom jets and a flight of Skyraiders. Behind them we have Hueys for exfil. Toss smoke again and give us targets to clear the LZ. Copy?"

"Copy. Smoke out."

The next twenty-five minutes was an air show in which the aircraft made pass after pass of bomb and strafing runs as Ed Ziobron directed them to targets. At the end, six helicopter pilots from the 170th Assault Helicopter Company radioed to Sundance. "Sundance, this is Bikini One, Two, Three, Four, Five, and Six. We are coming in to get you. Pop smoke."

Ziobron replied, "Bikini leader, this is Sundance, smoke out. Identify."

"I see orange."

"Good copy."

"Roger, Bikini One coming in."

The first Huey came in seconds after it could be heard, dipping through the thin fog. The NVA heard it also and their guns from the ridge and surrounding tree line opened up with furious fire, but the Skyraiders and Phantom jets hit them hard with unrelenting rockets and bombs. Ziobron had just hobbled into the clearing with a marker panel when Bikini One touched and six men of the company Bright Light force leaped to the ground and ran toward him at a crouch. The first person he saw was SFC Platz who greeted him with a grin and a firm handshake. "We are here to bring you home. Where can you use us for now?"

"We are nearly out of ammunition so we could use you at the edge over there. We are getting the biggest pressure from that side. I'll get my people busy loading up."

"Zab," he shouted. "Take some of our able-bodied ones. Get

Smith loaded up and six of our worst wounded."

Zaborowski and two reluctant strikers lugged Smith to the deck of the chopper and were followed by six badly wounded but very eager little people. They had not cleared the trees when Bikini Two glided in and received eight more injured men who leaped aboard. It lifted and climbed, only to be struck by enough anti-aircraft fire to force it to land at Ben Het Special Forces camp. The next two helicopters received sergeants Zaborowski and Conkin and fourteen other wounded SCU. Bikini Five took the last of the Montagnards leaving only Ziobron and the reaction force.

As Bikini Six touched down, a dozen NVA attacked the helicopter on the field and were dispatched by the reaction force and Ziobron using his last magazine of ammunition. Ziobron wanted to board last and discovered, as he crawled to the strut, that he was, after four days of continuous fighting and being wounded four times, too weak to make it all the way in. The door gunner grabbed him by his harness and pulled him the rest of the way.

As Bikini Six lifted, two more NVA ran to the chopper and tried to shoot it down. The door gunner could not depress his machine gun down enough to engage them. Ziobron scrambled to the door on his belly and made deliberate aim, firing twice into each soldier. He counted the rounds as he shot: "One, two, three, four, click." They were the last four rounds he had.

Ziobron contacted Skymaster. "Request you napalm the LZ as soon as we lift off."

"Roger. Will do. Give smoke."

"Done."

"Purple."

"Affirm"

Bikini Six barely cleared the ridge and looked down through the fog at the knoll when the site of battle erupted in a long line of orange and yellow explosions and the white death of napalm.

Ziobron lay on his back on the deck of the chopper and thought. "That was the 26th NVA Regiment down there. We have mauled them for sure. Certainly, my people killed five hundred if not a thousand of them. But there are one or two thousand more down there, and we never did find their present complex. We need . . ." he thought as he reached for the radio.

Ziobron contacted FOB via Covey. "Sir, I strongly suggest an Arc Light strike on my target."

"Way ahead of you Sundance. One has already been ordered. Good work."

Two of the disabled Bikini helicopters and some of the support aircraft landed at Ben Het. Pilots and crewmen emerged from Skyraiders and Cobra gunships and ran to the group standing by. "Who is this 'Sundance'? We want to meet this guy!"

But Sergeant Edward Ziobron lay on his back on the cold metal deck of a shivering helicopter, with a length of fatty white tendon hanging from his boot swaying like a pendulum as the craft banked and maneuvered at greatest speed toward Pleiku hospital, the first of several such places that would care for his several wounds over the next year. He glanced at the red bandages that covered the bullet wound on the other leg and noticed the blood no longer flowed but seeped, and he wondered if his supply was running low; his drowsiness might attest to that. And he wondered also, as some brave men might at such a time, if he would have the strength to walk on his own power to the emergency room door. But he would learn it would be three months before he would take his next step, and a year before he left the long white halls of a hospital.

He received only a silver star and it took twenty-five years for it to be upgraded to a Distinguished Service Cross, a decoration, most believe, should have instead been the Medal of Honor.

# CHAPTER FOURTEEN
*Sebastian Deluca*

There is a place in the Old Testament, in the oldest book of the Bible, where Job, the grievously vexed man of God, sat on a dung heap and scraped his sores with a broken piece of pottery and said at the end of it all, "I am escaped with the skin of my teeth." Our people in SOG often came back from a mission with that same sentiment. We referred to one of those as a "hairy mission." We barely survived and making it back to base slid off our helicopters with rubber legs, eyes still glazed, our wounds blood-browned and dry in yesterday's bandages, our hearts slamming against the cages in our chests like clambering birds trying to get out. The crises our people endured were often so acute that our wounds were deemed of little importance. Courage which cannot be described on a page (perhaps aided by the ardent prayers of an old Sunday School teacher we forgot about) carried us through. We were in charge of our fears, masters of them. We finished the task and returned. It was later—after the hugs and handshakes, the congratulations of our peers, the fondness we lavished on the little people who followed and trusted us, after the de-briefing—then, in the quiet of the team room, lying on our bunks with our hands clasped behind our heads, that we relived how close it all was and only then let it out.

Some of our leaders in CCC were aware of the need for down time after certain missions. It was an easy thing for us. We had our own airplanes that supported us. They essentially flew to China and Thailand and a few other places with ample space for us Special Ops people. Our Blackbirds had such classified instrumentation aboard they were only serviced at a secret place in Nationalist China and we flew with them. We had several flights to Bangkok. The captain of Recon Company would say, "Sergeant Hanson, there is a flight going to Bangkok tomorrow if you want to go." Our officer in personnel would type the orders and I would be gone—on an Air America plane to Saigon, an evening in House Ten and a steak sandwich, and on the next day to Bangkok.

I do not remember what happened to warrant my trip to Bangkok this time. But I left Kontum on a Blackbird, spent the night in the safe house in Saigon, and was off to the capital city of Thailand. Most SOG people stayed at the Opera Hotel on Soi Somprasong. It was not large, two stories (less than fifty rooms), a small restaurant, and a modest swimming pool outside; quiet and pleasant.

I had a girlfriend whose grandmother owned most of the land of Pattaya Beach, one of the most sought-after places in Thailand and I think she expected us to marry and live there. Any tension I might have felt from the war was forgotten in Thailand. Linda and I went to the zoo with her two little brothers and I played tag with them in the grass. We went to the museums. We went to Asian movies. They did not offer popcorn at the counter. Mangos which the man deftly scored so we could eat them in slices was the fare, and dried squid, also scored to tear in strips and eat. The movies were mostly in Thai with translations in several languages written in white at the bottom of the screen. In many of the films, there would be a revered old man character with sightless, glassy eyes and a long white beard who hobbled on a staff. From the empty sockets he would cast beams against the villain. Though he could not see, his karate never failed.

We saw the temples, surfaced in gold. There were stone statues of white elephants and the white monkey in the frescoes. There was the gold Buddha, nearly ten feet tall and weighed five and a half tons of solid gold. "Dale," Linda said, "This Buddha was covered in plaster for two hundred years to hide its value, but a rope broke when they moved it and the plaster chipped off and they found the true value. Buddhist believers purchase thin strips of gold the size of a postage stamp. They go to the Buddha and rub the gold foil against the skin of the statue and the heat of their finger marries the gold to become one with the statue."

In the Grand Palace was the Emerald Buddha: the large statue carved from a single piece of jade on a gold pedestal and adorned with gold and jewels. It was precious to the country. In ceremony, the king of Thailand goes in four times a year and changes the clothing on the translucent green Buddha for spring, summer, fall, and winter. The fabric of each garment is of woven gold.

We ate at the Ginali restaurant. It was a steamboat from the Mark Twain days complete with paddlewheel, disassembled in America and reassembled on a tiny lake in the center of Bangkok. From a dock, customers would be rowed to the steamboat where wonderful meals were served.

Off Pattaya Beach, we rented a Chinese junk boat with ribbed sails and eased to a small Island in the Gulf of Siam. We dove, bathed in the sun, and beach combed. I spent a couple of hours on my knees at a large tidepool and dug for crab alongside a young boy. It was pristine; I only heard the soft lapping of waves from a boat that passed beyond the horizon. With our sticks we prodded the sand for whatever it was the boy was looking for. The sun felt good on my back. I glanced up and saw Linda smiling at my second childhood. We ate higher up the beach near the palm trees under a thatched hut with sides open to the offshore breeze: fresh cooked crab, rice, and Thai vegetables. A bottle of Coke was two and a half cents.

Any tension I might have arrived with washed off in the South China Sea.

We were back at the Opera Hotel in the restaurant. Linda picked for me from the Thai menu. It was quiet and I put five cents in the jukebox for five songs. I liked easy listening mostly, but there were a few current songs I liked. I pressed *Reflections of my Life*, and *Hitchin' a Ride*, and *Rainy Night in Georgia*. The latter song was popular when I was in jump school. I admired how skillfully the author and Brook Benton set the tone with the lyrics.

> *Hoverin' by my suitcase*
> *Tryin to find a warm place to spend the night*
> *Heavy rain's fallin'*
> *Seems I hear your voice callin' "It's all right"*
>
> *A rainy night in Georgia*
> *A rainy night in Georgia*
> *Lord, I believe it's rainin' all over the world*
> *I feel like it's rainin' all over the world*

Linda had to go home to her parents' north of the city and I was left alone. I dipped in the pool and crawled under a blanket in the air-conditioned room. I fell asleep listening to the radio station from Australia. The song was *Days of Wine and Roses* by Mancini.

It seemed I had but blinked and it was the afternoon. I went to the restaurant and found a couple of SOG guys. Mike Buckland was there. We talked about the news at Kontum. With our missions, big things happened in a day. The war seemed so far away.

A few of us SOG guys took a cab to the House of Pancakes. I wanted real American food and we found it. This was the largest House of Pancakes in the world, two stories. The food tasted exactly as it would in the States. I ordered it all: sausage, eggs, hashbrowns, oatmeal, the works. I looked around. Thai people, but mostly Americans, were there, Peace Corps mainly.

We went our various ways, places we enjoyed or wanted to see. The war was left behind. Deliberately. The sun always shined when we went to Thailand.

Mike and I were at the Opera Hotel sitting in a booth of the small restaurant. Strange how even here we did not want our backs to a door or a window and without thinking about it, each of us had the other's back. But that was not a spoken thing.

Someone else put money in the jukebox. It wasn't me, and they played one of my songs.

*How many times I wondered*
*It still comes out the same*
*No matter how you look at it or think of it*
*It's life and you just got to play the game*

*I find me a place in a boxcar*
*So I take my guitar to pass some time*
*Late at night when it's hard to rest*
*I hold your picture to my chest and I feel fine*

*But it's a rainy night in Georgia*
*Baby, it's a rainy night in Georgia*
*Lord, I believe it's rainin' all over the world*
*Kinda lonely now and it's rainin' all over the world*

I think we had a Coke and something to eat, probably Thai food, and we talked. I looked up as someone entered the door, another learned thing. It was someone we well knew, loved, and respected. It was Master Sergeant Sebastian Deluca, our old first sergeant from training group. You could not miss him. He was about five-six, slim and wiry, a ball of energy. I had never met a man who could so curse and reprimand his troops to correct order, who also so loved them. Under his hardness was utter softness of heart. He dearly loved his people. He would do all in his power for them. He fathered his people in discipline. He mothered his people in love.

One glance in our direction. "Hey! It is good to see you," he said, as we motioned him to our table.

"Last time we saw you was in training group when we got our berets," Mike said.

"How can we ever forget that command, 'Remove cap . . . don berets.'" I added.

Deluca laughed and shook his finger at us. "I remember you guys in that room. At least seven of you, I think. All went to SOG as I recall."

Mike pointed at me. "We are what is left."

Deluca sadly shook his head.

"And I remember," he said after a pause in which he considered what Mike had said. "I remember when you two moved over to the two-man room reserved for sergeants."

Mike said, "Well there were no sergeants in the billets so we just took it over."

"You have a great memory to recall us after this time."

Deluca looked at us as if we were his children. "I can tell you one better than that. I remember that padlock you made out of cardboard."

"I do too, Sergeant Deluca. The captain said that all foot lockers had to be padlocked. I didn't have the money to buy one so I made one out of the back of a legal pad and painted it with colored pencil. We used that for weeks and they never noticed."

"I did. One time we went in and when we shut the door the wind blew the padlock. That's how I knew."

We talked and caught up. He was both excited and worried about our assignment to C&C and glad about our increase in rank.

"What have you been doing over there, Sergeant Deluca?"

"Sebastian, call me Sebastian."

We watched as his face grew solemn. "I have been working in OP-35, your headquarters. I have been keeping track of our missing in action and our people who are prisoners. Not just ours but we know of hundreds of them. We know who they are, where they are, and their condition. We know if they are in those bamboo cages, or in a stockade, or in Laos, or Cambodia, or North Vietnam, or PAVN in South Vietnam, or Czechoslovakia, or even Russia." His voice grew louder. He looked around him, bent forward and lowered his voice.

"We know their names and everything about them. Some of them are not far away and are reachable if we want to rescue them. But they won't let us." He slapped the table with the palm of his hand and took a long breath to control himself.

We waited a moment to see where the conversation would take

us. Mike changed the subject for him. "Are you here on leave?"

Deluca raised his read and whispered to us like fellow conspirators. "I'm AWOL. I left SOG headquarters without permission."

We did not know what to say.

"I'm AWOL," he repeated. The words he next said were spoken in the very tone and resolve I felt when I read Charles Dickens' *Tale of Two Cities*. About to take the place of one condemned to die at the guillotine, the protagonist, Sydney Carton says, "It is a far far better thing that I do than I have ever done before."

"I'm AWOL. This will probably end my career. We have prisoners of war out there. We know exactly who and where they are. Our country is making no effort to get them. I cannot leave them to rot half-submerged in mud and starving in a bamboo cage." He slapped the table again with the palm of his hand. No one was around us, and he continued. "I know exactly where some of them are. Exactly! I have maps and coordinates. I cashed in all my money and gold. I am leaving tonight to northern Thailand, then east into Laos and I will either rescue or buy some of our boys."

He looked at us to see how we might take it.

"I leave in a few hours."

We didn't know what to say. We wanted to get him a dinner but he was anxious to tie up any loose ends. I thought of moles, enemy spies inside our headquarters. We wondered who in Saigon knew of his plans, who might tip off anyone of his intent. We were nearly speechless. In the end, he excused himself to finalize things. "I will link up with you boys before I go," he said.

I was alone in the restaurant later that day when he walked in to the Opera Hotel. He came directly to my table. "Coffee?" I asked, "It's strong."

He sat down with a sigh. How much can be said with a simple sigh? Wits-end, sorrow, anxiety, grief, complete satisfaction, weariness—so much with that simple release of breath. I looked into the sergeant's eyes. His sigh meant, "All is complete and ready to begin. The last sigh when you parachute from a plane."

"Can I do anything for you? What can I do? I can certainly pray for you."

He smiled. There was weariness in it, but more, a readiness to take on his mission whatever might happen.

"I think your purpose is so commendable and selfless. I so admire and respect you for what you are doing, Sergeant Deluca."

"Tony. My friends call me Tony."

"Tony." I said, honored for the privilege. "Tony."

"Dale," he said, calling me by my first name. "I might not make it through this. But I will have tried. I do not know how I could live with myself, maybe retire in a house in Fayetteville with the rest of us out to pasture, and throw the ball for my dog, ever aware I knew about those guys we left behind and I did nothing to bring them home. I just don't . . ."

There was a silence across the table as he kept himself from weeping.

"Tony, you cannot know how much I respect you. What you are doing . . ." And here I had to pause as well. "Can I tell you a story?"

He raised his head to listen.

"In the Old Testament, the greatest king, the most loved of the kings began as a shepherd, born and raised in Bethlehem. He was undoubtedly the most courageous warrior to live in the country. As it happened, the Philistines invaded the land. They were a vile and cruel people. They killed King David's predecessor and nailed his body to a wall so the people could jeer and revile him. When a Philistine warrior died in battle they buried him in an oval grave with his weapons at his side, thinking he was not really dead but would join them in battle later. Before the face of each warrior, they placed an open flask of perfume so he would not notice the rot of his body but come out to continue the fight. They were the ones who poked the eyes out of Samson and hitched him up instead of the oxen to turn the huge stone mill that ground the corn into flour.

"The Philistine army got between Bethlehem and David's army. They fought hard, and the end of the day King David leaned back and uttered to himself, 'Oh, what I would do for a drink of water from the well in Bethlehem.'

"He did not know it, but three of his warriors were nearby and heard it. His soldiers loved their king. On hearing the words, the three men fought their way through the entire Philistine army, made their way to the well and filled a bottle with water from the well. They then fought their way back through the Philistine army and presented the water to their king."

Deluca was engrossed in my narrative. He listened for fully a minute before he spoke.

"Amazing," he said, "I wished I could have met them."

"Tony, that story is true. It happened as I stated it. But I want you to know something, Tony. I believe you are that kind of man. What you are going to do in the coming days is your mission to the well."

Sebastain Deluca did not speak as he considered my words. Then I said that which would be criminal for me not to say.

"I can think of only one other person who did more. Jesus Christ when he went to the cross to die and took upon himself the punishment I deserved for my sins, that I could be forgiven if only I believed and asked him to save me."

A Thai man entered the doorway of the restaurant and looked around the room.

"My taxi," Tony said.

He stood to go. I looked at him as a hero and a friend. My eyes took in the vision of his face like a camera and made it indelible in my memory.

He read my mind. "Don't hug me. It is already hard for me to go." He reached out and took my hand and shook it gravely while looking into my eyes.

And he left.

It had been two or three days, and a couple of us were still on leave. Our day had been full and we sat in the same booth we always did, with the benches the color of file folders. There were just enough people talking at the tables that the hum of conversation lent privacy to those around. A couple of the guys we knew from Kontum came to our table and slid in. A third one pulled a chair from a table and slid it in at the end. The solemn seriousness of their demeanor could not be mistaken.

"Did you hear about Sergeant Deluca?" one of them asked.

I assumed that they were unaware of his self-appointed mission and waited for them to reveal what he had confided in Mike and me.

"He's dead. They killed him up north as he entered Laos."

They waited to see our response. I couldn't speak.

"He was shot full of holes. At least eighteen times. The word is that the CIA did it. They left his body in the ditch. The Thai police found him this afternoon."

Another one of the guys picked up the narrative, the one in the chair at the end of the booth. "Everyone says it was our own people. Somehow, they let it be known. They wanted us to know it was our people. Some think it was that they did not want someone from OP-35 wandering around up there where he could be captured and secrets could be tortured out of him."

Another one of the guys took over. "Others say it was because of the prisoners of war. The government does not want them found. They have had plenty of chances to get our people and did not try." The news was a black blanket which hung over us, a morgue blanket. The guys from our booth broke up shortly after, and we went to our places of solitude. In the morning, I got a ride to the airport where I hitched a plane back to Saigon, and from there, back to the war.

It did not take many days before the story had been sanitized. Not verified, sanitized. "He had been killed by bandits. They saw the gold chains around his neck that he hoped to use to purchase a prisoner. He showed too much money. Murdered, robbed, left in a ditch, and stripped of anything of value." That is the current and sanitized version that persists to this day. But looking back on the sad history of leaving our prisoners behind, I tend to the first report. As Kissinger said when he folded up the list of prisoners we knew they had and did not release at Operation Homecoming, "Those are acceptable casualties for peace."

# CHAPTER FIFTEEN
*Saigon: The Continental Hotel*

We were still a couple years from the fall of Saigon; the last shovel of dirt on the grave of Vietnam. A few of us SOG guys were in that city, returning from Bangkok, and from there back to the war. We spent the night in the safe house on Nguyen Minh Chieu Street. The streets there were broad, paved and pacific with tall trees along the sides. In the days of the French when it was "French Indochina," it was residential with large, spacious homes shaded by flowering trees and vines covering their terraces. With fingers of chalk, children drew squares on the street and played games. A pet dog stole their ball and ran with it, chased by angry young boys. That was practically yesterday.

Mike Buckland and I caught a ride from the safe house to Tu Do street, infamous in the evening for its bars, prostitution and flashing lights. Our destination was across the street from all of that, the Continental Hotel. We wore our berets. The red SOG patch was plain on our pockets, a major indiscretion. Headquarters for Special Operations and the CIA had sent the word down to the units; none of us were allowed to wear the Green Beret in Saigon and certainly the red patch must not be seen, lest the connection between the two be learned. An absurdity which fooled no one. Certainly, the enemy moles in those organizations that informed the enemy we were being inserted into those targets behind the lines, knew the connection.

We entered the Continental, to the dining area, the terrace with the open sides which let in the fresh air from the opposite side as the street. Frangipani trees and shrubs lined the interior. White and yellow flowers were in full bloom and sent their sweet fragrance throughout the area. Some say it is the scent of the Orient not only for the sweet smell but because it carried with it the warmth and moist air of that part of the world. This would be one of the odors of the Orient I would remember when my war was over; that, along with the dung-fertilized rice paddies and the verdant and fecund smell of the jungle. It is said the frangipani was favored at graveyards as a symbol of life after death. A broken stem of it left on the ground would root and bloom again even without being planted.

The dining area was empty of patrons, for the time to eat was not yet. "Sit where you wish, gentlemen," the waiter said with a half bow waving his arm to indicate the whole garden. We chose a place facing the street under the shadow of a lattice of vines. White tablecloths topped every table and centered on each was a vase of fresh flowers, while above, in the middle of the terrace, a huge wood fan—perhaps the prop of a French fighter plane—made its slow circuit.

"Cokes," we told him when he returned. The Continental was a symbol of French colonialism of the past, and of diplomats and government workers in recent years. It was also a picture of elegance. A Coke was a dollar there when it cost ten cents anywhere else.

Below us, outside, was Tu Do. Trucks and pedicabs hissed and sputtered in every lane, coughing as they changed gears and accelerated. Horns honked. An immense number of motorcycles maneuvered among the other vehicles passing in and around the larger vehicles. Men passed in their western shirts and black slacks while behind them an Asian girl in an ao dai rode behind, one hand holding her straw hat to her head. Once or twice as we watched, a whole family passed by on a single motor scooter; father, mother, and half a dozen children attached and balanced as a normal thing.

From the big trucks, thick black smoke rose from underneath; from the scooters it was blue, and with my eyes closed I knew the odor each produced.

The waiter brought us our drinks, the cubes clinking against the glass and frost rising on the sides.

"I heard somewhere, Mike, that reporters would eat here and they would order shrimp or lobster from the menu. If the waiter said it was temporarily unavailable, the reporter assumed the Viet Cong had cut the road between Nha Trang where they catch it, and here in Saigon. So, the reporter, depending on the news, would either enjoy a great dinner or report a Communist advancement to his newspaper."

Mike shook his head in disgust. He put his hand to his head. He had brain freeze from our drinks.

A peacock strolled in and stopped a few feet from our table. It looked at us with his beady eyes, cocked its head and glanced at the table. Nothing there.

"Another thing I heard, Mike. In the old days with the French the peacocks would stroll in when people were eating and when they were not paying attention would steal the bread from their plates." Mike just looked at me wondering what got me talking this morning.

"Just think. Peacocks live forty years. That one," I said pointing at it keeping my finger away from its beak, "That one right there, might have taken the bread from Charles de Gaulle's dinner plate."

Mike half smiled, "You're trying to tell me that this peacock flew all the way to France?"

"Let's talk about something else."

The two of us were about all that was left of our group that came here for the war. We often held it all in; at other times we talked, as I was doing that morning. For several minutes we did not speak at all. We looked down on Tu Do Street with its daytime bustle and crowded sidewalks and thought. Concepts and ideas spoke aloud in the quietude of our minds.

It was hard for me to reconcile the bustle and ant-like activity I was watching below. To them, the war might be on another planet. What bomb ever fell on their city? Which house had a bomb shelter? The war was kept far away.

I remembered walking that downtown street in Bangkok two nights before. The night, even after the sun set, was warm and humid. Vendors still sold their wares. People lay in their blankets on the sidewalk deep in sleep. I recalled an older woman who leaned against something and had a bowl beside her to receive money from passersby. One or two baht of folding money was in the bowl so those who passed by knew the purpose of the bowl. She had a child next to her, fast asleep, sprawled beside the woman, close enough that all knew it was hers, but laid judiciously so the child's leg and arm lay across the walk and could not be missed, stepped over. The tiny child did not seem real; more like the small girl was made of rubber, without bones under the taut skin. She was deep in sleep.

The woman was not a panhandler in a strict sense. She did not call out for alms. This was a business to her. Explained to me by a local I knew, that woman would rent a child for the night, rent it just to sleep beside her. That's all, a marketing tool.

I looked down on Tu Do Street. I never saw such a thing in Saigon. Perhaps the officials would not permit such publicity.

"Mike," I said, "Have you ever seen a wounded soldier in Saigon? A Vietnamese man missing a leg, an arm in a sling, or walking down the sidewalk with a bloody bandage?"

He turned to me slowly and answered as if the thought had just occurred to him. "No," he slowly said, "No, I never have."

"You would think with their nation at war, you would see their soldiers, their wounded."

"Come to think of it, Dale, I have never seen a patriotic poster. 'Come, your country needs you,' either."

"Two more," I said to the waiter, and held up two fingers.

"It would not be red, white, and blue, but saffron and yellow. They might make Ho Chi Minh look like a serpent with blood coming off his fangs," he added.

The waiter came with our Cokes, this time with a folded towel draped over his arm, perhaps as a suggestion, "Perhaps the gentlemen would like to have something to eat?"

"Hungry, Mike?"

"Not really."

I shook my head in the negative and he left the table, shushing the peacock away with the menu. I glanced about the garden. "I think of this place as the place where the colonials gathered, perhaps also the plantation owners and those who had the rubber plantations. A unique watering hole, some who might come in dinner jackets, others in their sweaty clothing of the field."

There was another hiatus of silence as we each were absorbed in thought.

"Mike, know what might be the finest first paragraph of any book I ever read? That is apart from, 'In the beginning God created the heaven and the earth.' I think it is the first paragraph of Hemingway's *A Farewell to Arms*."

He looked at me and waited.

"I read it so many times I memorized it."

"And I suppose you are going to quote it to me, aren't you?"

"Yes. Listen."

In the late summer of that year we lived in a house in a village that looked across the river and the plain to the mountains. In the bed of the river there were pebbles and boulders, dry and white in the sun, and the water was clear and swiftly moving and blue in the channels. Troops went by the house and down the road and the dust they raised powdered the leaves of the trees.

The trunks of the trees too were dusty and the leaves fell early that year and we saw the troops marching along the road and the dust rising and leaves stirred by the breeze, falling and the soldiers marching and afterward the road bare and white except for the leaves.

"What made you think of that?"

"Well, I was thinking of this place, the Continental, as a famous symbol and meeting place, and I thought of other ones like it where we have been. I thought of the Norfolk in Kenya, how the famous hunters and explorers ate there. And the writers like Ruark and Hemingway. I thought of them in Africa sitting at the same dinner tables you and I sat at, perhaps scribbling notes on the napkins for their books. And that took me to that paragraph."

He nodded his head in sympathetic understanding.

"His writing makes a contrast between the clear water and the dusty road, and the contrast between the people in the villa and the war on the other side of the mountains, like here outside the Continental Palace and us crawling in the muck of Laos or Cambodia.

"Three times he mentions troops passing, dust rising to the trees, not stopping, and there is nothing about the soldiers. No descriptions of them as individuals, just men going off to war. He mentions them passing with parts of sentences between so you can feel them going by one formation after another.

"The troops go on, Michael, like you and me. Perhaps, if you and I die and do not get back home, the only indication that we were ever at war, might be that at home the leaves fall early."

We were both quiet for a time, each thinking of the same thing.

"There are not many of us left are there?" Mike said and he paused before he continued. "And if we were given the choice to all of this again . . ." and there was a very long pause before he finished the thought. "We would do it all again."

I did not have to wait long to answer. "Yes, we certainly would. I've been thinking about Tony Deluca and what he did. Can't get it out of my mind. But he was like the rest of us, who would do it all over again. I was telling him about *The Tale of Two Cities* when Sydney Carton takes the place of his son-in-law at the guillotine, and you know what Mike? He just looked at me like he didn't know what I was getting at—that what Tony was about to do was just the normal, expected thing." I took a breath. "I think the guys on our missions are just waiting in line at the guillotine. Dennis, dead. Randy, dead. On and on."

Michael Buckland turned to me. "My parents were alcoholics. My brother and I literally got food from garbage cans outside a restaurant in Alaska. Before I met God, I filled my life with school and learning and memorizing things. Teddy Roosevelt's speech about the man in the arena had an immense impact on me.

"It is not the critic who counts; not the man who points out how the strong man stumbles, or where the doer of deeds could have done them better. The credit belongs to the man who is actually in the arena, whose face is marred by dust and sweat and blood; who strives valiantly; who errs, who comes short again and again, because there is no effort without error and shortcoming; but who does actually strive to do the deeds; who knows great enthusiasms, the great devotions; who spends himself in a worthy cause; who at the best knows in the end the triumph of high achievement, and who at the worst, if he fails, at least fails while daring greatly, so that his place shall never be with those cold and timid souls who neither know victory or defeat.

"I hope we live through this. I know this, that we and our brothers in SOG will aways do what is right regardless of the risk."

The waiter came by again. I held up my hand to say, "Thanks. We are leaving." I was humming. Mike smiled. We knew the tune and the words. He said them aloud.

> *In the clearing stands a boxer*
> *And a fighter by his trade*
> *And he carries the reminders*
> *Of every glove that laid him down*
> *Or cut him till he cried out in his anger*
> *And his shame*
> *'I am leaving, I am leaving'*
> *But the fighter still remains.*

*RT Delaware*

*Homer Hungerford*

*Jim Jones (Shortan) RT Delaware*

*Leghorn*

*Ed Ziobron*

*Ed Ziobron ready to go on a mission*

*Ed Ziobron's scout recon team six Montagnards (all killed)
Front row; Te Bai, and Nhet. Back row; Mop Bi, Hiep, Jai da, and Pui Don*

*Chester Zaborowski and Ed Ziobron*

*Clyde Conkin*

*Clyde Conkin on a mission*

*John Plaster*

*Glen Umera and John Plaster*

*Lloyd O'Daniel*

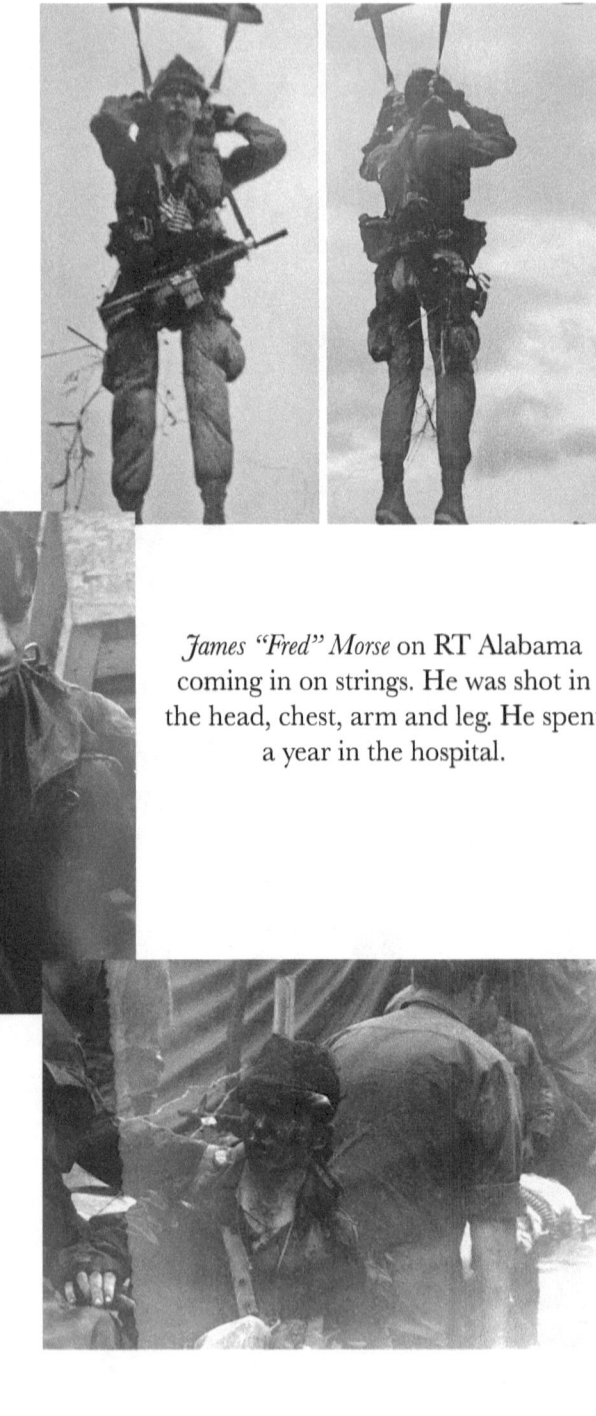

*James "Fred" Morse* on RT Alabama coming in on strings. He was shot in the head, chest, arm and leg. He spent a year in the hospital.

*Tony Deluca*

*Randy Rhea KIA*

*Im Nei Ksor and Ed Ziobron digging a fighting hole on an op in the tri-border, Cambodia, Laos and South Vietnam west of Du Co*

*Tel Bay with what we found in a very large cachet of rice and weapons*

*Ho Chi Minh trails, Communist headquarters hidden in Cambodia. (There is an enemy NVA soldier hiding)*

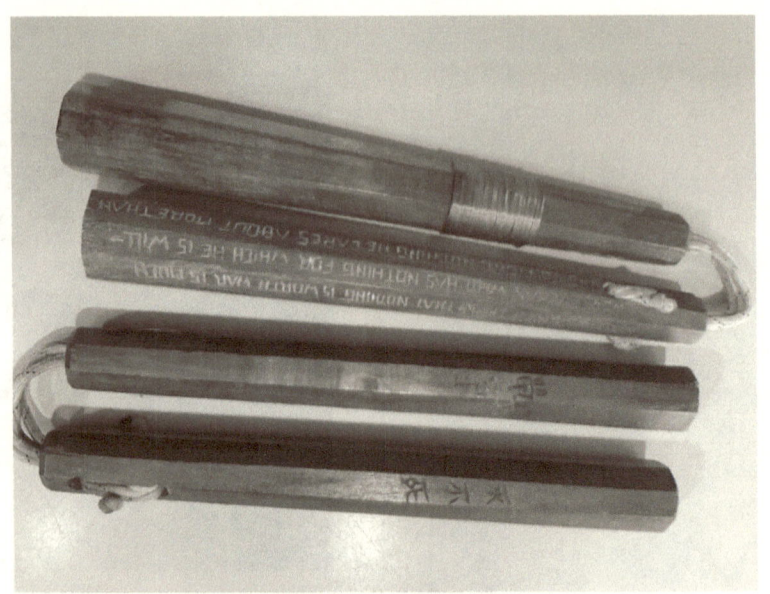

*Nunchakus Dale Hanson carried throughout the war and after*

*"House Ten" pass for the "SOG safe house" in Saigon during the war*

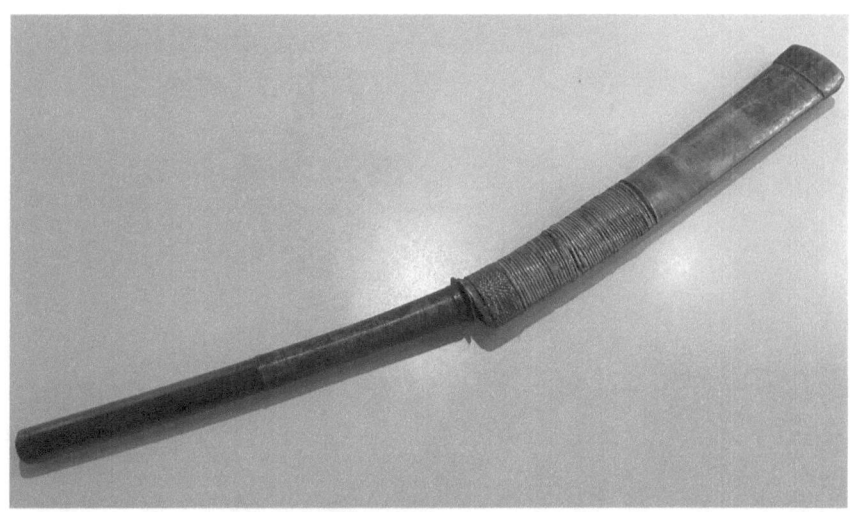

*Viet Cong sword captured after a battle*

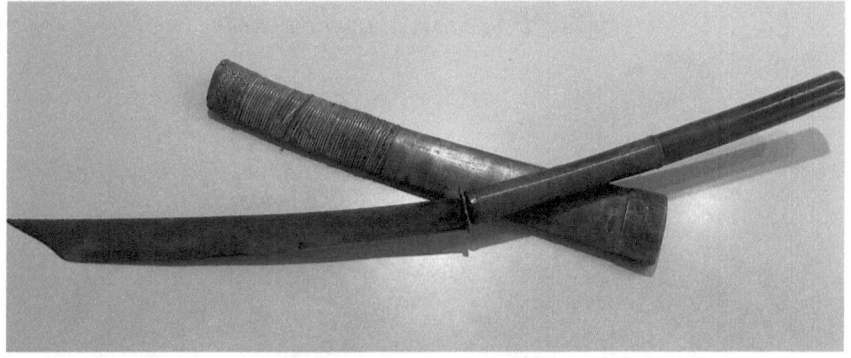

*The pilots of the SPAF (Sneaky Pete Air Force of CCC) They referred to themselves as "The Headhunters." From left to right; Claude "Phil" Phillips, Doug Kraut, Michael Buckland*

*Leaving by helicopter by ladder*

*Leaving by helicopter by strings*

# GLOSSARY

**AO** — Area of Operations

**ARVN** — Army of the Republic of South Vietnam

**Bright Light** — Code name for recon teams that were heavily armed and inserted behind enemy lines with the primary goal of rescuing downed pilots and recon team members, or locating and retrieving U.S. personnel who were KIA.

**CBU** — Cluster Bomb Unit

**CCC** — Comand and Control Central

***Chieu Hoi*** — Soldiers who defected from PAVN, Viet Cong, and their supporters and turned sides to fight with the Americans.

**COSVN** — Central Office for South Vietnam was the main North Vietnamese headquarters of the Communists in the war. Referred to as the "bamboo pentagon," it had overall command of all aspects of the war of Communism in Vietnam and Southeast Asia.

**Covey** — Call sign for the United States Air Force Forward Air Controllers who patrolled while SOG teams were on missions.

**Covey Rider** — Seasoned Recon soldiers who flew with Covey to communicate with teams on the ground and assist with providing coverage from the air when teams were in contact with the enemy.

**Dust Off** — Call sign for U.S. medical evacuation helicopter units that would extract wounded soldiers from missions on the ground.

**Hillsboro** — The United States Air Force 7th Airborne Command and Control Squadron. Tasked with coordinating and directing air coverage for recon teams on the ground during missions.

**Indig** — An affectionate term for the Indigenous members of the recon teams. Pronounced "in-didg," rhymes with "ridge."

**Leghorn** — SOG radio relay site in Laos.

**MACVSOG, SOG** — Military Assistance Command, Vietnam—Studies and Observation Group. The most dangerous, most decorated, and most secret project of the Vietnam war; so secret, the Special Forces soldiers signed twenty-year secrecy agreements.

**NBL** — No bomb lines

**NLF** — National Liberation Front

**One-Zero, One-One, One-Two** — Code names for the American Recon Team Leader, Assistant Team Leader, and Radio Operator, respectively.

**PAVN** — People's Army of Vietnam

**PIR** — Prepared Individual Rations, eaten while on missions.

**PRG** — Provisional Revolutionary Government of the Republic of Vietnam

**RON** — Remain Overnight. A location chosen by the One-Zero for recon teams on the ground to rest overnight while in the field. Spelled out when pronounced, "R-O-N."

**SCU** — Short for Special Commando Unit, a term of endearment for our indigenous troops. Pronounced with a silent "C," sounds like "Sioux," the American Indian Tribe.

**Sitrep** — Situation report. Radio reports provided by the recon teams while on missions.

**Slick** — UH-1 helicopters, also known as Hueys. They primarily were tasked with inserting and exfiltrating teams on their missions. Unlike gunships, Slicks did not have external weapon pods.

**STABO Rig** — Short for a Stabilized Body harness, which recon teams wore in order to be extracted on strings by helicopter when no landing zone was available (usually due to the canopy being too dense or the terrain being too hilly).

**Striker** — An informal, vernacular term referring to the indigenous members of a "strike force" in Special Forces, usually a platoon or company or group of men tasked to hit a target. Often a strike force may be referred to as a "hatchet force," "Mike Force," or some other designator.

**Strings** — Ropes suspended from helicopters that recon team members clipped into to be extracted from missions when helicopters could not touch down for teams to board.

# Other Titles by Dale Hanson

*Haiku: Flowers in the Grass*
*The Great Catch*
*The Last White Seal Hunter*
*Born Twice*

# About the Author

**Dale Hanson** is an accomplished sculptor who has led a life of adventure and enjoyed numerous accomplishments. He is a black belt martial artist, an author, a pilot of fixed wing and glider airplanes, has flown aerobatics and is a Special Forces underwater diver. He is a disabled veteran and a member of MENSA.

During the Vietnam War, Dale was a highly decorated Green Beret who served three years as a commando in the famous SOG program, whose mission involved extremely dangerous raids far behind enemy lines. This unit received more decorations and suffered higher rates of casualties than any American unit since the American Civil War. On one of these raids, Dale earned the first of several purple hearts as his right hand was mangled by a burst of machine gun fire. It is ironic that he became a sculptor, a field in which one's hands are so critical.

www.ingramcontent.com/pod-product-compliance
Lightning Source LLC
LaVergne TN
LVHW091654070526
838199LV00050B/2169